# PORTRAIT OF THE FAMILY
## within
## the Total Economy

### A study in longrun dynamics, Australia 1788–1990

## Graeme Donald Snooks

*Coghlan Professor of Economic History*
*Institute of Advanced Studies*
*Australian National University*

CAMBRIDGE
UNIVERSITY PRESS

Also by G.D. Snooks

*Depression and recovery: Western Australia, 1929-1939*
*Domesday economy: a new approach to Anglo-Norman history*
  (with J. McDonald)
*Economics without time. A science blind to the forces of historical change*
*Historical analysis in economics* (edited)

Published by the Press Syndicate of the University of Cambridge
The Pitt Building, Trumpington Street, Cambridge CB2 1RP, UK
40 West 20th Street, New York, NY 10011-4211, USA
10 Stamford Road, Oakleigh, Melbourne 3166, Australia

© G.D. Snooks, 1994
First published 1994

Printed in Australia by McPherson's Printing Group

*National Library of Australia cataloguing in publication data*
Snooks, G. D. (Graeme Donald).
Portrait of the family within the total economy.
Bibliography.
Includes index.
1. Economic history. 2. Australia—Economic conditions—
1788-1900. 3. Australia—Economic conditions—20th century.
4. Home economics—Australia. I. Title.
330.994

*Library of Congress cataloguing in publication data*
Snooks, G. D. (Graeme Donald)
Portrait of the family within the total economy: a study in
longrun dynamics, Australia 1788-1900/Graeme Donald Snooks.
    p.    cm.
Includes bibliographical references and index.
1. Households—Economic aspects—Australia—History. 2. Cost and
standard of living—Australia—History. 3. Home economics—
Australia—Accounting—History. 4. Australia—Economic conditions.
I. Title.
HC610.C6S66 1994
339.2'2—dc20                                          93-25974
                                                        CIP

*A catalogue record for this book is available from the British Library.*

ISBN 0 521 45203 1      Hardback

# Contents

# Tables

# Figures

Dedicated to my grandparents

| Thomas James Snooks | Alfred Charles Williams |
|---|---|
| 1890–1958 | 1896–1992 |
| Gladys Powell (née) | Violet Hilda Williams (née) |
| 1892–1943 | 1899– |

# *Preview*

The household sector is the forgotten economy of the Western World. Yet it is an institution that has always played a central role in the operation of economic systems, and in the way these systems have changed through time. By writing this book I hope to stimulate our collective memory about the role of the household economy in the process of 'total' economic change. This has been attempted not only by placing the household back within the context of the Total Economy, but also by identifying and analysing longrun dynamic processes in Australian society since the Industrial Revolution. Indeed, to fathom where human society might be going in the future, it is essential to understand the system of economic change operating in the past and present.

There is only one way that complex real-world dynamic processes can be understood—by *seeing* how they have operated in, and through, time. While deductive theory has had many successes, its major failure, in the social sciences in general and in economics in particular, has been the attempt to explore dynamic processes. Economic theory is useful as a general tool, but it must be combined with other techniques if we are to *see* and *show* how existing societies have been, and are being, transformed. This is the role of analytical economic history. Dynamic processes can only be fully understood by focusing on individual countries, or on the interactions between a group of countries that are closely related economically. In contrast, the growing fashion in 'global' studies commits scholars to an examination of comparative *outcomes* using mainstream static theory. This is usually done to provide confirmation of existing static theory and not to explore the nature of dynamic processes. In this study, however, I focus, not on abstract constructs of the mind, but on evidence concerning real-world processes of change that can be generalized to provide what I have called 'existential' models—models of existence. And the evidence employed involves a new system of social accounts that encompasses all economic activity, whether occurring in the household or in the market. This study is, therefore, a portrait of the Total Economy.

The portrait in this book is of the Total Economy in Australia over the longrun. The aim is to show how the household and market sectors have interacted with each other to generate economic development in Australia since

1788. The portrait in this book, therefore, attempts to expose the underlying economic character of Australian society—to penetrate beneath the institutional and shortrun features of this antipodean economy—rather than merely to highlight its transitory and superficial forms. To do this, a three-sector model—incorporating the household, private, and public sectors—has been developed. The forces exposed by this analysis are those that determined development, not just of Australia, but of the entire Western World over the past few centuries—forces, for example, that transformed modern market economies and led to that revolutionary shift of female workers from the household to the market in the second half of the twentieth century. Hence, as well as telling a new story about the emergence of the Australian economy since the late eighteenth century, the book also provides a general picture of real-world dynamic systems. In effect, general longrun dynamic relationships are examined within the particular circumstances of an individual economy—in this case the total Australian economy. It is to be hoped, therefore, that this study will be of general interest to those concerned with longrun economic dynamics, as well as those interested in the transformation of Australian economy and society.

The theme and methodological context for the book are provided in Chapter 1, entitled 'Economic portraits or reality exposed'. It will be argued that real-world dynamic processes cannot be encompassed by deductive models, only through existential models based on economic portraits—or economic time-scapes—that are constructed from quantitative data. This is the focal point for all that follows. The rest of the book is divided into two parts. Of these, the first—*The Forgotten Economy*—provides an empirical examination and interpretation of a new set of social accounts for Australia's Total Economy that in turn are presented and explained in Part Two. In Chapters 2 to 5 the household sector is placed within the wider economy, and the process of interaction between the household and market sectors is exposed empirically. In Chapter 6, an attempt is made to draw upon the various insights that emerge in the earlier chapters to provide a new portrait of Australian economic development from 1788 to 1990. To do so, a model of very longrun development, involving the household and market sectors as sources of economic expansion and economic growth respectively, was constructed. This marks a departure from the market-oriented approach to Australian economic development adopted by Noel Butlin in the late 1950s or, indeed, by Timothy Coghlan in the 1880s. The second part of the book (Chapters 7 to 9)—*Accounting for the Total Economy*—discusses the nature and construction of my estimates of household and Total Economy income and capital formation for the period since 1788. Basically this involves estimating annual units of household labour, capital, and land, and valuing them with the market factor prices that reflect their opportunity cost. Finally, Chapter 10, 'Retrospective', provides a brief review of what has been done and what remains to be achieved.

This presentation is not without its difficulties. These difficulties emerge from the possibility that the book's readers will fall into two broad groups— those primarily interested in the interpretations that it contains (Part One) and those primarily interested in the methods employed (Part Two). While I have no wish to interfere with the sovereign power of readers, those interested in the book's interpretations may wish to read progressively through the chapters in their published order. On the other hand, those readers who wish to satisfy themselves as to the soundness of the statistical building blocks before considering the interpretations constructed upon them, may prefer to begin with Chapter 1, which discusses the book's themes, philosophy, and methodology; then move forward to Chapters 7 to 9 in Part Two, which detail the estimation procedures; then back to Chapters 2 to 6 in Part One, for the interpretation; and finally, forward again to Chapter 10 for the retrospective. I trust that these suggestions will not discourage some readers from pursuing even more complex and idiosyncratic paths through this hall of mirrors.

One of the more obvious difficulties of this type of study is its nomenclature. There is, as yet, no universally accepted system of terms to cover the relatively new concepts required for a study of longrun market–household dynamics. Indeed, many of the terms currently used in traditional national accounting— such as 'household income' to mean the 'total [market] income' received by individuals normally resident in a nation state—are inappropriate and misleading, and need to be redefined.

In this study the word 'market' (rather than the ambiguous term 'formal') has been employed to define the portion of total economic activity that is bought and sold (for cash or kind) in the market place. This market activity is generated in either the 'private' (business) or 'public' (government or semigovernment) sectors. On the other hand, the portion of total economic activity that is undertaken in the family sector, which is neither bought nor sold in the market place, is called 'household' (rather than the less informative 'informal') production. Hence, marketability (rather than actual marketing) of goods and services is the test of 'economic' activity. If a clear distinction can be made between the activities of production and consumption—such as the production and consumption of meals or housecleaning services—then the goods and services produced should be regarded as 'economic', because they are potentially marketable and contribute to family 'income'. But if it is not possible to separate the activities of production and consumption—as in the case of television watching or chess playing—then they must be regarded as 'leisure' rather than 'economic' activities.

Further, the values of economic activity originating in the market and household sectors have been called 'gross market income' and 'gross household income' respectively. And the sum of both, which provides a measure of economic activity in the 'Total Economy' is called 'Gross Community Income' (or GCI). Finally, the various components of 'Gross Community Capital

Formation' (or GCCF) are defined in the same way. These definitions are discussed in greater detail in Part Two, and are gathered together in the Glossary of new terms and concepts at the end of the book. Inclusion in the Glossary is indicated by bold type in the text when the new or redefined term is first mentioned.

The book is more than just an outcome of a longstanding interest in the household sector and its relationship with the Total Economy. It is part of a larger investigation of the longrun dynamic nature of human society, that began with *Domesday economy* (1986), continued with *Economics without time* (1993), and which in the future will focus on the environmental constraints on economic growth. In the current work, I illustrate earlier themes about the limitations of deductive theory in exploring the real world, together with the need to examine reality directly—understanding through seeing rather than through speculation; and themes about the role of historical economic man in the continuous transformation of human society. The longrun analysis is also extended here by providing a wider view of both the process of economic change and of the nature and operation of the underlying driving force.

This study has been in progress for a decade. In that time it has both suffered and benefited from my wider interests in economic growth in the very longrun. It has suffered by being delayed by these wider interests, but it also has benefited by being exposed to them. Had this book been written even five years ago it would have been quite different and, I suspect, less interesting—at least to its author.

All scholarly work builds upon the ideas and sheer hard work of generations of earlier researchers. No advance in knowledge can occur in a vacuum. This is certainly true of the various attempts to measure and analyse the economic progress of nations. In the *Income of nations*, Paul Studenski traces the slow birth of national accounting for the market sector from the political arithmetic of Petty, Davenant, and King in late seventeenth-century England (actually there is a good case for extending that history back to the national accounts of William the Conqueror in 1086) to the modern world-wide system of social accounts of the 1950s. And the recent attempt to go beyond the traditional market-oriented national accounts to embrace the Total Economy by measuring the household sector has depended on important changes in economic ideas. But while acknowledging our general debt to earlier scholarship both applied and theoretical, it is also essential to critically analyse this work in the attempt to extend the existing body of knowledge. The intent is not to denigrate the work of others, but to prepare the ground for new structures that, in their turn, will be the subject of further critical scrutiny.

During the past decade, I have accumulated many personal intellectual debts. The first of these is to an old friend and colleague, Rod Maddock who, in 1982, invited me to contribute a paper on unpaid work to a conference in Canberra. The distance, in all senses of the word, between that paper and this book is greater than either of us could have imagined at that time. Secondly, I am indebted to those colleagues who have patiently endured a number of seminar presentations on my household project. In particular I wish to thank Geoff Brennan, Stan Engerman (who heroically read the entire manuscript), James Foreman-Peck, Bob Gregory, Bob Jackson, Max Neutze, Avner Offer (who has been a constant source of encouragement and support), Adrian Pagan, Jonathan Pincus, and John Treble (who reminded me of the achievements of labour economists). Their criticisms, as always, have been well directed. I am also indebted to two anonymous referees, who provided unusually detailed and incisive comments on an earlier draft.

I wish to thank those who have assisted, either directly or indirectly, with the project's research, and to acknowledge the Australian Research Committee and the Institute of Advanced Studies for financing their assistance. I benefited particularly from regular discussion with Chris Nyland and Deborah Jordan, who I was fortunate enough to employ as National Research Fellows on this project in 1987–88 and 1988–89 respectively. They have since gone on to develop aspects of the household project that captured their imaginations— Chris on the history of ideas in this field and Deborah on the Aboriginal household economy. Publications on these topics are eagerly anticipated. And finally I wish to acknowledge the debt I owe to members of my Department at the Australian National University: to a number of dedicated research assistants and programmers—Jane Berkley, Miriam Landau, Wayne Naughton, and Raha Roggero (and, earlier, Glen Lehman and Helen Smith in Adelaide)— who refused to be daunted by the magnitude of the task; to the office staff— Jeannie Haxell, Ann Howarth, and Barbara Trewin—who have expertly and cheerfully coped with the demanding work of word processing and formatting; to my editorial staff—Barry Howarth with the assistance of Barbara Trewin— for the essential task of proofreading and copyediting the various versions of the typescript; to Barry Howarth for compiling the index; and to Emmett Sullivan—one of those students from whom one learns as much as one teaches—for assistance with some of the econometric work. The book is dedicated to my grandparents who provided the first snapshots for my family photograph album.

Sevenoaks                                                                    G.D. Snooks
Canberra

A picture is a model of reality
                                —Wittgenstein, *Tractatus*

# 1

## Economic portraits or reality exposed

### Remembering the forgotten economy

The household is an economy forgotten in all senses of the word. Despite being the core of all economic systems—whether primitive or sophisticated, modern or medieval—the household economy has been neglected, disregarded, slighted, and put out of the collective mind.[1] Indeed it was put out of the collective mind before its form and function were ever really known or understood. Memory was lost, not because the household economy was regarded as trivial or *passé*, but because it was too elusive. Remembering the forgotten economy requires new concepts, new data, and a great deal of new analysis. But the rate of return on this effort is high because, in the process, the developing image of the **Total Economy** emerges revealingly out of the darkness.

What do we know about the longrun role of the household sector in the Total Economy? What is the nature of the dynamic relationship between the market and household sectors over the last 200 years? How has the household economy contributed to the transformation of human society since the Industrial Revolution? And what role have household workers played in this transformation? Owing to the virtual absence of appropriate estimates of household, and hence total, activity it has not been possible in the past to answer these questions with any precision or authority. This study, therefore, marshalls a large quantity of data in order both to answer these bigger and more general questions, and to deal with the smaller specific questions of time and place. In this process of remembering that which was lost, we obtain a clear idea of the shape and function of the Total Economy since the Industrial Revolution. While the issues are universal, the case study focuses upon a resource-rich society of the antipodes—Australia from first white settlement in the late eighteenth century to the last decade of the twentieth century. When similar longrun estimates are made for other countries it will be possible to place antipodean experience within the global context.

It is a quantitative history that tells a simple story. A story about the economic context in which household workers contribute to that larger entity, the Total Economy. And it is a quantitative history that is more concerned with economic reality than with a display of economic techniques. The last time a new story was told about the Australian economy was in the early 1960s, and it was a story about the shape, role, and function of the market economy. Since then all work on Australian economic history has taken place within the statistical boundaries sketched over thirty years ago by N.G. Butlin.[2] And even Butlin followed in the giant footsteps of that remarkable pioneer of applied economics and economic history, T.A. Coghlan, who dominated the field from the mid 1880s to the First World War and beyond. In fact, as discussed in Chapter 7, it was Coghlan who officially drew that fateful distinction between the market and household sectors—between 'breadwinners' and 'dependents'—that has formed the basis of modern national accounts ever since. It was Coghlan who set the market sector adrift from the Total Economy because, despite his brilliance as an applied economist, he was unable, or too busy pioneering modern national accounts, to resolve the problem of how to measure non-market economic activity. It was Coghlan, therefore, who led us to forget before we had ever really known. And, in the main, we have followed his lead ever since. But the failure to remember is our failure, not Coghlan's, because for some time we have possessed the knowledge, which he lacked, to measure non-market economic activity in the longrun.[3] This study, as far as the Total Economy is concerned, is a longrun quantitative exploration in the remembrance of things past.

# Existential versus logical models: a new perspective

The objective of the study is to reconstruct both the process of household production and the dynamic relationship between the household and market sectors over the longrun. For this purpose it has been necessary to quantify household economic inputs—of labour, capital, and land—together with the outcomes of these economic processes. The *raison d'être* of this exercise is that one can learn more about the reality of past, present, and future in this way than by relying solely upon deductive theory. This is not to deny the usefulness of deductive theory in reconstructing past and present reality, just to question the use of theory as if it were the end rather than the means. The exposure of reality is an act of seeing, not of conceptualizing.

Some of these issues were raised in my recent book, *Economics without time*. What I will do here is to go beyond that methodological discussion by exploring the nature of reality reconstruction, and by contrasting it with the construction of deductive models. This will be attempted both discursively and metaphorically, which in the latter case will involve considering quantitative economic history as photo-realism—as an act of seeing.[4]

## *The existential model*

First we need to draw out the similarities and contrasts between the 'inductive' and 'deductive' approaches (to be thought of in a relative rather than an absolute sense, as social science is always a mixture of both). Clearly the concern of both methods is to create models in order to understand and explain reality. In *Economics without time* I did not explicitly explore the process of reality reconstruction, and may have unintentionally given the impression that I thought it was possible to actually reconstruct reality. This, of course, is not possible or even desirable. What can be reconstructed is not reality—actual existence—but an empirical model of reality, which I will call an **existential model**—a model of existence—to distinguish it from a logical model, which is a construct of the mind.[5] An existential model has many of the characteristics of a scaled-down representation of physical reality—it is like a planner's computerized scale model of a town or city. The reason for constructing an existential model is to portray reality through the correspondences between the characteristics or structure of this model and those of the real world, both past and present. Hence the existential model is not reality, but it corresponds to reality; it *shows* visually what reality is like. As Wittgenstein argued in *Tractatus*:

2.12   A picture is a model of reality.
2.13   In a picture objects have the elements of the picture corresponding to them.
2.131  In a picture the elements of the picture are the representatives of objects.
2.14   What constitutes a picture is that its elements are related to one another in a determinate way.
2.141  A picture is a fact.
2.15   The fact that the elements of a picture are related to one another in a determinate way represents that things are related to one another in the same way.[6]

We can accept this reasoning without accepting Wittgenstein's argument, later abandoned, that a logical proposition must be a picture of the reality it describes—a commonality of structure between language and the world. The problem with this argument is that Wittgenstein moved from the world of objects to the world of language. It still makes sense, however, for the world of objects.

In this study, existential models are constructed inductively from numerical building blocks that correspond to key aspects of the reality in which I am interested, namely the longrun process of household production and the dynamic relationship between the household and market sectors. Numerical symbols represent household workers, or the goods and services they produce, and these numbers are used to draw pictures or, what I have called, timescapes that correspond to reality. These **economic timescapes** *show* the numerical relationships between important economic variables. And this showing is the beginning of understanding. But the inductive approach involves an additional step. It is necessary not only to *see* causal relationships but also to explain them by constructing existential models from the timescapes. This explaining will involve both the use of theory (logical models) and empirical modelling and testing. But it is important to ensure that the existential models or empirical explanations that are to be tested emerge from the data and not from *a priori* expectations. Formal empirical testing of existential models merely amounts to the application of generally accepted ways of observing the numerical variables, of reporting what we see, and of checking the nature of the statistical results (diagnostic tests) so as to reduce the subjectivity of seeing. Econometrics, therefore, should be an aid to the process of seeing, not a blinkered substitute for it. The important point is that, in the case of the existential model, seeing comes before explanation, while in the case of the logical model explanation comes before seeing (the application of theory) and may even be a substitute for it.

The picture of reality that I have attempted to expose in this book is not a picture of the external or temporary features of the economy, but rather one of the underlying dynamic processes of economic change. While this study deals with central institutions in Australian society—including the family, the firm, the bureaucratic department, and various commodity and factor markets that facilitate interaction between them—it does so in a general way because they are treated here as a vehicle of change rather than as a source of change.

Institutions are important. The unique character of any society is the outcome of interactions between fundamental economic forces and the cultural values embodied in the central institutions of that society. A distinction should be made, however, between the superficial character of institutions and their functional role. While the superficial features are interesting—like the background to a well composed portrait—it is only the underlying functions of institutions that need detain us here. Institutions differ between cultures, even functionally, because there is usually scope for different institutional response to changes in fundamental economic forces. There is no historical optimal development path for societal institutions. Institutions are important in the process of change, but not as important as underlying economic forces such as the demand and supply of commodities and factors of production. They are important because they facilitate economic change. Economic forces transform institutions, but institutions do not transform economic forces. Indeed, if institutions are inappropriate or inflexible—such as those in the former USSR—and they stand in the path of changing economic forces, those institutions will be swept away and replaced. It is these fundamental economic forces that I wish to expose through the timescapes and existential models in this book—models that focus on the general, rather than the unique, character of society.

Existential models are, nevertheless, specific to time and place. They tell us what logical models can never tell us—which of all logical possibilities, depending on the combination of assumptions made, is the one that was, and is, relevant to the development of human society. They can even tell us about economic issues that have been completely overlooked by theorists, or that cannot be handled successfully by the logical models that economists employ. These include, as was observed in *Economics without time*, the big issues of change in human society in the very longrun; those important issues of society, such as the household economy, that are not incorporated into the body of mainstream economic thought; and complex issues such as population increase, economic growth, and environmental change.

Economic growth is an interesting illustration of the limitations of theory. Because real-world change and growth is a complex process that involves many regional-specific variations, it must be observed before it can be explained. There is no universal growth process that can be worked out logically and applied in all cases. As the logical model does not observe before explaining, it cannot—and does not—tell us much. What the logical model can do is to specify the conditions under which certain outcomes will occur—such as stagnation, instability, equilibrium, exponential growth—or to state the central assumptions—such as decreasing, constant, or increasing returns—and determine the outcome. This is true not only for mainstream economic theory, but also for logical models derived from the new evolutionary/biological perspective in economics. In contrast, the existential model can tell us a good deal about real-world growth processes. By presenting an array of numerical variables over long periods of time, the existential model can *show* how an economy changes, in terms of its pattern, structure, and key relationships. This showing is a prerequisite to explaining the nature of the growth process.

## *The logical model*

The **logical model** is a construct of the mind that is intended to synthetically establish the probable relationships between key variables abstracted from reality. It is constructed not from data corresponding to real world features, but from abstract mathematical symbols that are brought together deductively into a logical system. Logical models correspond to reality only in the minds of those who create them and who continue to have faith in them even when attempts to apply them to reality are unsatisfactory—unsatisfactory in terms of both explanatory and predictive power, and in terms of policy successes. Their strength is their elegance and rigour, but their weakness is their simplicity and artificiality. They fail to formally recognize the real world because they are not constructed from tangible building blocks. Indeed their methodology is, on its own, self-defeating, because they attempt to explain without showing. The only reason that some economic models provide insight into the real world is because of the great intuition possessed by very few theorists—such as the ahistorical intuition of Keynes—that may partially compensate for the lack of historical seeing. But this is rare. When ordinary economists, who make up the bulk of the profession, attempt to emulate this performance, their lack of intuition is reflected in the lack of relevance of their theoretical attempts. A safer procedure is to place seeing before explaining.

The logical model, therefore, is driven by the nature of logical thought, while the existential model allows the real world to suggest its own relationships. Accordingly, the existential model enables us to explore complex, unexpected, and forgotten issues. But this should not be a choice between competing methodologies, rather there should be a *rapprochement* between them.

## Deductive theory

To illustrate the theoretical approach to reality we need, given the subject of this study, to look no further than that remarkable book, *A treatise on the family* by Gary Becker. A book of major importance, it is also a curious mixture of 'stylized' facts, intuition, rigorous logical thought, and largely undigested recent (since 1950) statistical data added at the end of the book almost as an afterthought. The contrast between the rigour of the formal models and the casual empiricism is striking. It is a contrast shared with many other important theoretical works.[7]

Becker begins by preparing the scene for what he is really interested in— the logical exploration of selected theoretical issues concerning the hypothetical household. He begins by telling us what the world is like, but only in very general and imprecise terms. We are told, for example, that: 'The *large* growth in the labor force participation of married women during the last 35 years has been accompanied by a *steep* fall in fertility and a *sharp* rise in divorce rates'.[8] No attempt is made to test the causes of loosely observed phenomena—indeed he admits that he 'is not primarily concerned with the causes of the increase'[9] and will leave that to others.[10] Basically his concerns are not with the interaction of the household and the market sectors but with decision-making within the household, similar to the interests of the traditional microeconomist in the theoretical (rather than the actual) firm. These theoretical issues include the gender division of labour, polygamy and monogamy, assortative mating, the demand for children, marriage and divorce, and non-human families. As he says:

> Although the main emphasis of the book is on analytical development, most chapters also contain empirical evidence: statistical data for recent periods; historical studies of particular villages, cities, and countries; information on Islamic, African, and Oriental societies; and anthropologic ethnographies of primitive societies. The evidence is covered much less systematically than the theory.[11]

It is, in fact, a pot-pourri of bits and pieces of fact (and even fiction) used unsystematically to *illustrate*, rather than to *demonstrate*, the relevance and importance of his theoretical concerns.

This illustrative method is only a background for Becker's theoretical 'games'—as serious as those games may be—which involve throwing off 'implications' from his model, with no attempt—other than through argument—to show how realistic or empirically important they are. He also uses these untested 'implications' to develop future scenarios.[12] This type of mainstream theorizing, however, does not provide a sound basis for predicting the future, because it is not grounded in reality. Becker's 'implications' are merely speculations. To say anything persuasive about the future, we need to examine systematically the *dynamics* of the system. Static economic analysis of the type employed by Becker and other deductive economists may provide interesting insights regarding relationships within the household at a point in time, but it tells us little about household dynamics over time, and nothing about the dynamics of household/market interactions. Nothing, in other words, about how societies travel through time.[13]

## *Applying deductive theory*

The failure of theoretical economics to capture the dynamics of economic change in its mental constructs, has led applied economists into difficult and uncharted waters. The toolkit of the applied labour economist contains a number of partial and general equilibrium models, but not a satisfactory dynamic model of economic change. While applied economists employ data sets that may range over fifteen years or so, they do not really take a longrun approach to contemporary models. Indeed the length of the timeseries is usually dictated by the number of observations required to satisfy the diagnostic tests of econometric analysis. And with the availability of quarterly data, the need to probe very far back into the past diminishes. Thus applied economists do not gain an effective perspective on current circumstances, and they run the risk of using data from an atypical period (such as the 1950s and 1960s). But even worse, the applied economist's interpretation of this data is necessarily one-dimensional, because it is not viewed as part of a dynamic process, and certainly not part of a dynamic process that involves an interaction between the household and market sectors. This can be illustrated by reference to the work of labour economists, during the last few decades, on the changing market participation of married females.

Since the pioneering applied work by Jacob Mincer in 1962 on the supply of female labour,[14] there has been a flood of supply-side analysis in the USA inspired by human capital theory.[15] An Australian example is provided by Gregory *et al.* (1985).[16] In this work, the changing participation of females in the market is explained largely in terms of female and non-female market income by employing a static framework. Little or no consideration is given either to demand forces or to dynamic processes. This one-sided approach can, unfortunately, produce idiosyncratic explanations of what is the greatest change in capitalist economies since the Industrial Revolution—the major shift of married women from the household to the market sector. Some have characterized this shift, not as a response to changes in the technological base (including the sectoral structure) of the economy, but as resulting from institutional—and even irrational—forces responsible for exogenously determined wage rates.[17]

An attempt has been made in this book, especially in Chapter 5, to show that, by taking a longer view, by attempting to visualize the complex process of change, and by focusing upon the Total Economy rather than the market sector, it is possible to view the Australian economic system as being driven by rational decisionmakers and in which economic variables, including the gender structure of labour demand (totally overlooked by Becker and those that have followed him) and the female/male wage ratio, are endogenously determined. But that is the subject of later chapters. For the remainder of this chapter we will consider further the nature of economic timescapes and existential models.

# Quantitative economic history as photo-realism

The distinction between seeing and explaining needs to be further explored. Economists, as has been argued, are familiar with logical explanations, but not with the understanding that emerges from seeing patterns in reality—an understanding that comes before full explanation. A revealing way of exploring the concept of understanding through seeing is by employing the metaphor of photo-realism. An appropriate embodiment for this metaphor, given the subject of this study, is the family photograph album.

The archetypical family photograph album contains individual and group portraits together with snapshots of daily home life, leisure activities, holidays, and touring expeditions throughout the countryside and even abroad: snapshots taken at different points in time over a generation or more. Each photograph reflects a passing fragment of reality—a reflected fragment of the outside physical world fixed on paper through the indifferent lens of the *camera obscura*. Each photograph means little on its own. But a sequence of related photographs—related by the unity of the family—will show not only how the life of the household has changed but also how relationships between members of the family and with the outside world have developed. Changes in the economic, social, and cultural situation of the family are reflected in changes of clothing and personal styles, changes in housing and possessions, and changes in leisure and holiday activities. And changing relationships within the family can be seen in the shifting balance between ageing parents and growing children; between the gradual disappearance of grandparents and the steady emergence of grandchildren and even great grandchildren. Changing relationships between our family and other families are also recorded: an assortment of friends and acquaintances make their appearance—some briefly, some regularly—and then depart, forever.

By flicking through the pages of the family photograph album these reflected fragments of reality project onto the mind's eye an overall picture of a wider reality. This procedure provides an animated sequence of mirror-like fragments that correspond to the dynamic process of the family's real life. It provides an overall picture, showing the changing relationships within and without the family over long periods of time. To see this animated sequence of life-reflecting surfaces fixed in time for all time, is to understand something of the real process of change. This is understanding through seeing, a process that precedes any formal explanation. Full understanding, however, requires the generalizing (existential modelling) and testing of what we see to ensure that our eyes are not playing tricks on us—that there are no flaws in the glass. Aspects of this conceptualization can be found in Susan Sontag's philosophical essay on photography. When discussing the function of the camera in extracting an isolated moment from the flow of life, she says that 'The camera makes reality atomic, manageable, and opaque', and again, 'The force of a photograph is that it keeps open to scrutiny instants which the normal flow of time immediately replaces'.[18]

The metaphor can be further developed by comparing the family photograph album with an oil painting of the family. If the artist is competent, the painting will be technically impressive. We will be dazzled by the perceptive subjective interpretation of the relationship between its members; by the contrasting highlights and shadows; by the outward appearance of cohesion but with a subtle hint of something darker, even tragic. The artist may even treat us to a series of paintings on the same theme in order to explore the changing relationship between family members and with the outside world, but a painting or a series of paintings cannot show us what reality is like, only what the artist *thinks* it is like. The selective eye of the artist has replaced the indifferent lens of the camera (despite the obvious controlling influence of the photographer), such that the degree of subjectivity underlying the painting is far greater. And finally, the essential quality of painting lies in its static rather than dynamic vision of life: it presents a picture of life in equilibrium.

The metaphor is apt. In quantitative economic history, the individual snapshots are the annual estimates of economic inputs and outcomes—the mirror-like fragments that reflect an unknown reality. These fragments are fixed on paper in camera through our very visual, but sometimes far too obscure, craft. And because reflections of reality have been extracted at regular intervals from the relentless flow of time, they are impressed on our memory and our understanding. The broader picture of real-world relationships—what I have called timescapes in this study—is provided by a series of annual statistical estimates comparable to an animated sequence of mirror-like fragments reflecting reality. Why pictures rather than tables? Because pictures, rather than tables, appeal directly to our visual-intellectual faculty of understanding through seeing, and because pictures rather than tables are more acceptable to the general reader. Pictures have universal appeal, while the appeal of tables is definitely limited to the initiated. In this way we see, and begin to understand, the relationships between economic agents over time. And out of this understanding we construct hypotheses—our existential models—that can be formally tested.

But we need not only to *see* the pattern of real-world processes, we also need to think imaginatively about what we see. There is, however, a danger here. We must seek explanations for what we see in what we see, not in what theory conditions us to expect. To interpret our hard-won data through the eyes of deductive theorists is to distort the picture of reality—or, in William Cunningham's words, to 'pervert economic history'.[19] Theory should be used either as a sorting device to exclude the irrelevant, or as a test of the logic of our argument, but not as a way of seeing. Indeed there is little point in going to great efforts to extract large quantities of data merely to use it to *illustrate* the simple models of economists. The data must be interpreted according to its own lights, and so the empirical, or existential, models that we employ, while they should be informed by theory, must emerge inductively from the observed relationships, from the timescapes. In this process, econometric technique must be employed imaginatively as an aid to the process of seeing—of induction—not as a blind substitute for it in the service of deduction. Ultimately theory may prove to be more important in the selection of data than in its interpretation, and econometric method may prove to be more effective as a test of the objectivity of seeing rather than as a test of logical relationships.

If quantitative economic history has much in common with the study of photo-realism—the attempt to record the fleeting image of reality objectively—then deductive theory has much in common with abstract painting. Intelligently crafted theory expressed in mathematical terms has an elegance and simplicity that matches the highest artistic achievement. And it stands in stark contrast to the complicated, brutal, and largely unpredictable reality of the world. It is the different degree of control exercised by human agents that underlies this contrast between the real and the theoretical worlds. While the theoretical world is dominated by the aesthetic shaping influence of the theorist, the real world of economy and society is the outcome of competing groups of people operating in an uncertain world that is periodically subjected to disruptions caused by environmental and biological forces beyond human control. There is, therefore, a fundamental mismatch between the nature of theory and the nature of reality.

# Seeing is the beginning of understanding

Despite the dazzling display offered by deductive theory, it cannot show us what reality is like, only what the theorist thinks it is like. We should not be overwhelmed by the technical sophistication of theory, because the world of the economist is simple in the extreme—a static two-dimensional world in which economic change is a timeless notion associated with longrun equilibria. And because possibilities in the economists' world are constrained by what the deductive theorist expects to encounter, formal economic models omit both the unexpected, and the larger, issues that lie beyond the personal experience of the profession's practitioners.

Insufficient comparison is made with reality before economic theory is used for policy purposes, generally because the simple elegant mathematical models cannot cope with the complex, often bizarre, processes of the real world. Theory is only at its best when economic systems are in equilibrium and when those systems are dismembered sufficiently to isolate economic activities of manageable proportions. And even if a comparison is made and the theory is found wanting, it is generally the data *rather* than the theory that is rejected. This is a legacy of the theorist's habit of explaining before seeing. Theorists are indoctrinated about causal relationships in the real world, before they consult the real world. Is it surprising, therefore, that these theoretical relationships attain the status of the *idée fixe*? Theory is rarely rejected, it just becomes used less often as new, equally untested, theories become fashionable. Like so many other areas of human endeavour, the world of the economist is the world of fashion. This highlights the dangers of explaining before seeing, and demands the reversal of our priorities.

In this study, real-world data are treated seriously. A vast array of data has been employed to construct quantitative pictures of the nature of household production, of the changing relationship between the household and market economies, and, finally, of the Total Economy.

Those who need to satisfy their curiosity about the manner of their construction may wish to advance immediately to Part Two and then return to pick up the threads of the story beginning in Chapter 2. These economic timescapes of Australia's Total Economy are employed to construct existential models that provide realistic explanations for the observed changes. In the process, I hope to show that seeing is the beginning of understanding. As such, this study is a portrait of, rather than a treatise on, the family within the Total Economy.

# Part One

---

## The Forgotten Economy

# 2

---

# *The Total Economy*

$T$he challenge being issued in this work is to look at the economy—in this particular case the Australian economy—in a new way. Economists since the Industrial Revolution have become accustomed to viewing the market sector—with many focusing on just the private part of the market sector—as the entire economy. It is as if we had forgotten that the private sector, or indeed the entire market sector, is only part of a wider economy. To avoid any ambiguity I refer to the wider economy as the **Total Economy**—total in the sense of encompassing all forms of economic activity whether or not they pass through the market. We need to treat the Australian household and market sectors not separately, but as one economy: as the Total Economy. The purpose of this chapter is to survey an integrated series of timescapes—based on the total national accounts presented in Part Two—for the household, market, and total economies of Australia between 1788 and 1990, and to construct and test existential models concerning the dynamic relationship between the household and the market.

## A tale of two revolutions

Over the past 300 years there have been two radical changes in the role of the household in the Total Economy. The first was a product of the Industrial Revolution, and the second resulted from the emergence of the post-industrial transformation, which I have called the **new economic revolution**, after the Second World War. In England during the time of Gregory King—the late seventeenth century—the household was the focus of economic activity for both males and females as they moved into and out of the market. Indeed, King's estimates of national income were constructed on a household basis.[1] Both male and female family members worked in and around the house without pay; they worked on any family land for both sustenance and the production of goods for the market; they took advantage of the common land to graze their animals; they worked part-time for wages on nearby farms or in nearby towns; they sold the results of cottage-industry activity; and they worked seasonally on the seas and in the mines. And the household was the organizing principle for all these various part-time and seasonal activities by adults and children, males and females. There was a gender division of labour in both sectors, but it was based on a biologically determined comparative advantage, not on a market/male and household/female distinction. The female members of the family generally adopted a supportive role in which they helped their husbands, fathers, and brothers in these various activities by undertaking the less physically demanding tasks.[2]

The British Industrial Revolution of the late eighteenth to early nineteenth centuries, however, created a new gender division of labour, this time on market-household lines. It also reduced the seasonal and part-time nature of work, and led to the market becoming the main determinant of the use of family time. In particular, the change in the market participation of married women was just as dramatic then as the change that has occurred since the Second World War, but in the opposite direction.[3] During the second half of the nineteenth century, household work became regarded as women's work, and market work was deemed to be primarily men's work. As will be argued below, this was largely technologically determined. Only after 1950 was this situation reversed. As we shall see, it took a further major technological change to enable women to take their place once more alongside men in the market.

The contemporary economic and social revolution that has centred on an increasing market participation by women—particularly married women—throughout the Western World, is vividly pictured in Figure 2.1. Only those OECD nations not devastated by the Second World War have been included because of the massive but temporary impact of post-war reconstruction on female participation rates in countries such as Germany, France, and Japan.[4] In general, the market participation of all working-age females in this sample of countries—USA, Canada, UK, and Australia—increased from 25–40 per cent in 1950 to 60–68 per cent in 1990, a two-fold increase in forty years. While the data for 'married' women are less reliable, and less readily available, they suggest that the market participation of household workers in the Western World increased from 10–20 per cent in 1950 to 45–60 per cent in 1990— more than a threefold increase over the same period. Yet this change was not one of steady growth throughout, particularly for the decade after the mid 1970s when a slow-down occurred, and particularly for Australia and the UK. Hence the impact of the new economic revolution was relatively greater for married women (and thereby for the household) than for all women. A fascinating international outcome of the new economic revolution is a convergence of female market participation rates throughout the Western World. In 1950 the range of participation rates was quite wide (60 per cent of the lower bound in the case of all females) whereas by 1990 it was quite narrow (13 per cent of the lower bound). This convergence is probably due

**Figure 2.1 Female market participation in the Western World, 1950–1990**

(i) All working-age women (15–64 years)

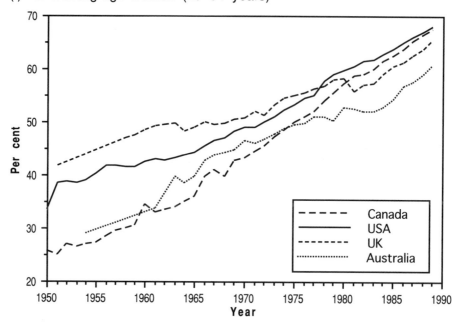

(ii) Married women

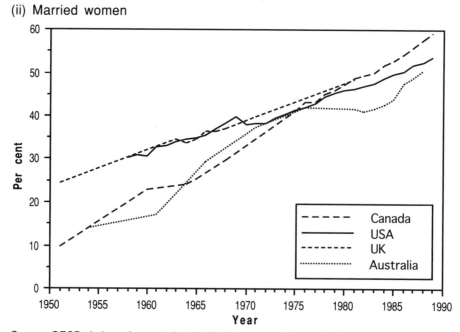

Source: OECD, *Labour force statistics*; UN, *Demographic yearbooks*.

to the greater structural comparability of economies in the tertiary, as opposed to the secondary, phase of development—particularly as between old and new countries. There is an element of economic leap-frogging here. Finally, as the great change in female market participation in Australia was similar to that in other Western countries, the analysis in this book should be of general interest.

# A model of the Total Economy

The Total Economy in both the past and the present is a more complex entity than the market sector, and the interactions between its various parts need to be carefully considered. Figure 2.2 provides a very simple diagrammatic macro-model of a closed Total Economy consisting of three sectors—household, private and public—and of the main flows of goods, services and factors, together with reverse flows of cash payments and factor returns. The dominant feature of this model is a composite household, with its own set of internal relationships, consisting of the **household economy** on the one hand, and family leisure activities on the other. Goods and services produced in both the market and household economies are combined with family leisure time to produce new and regenerated labour that passes back into the Total Economy through the household economy. Given the relative size of the household economy—35.8 per cent of Australian **Gross Community Income** (the sum of market and household income) for the whole period 1860 to 1990—together with its wider importance as being the only supplier (in the closed system) of new and regenerated labour, it is difficult to understand how it could have been so neglected by mainstream economics for so long.[5] This is particularly the case if we think of the private and public sectors as an outgrowth of a primitive and all-embracing household sector (as in the age-old Australian aboriginal economy)—in the beginning was the household.[6] From this perspective the emergence of separate private and public sectors can be interpreted as resulting from a process of contracting-out former household activities to specialists who, through division of labour and accumulation of specialist capital, were able to achieve higher levels of productivity and to pass on some of the benefits to households in the form of higher consumption standards. This contracting-out occurs, as discussed in Chapter 3, because households are unable directly to take advantage of economies of scale owing to the difficulty of imposing market-type supervision on a household of related workers. Household size has, in fact, remained remarkably constant over very long periods of time.

The importance of the household sector, therefore, is not merely quantitative. It is the strategic centre of the Total Economy, and of society as a whole. Decisions made in the household determine the amount and type of society's labour that is divided between the household and the market place; it

**Figure 2.2 The closed Total Economy**

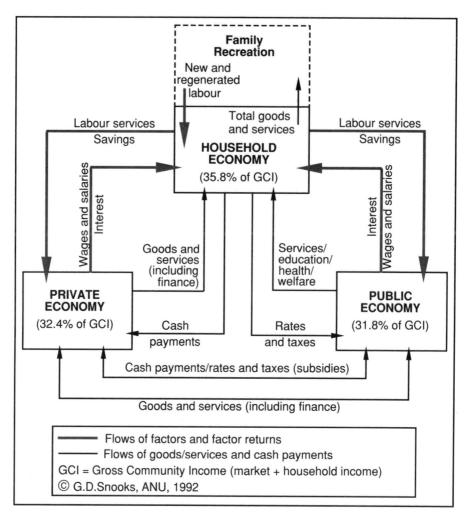

Flows of factors and factor returns
Flows of goods/services and cash payments
GCI = Gross Community Income (market + household income)
© G.D.Snooks, ANU, 1992

determines what proportion of total household income is consumed, what proportion is saved, and where the surplus is to be directed; it determines what goods and services will be purchased from the market place both private and public; it determines what political, economic, and social objectives are to be pursued by society—it is, as we shall see, the driving force in society and hence in history. Clearly, not all individual households have an equal say in these matters—it depends on their control of resources. Throughout history, the socio-economic class in which the ruling families are to be found has varied, from the small but powerful landowning elite of feudal society to the large consuming class of post-industrial capitalism.

The other two sectors in our model are the private economy, which in the Australian case has contributed only 32.4 per cent of Gross Community Income over the last 200 years, and the public economy, which has contributed the final 31.8 per cent of Gross Community Income. Figure 2.2, therefore, provides a snapshot, in simple but bold profile, of the main macroeconomic interactions between these sectors. It shows the household sector providing labour services and savings to the private and public sectors in return for wages, salaries, interest, and dividends. From the point of view of the household this is the supply side of sectoral interaction. On the demand side are the goods and services (including public utilities, education, health, and welfare) consumed by the household which are balanced by reverse flows of cash payments, rates and taxes.[7] And finally between the private and public sectors there are the flows, in both directions, of goods and services (including finance), and balancing flows, also in both directions, of cash payments and rates and taxes/subsidies. Equilibrium between the household, private, and public sectors at any point in time will depend upon available natural resources, technology, and the prevailing set of factor prices.

The closed macroeconomic model in Figure 2.2 can be extended to include the usual interactions with the world economy. These involve exports and imports of goods and services, and flows of factors of production as well as returns to factors (which, in the case of labour, generally remain in the host country, although there are many examples of the remittance of earnings back to the country of origin where the extended family claims property rights over individuals when they leave). Of course, when the Total Economy is opened to international influences, the household ceases to be the only direct source of new labour for the private and public sectors. And equilibrium between the three sectors also depends upon external conditions of trade and international factor flows.

As Figure 2.2 is a macroeconomic model it does not show relationships between economic agents—individual households, firms, and government instrumentalities—either between sectors or within the same sector. Nor does it tell us anything about the decision-making process in any of the sectors. That would require a set of microeconomic models. While economics gives much attention to the theory of the firm, and to the theory of public choice, less attention is paid to the theory of the household. The most notable, but not the only, contribution to the theory of the household is Becker's *A treatise on the family*. Although his model will be formally discussed in Chapters 3 and 7, a brief informal discussion is helpful here. In most modern economic systems, family time is utilized in three main ways: working in the market sector for a money wage; working in the household sector to produce goods and services not for sale but for direct consumption (there may be, however, some barter of surpluses between households); and involvement in leisure activities that are ends in themselves. The allocation of time between these three main activities takes place via the market mechanism. It is possible to illustrate this by focusing on two of these three activities—market work and household work—and assuming that, on average, households act in an economically rational way. Assume also that we begin from a position of equilibrium, so that each household is satisfied with its allocation of time between various activities. This equilibrium will be disrupted if, say, there is an increase in real market wage rates, because the marginal utility of time devoted to market work will exceed that used in household work. This means that households can increase their total utility from the use of time by working more hours in the market and fewer hours in the household. Accordingly there will be a flow of labour services from the household and to the market, which will reduce the hourly wage of market work and increase the shadow wage of household work. In the absence of any further underlying economic change, this flow of labour will continue until there is no household that believes it can improve its material position by shifting its labour time from one sector to the other. The economic system will be in equilibrium once more, with the marginal utility of time being equal in both sectors. It is a simple matter to extend this model to include leisure as well as paid and unpaid work.

As the model in Figure 2.2 is only a snapshot taken at a point in time, it cannot explain how the Total Economy changes through time. Indeed economists have been unable to successfully model real-world growth processes because of the complexities involved.[8] But they have been able to indicate the key forces in this growth process—capital formation, population growth, technological change, increases in factor quality, new natural resources, changing relative factor prices, and trade. What they have not adequately discussed are the changes occurring within the household that have contributed, through the various interactions outlined in our model, to the overall process of economic development: changes that include investment in new housing and renovations, expenditure on household equipment, factor substitution, changes in household organization and, most significantly over the last forty years, the outflow of married females from the household to the market sector. Although these changes have been dependent on the dynamics of the market economy, the household sector has played a central role in facilitating them. Further, these changes have had an important impact on the economic development of the Total Economy both directly and through interactions with the private and public sectors. Indeed, it is just not possible to understand the process of economic change by excluding the household sector from consideration.

It is with the interactions between these sectors—with the dynamics of the Total Economy—that this study is primarily concerned. If, for example, the equilibrium portrayed in Figure 2.2 is disturbed by a change in any one of these sectors—say by an innovation in the private economy, or by a change in demand for goods and services by the household sector, or by a change in investment policy of the public sector—a process of disequilibrium will be set in motion that will communicate itself to the other sectors through the flows of goods, services, factors, and the various payments for such. Clearly the strongest effects will be felt through forces that lead to changes in demand for the products and resources of other sectors, but changes on the supply side that affect the quantity and quality of the factors of production available to the market sector, will also have an important impact upon the Total Economy. It is in this way that the pictures of change—the economic timescapes—presented in this chapter are to be viewed and interpreted.

In addition, there is an even more fundamental dynamic relationship between the household and market sectors. As shown in Chapter 6, while the market sector is the source of economic growth, the household sector is the source of economic expansion, and both are part of a wider dynamic process of economic transformation. Indeed, the fruits of economic transformation— increases in total income per household—are used by the family to finance either an increase in the number of households through procreation, or an increase in the level of consumption per household, or both. This unexpected relationship is the basis of the model developed in Chapter 6 to explain the process of Australian economic development in general over the past 60,000 years, and in particular over the past 200 years.

# New pictures of reality

The statistical estimates presented in Part Two of this work are the basic components of the new pictures of reality that are developed and explored in this section. These quantitative sketches are the economic timescapes discussed in Chapter 1, and are concerned with the outline of longrun processes of change in human society and particularly with the structural relationships involved in this process. There are a number of ways in which the key relationships in the process of economic change can be explored both pictorially and analytically—from the net income produced in those sectors, and from the fixed capital expenditures that they generate. These timescapes will be discussed in a general way in this section, and in the next they will be employed to construct both aggregated and disaggregated dynamic existential models— models of real-world economic change.

## *Economic expansion*

The structure of the dynamic relationships between the household, market, and total economies is graphically shown in Figure 2.3. Dynamic pictures over long periods of time are best composed in logarithmic rather than arithmetic form, as the latter (Figure 2.3(i)) always give the impression that the fastest growth has occurred in the last quarter of the period under study—that nothing happens for most of the period and then, at the last moment, everything takes off vertically. Nothing could be further from the truth. As Figure 2.3(ii) shows, the *rate* of economic expansion (reflected in the slopes of the curves) was far more impressive prior to 1860 than it was thereafter. The focal point from

**Figure 2.3 Gross Community Income by sector, (constant prices) Australia, 1800–1990**

(i) Arithmetic scale

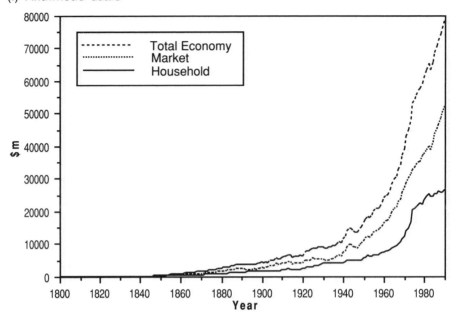

(ii) Logarithmic scale

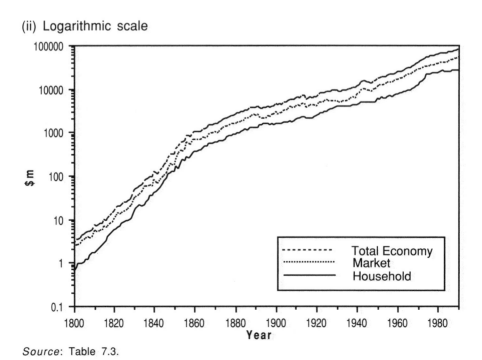

*Source*: Table 7.3.

which the data are viewed, therefore, can affect the perspective one has of reality. Provided we keep in mind the scale effects, a semi-log graph (as in Figure 2.3(ii)), in which growth rates are represented by the slopes of the curves, provides the most informative picture of the shape and structure of longrun dynamic relationships.

The fastest rate of expansion of the Total Economy was achieved before 1860, when the vast underutilized resources of Australia were brought into the British mode of capitalist production (Figure 2.3(ii) and Table 2.1). While the economic base was small in the early nineteenth century, the initial difficulties in constructing the foundations for a capitalist economic system in Australia were large, and so the achievement was impressive. This was particularly true between 1830 and 1850 when economic expansion was about as rapid as that achieved during the goldrushes of the 1850s. Between 1860 and 1890, however, the rate of expansion slowed considerably as the vast land resources of the Australian continent were brought increasingly into the newly established European capitalist economy. Expansion slowed even more during the years 1890 to 1939, a period when the economy was subjected to severe internal and external shocks—two major depressions, a major drought, and a world war. But rates of expansion comparable to those in the second half of the nineteenth century were reattained after the Second World War, at least until the mid 1970s. Since that time a new phase of slower expansion, comparable in growth-rate terms to the 1903 to 1939 period, has been experienced.

The original quantitative snapshots of the market economy were taken by Noel Butlin in the 1950s.[9] What is not known is the nature of the dynamic relationship between the market and household sectors, and how this produced changes in the Total Economy. We need to build up a new sequence of pictures of reality to both augment and replace those we already have. Figure 2.3(ii) (and Table 2.1) provides our first general view—more detailed aspects will be provided later—of **market/household dynamics**. The first feature to notice is the changing relative importance of the household sector in the expansion of the Total Economy over the last 200 years. Between 1800 and 1861 the household sector grew (10.02 per cent per annum) slightly more rapidly than the market sector (9.79 per cent per annum). From 1861 to 1889 the market (4.71 per cent per annum) and the household (4.56 per cent per annum) increased at similar rates, but between 1889 and 1939 the household sector (2.22 per cent per annum) forged ahead of the market sector (1.79 per cent per annum). Once again, between 1946 and 1974 the household sector (5.86 per cent per annum) increased its size more rapidly than the market sector (4.63 per cent per annum), and only between 1974 and 1990 did the market sector (2.78 per cent per annum) turn the tables on its old competitor the household (1.34 per cent per annum). Our first glimpse of the market and household sectors in harness, therefore, suggests that there was a considerable degree of ebbing and flowing between them, and that a measure of market activity—such as real GDP—cannot adequately capture the economic outcomes let alone the dynamic processes that gave rise to them.

**Table 2.1    Real rates of growth for the market, household, and total economies, Australia, 1800–1990 (per cent per annum)**

|  | Market income* | Household income* | Gross Community Income* | Household income | Gross Community Income | GDP* | Population | Number of households | GDP per capita* | GCI per capita | GCI per household |
|---|---|---|---|---|---|---|---|---|---|---|---|
| **1800–1990** | 5.47 | 5.48 | 5.47 |  |  | 5.55 | 4.33 | 5.02 | 1.18 | 1.10 | 0.43 |
| **1861–1990** | 3.43 | 3.34 | 3.40 | 3.45 | 3.43 | 3.50 | 2.08 | 2.44 | 1.39 | 1.33 | 0.93 |
| **1946–1990** | 4.03 | 3.89 | 3.98 | 4.26 | 4.11 | 4.19 | 1.82 | 2.52 | 2.32 | 2.24 | 1.43 |
| **1800–1850** | 9.24 | 9.81 | 9.44 |  |  | 9.50 | 8.92 | 10.22 | 0.54 | 0.48 | -0.71 |
| **1800–1861** | 9.79 | 10.02 | 9.87 |  |  | 9.89 | 9.13 | 10.56 | 0.70 | 0.61 | -0.63 |
| **1830–1850** | 8.77 | 11.07 | 9.55 |  |  | 9.19 | 8.72 | 11.25 | 0.43 | 0.76 | -1.57 |
| **1861–1889** | 4.71 | 4.40 | 4.60 | 4.56 | 4.66 | 4.76 | 3.38 | 2.84 | 1.34 | 1.24 | 1.73 |
| **1889–1939** | 1.79 | 2.33 | 1.99 | 2.22 | 1.94 | 1.75 | 1.64 | 2.24 | 0.11 | 0.30 | -0.24 |
| **1903–1914** | 4.39 | 3.56 | 4.11 | 3.37 | 4.06 | 4.76 | 2.01 | 2.51 | 2.71 | 2.00 | 1.63 |
| **1903–1939** | 2.26 | 2.95 | 2.52 | 2.65 | 2.40 | 2.32 | 1.58 | 2.32 | 0.73 | 0.80 | 0.23 |
| **1919–1925** | 4.23 | 4.41 | 4.30 | 8.17 | 5.55 | 3.09 | 1.79 | 2.60 | 1.29 | 3.71 | 1.56 |
| **1939–1946** | 4.64 | 1.67 | 3.50 | 1.45 | 3.52 | 5.06 | 0.89 | 0.90 | 4.14 | 2.62 | 2.44 |
| **1946–1974** | 4.63 | 5.13 | 4.81 | 5.86 | 5.07 | 5.08 | 2.07 | 2.69 | 2.95 | 2.94 | 2.07 |
| **1974–1982** | 2.22 | 2.38 | 2.28 | 2.10 | 2.17 | 2.07 | 1.12 | 2.11 | 0.94 | 1.04 | 0.16 |
| **1974–1990** | 2.78 | 1.58 | 2.34 | 1.34 | 2.25 | 2.44 | 1.30 | 2.08 | 1.12 | 0.93 | 0.26 |
| **1982–1990** | 3.03 | 0.60 | 2.14 | 0.43 | 2.07 | 2.53 | 1.33 | 1.82 | 1.18 | 0.72 | 0.32 |

*Notes:*    Columns marked * were deflated using the implicit GDP deflator (1966/67 prices). Those colums unmarked were deflated using the implicit GDP deflator for the market sector, and the final consumption deflator for the household sector. The final consumption deflator is not available for years prior to 1861. The latter are the preferred series.

*Sources:*    Calculated from Tables 7.3, 7.4, 7.5, 7.9, and 8.1; population from the ANU Clio database.

## Economic growth and community living standards

Inevitably growth—defined as changes in real per capita income—and changes in average living standards, are of greater interest than the mere expansion of economies. Our quantitative picture (Figures 2.4 and 2.5, and Table 2.1) of real Gross Community Income (GCI) per capita and real GDP per capita tell a different story. Figure 2.4 suggests that, over the 200 years since 1800, real GCI per capita increased via two giant permanent steps from 1850 to 1889 and from 1946 to 1974. These bold steps stand out against a background of stagnation (and even negative growth in terms of GCI per household) in the period 1800 to 1850, and instability between 1890 and 1939 (small tentative advances from 1904 to 1914 and from 1920 to 1925 were followed by retreats during the First World War and the Great Depression). No matter how much some scholars[10] wish to revive the status of the period 1890 to 1939, particularly in relation to the second half of the nineteenth century, it must be seen as adding little of a permanent nature to average material standards of Australian society. As Table 2.1 shows, the rate of growth of GCI per capita during 1889 to 1939 was 0.3 per cent per annum, compared with 1.2 per cent per annum from 1861 to 1889, and 2.9 per cent per annum from 1946 to 1974 (and even 0.9 per cent per annum from 1974 to 1990). Only briefly during the 1900s and 1910s (2.0 per cent per annum) and the first half of the 1920s (3.7 per cent per annum) did it rise to respectable levels. And, as shown in the final column of Table 2.1, GCI per *household*—the most appropriate measure of average living standards—actually *declined* by 0.2 per cent per annum in the interdepression period. GCI per *household* is used throughout this study as an indicator of the growth of the Total Economy because, as shown in Chapter 6, it is the central variable in the wider dynamic process of economic change.

This is not to say that the quality of life did not improve in this period. Various indicators of the quality of life, such as mortality, morbidity, and leisure show that it did improve significantly.[11] It is important, however, to emphasize the fact that the acquisition of material goods and services did not much improve, because it is the command over material goods and services that gives human society the resilience to survive in the longrun. In the past, societies that have failed to achieve **economic resilience**—failed to compete successfully in the race for economic power—have not survived. Economic resilience, not the acquisition of non-material gains, is the underlying objective of viable societies. This critical issue, which is discussed further in Chapter 3, appears to have been overlooked by previous scholars when discussing the issue of growth and living standards.

Before moving on, it is worth considering the contrasts between the earlier picture of economic expansion (Figure 2.3(ii)) and that of economic growth (Figure 2.4). Interestingly, the rapid expansion prior to 1861 (9.9 per cent per annum) was not translated into sustained economic growth (0.6 per cent per annum). It was a period dominated by the attempt to develop an economic

**Figure 2.4 Real GDP per capita and real GCI per capita, Australia, 1800–1990**

*Source*: Tables 7.5 and 7.9.

system that would facilitate the exploitation of Australia's vast natural resources, rather than a system that would improve economic efficiency. Also the expansion (whether in terms of real income or population) after the Second World War, which occurred at a similar rate to that achieved in the second half of the nineteenth century, gives little hint of the unprecedentedly rapid growth of per capita income achieved. Clearly there has been a marked improvement in the efficiency of the Australian growth process over the past 200 years.

Of particular interest is the picture of Australian economic growth that emerges when using estimates of GCI rather than the existing estimates of GDP. Figure 2.5 which is a collage created by superimposing the series of real GDP per capita on the series of real GCI per capita, presents the difference between these series by the shaded area. Here we have a clear picture (backed up by the alternative growth rates in Table 2.1) of the differences between these two series, which in turn reflects the role played in the Total Economy by the household sector. We can see that GCI grew faster (or declined more slowly) than GDP: during the booms of the 1860s and 1870s, the 1920s, and the 1950s; during the slower growth between the early 1970s and the early 1980s; during the depressions of the 1890s and 1930s; and during phases of the First and Second World Wars. The important point to note is that there were other periods—notably the 1850s, the 1880s, the early 1900s, the 1960s to early 1970s, and the latter part of the 1980s—when the market sector dominated.

**Figure 2.5 Gap between GCI per capita and GDP per capita, Australia, 1800–1990**

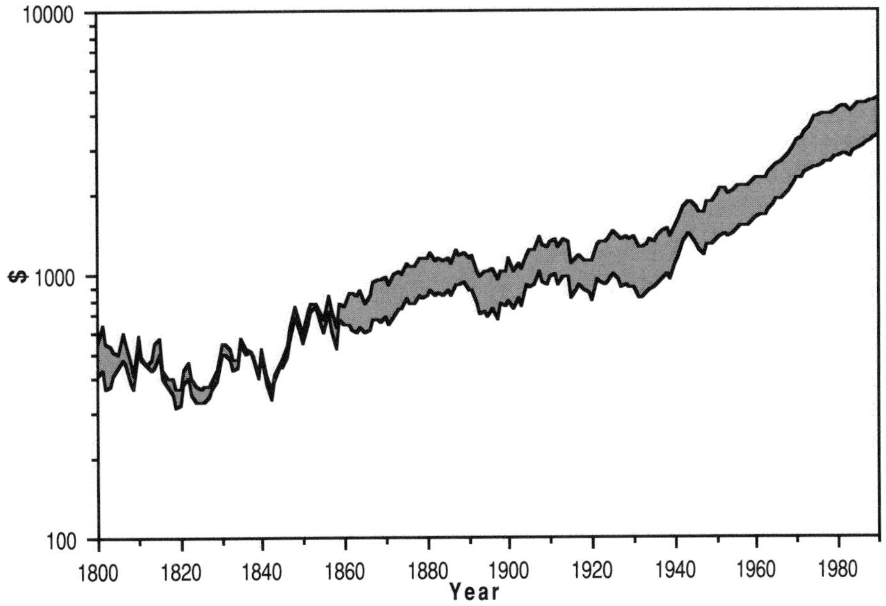

*Source*: Tables 7.3, 7.5 and 7.9.

Therefore, not only are there significant differences between GDP per capita—the traditional hybrid measure of economic growth—and GCI per capita—a new measure of growth in the Total Economy—but that these differences fluctuate quite dramatically. Accordingly, GDP per capita cannot be regarded as an appropriate proxy measure for total economic activity, or even for the market economy. A new measure of economic activity—a measure of Gross Community Income—is essential. This, however, is not the main justification for a measure of total economic activity—the main justification is that it enables us to analyse the dynamic process of household–market interaction.

## Productivity in the household and market

Productivity is a central issue in any discussion of the relationship between the household and market sectors. As I mentioned earlier, the *raison d'être* for a specialized market economy is that through market specialization it is possible to raise productivity levels, in the production of goods and services, above those possible in the household sector. One would anticipate, therefore, that labour productivity levels in the market sector would be significantly higher than those in the household sector. This prediction is borne out by the data. The selected years in Table 2.2 show that, apart from 1861 when market labour productivity levels were strongly influenced by the effects of the goldrushes (a predominance of small-scale economic activities), household productivity ranged from about half to two-thirds of that in the market sector. Clearly the market sector had an absolute advantage in the production of *some* goods and services, particularly those that could be mass produced using specialized labour and capital, and that were without special family significance.

In view of this substantial **productivity gap** between the market and household sectors, the interesting question is: why does not the household sector continue to contract out household activities until the market sector becomes the dominant, or even the only, economic sector in society? Certainly, there is no evidence of any tendency in this direction over the past 150 years. The reasons are two-fold. First, the productivity advantages possessed by the market sector arise from the large-scale production of rural and urban goods, rather than from the personal services in which the post–Industrial Revolution household has specialized. In the field of personal services the productivity gap does not appear to be so great. Second, a small productivity gap in personal services is not sufficient to overcome the preference of the vast majority of people to produce and consume them in the home. What the home provides is recreation in the sense of a renewal of the spirit. And there is no perfect market substitute for this.

A further issue of importance is how household productivity has changed, both in the short and long terms, over the last century or so. Figure 2.6 suggests that gains were made in two phases: one at the beginning and one at the end of the period between 1860 and 1990. Household productivity advanced steadily between 1861 and 1889 (by 22.7 per cent), and even more rapidly between 1950 and 1974 (by 97.1 per cent). It is also interesting that after each of these extended periods of productivity gain, levels declined slightly—by 11.5 per cent between 1889 and 1910 and by 6.4 per cent between 1974 and 1990. This is the natural outcome of a process of economic growth that takes place through long booms in which considerable imbalance occurs, and shorter periods of adjustment in which equilibrium is regained. The effects of retarded market activity for the period between 1889 and 1939 on household productivity are clearly seen in Figure 2.6. By the late 1930s the peak reached in the 1880s had only just been regained.

**Table 2.2   Household–market labour productivity levels, Australia, 1861–1990** (ratio of household to market)

| 1861 | 0.83 | 1921 | 0.54 | 1961 | 0.48 |
|------|------|------|------|------|------|
| 1871 | 0.55 | 1928 | 0.64 | 1966 | 0.47 |
| 1881 | 0.65 | 1933 | 0.69 | 1974 | 0.66 |
| 1891 | 0.61 | 1944 | 0.44 | 1981 | 0.64 |
| 1901 | 0.69 | 1947 | 0.55 | 1986 | 0.59 |
| 1911 | 0.56 | 1954 | 0.48 | 1990 | 0.54 |

*Note:*     Labour productivity levels in both sectors are gross income per worker (male and female).
*Source:*   Calculated from Table 9.11.

**Figure 2.6 Household and market labour productivity, Australia, 1861–1990**

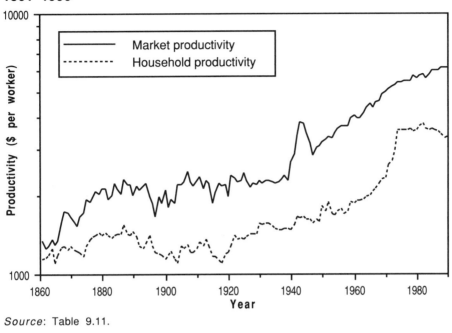

*Source*: Table 9.11.

How does this compare with market productivity? Generally speaking the longrun experience of both sectors is similar—steady advances in the second half of the nineteenth century followed by slight decline and stagnation until the Second World War, then a new phase of more rapid productivity gains lasting until the mid 1970s. As Figure 2.6 shows, the main contrasts are that market productivity gains were greater between 1860 and 1889, and that slower growth rather than decline was experienced after the mid 1970s. Also wars and depressions brought out contrasting cyclical experience, with the market doing better during the wars (when working hours were increased) and worse during the depressions (when the household sector became the mainstay of the unemployed). These long swings in productivity performance compare closely with those in the market capital/labour ratio depicted in Figure 4.3, p. 87, and reinforce the view that the interdepression period was one of stagnation and decline.

It is interesting that household productivity kept pace with market experience during the twentieth century, particularly between the Second World War and 1980. This shared productivity experience owes much to the close interaction between these two sectors, which involved a continuous response of households at the margin to changing relative prices for goods, services, and factors of production. Just as the growing costs of urbanization and of instability during the interwar years spread throughout the Total

Economy, so the benefits of stability and technological change in the private sector after the Second World War were shared by the household sector.

# Household–market dynamics

From this picture of longrun change in the Total Economy, it is possible to develop simple existential models of the dynamic process. This can be done at both the aggregated—household and market sectors—and disaggregated—household, private, and public sectors—levels. These existential models serve two functions: first, they provide a framework for the detailed analysis (in Chapters 3 to 5) of the way the household economy works, and the manner of its interaction with the market economy; and second, they provide a basis for a more comprehensive analysis of the longrun growth process (in Chapter 6).

## *Aggregated model*

### *Secular and cyclical features*

In this analysis, both the longrun and shortrun relationships between the household and market sectors will be explored. There are a number of questions that need to be asked. First, what is the longrun relationship between the household and market sectors? To answer this central question, we need to examine the longrun series concerning market and household income (in constant 1966/67 prices) presented in Figure 2.7 (and Table 2.1). The main longrun features are:

- a similar rate of growth of household income (5.48 per cent per annum) and market income (5.47 per cent per annum) for the last 200 years;
- a slightly more rapid growth of household (10.02 per cent per annum) than market (9.79 per cent per annum) income between 1800 and 1861;
- a slightly more rapid growth of the market (4.71 per cent per annum) than the household (4.40 per cent per annum) from 1861 to 1889;
- a significantly faster growth of household (2.33 per cent per annum) than market (1.79 per cent per annum) income in the long interdepression period 1889 to 1939;
- a slightly more rapid growth of the market sector (4.03 per cent per annum) than the household sector (3.89 per cent per annum) between 1946–1990, with the exception of the late 1960s and early 1970s.

The striking longrun feature of Australian economic development, therefore, is the slight ascendency of the market sector during periods of rapid growth—such as the two long booms of the second halves of both centuries—and the more significant ascendency of the household sector during periods of much slower growth or stagnation—such as the interdepression period. This

**Figure 2.7 Gross Community Income by sector (1966/67 prices), Australia, 1861–1990**

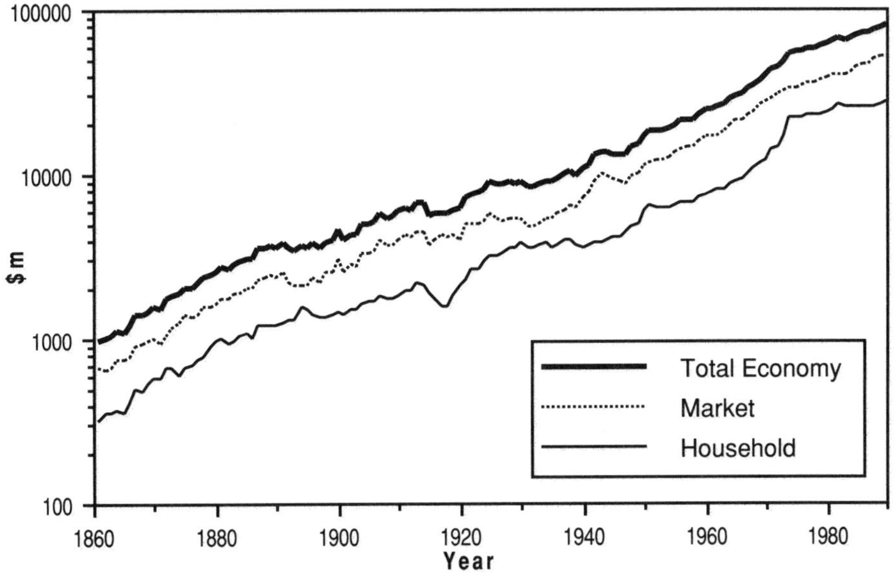

Source: Table 7.4.

suggests that rapid longrun growth requires market leadership, but that the household sector possesses an internal dynamic, involving natural population increase, that becomes apparent during long periods of retarded market development. During these periods of slower growth, therefore, the household sector plays a compensating role by expanding more rapidly than the market sector. The dynamic process internal to the household sector is examined in Chapters 3 and 6.

Second, the notable shortrun aspect of our story is a convergence between the market and household sectors during the depressions of the 1840s, 1890s, and 1930s, and during the First World War. Why should this be so? The main answer, which will be tested below, appears to be that any downturn in the market economy leads to a reduction in the market workforce of both part-time and full-time female and male workers who retreat back into the home, substituting household goods and services for market goods and services. Actually, the sequence of shedding labour in recessions appears to be more complex than this suggests, and has changed since the Second World War. Before the 1940s, when males dominated market-sector employment, the sequence appears to have been as follows: initially part-time workers, (only a very small percentage of the total workforce) were put off; then, as the recession deepened, full-time male workers were retrenched; but as recession gave way to depression a substantial proportion of the remaining full-time jobs were converted into part-time jobs—'robbing Peter to pay Paul'.[12] Since the 1940s this sequence has been complicated by the shift of married women into the market economy, mainly on a part-time basis. Recent severe recessions (early 1980s and early 1990s) suggest a new sequence of shedding labour: initially some part-time female (and male) workers are put off; then as the recession deepens, full-time female and male workers are retrenched; but as the recession begins to approach severe proportions (with unemployment about 11 per cent of the workforce), full-time female jobs are converted into part-time positions—a matter of 'robbing Mary to pay Maude'.[13] This suggests that we should also give some attention in our more formal analysis of the interactive relationship between the market and household sectors, to the female labour market.

In both periods—the 1980s and 1990s as well as the 1930s—the household sector has expanded as the market sector has contracted. Once recovery is underway, these sequences are reversed. In the shortrun, household economic activity increases directly as a result of a contraction of market activity. The Total Economy, therefore, possesses an inbuilt mechanism for reducing the severity of market downturns. As the household has a dampening effect on the trade cycle, fluctuations in the market sector are not reflected so severely in the Total Economy. It is unfortunate that this mechanism is not discussed, let alone analysed, by economists when examining economic fluctuations, because it has important implications for counter-cyclical, and unemployment, policy.

Hence the dynamic relationship between the household and market sectors involves two distinct—but not unrelated—processes: one secular and one cyclical. In the longrun economic process, rapid growth is driven by the market sector, but the household sector plays a positive (particularly during periods of stagnation) if secondary role; whereas in the cyclical process the household's role is much more reactive. This is the picture of reality provided by our time-scapes. We can now test what we have seen by employing a simple econometric model.

*An econometric analysis*
Any model to explain the dynamic interaction between the market and household sectors should, as we have seen from our timescapes, include both shortrun cyclical variables and longrun structural variables. On the shortrun fluctuations side, the above examination suggests that an inverse relationship exists between the level of real market activity, and the household/market ratio, a suggestion that is borne out by Figure 2.8(i). During a boom, underutilized household labour is attracted into the market, reducing the household/market ratio, whereas during a slump the reverse occurs. Two variables have been used to measure this effect—one reflecting fluctuations in real economic activity, and the other reflecting fluctuations in the female labour market. In the absence of adequate unemployment figures before the Second World War, and particularly before the 1910s, data on the fluctuations of real market income around a fitted trend (RMF) have been used. The best fit ($\bar{R}^2 = 0.995$) was obtained from a third degree polynomial. It was anticipated

that there would be an inverse relationship between this proxy for fluctuations in real market activity and the household/market ratio, because of its direct impact. The second short term measure, (see Figure 2.8(ii)), is the deviation of real female wage rates around a fitted trend (RFWF)—also a third degree polynomial ($\bar{R}^2 = 0.917$)—which is sensitive to shortrun changes in demand (and supply) for female labour. Owing to the indirect impact of changes in wage rates on the household/market ratio through changing female market participation, we cannot predict in advance whether the relationship will be positive or inverse (see discussion below).

To take longrun structural changes into account, two variables that should reflect fundamental changes in the market economy have been included. The first (see Figure 2.8(iv)) is an index of relative factor prices (Kp/Lp), which reflects the technological foundations of the market economy (RFP). It can be thought of as determining the level of job opportunities for females. The second (see Figure 2.8(iii)) is the change in the female/male wage ratio (ΔFMW), and can be interpreted as determining the response of households at the margin.[14] Both fundamental economic variables can be expected to influence family fertility—an expectation that is confirmed in Chapter 3— and hence the internal dynamics of the household sector. As structural changes are far more complex than cyclical fluctuations, it is difficult to predict what the outcome will be from any given change in these variables. However, it is possible to isolate the main effects—which I have called labour-shift effects, factor substitution effects, and wealth effects.

For example, what will be the impact on the household/market income ratio of an increase in the female/male wage ratio? The labour-shift effect describes the shift in female labour from the household to the market, which should increase the relative size of market income. But we must also take into account arrangements made in the household to maintain family 'income' at former levels—these are the factor substitution effects. These arrangements can involve the substitution of either paid domestic labour, other household labour (males and children), or household capital, for female labour, and will depend on conditions concerning relative factor prices (RFP in Table 2.3). Then there is the wealth effect, when households experiencing 'permanent' increases in income purchase larger houses with more equipment and hence increase household income. The outcome depends upon the particular economic circumstances prevailing in any period. It is a matter of empirical examination in each case.

The ordinary least squares (OLS) regression results for the entire period and the four sub-periods are presented in Table 2.3, and the diagnostic tests (which are highly satisfactory) can be found in the endnotes.[15] As there is little change in the household/market ratio before 1900, and as the explanatory variables experience cyclical change during this period, the model does not provide a good explanation ($\bar{R}^2 = 0.11$) for the nineteenth century. But after the 1890s depression the model is able to explain 65 to 71 per cent of the interaction between the two sectors, with the main cyclical and structural

### Figure 2.8 Determinants of household–market dynamics, Australia, 1868–1990

(i) Real market income fluctuations around trend

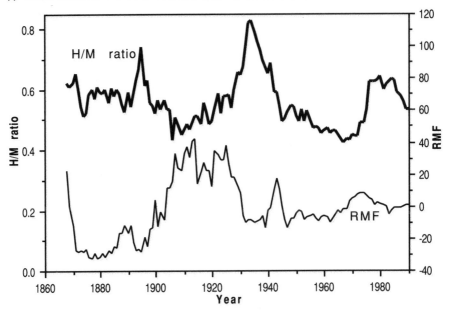

(ii) Real female wage fluctuations around trend

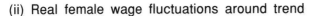

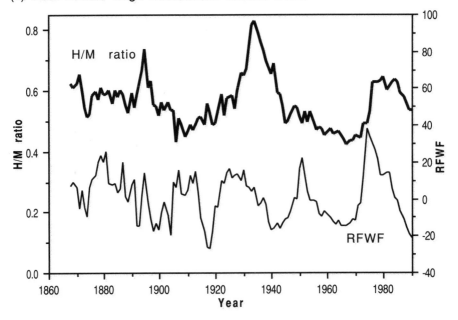

**Figure 2.8 continued**

(iii) Change in female/male wage rate ratio

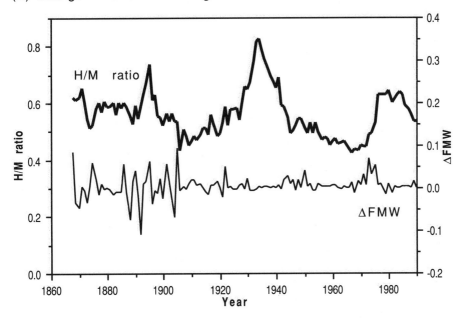

(iv) Relative factor prices ($K_p/L_p$) ratio

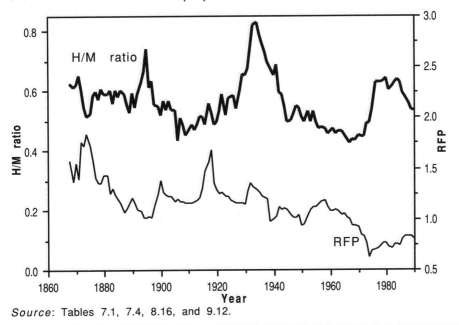

*Source*: Tables 7.1, 7.4, 8.16, and 9.12.

variables being highly significant. The Durbin–Watson statistics suggest that autocorrelation is not a problem during the twentieth century. The influence of the cyclical explanatory variables on the household–market relationship differed markedly. As expected, the impact of our proxy for real market fluctuations (RMF) was negative, whereas real fluctuations in the female labour market had a positive influence (suggesting that, in the shortrun, the factor substitution effects of a change in real female wages are more important than the labour-shift effect). The partial elasticities suggest that real market fluctuations are considerably more important than fluctuations in the female labour market. Of the structural explanatory variables, changes in the gender wage ratio (female/male) had a strong negative impact (suggesting that in the longrun the labour-shift effect was more important than the factor substitution effects), while relative factor prices (Kp/Lp) had a negative impact. As suggested earlier, the gender wage ratio is influenced not only by the usual demand and supply forces, but by the internal dynamics of the household sector; while relative factor prices reflect change in the technological base and structure of the market economy. As the partial elasticities for relative factor prices suggest that a 1 per cent reduction in the price of capital relative to labour led to a 0.8 per cent increase in the household/market ratio, funda-

**Table 2.3   Determinants of household–market dynamics, Australia, 1868–1990**

| Period | | Constant | RMF | RFWF | ΔFMW | RFP | $\bar{R}^2$ | DW |
|---|---|---|---|---|---|---|---|---|
| 1868–1990 | β | 0.538 | −0.001 | 0.002 | −0.179 | 0.018 | 0.112 | 0.255 |
|  | t | 15.323 | −3.217 | 2.718 | −0.626 | 0.592 |  |  |
|  | E |  | 0.004 | 0.002 | −0.001 | 0.036 |  |  |
| 1868–1889 | β | 0.605 | 0.0006 | 0.001 | −0.061 | −0.013 | −0.049 | 1.116 |
|  | t | 10.719 | 0.983 | 1.320 | −0.251 | −0.341 |  |  |
|  | E |  | −0.024 | 0.017 | 0.0001 | −0.032 |  |  |
| 1903–1939 | β | 0.327 | −0.006 | 0.004 | −0.232 | 0.270 | 0.659 | 1.407 |
|  | t | 2.303 | −8.512 | 3.305 | −0.469 | 2.347 |  |  |
|  | E |  | −0.149 | 0.011 | −0.001 | 0.576 |  |  |
| 1946–1990 | β | 0.942 | −0.009 | 0.001 | −0.913 | −0.474 | 0.710 | 1.501 |
|  | t | 17.056 | −4.672 | 2.473 | −2.139 | −7.419 |  |  |
|  | E |  | 0.035 | 0.001 | −0.013 | −0.831 |  |  |

*Notes:*  (1) β is the parameter estimate of the intercept or constant and the following explanatory variables: real market income fluctuations around the trend (RMF); real female wage rate fluctuations around the trend (RFWF); changes in the female/male wage rate ratio (ΔFMW); and relative factor prices [Kp/Lp] (RFP).
  (2) t gives the conventional t-ratios.
  (3) E gives the partial elasticities of the household/market ratio evaluated at the sample means of the explanatory variables.
  (4) The starting year of 1868 has been chosen because the fitted trend (3rd degree polynomial) does not cope very well with the 1860s. The resulting deviations before 1868, therefore, are artificial.

mental forces in the market sector clearly were a major driving force in the interactive relationship between the household and market sectors.

The econometric results in Table 2.3, therefore, confirm our understanding of the relationship between the household and market sectors, which has been based on the construction and inspection of a series of economic timescapes. These cyclical and structural forces can explain up to 71 per cent of an interaction which is at the very heart of the complex process of dynamic change in the Total Economy.

## Disaggregated model

The investment data for the Total Economy bring the household sector into particularly sharp focus because, unlike the income data, they can be organized into the economy's three main sectors: household, private and public. By timescaping and analysing these three sectors we gain, for the first time, a complex disaggregated view of the dynamic process of change in the Total Economy. This existential picture is unique because it could not have been developed deductively. The real world is far too complex to be adequately comprehended primarily through logic, even when assisted by the type of applied work inspired by deductive models.[16]

The dominating, indeed exciting, feature of this overview is that the process of Australian economic development since 1860 has been dominated by three *roughly equal* sectors—the household, public, and private sectors (Figure 2.9). Decade after decade these three sectors have grown and fluctuated together in a broadly similar and, as suggested earlier, close knit way. Naturally there are differences to be noted when we zoom in on detailed sections of the timescape, but this fails to alter the fact that, in the longrun, these three sectors were intimately involved in a dynamic economic process that generated a broadly similar pattern. Looking more closely, we can distinguish three distinct phases in the process of total capital formation since the middle of the nineteenth century. And each of these phases was dominated by a different sector—the household sector during the rapid expansion from the goldrushes to Federation; the public sector during the retarded development from Federation to the Second World War; and the private sector in the atypically rapid growth between the Second World War and the first international oil crisis. Each of these phases is also of roughly forty-years duration, and in each the household sector displays a conspicuous prominence.

The central question about the economic development of Australia becomes, therefore: what accounts for the emergence of different dominant sectors in each of these forty-year periods? The answer is complex and can only be rehearsed here,[17] but the major issues come clearly into focus as we sequentially blow-up the size of the three parts of the investment picture.

*1860–89.* During the 1860s and much of the 1870s the dominant sector in terms of size (but not in terms of rates of growth) was the household. Only

**Figure 2.9 Total capital formation by sector (1966/67 prices), Australia, 1861–1990**

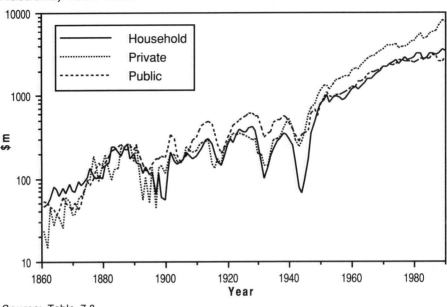

*Source*: Table 7.8.

in the second half of the 1870s and the early 1880s was it challenged by the other two sectors. At first glance it is surprising that the household sector would be more important than the private sector during a period of rapid expansion of foreign and domestic markets for private goods and services. While this issue will be explored further in Chapter 5, the short answer is that it stemmed from a successful attempt by the Australian colonies, particularly Victoria and New South Wales, to house the great influx of population during the goldrush decade and the decades of boom that were to follow. As can be seen from Table 8.2, the number of households in Australia increased remarkably by a factor of eight from 69,314 in 1850 to 551,672 in 1889.

It is important to realize that the expansion of the household sector was associated largely with the expansion of the urban rather that the rural economy. From 1861 to 1891 the urbanization of Australian population increased from 38 to 51 per cent.[18] Hence to omit the household sector is not only to ignore one-third of the Total Economy, but also to underplay the role of the urban sector. To a significant degree this was recognized by Noel Butlin[19] in his important work on residential investment, but Butlin not only failed to analyse this issue within a household–market context— his mindset was conditioned by the traditional nature of national accounts at the time, which dictated that residential investment be included idiosyncratically in GDP—but also neglected entirely to take the value of household labour services into account. Even Butlin, who excited our interest in cities in Australian economic development, overlooked the full significance of the urban economy.

The relationship between the three sectors in this period can be quantified by regressing household investment on investment in the private and public sectors. Those regression results, for which all coefficients are positive, suggest that household investment was much closer in pattern to that in the public ($\bar{R}^2 = 0.84$) rather than in the private ($\bar{R}^2 = 0.49$) sector. It is reasonable to suppose, therefore, that the household interacted more closely with the public sector in this period—more closely than with the private sector. In other words the household economy responded more energetically to social overhead capital associated with the massive inflow of migrants than with those investments undertaken in the private sector. Our pictures of the past—our economic timescapes—reveal an interesting aspect of colonial socialism.

*1900–39.* The dominant sector throughout this period of retarded development was the public economy, with the household just edging out the private sector. On reflection this outcome is indicative of the fragile state of the Australian economy throughout the half century prior to the Second World War. In a sense the public economy was the leading sector by default. Not only was the private sector the least buoyant of the three, it was also the most sensitive to those internal and external forces underlying short-term economic fluctuations, declining earlier and more rapidly than the other two sectors during recessions in the 1910s and 1920s. This was particularly the case in the 1920s. The private sector began its long journey into the night of depression as early as 1924, whereas the household and public sectors continued expanding until 1928. From this evidence we can draw the important conclusion that the household sector, as well as the acknowledged public sector, played a significant role in containing the economic and social impact of the private business cycle. The interactions between the private and household sectors, as discussed earlier, operated as an automatic countercyclical mechanism to dampen the effects of depression.

Once again the household's relationship with the public sector was stronger, but at that time only slightly so, than that with the private sector. A few simple regressions confirm the visual impression gained from Figure 2.9: the $\bar{R}^2$ from regressing household investment on private investment was 0.86 compared to 0.92 for public investment in the period 1900 to 1939. The fact that these values are much closer in the interdepression period than in the nineteenth century is a result, not of a closer real relationship between the household and private sectors, but of a closer relationship between the public and private sectors. Such an outcome is not surprising in a period when governments dominated economic activity, and private markets—both domestic and foreign—were subdued. In these circumstances both the household and private sectors depended heavily (but in different ways) on government investment programmes—generating both urban and rural social overhead capital—aimed at setting large, if erratic, inflows of migrants, and coping with the drift of households from rural to urban areas.[20] The public sector generated a demand for goods and services from the market sector and for factors from the household sector (stimulating further immigration) as well as facilitating the establishment of further migrant households.

*1947–90.* During the second half of the twentieth century, private enterprise became, for the first time in Australian history, the dominant, indeed leading, sector in the development of the Total Economy. The struggle for dominance began during the Second World War at a time when the household economy declined dramatically owing to the central redirection of resources, both labour and capital, from the home front to the war front.

With the unexpected return of buoyant economic conditions after the Second World War, the private sector supplanted the public sector as the economy's driving force, and the household economy, for the first time, failed to keep pace. The question we need to address is: what was responsible for this unique phase of Australian economic development? It is not difficult to explain the contrasting development paths between the two halves of the twentieth century—it was a matter of buoyancy in the international and domestic markets that produced different roles for the public and private sectors. But we know that the second half of the nineteenth century was no less buoyant than the second half of the twentieth century. Resolution of this apparent paradox lies in the differing scale of population growth in our first and third periods. Between 1851 and 1891 the Australian population increased by a factor of 7.3, whereas between 1947 and 1987 it increased by a factor of only (this is a relative only!) 2.1. The implications are twofold. First, the role required of the public sector in providing the necessary infrastructure after the Second World War was relatively modest in comparison with that after the goldrushes of the 1850s. Second, the relatively slower rate of increase of population in our third period in comparison with the first implies a less burgeoning household economy owing to the strong relationship between the household and public sectors.

Throughout the second half of the twentieth century (see Figure 2.9) the private sector steadily pulled away from the other two, which experienced similar longrun development paths. By regressing household investment on investment in the other two sectors we achieve a goodness-of-fit value ($\bar{R}^2$) of 0.94 for the public sector and 0.97 for the private sector. The safest conclusion to be drawn is that, in these generally buoyant conditions, the three sectors were interacting more closely with each other. Certainly the household and private sectors appear to have been more in concert with each other, no doubt due to the unique flow of married women into the private market place, which was facilitated by the substitution of household equipment on a large scale (to be analysed in Chapter 5).

# Conclusions

The snapshot of the Total Economy provided in Figure 2.2 at the beginning of this chapter shows a simple, static, and closed economic system that is in equilibrium. With the introduction of time into the story, in the form of a sequence of annual snapshots, as was attempted in this chapter, we are forced to consider a process of dynamic disequilibrium that may or may not reachieve equilibrium before the onset of further disruptive influences. Disruption of equilibrium could result from changes within any of the three sectors or, indeed, from outside this system: such as a sudden increase in household formation owing to immigration; a major technological change in the private sector; a significant change in public policy; or significant external disruption in the form of changing patterns of demand for domestic produce or resource flows, or of supplies of key imports. An attempt has been made in this chapter to expose the bold quantitative outlines of this process, and to consider its main determinants. It is suggested that the interaction between the household and market sectors over the last 130 years is driven in the longrun by fundamental changes in the structure of the Total Economy—particularly those affecting the gender demand for labour—and in the shortrun by fluctuations in market demand. During the new economic revolution after 1950, these structural and cyclical forces explain up to three-quarters of an interaction between the household and market sectors that is at the very heart of dynamic change in the Total Economy. The basic mechanism of this dynamic process is considered in Chapter 6, while the changing nature of the household economy and its relationship with the market sector is explored in Chapters 3 to 5.

# 3

# *The household economy*

*T*he family, or household, is the central institution in human society.[1] It is the prime source of economic motivation, the generator and regenerator of human resources, and the ultimate bestower of economic purpose. Yet, despite the important research of some social scientists, we know very little about how the family works as an economic system, or what role it plays in the Total Economy through its dynamic relationship with the market sector. An attempt was made in the last chapter to provide a general picture of the family within the Total Economy of Australia during the past two hundred years. It is a picture that focuses upon the interactions between the household, private, and public sectors. To expose the forces underlying these dynamic relationships we need to take a series of separate close-ups of the household and market. This chapter, therefore, will focus on the forces driving the household economy throughout the longrun; the determinants of family formation (by employing an econometric model); the respective roles of physical and human capital in this process of change; and the implications of rising average incomes for the household economy. The following two chapters will be concerned with household workers and with market demand for female labour.

## The ruling behavioural principle

To understand how the household economy works and how it interacts with the market sector over time, we need to understand its ruling behavioural principle. While some leading economists, such as Gary Becker, have explored the important issue of family motivation, most have ignored it entirely. Indeed, apart from a relatively small band of enthusiasts over the past few decades,[2] the household economy (other than as a hypothetical basis for consumer demand theory) has been surprisingly neglected by the economics profession.[3]

But there are signs that this is changing. In this section, the existing interpretation by mainstream economics of household motivation is reviewed. Some
modification and extension that will provide a basis for the following analysis
of Total Economy dynamics is suggested.

## *Static economic man*

Just as mainstream economics focuses largely on static theory, so the main
assumption underlying this theory is the concept of, what I have called, **static
economic man**. Further, recent theory of the family interprets the motivation
underlying economic activity in the family as being radically different to that
underlying economic activity in the market. As a starting point, consider the
claim made by Gary Becker in *A treatise on the family* about the ruling principle
in the household economy:[4]

> Sophisticated models tracing the economic effects of selfishness have been
> developed during the last 200 years as economic science has refined the insights
> of Adam Smith. Much is now known about the way selfishness allocates resources
> in different markets. Unfortunately, an analysis of equal sophistication has not been
> developed for altruism.

For it is 'altruism', Becker claims, that dominates family life. He goes on to
say:

> If I am correct that altruism dominates family behavior perhaps to the same extent
> as selfishness dominates market transactions, then altruism is much more important
> in economic life than is commonly understood. The pervasiveness of selfish
> behavior has been greatly exaggerated by the identification of economic activity
> with market transactions.

And he concludes this theme by adding: 'Even if altruism were confined to
the family, it would still direct the allocation of a large fraction of all resources'.
   This amounts to a strong claim for a new way of viewing economic behaviour
in the household.[5] Becker appears to claim that, while the maximization of
individual utility is the ruling principle in the market sector, it has little
relevance to the household sector. In other words, the economic man
traditionally subscribed to by theoretical economics is, according to Becker,
only part—and a contrasting part—of total social man, just as the market sector
is only part of the Total Economy.
   In order to evaluate this claim we need to understand exactly what Becker
means by the words 'selfishness' and 'altruism'. 'Selfishness', according to
Becker, is the principle that dominates market activity, with firms attempting
to maximize profits and consumers attempting to maximize utility derived from
the consumption of market goods. 'Selfishness' is equated with the maximization of *individual* utility. ' "Altruistic" ', on the other hand, 'means that
$h$'s utility function depends positively on the well-being of $w$ . . . and
"effectively" means that $h$'s behavior is changed by his altruism.'[6] In other

words, the altruist gains utility from seeing other family members increasing their utilities, and that this has an important influence on his economic decision-making. He further claims, without evidence, that while selfishness dominates market behaviour, altruism dominates household behaviour.

The implication of Becker's argument appears to be that rational economic man possesses two very different hats, one for work and the other for home; and that he/she behaves very differently when wearing one or other of these hats. This impression is reinforced by the introductory and concluding remarks in his altruism chapter, where he makes wide-ranging claims for the implications of these different behavioural responses. But, in the body of the chapter, Becker focuses entirely upon a number of narrow technical conditions of behaviour that he quite misleadingly calls 'selfish' and 'altruistic'. In other words, while he makes large claims for the implications of his altruism principle in society, his theoretical use of the term is narrowly and technically directed. As if in anticipation of this type of criticism, Becker writes:

> Since an altruist maximizes his own utility (subject to his family income constraint), he might be called selfish, not altruistic, in terms of utility. Perhaps—but note that $h$ also raises $w$'s utility through his transfers to $w$. I am giving a definition of altruism that is relevant to behavior—to consumption and production choices—rather than giving a philosophical discussion of what 'really' motivates people.[7]

But this is attempting to have one's cake and eat it too.

Becker's technical definitions of 'selfish' and 'altruistic' are very different from the normal meaning attached to these words, and they are also inconsistent with the more general, and empirically unsupported, conclusions he draws from his analysis. The word 'selfish' implies abnormal behaviour, and is inappropriate as a description of the normal human behaviour involved in attempting to maximize either profits or the utility derived from consumption. Selfish behaviour only occurs when an individual pursues self-interest to an irrational extreme, and (ironically), in the process, fails to maximize utility owing to the hostility generated in others. In the generally accepted sense of the word it is not selfish to maximize one's individual utility through individual action. Nor is it altruistic to cooperate with other people (related or not) in order to maximize individual utility even if, in the process, an individual's self-interested action leads to an increase in the utility of other people. Individual and cooperative actions are just different *means* applied in different circumstances to achieve the same *end*—the maximization of individual utility.

This is not just an argument about the meaning of words. It is an attempt to resolve the confusion that Becker causes by inappropriately drawing wider implications from his technical analysis. The issue is very important and must be resolved because he gives the impression that households operate on fundamentally different principles from those governing the behaviour of firms. Becker says, for example, that 'the same persons are altruistic in their families and selfish in their shops and firms'.[8] A less confusing, and admittedly less exciting, term than 'altruism' is **cooperative behaviour**—cooperation between individuals in order to maximize their separate utility functions by maximizing their joint objective function. Such behaviour is as relevant for firms as it is for households. Indeed it is difficult to imagine a successful firm composed of uncooperative individuals, precisely because their individual returns depend on their ability to work together for the good of the group. It is not helpful, as Becker has done, to compare the relationship between members of an individual household on the one hand, with the relationship between individual firms in the market place on the other. The relevant comparison with the household is not the market, but the firm in which teams of individuals attempt to maximize individual returns by maximizing the firm's objective function.

Yet, as a theory of 'cooperative' (rather than 'altruistic') behaviour, Becker's static analysis provides some interesting hypothetical answers to some equally hypothetical questions. Unfortunately, those technical questions and answers—dealt with by familiar static indifference curve/budget constraint analysis—are of little relevance to dynamic issues of household–market interaction (which Becker does not consider in his *Treatise*), or of longrun processes of change. What he does accomplish, however, is a clarification of the technical conditions under which household members will cooperate in order to maximize family income. The minimum condition identified by Becker is the willingness of one of the principal family members to act in a cooperative ('altruistic') way, by regarding his partner's utility as part of his own utility function. This will lead other family members—even those he labels as 'envious', 'selfish', and 'rotten'—to cooperate, because failure to do so will prevent the maximization of family, and hence individual, income. While there is nothing particularly unexpected about this finding, it is useful in explaining both the nature of cooperative behaviour and the distribution of family income. Nevertheless, it is a little odd to argue that one 'caring' individual is required to induce others to act in their own self-interest. Most people appear to recognize where their self-interest lies.

Ultimately we are led to ask: how helpful, in the explanation of dynamic issues, is a theory of the family that is based on a static and disembodied version of economic man? Becker, in the company of other mainstream economists, admits that he is concerned, not with human motivation that drives the economic system, but with behavioural outcomes. The static economic man underpinning his analysis is not a dynamic force in society, but rather an abstract collection of preferences and rational choices about consumption and production. Economic theorists have divorced these behavioural outcomes from more fundamental human motivational impulses. Becker goes as far as objecting to the suggestion that there might be some confusion in the terms 'selfish' and 'altruistic' on the grounds that any such discussion is a matter of philosophy, not a matter of economics. I will argue that, to the contrary, it is not a matter of philosophy but rather a matter of reality. The economists' disembodied economic man has no real-world substance—he is merely a cardboard cutout. In order to understand the role played by the household sector in the development of the Total Economy over the past 200 years we need to rediscover an economic man of real substance. Owing to their myopic and static theoretical analysis, economists have lost sight of the wellspring of economic change. Only through longrun analysis will dynamic or historical economic man re-emerge.[9]

## Dynamic economic man

A realistic discussion of human motivation, rather than hypothetical behavioural outcomes, is important if we are to understand real-world economic processes in the household and market. My interpretation of historical evidence,[10] is that the major driving force in human society throughout time is economic man—but an economic man of real substance. This section is concerned, therefore, with a search for historical or **dynamic economic man**—the substance, not the shadow, of dynamic change in human society.

### Rationality in open and closed societies

The nature of economic man's influence on society depends on the degree to which an economy is open or closed to outside competition. There are two extreme cases: the completely closed economy, such as the Australian Aboriginal economy for the tens of thousands of years prior to white settlement in 1788; and a largely open economy, such as Britain after the Industrial Revolution. These are, of course, only tendencies; there are no absolute states in human society. Even the Australian Aboriginal economy before 1788 had long witnessed unsystematic landings by Europeans along the northwest and northern coasts, and latterly on the southern tip and eastern edge of the continent, together with seasonal visits from Southeast Asian fishermen;[11] and the British economy did not fully achieve its briefly-held ideal of *laissez-faire* in international (or domestic) economic matters. Also in all societies (as I argue in *Economics without time*) there is a constant tension between the forces of order—the attempt of established elites to protect their wealth and power—and chaos—the attempt by those outside the protected circle to break in. The battle between these forces was certainly raging in English society after 1788, and was probably present, although to a radically different degree, in Australian Aboriginal society before 1788. As these two societies were involved in a fatal clash in Australia after 1788, they provide a relevant illustration of my argument.

In the closed economy of Aboriginal Australia before 1788 there had been little or no external competition or pressure for tens of thousands of years. Indeed in those parts of Australia—particularly Tasmania after it was isolated from the mainland by rising seas about 12,000 years ago—where even irregular and unsystematic contact with outsiders passed unnoticed, the coastline of Australia must have seemed like the edge of the world. Under these isolated conditions, economic rationality, which would appear to motivate all successful human societies, manifested itself in an entirely different way to that in Europe. Without the continuous stimulus of outside competition, it was economically rational—using an intuitive cost/benefit calculus—to attempt to maximize immediate material returns by establishing a system dominated by order and consensus. By employing a traditional technology—that changed impercept-ibly from generation to generation and only gradually from century to century and even millennium to millennium—and by deliberately controlling popu-lation to prevent it from exceeding accessible natural resources—food, hides, wood, etc.—Aboriginal tribes were able to achieve, on average, a comfortable lifestyle with an adequate and healthy diet, with considerable leisure (they may have worked as little as five hours per day), and with a rich cultural life.[12] What they lacked was a living standard that included material assets and fixed capital, either private or public. Noel Butlin, according to his own estimation, made a very rough estimate that, just prior to white settlement in 1788, Aboriginal GDP per capita might have been about half that in England.[13] A significant improvement in the Aboriginal living standard would have required considerable extra effort (with a corresponding reduction in leisure) both in developing and applying a radically new technology and in working longer hours and probably in a more regimented way. Clearly, without the external threat of invasion, the benefit to be gained from such a radical change would not have been worth the cost of the extra effort involved. Australia's original inhabitants had developed a workable system down through the millennia in which the marginal utility of work and leisure was in *very*, very longrun equilibrium. Only the real threat of dispossession and destruction of their way of life—as has always existed in Europe—could change their intuitive benefit/cost calculation in favour of economic development. What was lacking in Aboriginal Australia was not the ability to respond creatively to changing circumstances,[14] but rather the incentive to transform their rational ben-efit/cost calculation.

Aboriginal society, however, had not always operated within the context of very longrun equilibrium. Beginning with the period of migration, possibly some 60,000 years ago,[15] Aboriginal people gradually spread throughout the Australian continent. As discussed more fully in Chapter 6, this process of economic expansion involved an increase in the number of Aboriginal 'households' (or family units) through procreation so as to exploit unused natural resources. The driving force behind household expansion was the attempt to maximize family 'income', and hence individual income, in order to maximize the probability of survival. Family income could be maximized over time—the goal of dynamic economic man—by producing children who would eventually form family units of their own and thereby increase the economic resilience of the extended family group or tribe. This behaviour was based on a benefit/cost calculation—the discounted future benefit of an extra family unit had to be balanced against the cost in household time and resources involved in raising an extra child. While there was easy access to unused natural resources, the numbers of 'households' would increase and the frontier of Aboriginal occupation of the land would expand. But once all the natural resources of Australia had been fully utilized with the technology possessed by this hunter–gatherer society—a stage reached some tens of thousands of years before European settlement—the production of children was limited in order to prevent a reduction of living standards. Although economic expansion gave way to the stationary state, the economic motivation remained unchanged—the maximization of family/tribal, and hence individual, material returns.

The contrast in the late eighteenth century between Aboriginal Australia and England is stark. European tribes had experienced the threat of wars and invasions for thousands of years before 1788. Tribes from Eurasia came, saw, conquered, settled, traded and, in their turn, were overrun. In the process, networks of trade were developed, which were based on shipping links in the Mediterranean, the North Sea, and the great rivers of Europe. Enterprising adventurers and traders even went as far afield as China, India, Southeast Asia and the Americas.[16] In this context the existence of aggressive competition transformed the early European societies' primeval benefit/cost calculus concerning the introduction of new techniques of production, the increase in population, and the accumulation of fixed capital. As this dynamic process involved economic growth, as well as economic expansion, the nature of household choice was widened to include an increase in levels of consumption as well as an increase in family units or households. But nonetheless the objectives were just the same as those in Aboriginal society—the maximization of material gain. The outcome of this process of economic change, at least until after the Industrial Revolution, was to increase the economic resilience and power of European societies rather than to increase the living standards (except those of the ruling elites) of its populations. And it is this increase in economic resilience that has been critical to the survival of the open European society.

When these two societies—the European and the Australian Aboriginal—finally met in 1788, inevitably it was the closed culture that was destroyed. Clearly Aboriginal decision-making could not factor this eventuality into their primeval benefit/cost calculus, because they had no idea that, 13,000 miles away, a potential aggressor was unconsciously steeling itself down through the millennia for just such a meeting. Aboriginal society, in company with other closed societies around the world, paid tragically for its isolation.[17] Yet within its isolation Aboriginal society acted rationally.

Any attempt to explain the nature of historical, or dynamic economic man, must take into account the diverse circumstances that human society has encountered. While the everpresent goal is to maximize individual material advantage, the ways in which this can be achieved are extremely varied, as is suggested by the number of different economic systems that have existed in the past. I have already suggested that the operation of economic man in open and closed societies can lead to entirely different, but rational, outcomes in terms of the structure of society and economy, the allocation of time between work and leisure, the introduction of new ideas to the process of production, and the nature of economic performance. Elsewhere I have discussed the role played by economic man in a competitive feudal society in generating a surplus that was employed to extend the economy's infrastructure; to introduce new productive and organizational techniques; and to widen the extent and influence of commodity and factor markets. In the process, this system of feudalism was transferred into mercantile, and then industrial, capitalism. It was this industrial capitalist system that was introduced into Australia after 1788.

## Cooperative and individualistic behaviour

The degree to which the individual needs to cooperate with others in order to maximize his or her utility varies with the type of economic system under consideration. In a completely closed society, such as pre-1788 Aboriginal Australia, the economy will be based on an extensive set of cooperative relationships. The decision-making individual will be only able to maximize his or her utility by taking into consideration the utility of other members in their kinship group. This is not to deny the rivalry that existed between different kinship groups over adjoining land and the game thereon, or that this rivalry sometimes ended in ritualistic (and occasionally serious) combat.[18] At the other extreme, in modern westernized societies, there is greater scope for individuals to pursue their own self-interest with less extensive cooperation with others. Nevertheless, one should not overemphasize individualistic behaviour, because, even in the most modern society, a degree of cooperation (in the form of monopsonistic behaviour) is required to maximize individual utility, not only in the home, but also in the factory, shop, or office. And of course, in between these two extremes, such as feudal Europe, cooperation (in the form of monopsonistic behaviour) was required both within and between manors for individual economic decisionmakers to achieve their objectives. But at the same time there was also considerable individual initiative on the part of medieval decisionmakers, which often led to open conflict between manorial lords.[19] Many other examples could be provided.

Within different sectors of an individual economic system, a mix of cooperative and individualistic behaviour can be detected. Indeed it is difficult to imagine any economic sector in any real economic system in which one type of behaviour dominated the other. The problem with Becker's analysis is that he overemphasizes both the role of cooperation (misleadingly called 'altruism') in the household, and the role of individualism (misleadingly called 'selfishness') in the market place. Individualism and cooperation exist in both spheres of the modern (or indeed the ancient) Total Economy. Firms, just as much as homes, require cooperative effort between members in order to maximize individual incomes by maximizing firm profits.[20] This is not diminished—to the contrary it is actually enhanced—by the competition between firms in the market sector. And, for that matter, households also compete with each other—although in an informal way—just as aggressively as firms in the market.

## A general model of economic behaviour

The upshot of this discussion of economic man in history is that we require a simple model of behaviour that can encompass the interaction between individualistic and cooperative ways of maximizing individual utility. As historical economic man is not schizophrenic we need a model of behaviour that is holistic rather than dualistic—that can explain decision-making in closed and open economies, as well as in market and non-market sectors.

I wish to propose a simple model in which the individual is at the centre of a set of concentric circles or spheres that define the varying strength of cooperative relationships between him or her and all other individuals and groups in society. The strength of the relationship between the central individual and any other individual or group—which could be measured by what I will call the *economic distance* between them—will depend on how essential they are to the maximization of the individual's utility. Those aspects of the individual's objective function that require the greatest cooperation— such as the generation of love, companionship, and children—will be located on circles or spheres with the shortest economic distance from the centre. But even in this case the economic distance will be greater than zero, implying that the individual will always discriminate between himself and even those closest to him. For the typical individual, spouse and children will occupy the circle closest to the centre, with other relatives, friends, colleagues, neighbours, members of various religious and social clubs, other members of his socio-economic group, city, state, nation, group of nations, etc., occupying those concentric circles that progressively radiate out from the centre. As the economic distance—a measure of the importance of others, in maximizing the central individual's utility—between the centre and each sphere increases, the degree of cooperation between them diminishes.

There is always tension between the centre and the periphery no matter how short the economic distance may be, because all personal relationships are built up by the central individual during his or her lifetime in order to maximize his or her utility. While one must cooperate with others to maximize a joint objective function in order, in turn, to maximize individual utility, other cooperating individuals are still perceived to be a constraint on what one can achieve. Hence the persistence of tension in economic and social relationships. And the degree of tension appears to be inversely related to the economic distance, with most conflict and violence occurring between people who are closely associated with each other.

This is not a static model of behaviour. Individuals and groups on the various spheres are constantly changing, in response to changing economic circumstances. And the economic distance between these spheres of relationships, and even the order of those spheres, will change over time. Like indifference curves these circles or spheres will not intersect, but unlike indifference curves higher spheres represent weaker relationships and diminished cooperation.

As this model transcends different sectors and different economic systems, it is possible to make sense not only of what is happening in households and firms but also of the dynamic relationship between these two sectors. We are not dealing with economic agents that have different objectives depending on whether they are working in the household or the market. There are no rigid barriers between these sectors. The interchange is a fluid process. Becker's insistence on a sharp distinction between 'selfishness' in the market and 'altruism' in the household is not only artificial, it is also a barrier to an analysis of the dynamic relationship between them. The Total Economy is one economy, integrated by economic agents, who attempt to maximize individual utility in both the market and the household. Accordingly we need one model of economic man to analyse it. This model underlies the discussion, in the remainder of the book, of the operation of the household economy (Chapters 3 and 4), the interaction between the household and market sectors (Chapter 5), and longrun economic development of Australia (Chapter 6).

# Internal household dynamics

As economic agents behave in a similar way in both the household and the market, we can expect the household sector to possess a dynamic system that is both responsive to economic signals and that can achieve a certain momentum of its own. While the household dynamic system will have much in common with that of the market sector, it will also exhibit some marked contrasts.

The unique characteristic of the household economic system, which is examined in detail in Chapter 4, is its inability to achieve economies of scale through specialization and division of labour. Improvements in household productivity can only be achieved through the adoption of labour-saving equipment originating in the market sector, and even this has only been possible on a widespread basis since the 1940s. Hence the scope for economic *growth* (increases in output per unit of input) in the household sector has, until relatively recently, been very limited. On the other hand, the possibilities for economic *expansion* have been limited only by the growth of 'potential' real market income per household (or average living standards), which is required to finance the increase in household numbers. It is important in this context to make a distinction between 'potential' and 'actual' GDP per household. 'Potential' GDP per household is the level of average market income that would have been achieved in a *ceteris paribus* world if the number of households had remained unchanged between two points in time, and 'actual' average income is the level actually achieved when both GDP and the number of households are free to change. The difference between these measures is the income required to finance the actual increase in household numbers.

It is possible to translate this conclusion into an imaginary primeval world where the household economy *is* the Total Economy. A world where the market economy has yet to emerge. In such a world, economic expansion, which is driven by economic man, would be generated within the household economy. This expansion would take the form of natural increases in population and, hence, households, as hunter–gatherer families and tribes spread out to exploit existing natural resources; and this would continue until those natural resources were fully utilized. Once the natural resource limit was reached, economic expansion would cease, because further population and household growth would reduce living standards below an acceptable level (possibly even below subsistence). This would appear to be a good characterization of the migration of Aboriginal families and tribes from Southeast Asia to the Australian mainland, beginning possibly 60,000 years ago, and of their gradual occupation of the Great Southland until, given the limits of their hunter–gatherer technology, the natural resources were fully utilized at some time in the distant past. At this time the Aboriginal population may have been about one million—the level that probably existed when white settlement occurred in 1788.[21] In the intervening period, probably covering tens of thousands of years, the Aboriginal tribes deliberately limited the size of their populations to match the slow change in Australia's natural resources, in the disease environment, and in their evolving technology.

The household dynamics story, down through the ages, therefore, is a story largely about economic expansion—at least until the last millennium of human history. Modern market economic growth, however, has released household multiplication from a dependence on unused natural resources. Instead, an increase in household numbers can be financed through an increase in 'potential' GDP per household. In the case of the modern family economy, this suggests that household numbers will continue to increase provided real income per household is not depressed below the level required to maximize family utility, which involves the consumption of material goods as well as the rearing of children. Or to put it another way, the household economy will continue to expand provided the resultant increase in non-household labour does not depress real wage rates below the utility-maximizing level. To go beyond this critical point would be economically irrational. And as I suggested at the beginning of this chapter, the typical household cannot be regarded as being driven by irrational motivation. The upshot of this discussion, therefore, is that fertility—the key to household demographics—is subject to economic incentives and constraints.

Hence, the internal dynamics of the household economy involves an increase in the number of families through natural increase and immigration, in response to the market demand for labour and the supply of other household resources. The constraint on this expansion is the growth of real market income per household. It is probable that the economic momentum generated by this dynamic system will enable the household sector to achieve a degree of independence from the market sector. Indeed, this has been observed in Australia (in Chapter 2) during the slower market growth of the interdepression period, when the household sector grew at a faster rate than the market sector.

It is possible to test this hypothesis about the subjection of family demographics to market economics, by examining data on changes in both real wage rates and the quantity of labour employed in the market. The real male wage rate index in Figure 3.1 shows that real wages increased steadily (by a factor of 2.3) throughout the period 1861 to 1990 (and even during the interdepression period) at a time when the quantity of market labour increased by a factor of 12.5. When cast in the familiar demand–supply analytical framework, this evidence suggests that the market demand for labour schedule (or marginal product of labour curve), shifted out more rapidly than the supply of labour schedule. In other words the increase in population was driven more by market demand forces (changes in the production function), than by household supply forces. Hence, family demographics are endogenous to the dynamic economic system outlined in this study.

# Portrait of the household economy

## Growth and productivity

The broad economic profile of household development was exposed in the previous chapter. We saw (in Figure 2.3) how household activity went through four main phases: 1800 to 1860, when the household sector grew very rapidly (10.0 per cent per annum); 1861 to 1889, when the growth rate (4.4 per cent per annum) halved, as did that for the market sector; 1890 to 1939, when the household growth rate (2.3 per cent per annum) halved again, but still exceeded that of the market sector; and 1940 to 1990 when the growth rate (5.9 per cent per annum) doubled to 1974, then stalled. The basically similar pattern of fluctuations (Figure 2.9) in the three main sectors—private, public, and household—of the Total Economy, attest not only to the close interaction between these spheres of economic activity, but also to the common driving force underlying them all. In fact, as well as in hypothesis, the Total Economy is not a dual economy, as it is usually treated by economists and historians, but one unified economy.

The longrun development pattern of the household economy was a function of a steady growth of household workers and a more unstable pattern of household labour productivity (Figure 3.1). For much of the long period 1860 to 1990, household labour inputs grew at a fairly steady rate. The exceptions were the periods 1860 to 1890 when the rate of growth was higher than the longrun trend, and 1935 to 1950 when it was lower. In contrast, household labour productivity increased significantly in only two periods: moderately

**Figure 3.1 Household productivity (1966/67 prices), Australia, 1861–1990**

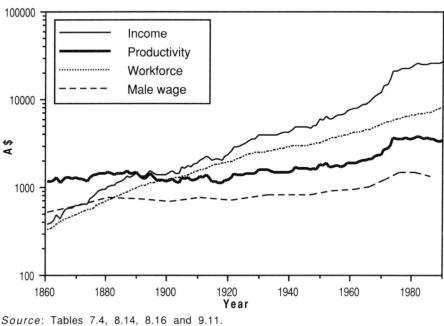

*Source*: Tables 7.4, 8.14, 8.16 and 9.11.

from 1860 to 1889, and more rapidly from 1950 to the early 1970s. It even appears to have declined in between these two periods. The evidence for relative, even absolute, stagnation in the half century between 1890 and 1940 is difficult to ignore.

Looking beneath the surface, it is clear that the expansion of household labour for much of the 130 years was determined largely by the rate of household formation (Figure 3.2). In turn this owed much to initiatives promoting high rates of immigration which arose within the market sector, both private and public. It will be seen also in Chapter 5 that household demographics were the effect rather than the cause of market economic forces.

What about productivity change? What accounts for the two bursts of expansion of about twenty-five to thirty years duration at the beginning and end of this long period? The answer can be seen reflected in the household capital-formation picture in Figure 3.3. Basically, these were the only two periods of sustained increase in expenditure on household equipment, which was not only labour saving but, after the Second World War, also embodied a new household production function. The significantly more rapid growth of productivity in the 1960s and early 1970s, owed much to the widespread adoption of labour-saving electrical household equipment that will be discussed in more detail below. It is also interesting to notice in passing that a broadly similar pattern can be detected in the picture of market productivity shown

**Figure 3.2 Household formation and household labour, Australia, 1788–1990**

*Source*: Tables 8.2 and 8.14.

in Figure 5.1 (p. 105). The main difference is that, after the First World War, market productivity kept pace with the growth of the market labour force, whereas, over the same period household labour inputs grew more rapidly than household productivity. In part this was due to the weaker investment performance of the household sector than either the public sector in the first half of the twentieth century, or the private sector in the second half.

## *The role of physical capital*

The recent revival of interest in the household by economists has led to an oddly focused picture of its production function. While Becker's analysis correctly draws our attention to the household's human capital, he has done so by ignoring its fundamentally important physical capital. Becker's picture of the family focuses quite clearly on the human characters, but consigns their physical environment to a blurred background. This is a major omission in a period (since the Second World War) when the dynamics of societal change have been dominated by changes in the physical, rather than the human, capital stock. This claim, which may be regarded by some as radical, even heretical, arises from the analysis in Chapter 5. A greater resolution to the role of physical capital, an important player that has been placed in

**Figure 3.3 Components of household capital formation
(1966/67 prices), Australia, 1861–1990**

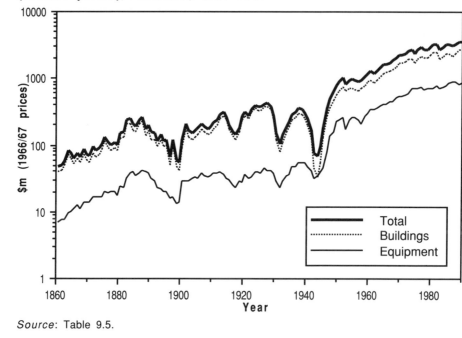

*Source*: Table 9.5.

the background by recent developments in mainstream economic theory, needs to be given. This must be done whilst keeping in focus the development of human capital—examined in Chapter 4—in this family portrait. A greater depth of field than has been given to this subject in the past is required.

A fundamental issue in any study of the household over time is the role played by physical capital in both the household and market sectors. Basically this is a story about the substitution of capital for labour—both hard physical labour and skilled labour. To tell this story we need to estimate, as has been done in Chapter 9, the changing stock of capital. Of course, capital is not the only factor that can be (and was) substituted for household labour—paid domestics have also fulfilled this role in the more distant past—but this can be left to the next chapter.

A revealing picture of household capital/labour ratios is provided in Figure 3.4. There are three interesting features captured by this timescape. The first involves the modest fluctuation of total household capital/labour ratios around a largely horizontal trend during the second half of the nineteenth century. Only in the 1880s did this ratio increase significantly (by 40 per cent) and, even then, temporarily. The second feature involves a surprisingly steep decline in the ratio by 12 per cent between 1890 and the 1930s, while the third shows a dramatic increase in the ratio after the Second World War (by over 150 per cent).

We need to look beneath the total capital/labour ratios to their constituent parts. The fact that equipment per worker in the household declined significantly between 1890 and 1940 is particularly interesting because it occurred against a background of declining (except during the First World War) prices of equipment relative to wages. In the absence of unusual circumstances, the relationship between these two variables is inverse (negative) rather than direct (positive) as shown in Figure 3.4. The unusual circumstance that reversed this normal relationship was the longrun stagnation in market income per capita, and its absolute decline during the depressions of the 1890s and 1930s. This is further evidence concerning the real and profound nature of the stagnation and decline of material standards of living during this half century. Despite the growing availability of electrical household equipment during the interwar period, and the significant decline in the relative prices of equipment to labour, the stock of household equipment was actually allowed to run down. There is just no solid basis, therefore, for any optimistic interpretation of this period.

The other interesting part of this story is the major substitution of equipment for labour in Australian households after the Second World War. As Figure 3.4 shows, this dramatic increase in the household capital/labour ratio coincides with an equally dramatic reduction in relative factor prices. As we shall discover, the wider process of change in the Total Economy was

**Figure 3.4 Household capital/labour ratios, Australia, 1861–1990**

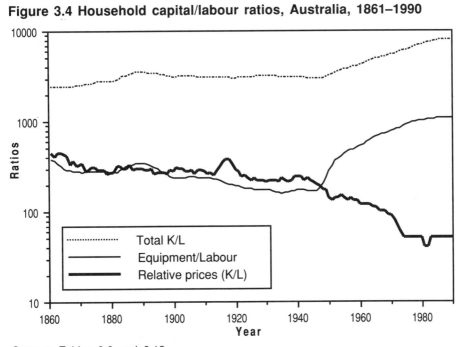

*Source*: Tables 9.9 and 9.12.

more complex than this simple relationship suggests. The substitution of capital for labour in the household was also strongly motivated by forces on the demand side—the market sector's dramatic increase in demand for married female labour, largely part-time.

The introduction of electrical household equipment does two things. First, it reduces the amount of time that household workers *need* to devote to housework, which provides more time for paid work and/or leisure. If the major impetus for the introduction of this new equipment comes from the supply side (relative factor prices) we would expect an increase in married female leisure; whereas if it comes largely from the demand side (a change in the gender structure of labour demand) we would expect an increase in paid-work by married females. The evidence, as we shall see, supports the latter hypothesis. Second, the introduction of household equipment reduces the energy demands of housework.[22] This makes it possible to undertake market work in conjunction with household work, or to service larger houses without an increase in the time or energy spent on housework.

The size of houses is an interesting issue. Figure 3.4 shows that, for the first half of the twentieth century, the total capital (buildings plus equipment)/labour ratio increased while the equipment/labour ratio declined. This implies that the energy demands on household labour actually increased. This has further, previously unanticipated, implications for living standards in this period of stagnation, particularly for married females, who would have experienced greater fatigue and probably less leisure. After the Second World War, the slower growth rate of the total capital/labour ratio in comparison with the equipment/labour ratio, suggests that the total energy demands on household workers actually declined, despite the increase in dwelling size. Indeed it is reasonable to conclude that the growth of equipment per worker contributed to the growth of housing stock per worker. Certainly a closer focus on investment in household equipment is justified.

## The nature of household equipment

A close-up of household capital formation in the twentieth century is provided by Figures 3.3 and 3.5—which are based upon estimates discussed in Chapter 9—showing the relationship between investment in residences and equipment. Not surprisingly, equipment expenditures described a broadly similar pattern to residential investment, albeit at a lower level—a level that fluctuated between one-quarter and one-third of total household capital formation. But from time to time it dropped below that level. The 1920s is an interesting case in point. In the 1900s the equipment/total household investment ratio was about 30 per cent, whereas during the 1920s it fell by half to 15 per cent, rose to about 27 per cent in the late 1930s, and maintained that level during the 1950s and early 1960s. Only after the mid 1970s did the ratio fall again to 18 to 20 per cent. Hence the 1920s stand out, once again, as a period of reduced circumstances. The growing population had to

**Figure 3.5   Household equipment by major item, Australia, 1901–1985**

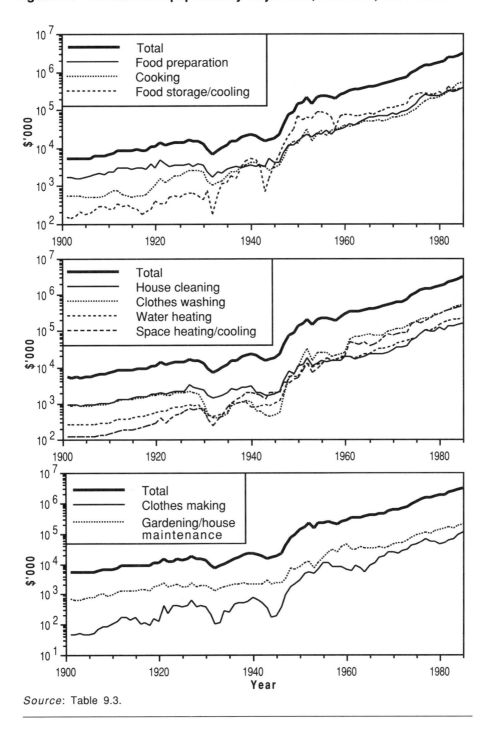

*Source*: Table 9.3.

be housed, but they did without the standard of household equipment that their parents and adult children experienced. This is yet another index of the stagnation, and even decline, in Australian material living standards during the interwar period.

Investment in household equipment increased steadily between 1901 and 1940, with the exception of the Great Depression and the Second World War. But this expenditure, as we have just seen, did not keep pace with the increase in household labour and the eroding force of depreciation. The leading sectors in this modest growth of expenditure on household capital (as can be seen from Figure 3.5) were clothes-making equipment, food-cooling equipment (ice chests, Coolgardie food safes, etc.) and space heating and cooling equipment. The much faster growth of equipment expenditure after the Second World War involved the widespread adoption of electrical equipment that had been pioneered in the 1920s,[23] but which had made little previous headway during a period when neither demand nor supply forces were particularly encouraging. In the first place, the gender structure of market demand for labour did not change radically until after the 1940s. Only during the second half of the twentieth century was there a major change in the range of jobs available for females. This was due to both technological and structural change. The resulting movement, on a large scale, of women into the market led, for the first time, to a widespread substitution of electrical household equipment for female household labour. Second, demand for an improved physical environment in the home arose from a rapid growth in market income per capita after the 1940s and the concomitant decision to reduce family size. Third, as we have seen, a marked change in relative factor prices, which under normal circumstances will encourage factor substitution, did not occur until after the 1940s.

The leading sectors in the post 1940s expansion of equipment expenditure were in the areas of clothes-making, refrigeration, water heating, and space heating and cooling. Less significant, although still important, were the growth of expenditures on equipment for food preparation, house cleaning, gardening, and house maintenance. Owing to these capital expenditures, the household production function was radically transformed, and the physical environment, both in terms of quantity and quality, was dramatically improved. Hence, the neglect of physical capital in the household by Becker and the human capital school, is most misleading.

## Family formation

The picture of family formation over the past 200 years is composed from the number of households, together with the average size, organizational structure, and demographic features of these households. We are interested, in other words, in the changing structure of the Australian family, its changing role as a source of population growth, and its evolving internal relationships.

## Family growth

Longrun growth in family formation is mirrored in Figure 3.2 which shows the number of Australian households over the entire period 1788 to 1990. The striking feature of this timescape is the sharp break—the fascinating kink—in the growth rate of households that occurred around 1860. In longrun terms, there have been two entirely different growth rates operating either side of the watershed year 1860. These growth rates, which are pictorially represented by the slopes of the household-formation curves, are 11.6 per cent per annum before 1860, and 2.5 per cent per annum after 1860. While closer inspection reveals shortrun differences in these growth rates, the deviation around the mean is not very marked.

Before 1860 the rate of family formation was rapid in the extreme. During the generation before that watershed year, the number of Australian households increased from 12,300 to 232,800—a factor of 19. It took a further 4.8 generations to emulate this feat. Interestingly, the explosive rate of family formation was not solely due to the goldrushes of the 1850s. As can be seen from Figure 3.2 the goldrush period does not stand out as exceptional in terms of *rates* of change of family formation. This suggests, therefore, that the economic forces operating in all periods—the period as a gaol, the years of the early export staples and convict agriculture, the age of pastoral expansion during the 1820s, 1830s and late 1840s, and the epoch of the goldrush years—

**Figure 3.6 Household formation by colony, Australia, 1788–1900**

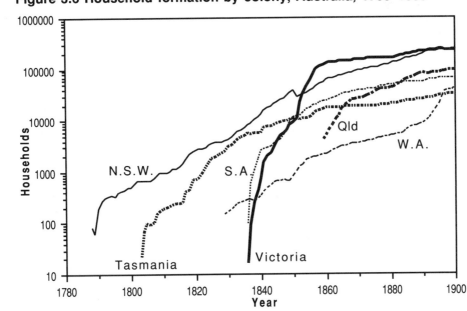

*Source*: Table 8.2.

had similar outcomes in terms of rates of economic expansion, which is appropriately measured by the increase in household numbers. But of course, as the scale of the economy increased between 1800 and 1860 the absolute impact of each phase of market expansion had to increase geometrically. In *absolute* terms, therefore, the impact of gold on family formation won hands down. As we shall see, after 1860 it was not possible to continue expanding the absolute scale of the economy in a way that would allow the achievement of a constant *rate* of growth of households. But a new and slower longrun equilibrium *rate* of family formation was achieved after 1860.

A family portrait—a colonial close-up—of the six settlements before Federation, is provided in Figure 3.6. While household formation was rapid in the older colonial family members of New South Wales and Tasmania (the latter experienced faster growth than New South Wales between 1815 and the early 1830s), it was the sudden appearance of the newer and amazingly virile members of the colonial family—namely Victoria and South Australia— that imparted such a steep slope to the total Australian family formation curve before 1860. This virility arose mainly from the application of a post– Industrial Revolution technology—particularly in transport (railways) and agriculture—to large areas of underutilized natural resources, and from the impact of gold, direct in the case of Victoria and indirect in the case of South Australia. But, after 1860, these two colonies settled down and they approached the rate of family formation of the older colonies. The exception was Western Australia in the 1890s, once again due to the impact of gold. Gold radically transformed the scale, if not the rate of change, of total economic activity in Australia during the mid and late nineteenth century.

Clearly there were shortrun surges in the 1880s, 1910s, and 1920s, together with downturns during the depressions of the 1890s and 1930s, and the world wars, but the longrun outcome for the period after 1860 was rapid and relatively stable growth in family formation. Between 1860 and 1990, the number of households increased by a factor of 24, from 0.23 million to 5.62 million. Although slower than pre-1860, it was still faster than the rate of family formation in most other western societies.[24] During these years (1860 to 1990) family formation occurred most rapidly in the initially smaller colonies/states of Western Australia (a factor of 155) and Queensland (a factor of 145), and much less rapidly in New South Wales (28) South Australia (19), Victoria (14), and Tasmania (6). Owing to their size, and the range and quantity of mineral resources they contain, Western Australia and Queensland have the greatest potential for future expansion, and may well become the most populous states by the end of the twenty-first century.

What accounts for the fascinating kink in the growth profile of household formation? The answer to this question is a central part of the dynamic model of the Australian economy developed in Chapter 6. But some explanation is required at this stage. A short period centred around 1860 marks the watershed between two very different types of economic development. Prior to about 1860, the economic development of Australia was dominated by a process of economic *expansion* that involved a rapid multiplication of households as the natural resources of this ancient land were brought into a system of production based on the state of technology reached during the British Industrial Revolution. This was achieved without any increase in average living standards—that is, without economic growth. Indeed market income per *household* actually declined between 1800 and 1860. By about 1860, therefore, most of the accessible natural resources in Australia were being utilized with the existing technology, and the ancient Aboriginal economy had been completely displaced. After 1860, further economic *expansion*—which, as shown in Chapter 6, is the result of household multiplication—depended on the technological base, and the fruits, of Australian economic *growth*. In other words, subsequent household formation depended on a more intensive employment of utilized natural resources arising from the technological change underpinning economic *growth*,[25] and a growth of real income to finance procreation and immigration.

The point of this discussion is that economic expansion based on the exploitation of 'unused' (after the defeat of Aboriginal resistance) natural resources can occur far more rapidly (by a factor of 4.6) than expansion based on the more intensive use of already utilized resources, and on the returns to economic growth. Interestingly, the evidence of this study suggests that the natural rate of 'extensive' resource exploitation in Australia is 11–12 per cent per annum, and the natural rate of 'intensive' resource exploitation in Australia is 2–3 per cent per annum. The kink in the growth profile of household formation suggests that the transition from one dynamic process to the other occurred suddenly.

## Household size

What determines the size of households? And have these forces changed over time? Becker has some interesting speculations on the first of these questions. As he points out, the gains from specialization—economies of scale—provide pressure to increase the size of the production unit. Certainly manufacturing establishments have increased in size since the Industrial Revolution. In Australia over the period 1861 to 1990, the average size of manufacturing establishments increased from about 16 to 26 workers.[26] Quite obviously households have not grown so large. Why? Becker's answer is that increasing returns from specialization in the household are outweighed by diseconomies arising from 'malfeasance' (shirking, pilfering, cheating, etc.) owing to conflicting loyalties in the extended family, from the costs associated with the invasion of individual privacy whenever an attempt is made to supervise family production, and because firms are more capital intensive than households.[27] But Becker is not convincing on this issue because he fails to draw a clear distinction in his theoretical analysis between the economic and non-economic activities of households. Rather than focus just on the economic activity of families, he employs economic analysis to examine all family activities, whether economic or non-economic. He is concerned not with the production of economic goods and services, but with the creation of higher 'commodities' of which economic goods and services (from both the market and household sectors) together with non-economic time, are inputs (see Figure 2.2). While this holistic approach is enticing it also involves a fundamental flaw.

The preferred argument to explain this contrast in size of market and household economic units, is that home economic activity cannot be supervised in the same way as factory activity, because family household workers have non-economic rights (and responsibilities) as well as economic ones. And it is these non-economic rights that are violated under normal economic systems of supervision. This is why, for example, in wealthy families the size of the paid domestic staff—which is really a market enclave operating within the household precincts—will be significantly higher than a household of family-related workers. Gregory King, for example, shows that in England in 1688 the size of middle class and working class households ranged from four to five people, whereas the size of upper class households ranged from eight for 'gentlemen', thirteen for knights, sixteen for baronets, twenty for 'spiritual lords', to forty for 'temporal lords'.[28] While economic systems of supervision, used to eliminate disruptive behaviour, can be imposed on paid domestics owing to their lack of non-economic claims on the household, the same system will not be tolerated by family-related household workers who possess non-economic rights. Hence households of family-related workers have a small optimal size—determined by a shared utility function—whereas households of paid domestic workers can achieve a size that rivals the average size of many market firms. Becker does not consider this point. Neither does he pursue the analytical distinction between the economic and non-economic interests of the family, and gives little attention to the physical/capital intensity of households. The weakness of theoretical speculation is that it can, and does, overlook some important real-world relationships that become apparent through historical observation.

But, it might be argued, the explanation offered here overlooks the role of family firms in the market sector. Not at all. Family market businesses bear no relation to households. In the first place both organizations operate under different constraints. To succeed, a family firm must be able to compete effectively with other firms, whereas a household must satisfy the non-economic, as well as the economic, aspirations of its members. Hence the constraints for the family firm are external, whereas those for the family are internal. Second, the structures of the family firm and the household are entirely different. The *successful* family firm, like other market firms, does not provide workers with non-economic benefits, because it is not profitable to do so. Family members enter the firm on the understanding that they will work in the same way as they would for other firms. In other words they relinquish any claims to non-economic rights. There are formal organization and legal structures to ensure that this occurs, as nepotism would ensure failure in a competitive environment. Third, successful family firms, unlike households, are not composed entirely of family members. While family members may hold key posts, the bulk of employees in a large firm must consist of non-family members. The more successful the firm, the smaller the proportion of family-related workers. Hence the fact that family organizations have been important in market dynamics in the past, does not affect this explanation of household size.

Interestingly, there are also constraints on any desire to *reduce* the average size of households. This arises from the discussion of family fertility in the section at the beginning of this chapter on the internal dynamics of the household. The historically optimal family size is about five persons. In the traditional household, this number could only be reduced by reducing the efficiency or productivity of the family to uneconomic levels—levels that would not maximize family utility. To reduce family size significantly below five persons required, not only changes in market demand for female labour and in living standards, but also a radically new household production function that involved the substitution of electrically driven household equipment for household labour. And this new technology was only effectively available after the Second World War. As can be seen in Figures 3.1 and 3.7, modest attempts to reduce family size led to a decline in household productivity. Only with the new technology of the second half of the twentieth century could family size be radically reduced and productivity actually increased. There were, therefore, very strong economic constraints operating on family size. Only once they were released by the new economic revolution was it possible for family demographics to change.

What about the Australian evidence on household size? As Australia was settled in 1788 by Great Britain, a brief review of evidence for that country over the last millennium provides an interesting backdrop to the Australian data. Recent evidence on the late Anglo–Saxon period suggests that 1,000 years ago the average household size was in the range 4.3 to 5.1 people.[29] In *Economics without time* I argue that the mean size of English households in 1086 was between 4.5 and 5.5 people, although the households of the very small ruling elite (which had little impact on average household size) were probably much larger, consisting of a high proportion of slaves, paid servants, and retainers. Manorial records in the thirteenth century also suggest a figure of 'nearly five per household'.[30] And for the period 1574 to 1821 the mean household size in England is reported to have been in the vicinity of 4.75 persons.[31] This suggests, therefore, that household size has been relatively constant—at about five persons—in English society over very long periods of time.

Before examining the Australian data, it must be emphasized that demographic circumstances before 1860 were atypical, owing to the transition from penal settlement to capitalist economy, and to the fact that, before this process had been completed, the disorienting influences of the 1850s goldrushes were experienced. In the unusual demographic circumstances of the pre–1860 period, as can be seen from Figure 3.7, the average (mean) size of households declined gradually from 10.8 to 5.9 persons. The special conditions of the early settlement, therefore, led to a doubling of the size of the average British 'household'. It is unfortunate that frequency distributions are not available, but we do know from qualitative data that convicts were housed in dormitories in government employ, in existing private houses as servants, and in simple shelters on farms.[32] And the unbalanced gender ratio suggests a higher than usual proportion of males living in boarding houses and hotels.

In the 1860s, once the goldrushes had subsided, the household size settled down to about five persons, a level that appears to have been the English historical norm for almost a millennium. This Australian average was maintained—apart from a slight increase to 5.7 during the rapid inflow of population during the 1880s—until the First World War. From then the average household size declined slowly from 5.0 in 1919 to 4.5 in 1928 and then more rapidly after the 1930s to 3.0 in 1990, a fall of 40 per cent in just 70 years. As the reduction in household size after the Second World War was a function of fundamental changes in the Total Economy, it can be regarded as a secular rather than a cyclical change. And, as it was part of the first major change in average household size in Western society in 1,000 years, its importance cannot be exaggerated.[33] It amounts to a radical change in the nature of the household economy, and reflects an equally radical change in the nature of the market economy owing to the new economic revolution.

**Figure 3.7 Household size, Australia, 1788–1990**

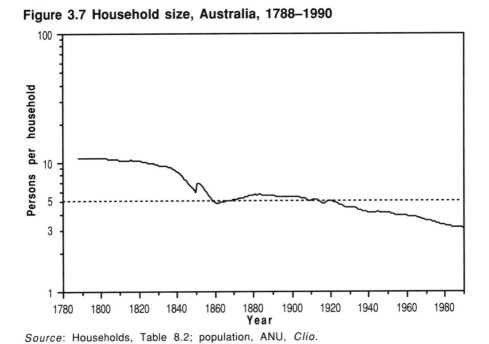

*Source*: Households, Table 8.2; population, ANU, *Clio*.

What were the reasons for this radical change in the nature of family organization in the mid twentieth century? At the immediate (or proximate) level it might be argued that the number of births per household had an important impact upon the size of families. But this is merely stating the obvious. More profoundly, we wish to know why the number of births per household fell steadily from the 1840s (see Figure 3.8). Once again, the evolution of the Australian family can be explained in terms of changes both in the technological base of the market economy and in the signals the market economy gives to the household economy. The hypothesis to be tested is as follows: the average size of the Australian family depends on the levels of both the market capital/labour ratio and the female/male wage ratio—one is a reflection of the gender structure of market demand for labour, and the other also reflects the supply response of households to this demand.

The regression results are given in Table 3.1. As expected, owing to the remarkable stability of household size before the 1930s and the normal cyclical variation in the explanatory variables, the model has only limited explanatory success until the second half of the twentieth century when the structure of the Australian family changed radically. An inspection of the results uncorrected for autocorrelation (i.e. $\beta_1$, $t_1$, $E_1$), reveals that while the goodness-of-fit statistics ($\bar{R}^2$) are quite high in the pre–Second World War periods, the explanatory variables are either insignificant, have the wrong signs, or suffer from a high degree of autocorrelation. Only after the Second World War are the explanatory variables highly significant and with the correct sign, but even then there is a high degree of autocorrelation. Clearly it is necessary to correct the regression results for this problem.

Table 3.1 also reports regression results corrected for autocorrelation (i.e. $\beta_2$, $t_2$, $E_2$) by autoregressing the dependent variable lagged by one and two periods (HHS$_{-1}$ and HHS$_{-2}$).[34] These results provide the basis for interesting, and distinct, stories about the two periods of long upswing in Australian economic history—the second halves of both the nineteenth and twentieth centuries. During the first of these periods there is evidence of a statistically significant inverse relationship between the capital/labour ratio and household size. By visually inspecting Figure 3.7 and Figure 5.2 (p. 109) it can be seen that between 1860 and 1870 an increase in household size is associated with a reduction in the capital/labour ratio, and that between 1870 and 1890 a reduction in household size is associated with an increase in the capital/labour ratio. But we must be careful not to jump to ahistorical conclusions. The relationship for this period is not as clear cut as for the post–Second World War years. There appear to have been two forces operating in the earlier period. First, there was a small change in the technological foundations of the Australian economy in the 1870s and 1880s, which is reflected in the modest, and temporary, increase in female market participation rates (see Figure 4.3, p. 87), and hence of a reduction in household size. But second, and more important, the very high rates of immigration experienced in the 1850s and 1860s placed great strain on the

**Table 3.1    Determinants of household size, Australia, 1861–1990**

| Period | | Constant | KLR | FMW | HHS$_{(-1)}$ | HHS$_{(-2)}$ | $\bar{R}^2$ | D-W |
|---|---|---|---|---|---|---|---|---|
| **1861–1990** | $\beta_1$ | 7.288 | 0.00005 | −4.860 | | | 0.885 | 0.279 |
| | $\beta_2$ | −0.013 | −0.000003 | 0.015 | 1.582 | −0.581 | 0.998 | 2.105 |
| | $t_1$ | 45.211 | 1.229 | −12.472 | | | | |
| | $t_2$ | −0.147 | −0.670 | 0.197 | 21.577 | −7.657 | | |
| | $E_1$ | | 0.021 | −0.626 | | | | |
| | $E_2$ | | −0.001 | 0.002 | 1.587 | −0.585 | | |
| **1861–1889** | $\beta_1$ | 4.598 | 0.001 | −0.256 | | | 0.569 | 0.135 |
| | $\beta_2$ | −0.271 | −0.0002 | 0.257 | 0.879 | 0.180 | 0.987 | 2.279 |
| | $t_1$ | 8.003 | 6.198 | −0.220 | | | | |
| | $t_2$ | −1.196 | −2.965 | 1.310 | 4.549 | 0.908 | | |
| | $E_1$ | | 0.153 | −0.023 | | | | |
| | $E_2$ | | −0.024 | 0.023 | 0.874 | 0.178 | | |
| **1890–1939** | $\beta_1$ | 7.867 | −0.0002 | −5.676 | | | 0.749 | 0.810 |
| | $\beta_2$ | 0.164 | 0.0000004 | −0.170 | 1.487 | −0.507 | 0.991 | 1.967 |
| | $t_1$ | 21.465 | −0.847 | −12.025 | | | | |
| | $t_2$ | 0.692 | 0.008 | −0.910 | 11.423 | −3.839 | | |
| | $E_1$ | | −0.041 | −0.548 | | | | |
| | $E_2$ | | 0.00007 | −0.016 | 1.496 | −0.513 | | |
| **1946–1990** | $\beta_1$ | 4.823 | −0.0002 | −0.808 | | | 0.988 | 0.393 |
| | $\beta_2$ | 1.031 | −0.00003 | −0.186 | 1.266 | −0.479 | 0.998 | 1.901 |
| | $t_1$ | 65.017 | −16.188 | −5.964 | | | | |
| | $t_2$ | 3.771 | −3.401 | −2.721 | 9.271 | −3.880 | | |
| | $E_1$ | | −0.164 | −0.177 | | | | |
| | $E_2$ | | −0.037 | −0.041 | 1.275 | −0.485 | | |

*Notes:*   (1) The results corrected for autocorrelation ($\beta_2$, $t_2$, $E_2$) are shown immediately below the uncorrected results ($\beta_1$, $t_1$, $E_1$).
(2) $\beta$ gives the parameter estimates of the intercept or constant and the following explanatory variables: the market capital/labour ratio (KLR), and the female/male wage rate in nominal terms (FMW).
(3) $t$ gives the conventional $t$-ratios.
(4) $E$ gives the partial elasticities of household size (HHS) evaluated at the sample means of the explanatory variables.
(5) D–W is the Durbin–Watson statistic to test for autocorrelation.

physical resources of the Australian colonies, and appear to have contributed directly to the temporary increase in household size and also to the decline in the capital/labour ratio. By the 1870s and 1880s, however, the Australian colonies had developed a system of mobilizing physical resources (particularly British capital) to cope more effectively with the high inflow of population, thereby contributing to a fall in household size (but only to the very longrun level of five persons) and an increase in the capital/labour ratio.

But the most dramatic story reflected in the corrected regression results is about the rapid secular decline in household size after the Second World War. For the period 1946 to 1990, our model can not only explain 99 per cent of the change in family size, but also all the variables are significant and have the correct sign, and the various diagnostic tests are satisfactory.[35]

The partial elasticities also suggest that the demand and supply determinants—the capital/labour ratio and the gender wage ratio—were approximately equal determinants of household size. Hence the first great change in the size of the Australian household in a century—or, indeed, of the Anglo-Saxon (and European) household in a millennium—can be explained virtually entirely in terms of fundamental economic forces.

## Inside the family—marriage, fertility, mortality

While family demographics are quite clearly driven by fundamental economic forces in the Total Economy, and hence should be regarded as endogenous to the dynamic system of economic change outlined in Chapters 2 and 6, they are the proximate cause of the observed nature and structure of the household. Marriage, fertility, divorce, and mortality are, for statistical purposes, usually compared with the size of the population or some subset thereof. But rates calculated in this way do not take into account changes in the rate of family formation. If, for example, the fertility rate—the number of births per 1,000 women of child-bearing age—increased significantly over a period of time, but the rate of household formation did not increase and we were not able to determine this (as has been the case in earlier studies), then we would be uncertain as to whether the change in fertility had taken place within the existing household system or had resulted from an expansion of the system itself. Clearly this is a major problem, particularly over long periods of time. The contribution of this section, therefore, is to discuss these demographic issues of family formation, not in an abstract context as done by Becker, or without recourse to the institution of the family as done by most demographers, but within the real context of the Australian family. As mentioned before, this is a living portrait of, not a hypothetical treatise on, the family.

A portrait of the changing demographic structure of the Australian family over the past 200 years is provided in Figure 3.8. We should note, but need not dwell upon, the erratic picture provided by the period before 1860. During these unsettled years of transition from gaol to capitalist economy, rates of marriage, birth, and death were not typical of British society, and they were highly unstable. While they are of interest to those who wish to focus on this period—and for this reason are provided here—they must not be used for longrun comparisons.

The general longrun perspective of the Australian family over the past 150 years shows a steady and parallel decline in the birth and death rates per family from the 1840s to the 1890s; a relatively stable marriage rate from the 1860s to the 1940s (if we ignore for the moment the shortrun effects of depressions and wars), that suddenly declined significantly (by 49 per cent) after the 1940s; a relatively steep increase in the divorce rate throughout the twentieth century, with large peaks after the wars and during the 'liberated' 1960s and early 1970s, and with a modest decline during the last few decades of the century; and, finally, a very steep decline in infant deaths from about 1890 to the end of the twentieth century.

What does this general picture show us about the Australian family over the past 150 years? Certainly, there has been a revolutionary change in the family, not only in Australia but throughout the Western World. As an institution—the central institution in the Total Economy—the structure of the average family appears to have been relatively stable in the second half of the nineteenth century and the early twentieth century, but that it began to change from the First World War—slowly until the 1940s, but then with revolutionary speed. A hint of this is provided by the number of divorces per family, which rose modestly from a low point of 4 in every 10,000 families in the 1900s to 14 per 10,000 families at the end of the 1920s, and then very rapidly after the Second World War to reach a peak of 153 in the mid 1970s, and finally to retreat to 76 by 1990. It was as if an early twentieth century desire for social change (largely amongst wealthier feminist groups) was held tightly within the vice-like grip of fundamental economic forces. Only once this economic grip was relaxed after the 1940s, due to forces that owed nothing to social concerns, did the social relationships within the family change—and change radically.

Despite the slow increase in divorce rates per family between the wars, the marriage rate did not begin a secular decline until after the 1940s. The marriage rate which was relatively stable at about 4 per 100 households over the century prior to 1950, suddenly began to decline, until by 1990 it was only about 2 per 100 households. In other words, after the Second World War there was a substantial and persistent increase in the proportion of households that did not enter into marriage contracts to 'protect' non-market workers against the financial implications of a breakdown of the household. Clearly this is associated, as others have pointed out, with the growing independence of women in this period as they became increasingly involved in paid market work, as birth rates declined, and as welfare payments increased.[36] At the same time, and for the same reason, the perception by males of their family responsibilities also declined. The growing financial security of women, combined with declining family responsibilities of both females and males—the result of fundamental changes in the Total Economy—reduced both the need and the desire for formal contracts of marriage, and the former reluctance to terminate them.

The declining family responsibility in the second half of the twentieth century deserves closer attention. Figure 3.8 shows that the average birth rate was fairly stable at about 20 for every 100 households during the second half of the nineteenth century, that it declined moderately to 14 per 100 households just before the First World War, that it was about 10 in the late 1920s and late 1940s, and then fell rapidly to 4.7 by 1990. The decline from the turn of the century coincides with a sharp reduction in infant deaths rather than with major technological and structural change which was not forthcoming until after the 1940s. But, the decline in the rate of infant deaths per family—

**Figure 3.8 Births, deaths, marriages and divorces per household, Australia, 1788–1990**

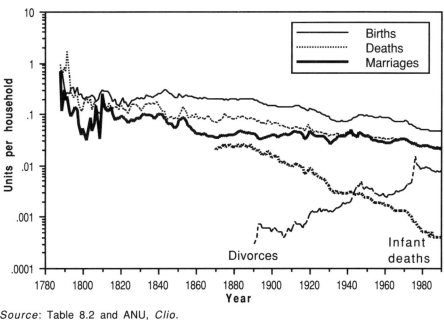

*Source*: Table 8.2 and ANU, *Clio*.

from 2.5 per 100 households in 1889 to 0.5 in 1928, and 0.04 in 1990—was still largely a function of economic growth. Rapidly rising Gross Community Income per capita in the 1880s reduced the rate of infant deaths both directly by increasing standards of nourishment and hygiene for mothers and babies, and indirectly through the virtual elimination of major infectious diseases by the construction of safe systems of water supply and sewerage disposal,[37] and the introduction of public health programmes. And a decline in infant mortality made it possible to reduce the number of births necessary to achieve a family of a given size.

The infant death rate continued to decline rapidly throughout the second half of the twentieth century, owing initially to advances in publicly funded medical science that began with the introduction of sulphonamide drugs in the 1930s, penicillin in 1941, and inoculations against various infectious diseases from the late 1940s.[38] But after the 1940s, as we shall see in Chapter 5, the major determinants of the reduction in birth rates were major changes in the market sector's technological base and its structure. These changes led to a significant increase in the demand for female labour together with an increase in the female/male wage ratio. The effect of these economic forces was to reduce the demand of households for children. As can be seen from Figure 3.9 the number of children per household declined from an average of about 2 between 1861 and 1901, to 1.5 by the late 1920s, to 1.0 by 1971, and 0.7 by 1986.

**Figure 3.9 Family size and real family resources, Australia, 1788–1990**

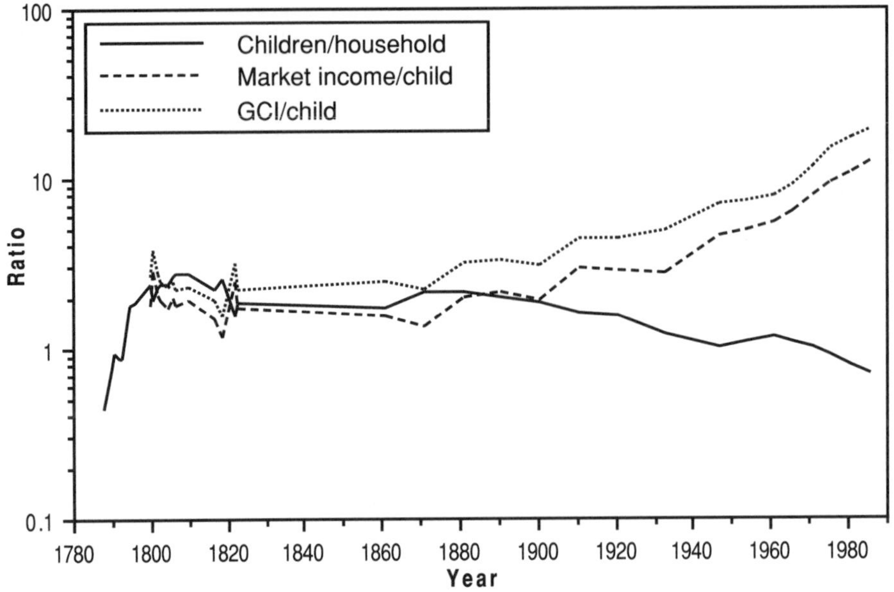

*Source*: Tables 7.3, 8.2 and ANU, *Clio*.

The implications for family living standards and human capital of the reduction in the number of children per household, are also reflected in Figure 3.9. Generally speaking, the number of children per household and real income per household, moved together until 1900 but thereafter they increasingly diverged. Neither real market income nor real Gross Community Income per child changed significantly in the first half of the nineteenth century, and even appears to have declined in the 1860s as a result of the relatively high birth rates in that decade. From the 1870s to the 1990s, real income per child increased in three steps. The first two, in the 1870s to 1880s and again in the 1900s, were relatively small: Gross Community Income per child was $3,141 in 1881 and $4,299 in 1921. In other words, in the forty years following the late 1870s, real income per child increased by only 37 per cent. It was, however, with the third step forward in real income per child that most gains were made. Between 1921 and 1990, real GCI per child increased from $4,299 to $19,377—an increase of over 350 per cent in seventy years. Hence, in the second half of the twentieth century, the quantity of children per household declined by half, while the resources available to each child increased by a factor of 4.5. As these resources have in large part been used to increase the living standards and human capital of children, as shown in Chapter 4, the decline in the quantity of children per household has been far outweighed by an increase in their quality. This outcome suggests that the market workforce of the future will be able to respond more creatively to the challenges that lie ahead.

## Conclusions

An attempt has been made in this chapter to provide a longrun portrait of the household economy in both macro and microeconomic terms. Owing to the limitations of static economic man in the existing literature, it was necessary to develop a model of dynamic economic man. This model portrays dynamic economic man as an integrated decisionmaker who does not have to change personality as he/she moves spatially from the market to the household, or temporarily from the market economy to the premarket economy.

At the macro level, consideration was given to the growth, productivity, and investment in physical assets experienced by the household economy. Of particular interest were the discoveries that there was a sharp break in the rate of growth of household formation in 1860 (which has important implications for the interpretation of Australian economic development in Chapter 6), and that physical capital (which has been overlooked in recent work on the economics of the family) may have been more important than human capital in the internal dynamics of the household. Finally, at the micro level the process of family formation was analysed, and it was argued that family demographics have been, and are, largely driven by fundamental economic changes in the market sector. In order to further explore aspects of the family, we turn to an examination of the role of household workers in the Total Economy.

# 4

---

# *Household workers*

## The lost tribe

Household workers are the lost tribe of the Total Economy. They are known to exist, but many economists, economic historians, and policy makers act as if they are irrelevant to the operation and development of human society. It is a strange case of collective amnesia. Most theoretical economists—with such notable exceptions as Gary Becker, Jacob Mincer, and their followers—appear to have little interest in the family, and most applied economists concerned with the market participation of married women appear to assume that they materialize from nowhere. While other social scientists, such as historians, sociologists, anthropologists, and feminists have for many years undertaken interesting and important research on the family and the role of women, the subjects of their studies have not been placed within the context either of the Total Economy or of economic forces that drive society and motivate political decisions.[1]

In order to rediscover the lost tribe and eradicate our collective amnesia we need to systematically examine the changing role of the household worker within the context of the wider forces acting on the Total Economy. And this must involve an examination of male as well as female household workers. If household workers are the lost tribe, then male household workers are the most neglected members of that tribe. This chapter, therefore, focuses on the changing composition of the household workforce, the reasons for the gender division of labour that we find (by employing an econometric model), and the changing nature of human capital in the household together with its implications for the future market workforce.

# The gender division of labour in theory: a new model

The gender division of labour attracted the attention of mainstream economists—including Stanley Jevons, Thorold Rogers, Henry Sidgwick, and even Alfred Marshall—towards the close of the nineteenth century. Their interest, however, was practical rather than theoretical, and coincided with a modest and brief increase in the market participation of married women.[2] They were concerned that any shift of married women into the market sector would reduce the quality of the next generation of market workers. Accordingly they advocated legislation to restrict the employment of women with young children. The next, and far more major shift of married women into the market economy, which occurred after 1950, also attracted the attention of economists, including the pioneering human capital theorists Jacob Mincer and Gary Becker. But on this occasion, possibly owing to the greater significance of the event, some attention was given to theoretical and empirical work as well as to policy.

The model employed in this study involves an extension of Becker's human capital model. This extension, however, is based not on the deductive theory of either Becker or his followers, but on an analysis of the empirical work in this study. This extension involves two dimensions, one static and the other dynamic. Becker's comparative static model has been extended to include demand-side forces—an aspect that my empirical investigation has shown to be dominant in the fortunes of the household and the market. Also an attempt has been made to sketch the outlines of a dynamic model suggested by the reconstruction of the longrun process of change in the Total Economy.

## *The static model*

Building on Adam Smith's concept of division of labour, Becker makes the important point that members of an 'efficient' household will specialize in either household or market work, in order to take advantage of increasing returns from specialization, *even if their labour skills are identical.* Hence, in a two-person household, one person will invest in market human capital and specialize in market work, while the other member will invest in household human capital and specialize in household work. They acquire, in Becker's terminology 'activity specific' human capital. Only in this way will the household maximize its utility function. It is, in other words, inefficient for *both* household members to invest and work in *both* sectors.

While questions of efficiency will dominate the typical household—and it is the typical household that drives the system—it should also be acknowledged that in *some*, albeit atypical, households, questions of equity are of equal or greater importance. Despite the fact that it is less efficient to do so, both adults in some households will invest in both types of human capital and will work in both sectors of the Total Economy. In these atypical households (generally of the younger professional class) it would have been possible to achieve a higher utility—possibly by the production of (more) children, or less tension, greater longevity, more leisure, or a higher level of consumption of more personalized home goods and services—by specializing according to comparative advantage. The non-specialized household may be more equitable, but it will be less efficient than the norm. There is, therefore, a conflict between efficiency and equity in the household economy, just as there is in the market economy.

## *Why women? Becker's story*

The concept of division of labour can explain why family members tend to specialize in either household or market work, but it cannot explain why women traditionally have remained in the home and men have sought paid work. Becker's argument on this matter has gone through two stages. In the first edition of the *Treatise*, Becker emphasizes the different biological roles of males and females. As women bear the children, they invest considerable thought, time, energy, and forgone earnings in reproduction. This central event in the lives of most families is responsible for the acquisition of household skills by females and market skills by males. Once this process of acquisition of gender-based skills is initiated it tends to be maintained, because of the costs involved for a household in switching its pattern of specialization, particularly as there will be insufficient time left before retirement for the household to recoup its new round of investment in human capital.

Clearly Becker is not entirely happy with this argument. It needs qualification if it is to explain his perception that specialization on a gender basis is not perfect. His *casual* observation suggests that males are also involved in work around the home and that sometimes this involves 'women's work'. As he says:

> Since the biological natures of men and women differ, the assumption that the time of men and women are perfect substitutes even at a rate different from unity is not realistic. Indeed, their times are complements in sexual enjoyment, the production of children, and possible other commodities produced by the household. Complementarity implies that households with men and women are more efficient than households with only one sex, but because both sexes are required to produce certain commodities complementarity reduces the sexual division of labour in the allocation of time and investments.[3]

In other words, if the time of men and women were perfect substitutes, there would be even greater specialization than can be observed in reality. Nevertheless, given that women have, in the main, specialized in household work, comparative advantage has been more important than these complementarities.

In the second, 'enlarged' edition (1991) of the *Treatise*, Becker expresses a number of concerns about his earlier argument, mainly because the 'huge increase in the the labor force participation of married women in developed countries should have encouraged much greater investment by women in market capital, which presumably would raise their earnings relative to men's'.[4] The fact that a considerable margin still exists between the wage rates of males and females in developed countries is puzzling to Becker. As he says:

> The modest increase in the hourly earnings of women relative to men during the last 35 years in the United States and many other Western countries . . . has been an embarrassment to the human capital interpretation of sexual earnings differentials.[5]

He briefly suggests that exploitation (where males *insist* that females work at home and that males work in the market) and the sudden release of females onto the market may have played some role in maintaining a significant gap between male and female wage rates. This unexpected real-world result, at least in terms of the human capital model, has caused Becker to be less assertive about the source of comparative advantage in the 'enlarged' edition of *Treatise*, and to claim only that 'investments in specialized human capital produce increasing returns and thereby provide a strong incentive for a division of labor even among basically identical persons'.[6] To reinforce this new, less confident, position he adds a theoretical discussion (in the Supplement to Chapter 2) of increasing returns to scale and advantages of specialization. Also when evaluating competing arguments (exploitation, childbearing—which may be less important due to social welfare—, etc.) for initial comparative advantage he says, defensively:

> No definitive judgement need be made for the analysis in this supplement, because it does not depend on the *source* of the comparative advantage of women at household activities, be it discrimination or other factors. It requires only that investments in specific human capital reinforce the effects of comparative advantage. Indeed, the analysis does not even require that the initial difference in comparative advantage between men and women be large: a small initial difference can be transformed into large observed differences by the reinforcing effects of specialized investments.[7]

To further bolster his ailing human capital model, Becker introduces a theory of the allocation of risk. He draws attention to the well-known fact that intensity of work, which he calls 'effort', differs between various economic activities. Basically his argument, which is not supported by evidence, is that female work in the household—particularly childrearing—requires a greater input of energy than the household work typically undertaken by males. As the supply of energy is limited, this leaves married women with less energy than males for work in the market. Accordingly married women seek less energy-intensive work in the market than do married men, and acquire less market human capital than their male counterparts *even when they work the same number of market hours*. This, Becker claims, is why the female/male wage ratio in the United States has failed to respond to the shift of married women from the household to the market since 1950.

## *Why women? A new story*

In what follows, a more general model to explain the gender division of labour is suggested—a model that does not have to be supported by a growing encirclement of special *ad hoc* arguments. The model includes variables from both the supply and demand sides, and has been arrived at inductively by empirically examining, through the use of timescapes, the interaction between the household and market sectors. This model is not developed using mathematical symbols, an approach which is often unnecessary and which limits its accessibility.

The general argument on the supply side about the division of family labour, which occurs in order to take advantage of increasing returns, is persuasive. Becker's initial argument, about comparative advantage based on biological differences, is a contributing factor, but not the only one (as discussed below). However, the special arguments about complementarities and 'effort'—that are introduced to explain away the embarrassing and contradictory real-world facts—are not convincing. The tendency in deductive economics to call on additional special arguments each time a new set of unaccommodating facts is discovered must be challenged. The problem with this procedure is that it will continue indefinitely until the initial theory is surrounded by a large number of special qualifying arguments. It is like the flying buttresses of a Gothic cathedral—remove them and the whole structure will collapse. But the flying buttresses are never removed and the initial theory is rarely discarded, even when it is unable to explain what is happening in the real world.[8]

The first special argument concerns complementarities. While suggesting that comparative advantage has been more important than complementarities in influencing the gender division of labour, Becker is forced to admit: 'Yet complementarities cannot be unimportant, especially in modern times; women are becoming less specialized in household activities, and men are spending more time at household activities'.[9] The argument about complementarities is introduced to explain away the fact, not anticipated by his core human capital model, that in reality a large proportion of women work in the market, and some men work in the home. But the argument about complementarities cannot bear the weight that is cast upon it. This dilemma arises from Becker's decision not draw an analytical distinction between economic and non-economic activities in the family. An economic activity is one that gives rise to goods and services that could be sold in the market and hence contribute to family 'income'. The only family activity that requires the input of both sexes—the production of children—is, in modern developed societies, a non-economic activity, as children cannot be bought or sold in the market, and as they rarely provide a positive rate of return to the household on the time and income expended on them (i.e. they are consumer, rather than producer, 'goods'). Therefore the complementarity argument explains very little about the household economy.

The second special argument, enlisted to support the ailing human capital model, concerns the allocation of 'effort'. This argument, however, is called on to carry a far greater burden than it can possibly bear, as it is vulnerable on both conceptual and empirical grounds. In the first place it can be argued, with equal force, that individuals, whether male or female, who are temperamentally suited to raising children are unlikely to find this type of household work unduly exhausting. Only those who resent what they are doing, namely those who wish to develop exciting and demanding market careers, are likely to become bored, frustrated, and hence exhausted. But it is just these people who are likely to invest most in market skills and to take on demanding market jobs in addition to family responsibilities. Second, it could be argued, quite reasonably, that the traditional male task of assuming responsibility for the financial and physical security of the family is just as exhausting—particularly for those males not suited to it—as childrearing. Third, the available evidence (which Becker does not consult) on energy input in various economic activities, suggests that, on balance, modern housework falls into the 'light' energy expenditure category (see Table 5.1), and is on a par with light industry. Also, work traditionally done around the home by males is more demanding, in physical terms, than that undertaken by women. Actually it does not matter how these competing arguments are resolved finally, just that Becker's argument about 'effort' can be challenged, and is not able to stand much scrutiny. He needs a great deal more evidence to support this special argument than merely claiming that: 'the care of small children use[s] much energy'.[10]

Of greater importance, however, is another argument that must be introduced into the debate. The ability to have children is not the only biological difference between males and females that influences gender comparative advantage, at a point in time, as well as changes through time. As will be discussed in more detail in Chapter 5, the ergonomic literature provides abundant evidence that, on average, adult females possess only two-thirds of the strength of adult males in the upper part of the body.[11] Clearly the range of physical activities, together with the number of repetitions in a given period, that can be successfully accomplished (without injury to muscles and spine), is significantly more limited for females than for males. If market economic activity—and here we obtain a glimpse of the demand side of the general model—requires a full range of physical strength, part of which is not possessed by females, then males are going to have a comparative advantage in market work and females in household work. When combined with the childbearing issue, the emphasis on biological differences between males and females becomes a powerful basis for determining initial gender comparative advantage. Accordingly there is no need, as Becker has done, to admit a significant role for discrimination or chance. This is not to deny, however, the desire for, or existence of, discrimination. Just that, in an open economy, while the desire for discrimination (of all types) certainly exists, the scope for its practice is very limited. The evidence for this claim is provided in Chapter 5.

But the explanation of the gender division of labour is not complete until the nature of market demand is considered. If the physical labour demands of the market economy fall within the range of physical strength possessed by the *average* woman, then the biological explanation is limited to an argument about childbearing. Accordingly the general model will collapse to coincide with Becker's human capital model. But if the physical demands of the market lie significantly outside the range of physical strength possessed by women, then the general model suggested here is essential to explain the gender division of labour. Both the ergonomic literature[12] and the study of market demand in Chapter 5, show that physical strength is an important determinant of this issue.

There are two dimensions to the argument about the gender structure of labour demand. The competitive market position of married women, particularly those who have specialized in childbearing and associated housework, as shown in Chapter 5, is limited both by a relative lack of market skills and by the possession of relatively less physical strength than married men. As the market requires both market skills and a wide range of physical strength, males have a substantial competitive edge in the market economy. Accordingly they have a wider range of employment opportunities and can command a higher wage. At any point in time males have a comparative advantage in market work. This is an outcome of both demand and supply forces.

## A dynamic model

The nature of gender comparative advantage changes over time. During the last fifty years, for example, the competitive market position of females has changed radically owing, as will be shown in Chapter 5, to a transformation of the technological foundations of the market economy and to a marked change in its sectoral structure. The increasing capital intensity of production in the market economy during that period, largely in response to the marked reduction in the prices of capital relative to labour, brought with it a substitution of physical capital both for market skills and for heavy labour. In both respects females possess a comparative disadvantage. As relatively unskilled female market labour commands a lower wage than the more highly skilled (both in terms of human capital and physical strength) male labour, the gender structure of market demand for labour has shifted increasingly towards females in the past half century. Linked to this issue is the changing structure of the market economy in favour of the tertiary, or services, sector, in which women have a comparative advantage, particularly as labour skills are being replaced by sophisticated electronic equipment.

Owing to the widening range of employment opportunities in the market for less strenuous and less skilled employment, married females, largely part-time,[13] have moved from the household to the market, attracted by the higher real wages than were traditionally available in the limited pool of occupations suitable for unskilled women. Males, who have greater market skills (both human capital and physical strength) on average than the females replacing them, have moved into other sectors of the economy where these skills are still in demand. In a static economy this would have slowed down the increase in male wages and would have reduced the gap between male and female wage rates, *even though females had not increased their investment in human capital*. In a dynamic economy, however, the outcome is less clear, but the pressure towards equality will be less intense. The persistent gap between male and female wage rates, therefore, can be explained largely as a response to the dynamic forces in the market economy that opened up job opportunities for women without requiring them to acquire extensive market human capital (apart from that which comes with experience).

The changing gender structure of market demand for labour has had a radical impact on the household economy during the last half century. In particular, the proportion of female household workers who also work in the market has risen dramatically (in Australia from 8.0 to 36.5 per cent). This has been a rational response of the household to changing market conditions mediated through the changing marginal utility of family time in all uses. But what impact did it have on the gender division of labour of the household? The answer is that the impact was interesting, and can be characterized in the following, highly simplified, way. Before 1950, owing to biological differences between men and women and to the skill (both human capital and physical strength) requirements of the market economy, men had a comparative advantage in market work and women had a comparative advantage in household work. The household work undertaken by men utilized the market skills—based upon physical strength, craft skills, and leadership skills—that they had acquired. After 1950, men still had a comparative advantage in full-time market work, but the position of women had changed quite dramatically. Although women did *not* have a comparative advantage in *full-time* market work they had a comparative advantage in either *part-time* market work combined with household work (owing to the introduction of electrical household equipment) or just full-time household work. The choice depended on the income of the full-time male market worker and the relative importance of market income/household 'income' in the household's utility function.

This general demand/supply model, particularly the dynamic version, is able to explain most of the changes in the gender division of labour, the acquisition of human capital, and the female/male wage ratio that so embarrassed Becker's static human capital model. And it is able to do so without recourse to special *ad hoc* arguments.

# The gender division of labour in reality: a new picture

A new picture of the gender division of labour in Australia is provided in Figure 4.1. A visual comparison of primary household workers, predominantly

**Figure 4.1 Primary and secondary household workers, Australia, 1788–1990**

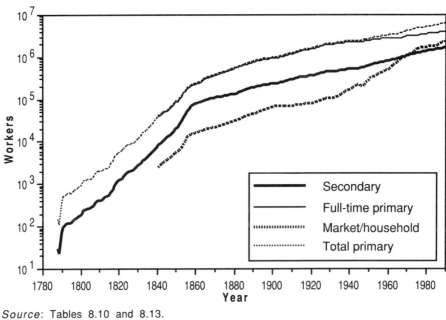

Source: Tables 8.10 and 8.13.

female, and secondary household workers, predominantly male, graphically shows the gender division of labour in the Australian household economy since 1788. Clearly, females provide the great bulk of the household labour force, ranging from 75.2 per cent in 1861, to 79.3 per cent in 1990. While secondary (male) household workers may have grown more rapidly than primary workers (female) before 1860, this trend was reversed from 1860 to 1940, after which both labour types grew in parallel fashion.

Beneath these aggregate figures lies a fascinating change. Until the Second World War, the predominant economic role of 'married' Australian females was as full-time household workers. As we shall see the number of females involved in market/household work was both absolutely and relatively small. There was, however, one brief episode during the late nineteenth century when 'married' females noticeably moved into the market place, but this was reversed during the early years of the twentieth century, and did not occur again until after the 1940s—but then on a massive scale.

Hence the traditional and typical family experience in Australia before the Second World War was for the division of labour along gender lines, with males specializing in the acquisition of market human capital and working full-time in the market sector, and with married females acquiring household skills and working full-time in the household. The main market involvement of females occurred prior to marriage, and even this was not universal, as a large proportion of single females remained in the family home to assist their mothers (see Figure 4.2). While males did play an important role as secondary household workers, they did so by undertaking those tasks, generally outside the house, that could make good use of their investment in market skills (both human capital and physical strength). These tasks included landscaping, building structures, renovating and repairing the house, maintaining the garden, and repairing machines and vehicles. But during and after the Second World War, a radical change occurred. Under the demands made by a wartime command economy (at least between December 1941 and October 1943), when output was more important than productivity, married females, less skilled than the males they 'liberated', entered the market workforce in significant numbers in order to take the place of their husbands who were drafted into the defence forces. After the war, with the return of ex-military personnel, an attempt to revert to more traditional roles was short-lived, owing to the fundamental changes taking place in the market economy. These changes, as discussed in Chapter 5, involved a major shift in the technological foundations of the market economy, a steep rise in the prices of labour relative to capital, a large-scale substitution of capital for labour, the de-skilling and 'de-physicalization' of some market work, a dramatic and permanent increase in the female/male wage ratio, and the widespread substitution of capital for labour in the household.

No amount of political rhetoric, social rationalization, or sexual discrimination could resist these fundamental and massive changes in what is basically an open society. This was a victory, not for feminism (which had failed when the economic changes around the turn of the century proved transitory), but for economic man. As shown in Chapter 5, available evidence suggests that social values are forged by economic change, not economic change by social values. No amount of feminist pressure in Edwardian times, and there was a good deal of it,[14] could have engineered the mass exodus of married women from the home and into the market that occurred in the second half of the twentieth century. And no amount of male chauvinism in the post–Second World War period could have prevented it.

# The household workforce

## *Economic portrait*

A close-up exposure of the household workforce reveals some interesting detail that invites more comprehensive analysis. The major issue is the persistent specialization of Australian married women in full-time household work for over three-quarters of the country's European history, and then, in the last half of the twentieth century, their sudden and dramatic shift into the market economy. Prior to the Second World War, the number of full-time unpaid household workers exceeded the number of households by between one-quarter and one-third (Figure 4.2). But with the sudden flow of married females from the home to the market, this ratio fell quickly to unity in 1961, and by the beginning of the last decade of the twentieth century, less than three-quarters of Australian households were staffed with a full-time female worker. The other side of this coin is the equally dramatic change in the proportion of female household workers who were also employed in the market sector. This ratio, which has greater analytical relevance than the participation rate of married females,[15] was largely static between 1861 and 1939, languishing in the range 5 to 7 per cent; but after the 1940s it rose dramatically to 10.3 per cent in 1950; 15.3 per cent in 1960; 25.6 per cent in 1970; 32.7 per cent in 1980; and 36.5 per cent in 1990. By the last decade of the twentieth century, therefore, almost 40 per cent of female household workers were also employed in the market. Of these, 53.3 per cent worked full-time in the market and 46.7 per cent worked part-time, averaging 37 and 16 hours per week respectively. This change is nothing short of an economic and social revolution— a change that involved a more sudden break with the past than in the USA where the market participation of married white women increased by a factor of four prior to 1950 and a factor of three thereafter.[16]

**Figure 4.2 Households and full-time household workers, Australia, 1841–1990**

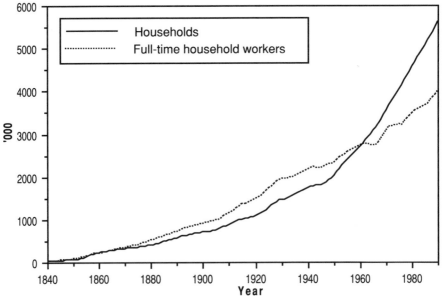

*Source*: Tables 8.2 and 8.10.

## An econometric analysis of female market participation, 1861–1990

How do we explain this dramatic transformation of the household economy? Was it the result of a major change in fundamental economic forces or of changing social attitudes? The answer is to be found in a major change in the nature of the market economy; and social attitudes, fighting and screaming all the way, followed along behind. From what we have already seen of the empirical relationships presented in various timescapes, the gender structure of market demand for labour, the sectoral structure of output and employment, and the female/male wage ratio are leading contenders for the economic determinants of the market participation of female household workers. But it is necessary to test the objectivity of our visual approach—of our seeing—by employing a simple regression model.

The simple reduced-form regression model, based on our observation of the economic timescapes presented in Chapter 2, characterizes the market participation rate of female household workers as a linear function of the market capital/labour ratio, and the female/male wage rate. To keep this demand/supply model as simple as possible, without violating the nature of causation suggested in the timescapes, quantitative measures of the fundamental changes taking place in the Total Economy are employed. The dependent variable is the proportion of female household workers who are also employed in the market economy. This measure is more appropriate than (although closely related to) the market participation rate of married females, as the household is the decision-making unit in this process. The demand-side explanatory variable—the market capital/labour ratio—is a measure of the fundamental changes taking place in the economy, including technological change, the substitution of capital for both heavy labour and skilled labour, and structural change.[17] Traditionally, the ratio of female to male wage rates has been treated as a supply-side variable. While it is true that this variable should pick up the effects of changing human capital stocks as between males and females and provide a measure of the growing opportunity cost to households of devoting female labour solely to household work, the evidence in this study suggests that the gender wage ratio is also strongly influenced by largely autonomous changes in market demand for female labour. Finally, consideration is also given in this model to changes in the birth rate, not as the ultimate source of change, but as a medium through which changes of a more fundamental nature are communicated from the market to the household.

In formal terms, the model to be tested is as follows:

$$MP = a + bKLR + c\Delta FMW + d\Delta BR$$

where *MP* is the market participation ratio of female household workers, *KLR* is the capital/labour ratio, $\Delta FMW$ is the annual change in the female/male wage ratio, and $\Delta BR$ is the annual change in the number of births per household. The level of *KLR* can be thought of as determining the job opportunities for females in the market economy, while changes in both the gender wage ratio and the birth rate can be interpreted as determining the response of households at the margin. Together they should explain much of the market participation of female household workers.

The regression results are presented in Table 4.1, and the main variables are pictured in Figure 4.3 (and Figure 3.8, p. 71, for household birth rates). It is essential to provide economic timescapes as well as the usual black-box statistical results, because formal statistical methods should be regarded as a

**Table 4.1   Demand and supply determinants of married female market participation, Australia, 1861–1990**

| Period | | Constant | KLR | $\Delta$FMW | $\Delta$BR | $MP_{(-1)}$ | $MP_{(-2)}$ | $\bar{R}^2$ | D-W |
|---|---|---|---|---|---|---|---|---|---|
| **1861–1990** | $\beta_1$ | 0.756 | 0.006 | 6.290 | 77.704 | | | 0.983 | 0.242 |
| | $\beta_2$ | 0.027 | 0.0004 | 1.592 | -7.555 | 1.634 | -0.696 | 0.999 | 1.804 |
| | $t_1$ | 4.200 | 84.427 | 1.417 | 2.428 | | | | |
| | $t_2$ | 0.637 | 3.561 | 1.649 | -1.059 | 25.252 | -11.126 | | |
| | $E_1$ | | 0.942 | 0.002 | -0.008 | | | | |
| | $E_2$ | | 0.063 | 0.0005 | 0.0008 | 1.602 | -0.669 | | |
| **1861–1889** | $\beta_1$ | 6.011 | -0.376 | 1.418 | 3.566 | | | 0.035 | 0.166 |
| | $\beta_2$ | 0.773 | -0.00004 | -0.021 | -0.553 | 1.143 | -0.286 | 0.964 | 2.372 |
| | $t_1$ | 33.485 | -1.604 | 1.000 | 0.309 | | | | |
| | $t_2$ | 3.363 | 0.805 | -0.088 | -0.278 | 5.563 | -1.587 | | |
| | $E_1$ | | -0.048 | -0.0 | -0.0002 | | | | |
| | $E_2$ | | 0.005 | 0.000005 | 0.00006 | 1.148 | -0.289 | | |
| **1890–1939** | $\beta_1$ | 5.453 | -0.350 | -0.128 | 32.867 | | | -0.024 | 0.115 |
| | $\beta_2$ | 0.059 | 0.0001 | -0.064 | 2.878 | 1.752 | -0.780 | 0.979 | 2.507 |
| | $t_1$ | 7.411 | 0.453 | -0.043 | 1.351 | | | | |
| | $t_2$ | 0.344 | 1.041 | -0.148 | 0.806 | 17.292 | -7.500 | | |
| | $E_1$ | | 0.060 | -0.00005 | -0.014 | | | | |
| | $E_2$ | | 0.020 | -0.00003 | -0.001 | 1.746 | -0.775 | | |
| **1946–1990** | $\beta_1$ | 0.614 | 0.006 | 21.716 | -81.560 | | | 0.978 | 0.288 |
| | $\beta_2$ | 0.229 | 0.0007 | 10.253 | -100.594 | 1.405 | -0.528 | 0.999 | 1.972 |
| | $t_1$ | 1.076 | 42.635 | 1.582 | -0.850 | | | | |
| | $t_2$ | 1.412 | 3.241 | 3.083 | -3.740 | 15.031 | -5.763 | | |
| | $E_1$ | | 0.963 | 0.007 | 0.003 | | | | |
| | $E_2$ | | 0.115 | 0.003 | 0.005 | 1.366 | -0.499 | | |

*Notes:*   (1) The results corrected for autocorrelation ($\beta_2$, $t_2$, $E_2$) are shown immediately below the uncorrected results ($\beta_1$, $t_1$, $E_1$).
(2) $\beta$ gives the parameter estimates of the intercept or constant and the following explanatory variables: the capital/labour ratio (KLR), the annual change in the female/male wage ratio ($\Delta$FMW), and the annual change in the household birth rate ($\Delta$BR). The dependent variable is the market participation of female household workers (MP).
(3) $t$ gives the conventional $t$-ratios.
(4) $E$ gives the partial elasticities of female participation evaluated at the sample means of the explanatory variables.
(5) D-W is the Durbin–Watson statistic to test for autocorrelation.

**Figure 4.3 Determinants of female market participation, Australia, 1861–1990**

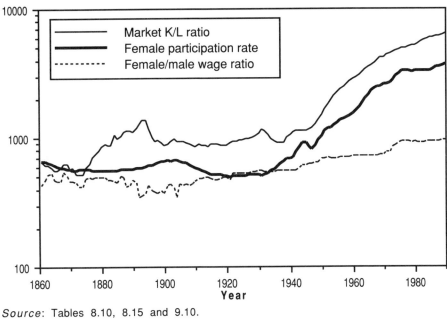

*Source*: Tables 8.10, 8.15 and 9.10.

way of testing the objectivity of our seeing. As anticipated, the stability, prior to the Second World War, of the female market participation rate together with the normal cyclical fluctuation of the main explanatory variables, means that our model does not come into its own until after 1946. An inspection of the results uncorrected for autocorrelation $(\beta_1, t_1, E_1)$ suggests that, while the model can account for 97.8 per cent of the variation in the participation rate during the second half of the twentieth century, there is a serious problem of autocorrelation.

The results corrected for autocorrelation $(\beta_2, t_2, E_2)$ by autoregressing the dependent variable lagged two periods ($MP_{-1}$ and $MP_{-2}$) are striking. For the post–1945 period, all the explanatory variables are statistically significant and have the correct sign; and the diagnostic tests are highly satisfactory.[18] The implication of these results is that the radical departure after 1946 of female market participation from what was essentially a stationary state, was due to a major change in the economy's technological base (as measured by the capital/labour ratio) and to the resulting change in the female labour market and in the family responsibilities of 'married' women, both directly in any given year and indirectly through their influence on the participation ratios in the two preceeding years.[19]

Do our results provide any information on the relative importance of demand and supply forces in determining female participation rates? There are two lions in that path. The first concerns the difficulty of determining the demand and supply determinants of the gender wage ratio, and the second concerns the difficulty of comparing elasticities on variables that have different transformations (levels and changes). One solution is to isolate a major explanatory variable (in this case the market capital/labour ratio), the nature of which is unambiguous (in this case a major demand-side force), and to regress the dependent variable on it. By doing so we find that the capital/labour ratio on its own accounts for 97.6 per cent of the variation in female participation results in the post–1946 period. While this is only a rough procedure, it does suggest that demand-side forces—more particularly, dynamic processes in the market sector—are largely responsible for driving the process of employment interaction between the household and market sectors.

This conclusion is of the greatest significance, because the dynamic processes of the market economy have, in this context, been neglected by theorists, applied economists, and by feminists. Quite clearly the issue of changing female market participation can be explained largely—up to 98 per cent—by reference to fundamental economic forces. This leaves little room (a mere 2 per cent) for the involvement of exogenous institutional forces or of economically irrational discriminatory policies. This is not to say that institutions were not influential in wage determination, just that they were sensitive to market forces; nor does it suggest that flagrant examples of discrimination do not exist, or that human beings (not just men) are not discriminationists at heart, just that irrational discrimination in an open economy is a luxury that the *average* employer or householder cannot afford. What it does say is that the Total Economy in Australia is a system driven by rational decisionmakers, in which the main demand and supply forces are endogenously determined. Both the stable gender division of labour between the goldrushes and the Second World War, and its radical change thereafter, resulted from rational responses of householders, both female and male, to dynamic processes occurring within the market sector. These dynamic processes will be studied more closely in the next chapter.

## Other econometric studies

The results of this longrun dynamic study are at variance with other Australian timeseries studies of participation rates by Dunlop, Healy, and McMahon (1983) and Gregory, McMahon, and Wittingham (1985). To illustrate this difference and the reasons for it, I will focus briefly upon Gregory *et al.* (1985) because of its widespread citation (including Becker) in the international and national literature as a correct characterization of the Australian labour market. They typically employ a model that includes, as explanatory variables, the real earnings rates of males and females, the unemployment rate of married females, the ratio of children (ages 0 to 5 years) to women (ages 15 to 44 years), the divorce rate, a time trend, and seasonal dummies; and they test it using quarterly data for the period 1964 to 1980. As most of these variables can be expected to respond to changes in the female/male wage ratio (as it changes the marginal utilities of time-use by the household) they will certainly boost the $\bar{R}^2$, but will generate unnecessary multicollinearity. On the other hand, no attempt is made to include a variable that measures the changing gender structure of market demand for labour resulting from dynamic changes in the technological and sectoral structure of the market economy. Hence, not only have they ignored the dominant determinant of changing female market participation, but their misspecified model is unlikely to generate meaningful coefficient estimates and $t$-statistics.

It is not terribly surprising, therefore, that none of their explanatory variables is significant or that some have the wrong sign, even after correcting for autocorrelation and after using various lags in the explanatory variables. (In my own regression analysis, the gender wage ratio and the birth rate only become significant in the presence of the proxy—the capital/labour ratio— for demand-side forces). They conclude that their 'disappointing results' must be due to institutional reasons, and that: 'We are led back to a view of the economy that stresses an exogenous relative wage change and a fairly rigid job segregation that protects female employment when their relative wage increases'.[20] In their view, married women move into the market (from where is not specified) not in response to a change in the female/male wage ratio as part of a process of rational family decision-making, but merely as market jobs which, for some unspecified reason, wax and wane. There is no vision here of a Total Economy in which the market sector is undergoing fundamental economic changes to which the household sector responds rationally, owing to changing marginal utilities of time-use, by redistributing their effort between housework, paid work, and leisure. This is the reason that married female unemployment does not fluctuate according to the business cycle. It should not have come as a surprise. What they have done is to overlook the central role that the household sector plays in the Total Economy as the major employer of married female labour. Their results are 'disappointing' largely because their model is badly misspecified. Had demand-side forces been included in their model, the gender wage ratio probably would have emerged as significant and with the correct sign, undermining their argument that wages are exogenously determined by arbitrary institutional decree.

This type of supply-side analysis is characteristic of the human capital approach to labour issues. Jacob Mincer, one of the pioneers of applied work in this field, attempted in the early 1960s to explain the market participation of married white US females over the period 1900 to 1950 in terms of a simple supply-side model in which the explanatory variables are the wage rate for married females and the income of their husbands (i.e. the relative female wage).[21] In Schumpeterian fashion, Mincer's innovative work inspired many followers. The resulting upsurge in econometric work on the supply of female labour has focused on human capital variables (particularly female and non-female market income) within a static framework.[22] More recently, Claudia

Goldin has extended this supply-side model to formally take account of demand forces.[23] Goldin's more general model is ingeniously derived from the familiar labour demand and supply analysis, in which rates of change have been substituted for the absolute values of wage rates on the vertical axis and female participation on the horizontal axis. This analysis, which requires assumptions about the elasticity of both the supply of, and demand for, female labour, is a rather indirect and non-historical way of incorporating 'demand forces'. Essentially, it is a static approach to the issue, and does not focus on the underlying nature of the 'demand forces' or the dynamic process of change. Rather, her analysis of historical changes in the market role of women incorporates a number of institutional and cultural factors.[24] Hence, despite the important contribution of the human capital tradition it has yet to meet the challenge, thrown down by Clarence Long some thirty years ago, to conduct 'an extensive inquiry into the *dynamic* behavior of labor force of wives'.[25]

# Human capital in the household

Although this study has attempted to refocus attention on the contribution of physical capital in both the household and market sectors, human capital must not be ignored. The contribution that a population can make to economic activity depends on the nature and degree of its education and general health. In turn this largely depends on the quantity of resources that are available to households to spend on formal and informal education, and on diet, recreation, etc.; and on the manner in which these resources are distributed within the household. These issues have important implications for the quality of the future market labour force, an issue in which governments are vitally, and quite properly, interested. Accordingly, this section will be devoted to an examination of changes in education and health, particularly of females, against a background of changing household income.[26]

## *Household living standards*

In examining household living standards it is important to examine not only market income but also Gross Community Income (GCI), *per household*. As can be seen from the timescape in Figure 4.4, GCI per household not only increased more rapidly than market income per household during the second halves of both the nineteenth and twentieth centuries, it also failed to fall as rapidly as market income during the major depressions. In other words, the household economy acted as a safety net during the depressions of the 1890s and 1930s. What our timescape shows is that income per household increased quite rapidly in the first and last forty years of this 130 year period, but that it stagnated and declined in the intervening fifty years. Possibly the most

**Figure 4.4 Real Gross Community Income and market income per household, Australia, 1861–1990**

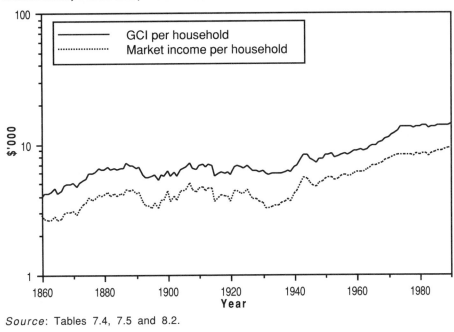

*Source*: Tables 7.4, 7.5 and 8.2.

interesting part of this overall picture is the fact that when income is viewed on a household basis, the *relative* stagnation revealed by Noel Butlin's estimates of per capita income becomes *absolute* stagnation; and the expansion after the Second World War appears less impressive. This is a fundamentally important point that reflects upon the dynamics of this period and has important implications for the interpretation of Australian living standards. Average household income is a more appropriate measure of average living standards than per capita income, because the family is the unit of final consumption.

This point is so important that it needs to be pursued in greater detail here, particularly because it is rarely raised in an empirical context. The reason that my income per household estimates change our interpretation of the 'inter-depression' period from one of relative stagnation (based on Butlin's per capita estimates of the 1950s) to absolute stagnation and decline, is that the number of households increased at a faster rate than the population after the 1890s, and particularly after the 1930s. This suggests that the changing structure of the Australian household has had an important impact upon family living standards.

In the period 1900 to the 1930s, the structure of the Australian household underwent significant change owing to the breaking up of the traditional extended family—of three generations living in the same household. This had important implications for the living standards of both young families and elderly couples, who, increasingly after the turn of the century, lived in separate establishments. My argument is that elderly couples and young families, both of whom were on the lower end of the income distribution curve, were separated from the more affluent middle-aged group. Hence the middle-aged group benefited financially from the breakdown of the extended family, while the elderly and the young groups suffered a reduction in average incomes, even with the development of social welfare. As a given income was spread over more households, average household income declined.

Since the Second World War, the changing structure of the Australian family has also had an impact on household income that is not reflected in per capita income. It was shown in Chapter 2 that, over the second half of the twentieth century, the rate of divorce has increased rapidly. One unfortunate consequence has been a rapid increase in the number of single-parent households, with households growing more rapidly than population. It is unfortunate because the living standards in these households, despite government attempts to redistribute income, is lower than that of two-parent households, both in market and total income terms. Accordingly, household income in the last forty years has grown less rapidly than per capita income.

This survey of the resources available to Australian households over the last 130 years suggests that, other things being constant, improvements in human capital were possible in two periods: the 1870s and 1880s and again, but on a much larger scale, after the 1940s. Needless to say other things were not constant. In the 1870s and 1880s the level of income, whilst sufficient to improve standards of diet and aspects of the physical environment, was not sufficient to greatly improve human capital. Indeed even the physical environment left a lot to be desired. The failure to adequately sewer Australian cities (particularly Melbourne or 'Smelbourne' as it was popularly known) before the 1890s, for example, led to regular and devastating outbreaks of infectious diseases such as typhoid.[27] While GCI per household declined in the interdepression period, so too did the number of children per household (see Figure 3.9, p. 72), which would have cushioned the impact of declining real family income. Without doubt, the period after the Second World War really was a golden age.[28] There was an unprecedented increase in income per household, and a dramatic reduction in the number of children per household, at a time when relatively inexpensive advances in medical science had a major combined impact on human capital and health. This contrasts starkly with the interdepression period, and can be illustrated by examining the statistical record on education and health.

## Education

Higher household incomes in the post–1945 years were clearly used, for the first time, to make major improvements to the stock of family human capital. Three sets of data can be marshalled to briefly demonstrate this point. First, data on enrolment in primary and secondary school can be used to provide a rough sketch (particularly rough in the nineteenth century) of changes in general human capital formation in Australian families. These statistics suggest that the proportion of all children under 14 years attending school was about 60 per cent in 1871, a level that remained largely unchanged until the Second World War. In 1949, for example, the proportion was still 67 per cent; but by 1971 it had risen to 77 per cent, by 1981 it had reached 82 per cent, and by 1986, 87 per cent. Hence, the expansion of basic schooling, which occurred only after the 1940s, coincided with the marked increase in GCI per household. It is unfortunate that available statistics do not allow us to sketch the increasing proportion of children attending kindergarten and other pre-school institutions. We do know from general sources, however, that considerable expansion in the formal education of pre-school infants increased dramatically after the 1940s.

The post–1940s period also experienced a rapid expansion of upper secondary schooling and of tertiary education. School students of 16 years and above as a proportion of total school enrolments, increased from negligible levels in the interwar period to 20.4 per cent in 1959, 32.5 per cent in 1970, and 35 per cent in the 1980s.[29] In an even more dramatic way, the number of students enrolled in technical education as a proportion of the total population increased from 1.0 per cent in 1905 to only 1.4 per cent in the late 1930s, but then increased dramatically (by a factor of 5.4) to 7.5 per cent in 1986. Similarly the number of university students (exclusive of Colleges of Advanced Education and Teachers Colleges) increased from 0.17 per cent of the population in 1938 to 0.24 per cent in 1955, 0.82 per cent in 1969, and 1.02 per cent in 1980. If we include all tertiary students, the participation rate (as a proportion of total population) increased from 1.23 per cent in 1969, to 2.10 per cent in 1980, and 2.82 per cent in 1990.[30] Clearly the correlation between income per household and formal human capital is strong.

There is a question central to this analysis: while there was a general increase in the human capital of families in the post–Second World War period, was there also a relative shift in family resources from males to females? Or in other words, did the changing gender structure of labour demand in this period lead to a significant increase in the education and training of females relative to males? The evidence suggests that a relative shift in the structure of gender human capital formation did occur, but that it was not as great as would be predicted on the basis of the change in female market participation, and was more of an academic than a technical nature.

While the female proportion of all 14 year-old school students increased only marginally (47.6 to 48.7 per cent) between 1960 and 1990, it increased more substantially (44.6 to 50.4 per cent) for the 15 to 17 year-old group (Table 4.2). In other words, the proportion of female students completing secondary school increased dramatically, particularly in the 1960s, until their numbers even slightly exceeded those of their male counterparts. The major change in the education of females, however, occurred at the tertiary level. Over the period 1950 to 1990, the proportion of female to total enrolments

**Table 4.2   Gender distribution of human capital formation, Australia, 1950–1990** (female as percentage of total student enrolments)

|      | School aged 14 | School aged 15–17 | Higher degrees* | Bachelor's degrees | Technical education | Apprentice- ships |
|------|------|------|------|------|------|------|
| **1950** | .. | .. | 12.1 | 18.3 | .. | .. |
| **1960** | 47.6 | 44.6 | 13.2 | 22.8 | .. | .. |
| **1970** | 48.3 | 55.6 | 16.5 | 30.7 | .. | .. |
| **1980** | 48.8 | 51.3 | 28.0 | 43.6 | .. | .. |
| **1990** | 48.7 | 50.4 | 39.5 | 51.1 | 44.7 | 14.6 |

*Notes:*   * Does not include diplomas.
       .. Not available.
*Sources:*  Grundy and Yuan, 'Education and science'; ABS, *Schools, Australia*; DEET, *Apprenticeship statistics*; DEET, *Selected higher education statistics*; TAFE and DEET, *Selected TAFE statistics*.

at the undergraduate level increased from 18.3 to 51.1 per cent, and at the higher degree level (not including diplomas) from 12.1 to 39.5 per cent. Also by 1990, 44.7 per cent of all 'technical' students (generally in non-industrial courses) were female. It must be realized, however, that this change in academic training was enjoyed by only a very small proportion of the female population—in 1990 only 3.9 per cent of all females over the age of 16 years were currently enrolled in institutions of higher education—with the great majority of women receiving no more than a basic school education.[31] On the other hand, a considerably larger proportion of males received formal vocational training. It is significant that, even in 1990, only 14.6 per cent of all apprentices were female.

## Health and physical wellbeing

The health of the workforce is of central importance to the economic performance of any society. This was effectively recognized by colonial and state governments around the turn of the century. Infectious diseases were directly attacked in the capital cities by public investment in the provision of pure water in the 1870s and 1880s, and through the introduction of deep sewerage by the 1890s.[32] And these facilities were extended to rural areas in the interwar period.[33] The 1890s also saw local governments introduce effective public health and pure-food legislation, and in NSW between 1898 and 1900 medical practitioners and dentists were required to be officially registered.[34] Further, before the First World War, state governments introduced medical inspections for schools, and after the war they built baby-care centres in urban and rural areas and encouraged school children and the general public to practice personal hygiene.[35] And the introduction of maternity allowances by the Commonwealth Government in 1912, together with child allowances in New South Wales in 1927 and the rest of Australia in 1941, was official recognition of the importance of the home, and of children, in providing an efficient future workforce. These simple, but effective preventative and supportive measures, were joined by major breakthroughs in medical science after the 1930s—penicillin in 1941, inoculations for a range of dangerous diseases such as diptheria, whooping cough, german measles, etc. from the late 1940s, and Salk vaccine to combat polio in the 1950s.

The impact of these measures on family health is reflected in Figure 3.8 (p. 71), which tracks the sharp decline in infant deaths, and all deaths, *per family* from the late nineteenth century, and particularly from the 1940s. As a result of these changes, the life expectancy at birth of males rose from 47 years in the 1880s to 71 years in the 1980s, and for females from 51 years to 78 years over the same period. As this increase in life expectancy was largely due to increases in living standards and hygiene in the home, we can expect that it also led to an improvement in family health, particularly of infants. Confirmation must wait until the data on the heights of school children, collected by various state education departments, is examined.[36] This evidence for both girls and boys will also cast some light upon the changing gender distribution of family resources.

A perusal of the death-rate data[37] (which are too detailed to present here) for diseases such as tuberculosis, venereal disease, other infectious diseases, respiratory disease, diseases of the digestive system, the genito-urinary system, and of skin, all suggest that peak levels were experienced before the First World War, and that they fell steadily during the interwar years, and rapidly after the Second World War. There are some death-causing diseases, however, that increased over those years, and even reached peaks in the post 1940s period. These include cancer and leukaemia, cardio-vascular disease, glandular and metabolic diseases, senile diabetes, musculo-skeletal diseases, and, of course, Acquired Immune Deficiency Syndrome (AIDS). Many of these diseases are the costs associated with higher consumption standards, lighter work, increased longevity, and changes in lifestyle. We have probably reached the stage in human development, when the costs (in terms of morbidity) to an individual of an extra year of longevity may have surpassed the benefits. Maximization of longrun utility from life may, in the 1990s, have been realized by the human race in the developed world.

Finally, it is illuminating to reflect upon working-age male deaths arising from 'injury and poisoning'. If we exclude the injury-prone 'tear-away' age group of 15–24 years, together with those over 65 years, who are no longer part of the market workforce, we find that deaths from injury fell by 45 per cent from the 1900s to the 1970s, with most of the reduction occurring after the Great Depression. Indeed, the average male death rate from injury in the period since 1940 was 29 per cent lower than the average rate experienced between 1908 and 1940. This has a greater significance than may be apparent at first sight. The marked reduction in the male death rate from injury and industrial poisoning is consistent with the changing technological nature of the economy: as capital is substituted for heavy labour tasks, the rate of injury can be expected to fall. This is another signal to employers and to households that the range of female job opportunities in the market is widening. Clearly it is now time to turn to an analysis of the dynamics of the market sector that generated the radical increase in demand for female labour after the Second World War.

## Conclusions

The dramatic change in the gender division of labour is examined in this chapter. It is a subject explored through the presentation of timescapes and through econometric analysis. Because of the limitations of the existing static supply-side (human capital) model, it was necessary to develop a general dynamic model. The general model includes forces on both the demand and supply sides. On the supply side, this study suggests that gender comparative advantage is significantly influenced by physical factors, and on the demand side allowance has been made for the impact of technological forces in the Total Economy. This model is considered in both a static and a dynamic framework.

The dramatic increase in market participation by married females after the 1950s is explained largely in terms of a fundamental change in the technological foundations of the market economy, and to a lesser degree by changes in human capital. In other words, forces on the demand side were more important than forces on the supply side in the changing gender division of labour. Nevertheless, consideration is given here to family human capital, which is seen as a function of changing household living standards. While there was clearly a redistribution of family resources to female members, evidence on increasing female market participation suggests that this was not as great as would be predicted by the human capital model. This outcome reinforces the demand-side explanation developed here.

# 5

---

# *The market and the household*

$F$ undamental longrun changes in the market economy have played a central role in the interaction between the household and market sectors. This has become apparent from both the economic timescapes and the results of formally testing the existential models presented in earlier chapters. The aim of the present chapter is to explore in greater depth those elements that have emerged as being important in the dynamics of the Total Economy. Accordingly, the chapter focuses on economic motivation in the market and how it relates to household objectives; why the market appears to undervalue female labour; how dynamic market processes have influenced the demand for female labour in the longrun; and what role discrimination and segmented labour markets play in the employment and remuneration of women. In the process, new insights regarding the dynamics of economic development in Australia are provided—insights that are developed further in Chapter 6.

## A model of market–household interaction

### *Market motivation*

Becker's claim that the ruling principles in the household and the firm are, respectively, 'altruism' and 'selfishness', has already been challenged. In Chapter 3, reasons were given for rejecting this dualistic approach to the Total Economy. Just as 'altruism' is an inappropriate description of the driving force in the household economy, so 'selfishness' fails to capture the ruling principle in the market economy. The pursuit of individual utility maximization is the dominant motivational force in both sectors, and in both sectors the attempt to achieve it is made through an opportunistic combination of both individualistic and cooperative behaviour. Hence the Total Economy should not be thought of as a dual economy, but rather as an integrated economy driven by the same forces, and involved in a close and continuous process of interaction of its component parts.

An appearance of duality is given by the obvious contrast between the home and the firm in terms of size, degree of specialization, dynamic interaction with markets in other regions, technological underpinning, and the capital intensity of production. But this is all a matter of appearances. In the beginning was the household. And out of the household was created the market sector both private and public.[1] The market sector had its being, and thereafter obtained its sustenance, from the household contracting out some of its activities in order merely to increase its returns. While there are obvious structural differences, motivationally and behaviourally the Total Economy is one economy.

## A general model of the home and the firm

We start with a simple general model. Begin with the assumption that the basic units of production in the household and the market sectors—the home and the firm—attempt to maximize their utility. In the case of the home, this involves maximizing the consumption of market and household goods and services (including leisure), and in the case of the firm it involves maximizing profits. Individuals in both the home and the firm attempt to maximize their own utility by cooperating with other workers in order to maximize the objective function of their organization. In a competitive environment, the firm will wish to employ the most cost efficient forms of labour, and the home will direct labour to household and market activities on the basis of comparative advantage so as to equate marginal utilities on the alternative uses of time. Although human beings are prone to prejudice and to discriminatory behaviour, mainly due to fear of material loss, the scope for actually behaving so is limited in an open and competitive society. In an open and competitive society, therefore, both the home and the firm will be forced to respond to fundamental economic forces, and the effects of job or wage discrimination will be contained within fairly narrow limits determined by the costs and benefits of fighting the forces of oppression. While the open society is the enemy of discrimination, the closed society is its accomplice.

In a period when fundamental economic change is slow, the gender division of labour based on comparative advantage will be encased within the cement of social rationalization and justification. This is how we justify our actions, both to ourselves and to others. Subsequent growth and structural change— such as the introduction of a new technology or access to new resources— that alters fundamentally the decisions of firms and households, will meet initial resistance, generally in the name of social standards, from those who stand to lose materially. In such circumstances, gender or racial discrimination may increase. But within a relatively short time this resistance will weaken as it becomes clear that those who respond to the new economic circumstances, both in the market and the household, are the economic winners, and those who resist are the economic losers. In an open economy this change will occur quite quickly, and a new set of social mores will be established to justify the new economic reality. Only in a closed economy will change be successfully resisted for a time, but even here change will eventually occur and, when it does, it will take place with great suddenness and possibly great violence as in Eastern Europe and the USSR in the early 1990s.[2]

Depending on the industry in which it is located, the firm will require a workforce with a specific range of attributes including human capital and physical strength. Human capital theory has focused on work skills that are acquired formally through investment in training programmes—either in educational institutions or apprenticeships—and informally through work experience. But little attention has been given to an equally important labour force attribute—physical strength. This matter is widely misunderstood. It is the subject of groundless suspicion by feminist groups, and it is strangely ignored by human capital theorists. The plain fact is that physical strength has been, and still is, an essential input in the production process of heavy industry, construction, mining[3], resource exploration and exploitation, agriculture, and crisis management.[4] And it remains important in a range of tasks— such as loading, carrying and shifting heavy objects, and rectifying production systems that get out of control—even in light industry, commerce, and service activities. Just as a firm requires a range of intellectual and manual skills, so it requires a range of physical strength. And just as some members of the workforce have a comparative advantage in work that requires intellectual or manual skills, others have a comparative advantage in work that requires physical strength. It is curious that this simple observation should be regarded as controversial.

At any point in time, the balance of market demand for labour with intellectual or manual skills on the one hand, and physical strength on the other, will depend on the technological base of the economy. Following the Industrial Revolution, which was based on a relatively labour-intensive technology,[5] the demand for a workforce possessing physical strength was considerable. Lighter industries, such as clothing and textiles, existed, but even here there were tasks that could only be performed with the use of considerable human strength. Physical power was essential to the success of the Industrial Revolution. In the case of Britain, there was only a very modest increase in the capital/labour ratio during the Industrial Revolution and, subsequently, the rate of growth of capital per 'man-hour' in manufacturing and commerce actually fell from the mid nineteenth century to the First World War. It even became negative during the interwar period. Not surprisingly, during these years relative factor prices changed little. Only after the Second World War, when the price of capital relative to the price of labour fell, did the British capital/labour ratio resume rapid expansion, at a rate double that achieved in the second half of the nineteenth century.[6] In the more rapidly changing USA, the capital/labour ratio increased by 80 per cent between 1870 and 1900, and a further 59 per cent between 1900 and 1939.[7] Yet, even the greater US capital intensity of production in the pre-1940s period often *increased* the demands for strength because of the accelerating speed of machine-controlled work, and the multiplication of processes placed under the control of single operators.[8] It was not until after the 1940s that large and permanent reductions occurred in the prices of capital relative to labour, not only in Britain and the USA, but throughout the Western World, encouraging a major substitution of automated capital for heavy labour. And from the 1960s there was a widespread introduction of sophisticated electronic machinery including computers, that involved a substitution of capital for skilled labour. Only after the Second World War, therefore, was there a large-scale expansion in the range of market jobs that were relatively undemanding in terms of physical strength and industrial skills.

## Physical strength as human capital

### The evidence

A useful introduction to the issue of physical effort in the workplace is provided by Table 5.1, which presents research results concerning the expenditure of energy (in kilocalories) by both males and females in five categories of work, ranging from light to very heavy work in both the market and the household.[9] The first point of interest is that energy expended on the same tasks is greater for males than females owing to their larger size and to the speed and vigour with which the work is done. Second, the range of physical strength required in the Total Economy is wide. This is reflected in the fact that the lower bound for 'unduly heavy' work is over six times greater than that for 'light' work. Third, the total effort expended is a function not only of the type of work, but also the rate at which it needs to be undertaken. For example, a male labourer would expend 2,400 Kcals of energy, either by working steadily at a moderate rate of 5 Kcals per minute through an eight-hour shift, or by working at a faster rate of 9 Kcals per minute for half the shift and then resting (at say 1.2 Kcals per minute) for the other half. Fourth, the greater the energy requirements of the work, in terms of either heavy individual tasks or a high repetition of moderate tasks, the greater the probability of worker injury from overstrain and accident. Finally, workers who are not physically suited to the energy demands of heavy work are clearly the most prone to injury. These workers will be more costly to employ, in terms of days away from work and through damage to the production process. Needless to say less strong workers will find heavy work unattractive.

The relationship between the energy demands of industry and the level of injury is well documented in ergonomic literature. The research of Monod and Zerbib, for example, leads to the conclusion that: 'Carrying loads is a particularly arduous form of work for man. It requires considerable muscular effort, imposes both static and dynamic stress on numerous groups of muscles and quickly becomes tiring', particularly for female workers as 'women have a maximum strength approximately 30–40% lower than that of men'.[10] Injuries

resulting from heavy work, which mainly inflict damage to the lower back—
the most debilitating of injuries—have received considerable attention from
researchers. In Sweden, for example, it has been found that:

> the back was the main part of the of the body injured in about 2200 occupational
> diseases and 13 000 occupational accidents in Sweden during 1980. Overexertion
> was an important factor in the majority of these cases. Fourteen per cent of these
> accidental injuries were a result of strenuous movements, 16% resulted from a fall
> and 55% occurred when objects were lifted.[11]

A similar outcome of heavy work has been noted in the UK. After examining
the UK accident data over the period 1976 to 1980, one researcher concluded
that: 'injuries related to handling [heavy objects] form a sizeable proportion,
between 20 and 30%, of over 3 day injuries in most sectors of U.K. industry'.
In 1980, for example, he found that 31.5 per cent of all injuries were caused
by 'handling goods' generally and 'overexertion' specifically. Of these, half
were back injuries.[12] Not surprisingly, the incidence of work-related injuries
has been found to differ between industries according to the degree of heavy
work involved. In Scandinavia during the 1950s, for example, it was discovered
that almost twice as much low-back disability occurred in 'heavy' as compared
with 'light' occupations.[13] And Snook, in reviewing the psychophysical
literature, reported that: 'several investigators have found that when workers
are asked to subjectively rate the degree of physical effort or strain in their
jobs, low-back pain appeared significantly more frequently in those who
believed their work to be harder'.[14]

Because of the effects of heavy work, many researchers are adamant 'that
the physical job requirement should be related to the strength of the worker,

**Table 5.1  Physical effort required in economic activity** (rates of energy
expenditure)

| | Males (Kcal/minute/65kg) | Females (Kcal/minute/55kg) |
|---|---|---|
| 1. Light | 2.0–4.9 | 1.5–3.4 |
| 2. Moderate | 5.0–7.4 | 3.5–5.4 |
| 3. Heavy | 7.5–9.9 | 5.5–7.4 |
| 4. Very heavy | 10.0–12.4 | 7.5–9.4 |
| 5. Unduly heavy | 12.5– | 9.5– |

*Notes:*  1. Light work: housework; modern capital intensive light industry such as printing, tailoring, shoemaking, garage work, electrical industry; food and drink industry; transport; laboratory work; retail trade; personal services; office.
2. Moderate work: old fashioned labour-intensive housework (e.g. scrubbing floors, cleaning carpets, washing clothes by hand, furniture polishing, etc.); machine-tool, metals and motor industry; chemical industry; woodworking; mechanized agriculture; forestry.
3. Heavy work: building and construction; iron and steel industry; heavy engineering; mining.
4. Very to unduly heavy: certain activities in iron and steel; construction; land clearing; mining.

*Source:*  Compiled from J.V.G.A. Durnin and R. Passmore, *Energy, Work and Leisure* (Ch. 4).

and that strength testing is a useful means of reducing back injury rates'.[15] In some countries ergonomic evidence has, in the past, led to the framing of regulations specifying different maximum load-carrying levels for male and female workers. Indeed, industrial regulation aimed at limiting the handling of heavy loads, particularly by women, has a long history going back to English laws of the 1830s that regulated the employment of females and children in mines and factories.[16] Especially revealing is a 1935 report of the US Women's Bureau, in which the connection between heavy work, fatigue, and accidental injury was recognized. The report considered it necessary to monitor the physical condition of workers in order to enable them to obtain the job for which they were physically suited, and to discourage physically unfit people working in physically demanding jobs. Particular concern was expressed about the physical aptitude of women for heavy work: it insisted that there be 'no prohibition of women's employment except in occupations proved by scientific investigation to be more injurious to women than to men'; noted approvingly 'laws regulating the employment of women with regard to lifting heavy weights'; found that two-thirds of injuries to women 'affected the upper extremities' (arms and shoulders) where the comparative disadvantage of women is greatest; and noted that 'increasing the number of machines that each worker must operate [meant that] less-adaptable women have suffered from nervous strain that has caused illness and loss of time'.[17]

More recently, in a study of the ergonomic data, Snook also noted that 'the maximum acceptable weights of lift were significantly less . . . for females than males' and 'the maximum acceptable forces of push and pull were also significantly less . . . for females than males'.[18] And with greater precision, a study by Rutenfranz that measured the energy expenditure (oxygen intake and heartbeat) of workers was able to establish a 'level of maximal aerobic power . . . needed for [building] workers if no over-strain is to happen'. By comparing this standard with the performance of males and females of various ages he found 'for different sex and age groups of the normal population, most of the female and several of the young male groups missed this criterion. At the age of 25, however, 84% of the male but only 3% of the female population had such a maximal aerobic power'.[19]

The ergonomic and industrial safety literature is not alone in emphasizing the link between heavy market work, the incidence of industrial injury, and its differential impact on the sexes. At least one econometric study of the labour market has come to similar conclusions. In a study of employment hazards, Viscusi uses cross-sectional data to analyse the determinants of workers' perceptions of job risk. One of his conclusions is that: 'As one would expect, jobs requiring substantial physical effort . . . irregular work . . . and overtime work . . . tend to be more dangerous, while those associated with a [physically] pleasant environment . . . are less hazardous'.[20] All these factors contribute to physical, and possibly, mental stress, which in turn leads either to injuries of joint or muscle, or to mistakes (or frustrations) that inflict injuries (or illness).

Adult women, who have, on average, about two-thirds of the upper-body strength of adult men,[21] are more prone to serious injury than their male counterparts in work that requires the lifting and carrying of heavy loads, or moderately heavy work done continuously and at speed. Not surprisingly, such work is not attractive to women, nor is it financially viable for employers if undertaken by women. Only since the widespread substitution of capital for heavy labour have women become economically competitive in sections of these industries.

## The model

Physical strength can be examined in a human capital framework. Indeed some forms of human capital (such as coalface mining) can only be acquired by those who possess unusually high levels of physical strength. There is, in other words, an interaction between physical strength and human capital in some occupations. Hence it is surprising that human capital theory has not been extended in this way by Becker and his followers. Young males with a comparative advantage in activities that require physical strength will specialize in those activities—professional contact sports and jobs in heavy industry, construction, forestry, and mining—because of the premium paid for such work, and will invest in formal (commercial weight and endurance training) and informal (private physical training programmes) strength-enhancing programmes including greater and more expensive food consumption. The return to this type of investment is relatively high, because only part of the workforce (predominantly male) is able to successfully undertake heavy, high risk (in terms of injury) jobs. In the past, considerable status within the working class was achieved by those men who could successfully undertake such work. Even with extensive substitution of capital for heavy labour, there is still a role, although somewhat reduced, for those men who are willing and able to accept work in mineral exploitation (e.g. on oil rigs), fire control, construction in difficult and dangerous environments, and in professional contact sports. These are still, and will probably always remain, male-dominated economic activities based on physical strength and the manual skills that can only be acquired by those possessing physical strength.

The main implication of this model is that, given the technological structure of the economy in the pre–Second World War period, the average male possessed a marked comparative advantage over the average female in market work owing to greater physical strength. This was in addition to the differential investment in human capital by males and females. Even in the absence of other biological differences (such as reproduction) and discrimination, this gender difference would have been sufficient to produce a sexual division of labour by which males invested in market human capital and specialized in market work, and by which females invested in household human capital and specialized in housework. Only in light industry (e.g. textiles) and sections of the service sector could women compete with men, owing to lower female wages as a result of market (surplus supply) and human capital forces.

But gender comparative advantage is not a static state. Since the 1940s, the growing capital intensity and capital sophistication of the market economy, together with its changing structure, has broadened the range of jobs available for lighter, relatively unskilled, labour. Capital has been substituted for both heavy labour and market skills in many industries. Hence female employment has expanded rapidly but, as yet, the relative female/male wage rate has not attained unity.

# Changing employment opportunities for women in Australia, 1788–1990

So far, our analysis suggests that the expansion of female employment opportunities is largely a function of the changing technological base, and the emerging post-industrial structure of the market economy, rather than of an exogenous change in institutional or 'cultural' forces. Both characteristics are, in turn, a function of the dynamic process of change in the Total Economy, a process to which we now turn.

## *Growth of the market sector*

A complex picture of the growth of the Australian market economy over the last 200 years is provided by Figures 2.3, 2.4, and 2.6 (pp. 22, 26 and 29). This long period can be viewed as a sequence of four wide-angled exposures. The first, from 1800 to 1860, shows the emergence of an immature capitalist economy from an embryonic form which consists of a centrally determined imperial core and a precariously growing free enterprise periphery. While this new economy is based on the export of wool, it possesses a strong urban sector. By the early 1840s this transition is largely complete and, as if to prove it, eastern Australia suffers the first of its three major depressions. By the time the economy emerges from crisis, it experiences the effects of a full-scale resource bonanza—alluvial gold—which transforms the infant economy's size, and sets its urban course for the next 150 years and beyond. Even now Australia is the lucky country, as its precocious wealth depends upon the easy returns of an abundant supply of natural resources.

The second picture, of the period 1861 to the 1890s, is a familiar picture of boom and bust. On closer inspection, the early 1860s still show signs of the economy's attempt to achieve equilibrium after the destabilizing impact of the goldrushes on population, prices, and output. But before this can be achieved the economy responds enthusiastically to the heady influence of a rapidly expanding export market for the products of our natural resources, and to an equally rapid inflow of British capital and labour. The new immigrants join with the diggers, who have decided to stay, and invest their human and financial resources in the rapidly expanding metropolitan areas. Once again the market economy, both public and private, is involved in a Schumpeterian disequilibrium process of economic change. The leading sectors in this growth and development process, as Noel Butlin has clearly shown, are the pastoral, urban, and public sectors, which override the countervailing forces (underlying the agricultural and manufacturing sectors) that could have led to equilibrium growth through a more balanced process of change. In the event, market productivity increases significantly (see Figure 5.1) as the income in this sector outstrips a labour force that is growing more rapidly than it was to do in the post–Second World War years.

The third picture, which spans the years 1890 to 1939, depicts a scene of relative stagnation. Whatever angle this picture is taken from, there is no escaping the fact that the market economy did not grow significantly in real per capita income terms. It is not, for example, valid to try to squeeze out more growth by employing partial price indexes as some have done.[22] And relative stagnation turns to absolute decline when we view the changes in real income in per household rather than per capita terms. It is true that temporary advances are achieved in the 1900s and 1920s, but they are achieved by import replacement—a sleight-of-hand through tariffs—and are negated by the depressions of the 1890s and 1930s and the contraction during the First World War. This contributes to the stagnation of labour productivity (Figure 5.1) as the efficiency of the production process declines to the point where income

**Figure 5.1 Market productivity (1966/67 prices), Australia, 1861–1990**

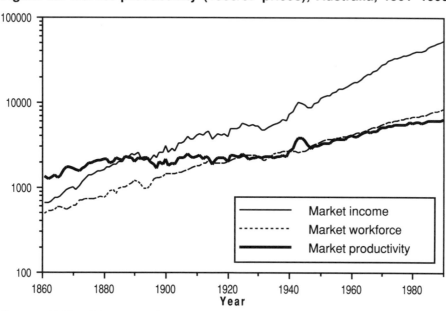

*Source*: Tables 7.3, 9.10 and 9.11.

grows no more rapidly than the labour force. A major problem confronting the economy during these years is that spluttering engine of growth— international trade—that had driven the nineteenth century economy, and the failure of urban-directed policies of protection to replace it with a new motive force based on self-sustained internal growth.

Our final picture, covering the years 1946 to 1990, is one of boom followed not by a bang, but by a whimper. The growth performance of the Australian market economy from the late 1940s until the mid 1970s, is the most impressive in our entire history. But this dynamic disequilibrium process contains a fatal flaw. The boom is in fact the logical outcome of the course set in the interwar years, but with the good luck this time of coinciding with an unusual degree of international buoyancy that is due in part to a sudden release from a generation of world depression and war. It is a picture of protected urban development against a background of high international demand for the exploitation of our natural resources. Accordingly, the sleight-of-hand that had been detected by some in the 1920s,[23] now goes virtually unnoticed. Only once the potential for import replacement is exhausted, do the costs of this development phase—of pulling oneself up by one's own bootstraps—become obvious, but even now only because it coincides with a falling off in expansion of world demand for the products of Australia's natural resource exploitation. Even so, the productivity performance of the market economy during this period surpasses even that of the late nineteenth century (Figure 5.1), largely owing to a new-found ability to achieve a higher rate of growth of income with a lower rate of growth of workforce. The end of the boom is marked by stagflation in the second half of the 1970s, and even worse, deep recession in the early 1980s and again in the early 1990s with average unemployment rates as high as 11 per cent, and with negative growth in several of these years. The decade-and-a-half after the end of the boom fails to do what it had always done before: to produce the short sharp shock that has always been necessary to bring the excesses of dynamic disequilibrium processes in Australia to an end, so as to clear the way for a new phase of expansion. The structural equilibrium achieved through the process of depression in the 1890s and 1930s does not occur during the second half of the 1970s. While our ability to manipulate the market economy, through monetary and fiscal means, prevents the short-sharp shock that would resolve the accumulating imbalance of extended boom, it cannot achieve the Herculean task of cleansing the economic stable. We have yet to achieve the most important goal of the economist's quest.

Our interest here is not with the process of market economic growth *per se*, but with the implications it has had for the employment opportunities of women, through changes in the market economy's technological base and structure. Each of these periods provided different opportunities for women and for the household. In the period before 1860, the market economy was struggling for a life of its own in a harsh and alien landscape, and in the face of severe depression and a dislocating goldrush. Economic development was rapid, but there was little scope for female market participation in this pioneering phase apart from in the traditional ways (mainly domestic service, see Table 5.2, which is discussed later in the context of the service sector) in towns and on established rural settlements. The gender imbalance reached its peak—142 males for every 100 females in 1851—in this period.

After the early 1860s the economic and social environment was normalized—by 1891 there were only 116 males for every 100 females—and the rapid growth, which was centred in the cities, provided scope for the traditional role of women as wives and household workers. Only towards the turn of the century was there expanding scope for female employment in industry, and then mainly in clothing, textiles, and leather working. The gender imbalance, as shown in Table 5.3, in this period was experienced mainly in the rural areas, disappearing quite quickly in the towns. Also there was a cyclical element to the expansion of female participation. In the 1890s the wives and daughters of unemployed males found work in middle-class households which was offered because of rising real incomes of those families not disrupted by the depression, and because of the declining female/male wage ratio. On the one hand female labour was being substituted for male labour in the market sector during the 1890s depression, and on the other hand, paid domestic labour and unpaid male labour were being substituted for unpaid female labour in the household sector.

From 1890 to 1939, the relative stagnation of the market sector provided little opportunity for a change in the economic role of women. The limited economic growth achieved—and this largely in the 1900s and 1920s—inhibited

**Table 5.2   Paid private domestic and manufacturing workers, Australia, 1881–1986**

|      | Private domestic service | | Manufacturing | |
|      | Female | Male | Female | Male |
|------|--------|------|--------|------|
| 1881 | 67,933 | 15,036 | 43,409 | 282,618 |
| 1891 | 83,980 | 15,662 | 59,719 | 359,726 |
| 1901 | 103,083 | 19,466 | 76,152 | 352,860 |
| 1911 | 103,335 | 12,299 | 109,261 | 459,871 |
| 1921 | 97,581 | 10,243 | 118,883 | 604,676 |
| 1933 | 123,517 | 4,333 | 137,779 | 728,392 |
| 1947 | 39,300 | 7,061 | 184,082 | 645,718 |
| 1954 | 30,763 | 6,703 | 227,063 | 800,268 |
| 1961 | 26,919 | 5,773 | 253,208 | 887,127 |
| 1966 | 27,829 | 5,789 | 323,548 | 988,577 |
| 1971 | 18,729 | 3,457 | 312,344 | 903,274 |
| 1976 | 14,463 | 2,550 | 290,766 | 847,762 |
| 1981 | 14,462 | 3,142 | 284,550 | 830,119 |
| 1986 | .. | .. | 261,911 | 714,352 |

*Note:*     .. Not available.
*Source:*   Australia, *Population Census* (various).

the changes in the structure and technological base of the economy that were required to significantly expand the employment opportunities of women. This is reflected in the dominant role played by paid private domestic service in female market employment throughout this period. Private domestic service remained the main source of employment for women until about 1911 (see Table 5.2), when manufacturing surpassed it for the first time. But even this lead was challenged in 1933, by the last economic charge of private domestic service, as the wives and daughters of unemployed males sought market jobs in middle-class households where real incomes were rising, but where lower domestic wage rates were being paid.[24] Notice that, by way of contrast, the paid male domestic workforce fell during the Great Depression. By 1947, however, manufacturing employed five times as many women as the private domestic service industry. The limited shift of the economy towards manu-facturing in the pre–Second World War period, provided a modest expansion of employment opportunities, mainly around the turn of the century and in the late 1930s.

Yet, it was only with the atypically rapid growth of the market sector between 1946 and 1973 that scope was provided for fundamental change in the economy both structurally and technologically. As we shall see, this fundamental change throughout the market economy provided a rapid increase for the first time in the number and range of jobs available for women, particularly in the service sector. We turn, therefore, to the underlying dynamic processes of economic change.

## Changing technological foundations of the market economy

A profile of the changing 'technological' foundations of the market sector in the longrun can be sketched with two key variables, relative factor prices and the capital/labour ratio.[25] These variables reflect longrun technological change in the economy, because of the intimate and complex relationship between technical advance, factor saving bias, factor substitution, and relative factor prices.[26] The profile, which is presented in Figure 5.2, shows the broadly

**Table 5.3   Gender balance, rural and urban areas, Australia, 1861–1891**
(males per 100 females)

|  | Urban | Rural |
|---|---|---|
| 1861 | 110 | 161 |
| 1871 | 101 | 137 |
| 1881 | 102 | 132 |
| 1891 | 102 | 130 |

*Source*:   Caldwell, 'Population', p. 40.

**Figure 5.2 Market capital/labour ratios and relative factor prices (K/L), Australia, 1861–1990**

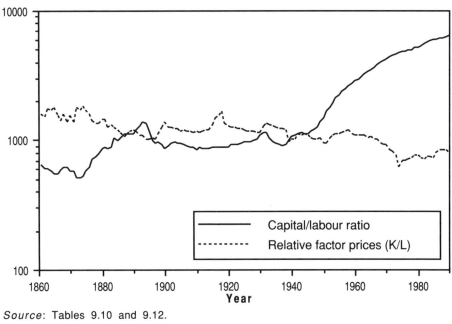

*Source*: Tables 9.10 and 9.12.

inverse relationship between these two variables over the last 130 years.[27] Closer inspection shows that from the mid 1870s to the early 1890s, the capital/labour ratio increased by 138.9 per cent, in response to a decline in the ratio between capital prices and wage rates by 38.9 per cent. If we ignore the First World War years, it can be seen that the secular trend in both variables between 1900 and 1939 was approximately horizontal. In the second half of the twentieth century the relative factor price ratio declined by 20.0 per cent, while the capital/labour ratio increased by 431.6 per cent.

What this picture shows us is, first, a modest change in the technological base of the market economy during the last few decades of the nineteenth century. This involved a limited degree of substitution of capital for labour that could have provided at least some opportunity for women to compete more effectively with men. It was, however, largely confined to manufacturing and agriculture because, apart from the mechanical typewriter, this technological change did not have a noticeable impact on the service sector. But, possibly offsetting this change, at least in part, was the fact that the machinery of the period, both in urban and rural areas, was heavy and dangerous to operate. We can expect, therefore, only a marginal change in job opportunities for women during these years.

Second, as expected from the stagnation of the period 1890 to 1939, the underlying technological base of the market economy remained largely unchanged. There was no significant substitution of capital for labour in this period. Indeed, Figure 5.2 shows that the peak level of the market capital/labour ratio achieved in the late 1880s was not exceeded again until the post–Second World War years. Yet this does not deny that technological change took place in certain industries, just that the introduction of new production functions was overwhelmed in the aggregate by the old ones. Certainly the newly re-established iron and steel industry (1915 by BHP), and a number of newer engineering industries that had been encouraged by the isolation provided by the First World War, introduced new technologies, but often even these were second-best practices from Britain.[28] Even in this period, the machinery introduced to replace work done exclusively by muscle power—such as the latest machinery introduced into concrete pipe making in Australia in the interwar period[29]—still involved the use of heavy labour, just less of it per unit of output. And virtually no progress was made in the introduction of automated machinery that could be substituted for labour skills.[30] Hence, there was little scope in the first four decades of the twentieth century for extending the range of employment opportunities for women.

The years after the 1940s, however, provided a remarkable contrast with all that had gone before. What amounts to a radically new economic change—the post-industrial 'revolution'—occurred in the second half of the twentieth century. This period experienced an unprecedented change in the technological foundations of the market economy in Australia. Not only was there a remarkable increase in the capital/labour ratio, but also there was a widespread introduction, for the first time, of automated machinery in manufacturing; power-driven load carrying machinery in construction, mining, forestry, agriculture, etc.; and sophisticated electronic machinery and computers throughout the economy. The evidence shows, therefore, that physical capital rather than human capital was central to the transformation of the market economy. Indeed capital has been substituted not only for heavy labour but also for a range of labour skills in all sectors of the economy. The post-industrial transformation of the market economy—the new economic revolution—has involved a powerful process of deskilling. Hence these fundamental changes in the market economy have radically widened the paid employment opportunities for women.

## Structure of the market economy

Employment opportunities for women also depend on the relative size of the service sector in the market economy, because in these industries women have a comparative advantage. Yet this should not be thought of as a straightforward issue. Many tasks in the service sector have traditionally required either physical strength or market skills not possessed by the majority of married women. While an expansion in the relative size of the tertiary sector will probably increase the job opportunities for females, on its own it would not account for the post-1950 increase in female employment in the various service industries. The substitution of capital for heavy labour and, particularly, for market skills in finance and administration has been an important additional factor. Structural and technological change are, in any case, intertwined in the dynamic process of economic change.

The change in the relative importance of the tertiary sector over the past century is captured in Figure 5.3. Basically the relative size of the tertiary sector in the market economy did not change significantly between 1891 and 1938. The narrower definition of 'services'—which includes finance, property, and a range of community, personal, and other services—provided 20.3 per cent of total market employment in 1891 and 20.9 per cent in 1938, compared with 39.6 per cent and 43.1 per cent for a wider definition that also includes wholesale and retail distribution, and trade and transport (but not construction). The main expansionary phase in the role of the tertiary sector, occurred after the Second World War. Between 1938 and 1989: the proportion of the total market workforce employed in the smaller service group more than doubled to 42.1 per cent, while the proportion employed in the wider service group increased by more than half to 68.1 per cent. This rapid expansion in the relative size of the service sector would have provided greater employment opportunities for women even if other market-based changes had not increased the comparative advantage of women in this area. It is interesting to compare

**Figure 5.3 Service employment as a proportion of market workforce, Australia, 1891–1990**

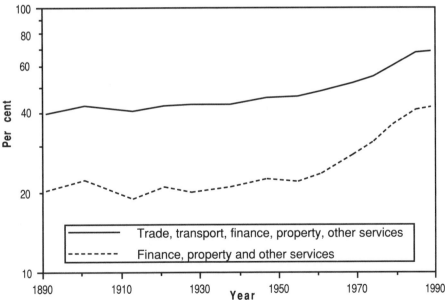

*Source*: Calculated from Australia, *Census* (various) and Butlin and Dowie,'Australian workforce'.

and contrast the timing of this post-industrial structural change in Australia with that in Europe and the USA. The USA was the clear leader in this transition to a service economy, a process that began in that country prior to the Second World War. Western Europe, like Australia, did not experience this transformation until after the Second World War, but when the change did occur it was rapid and the USA's lead was significantly reduced.[31]

## Structure of the working week

Before examining female market employment in detail, consideration should be given to the changing structure of the working week. While this is an important subject it will be dealt with but briefly here, in part because data are not available except for the last few decades, and in part because it is not involved in the longrun story told here.[32] The willingness of the market sector to employ part-time labour has also changed radically since the 1950s. This should be regarded as a response to, rather than a determinant of, more fundamental changes in the economy. Changed employer attitudes to using part-time labour is a function of the growing demand for 'light', lower-skilled labour—a function of the changing technological and structural characteristics of the market economy—which was only available on a large scale on a part-time basis. Clearly there is a cost associated with employing larger numbers of people to do a given job (in terms of on-the-job training, supervision, and administration), but this would appear to be offset by the benefit derived from gaining access to a lower cost source of labour that wishes to work on a part-time basis—female household workers. This is the significance of the expansion of part-time work since the 1950s.

The extent of part-time labour has grown rapidly since the Second World War. In the early 1950s, women working part-time made up a negligible proportion of the total market workforce, but by 1975 their contribution had increased to 11.6 per cent, and in 1989 it was as high as 16.4 per cent. Indeed by 1989, 40.1 per cent of female market workers worked part-time. In that year, all part-time female market workers undertook an average of 15.1 hours per week, compared with 36.7 hours by all full-time female workers.[33]

# Female market employment in Australia, 1890–1990

Over the past hundred years, female market employment in Australia—as shown in Figure 5.4—has been dominated by three main industries: community and personal services, distribution, and manufacturing. Since the 1930s these three traditional areas of female employment have been joined by financial and business services, and transport and communications. The

**Figure 5.4 Female market employment by industry, Australia, 1891–1990**

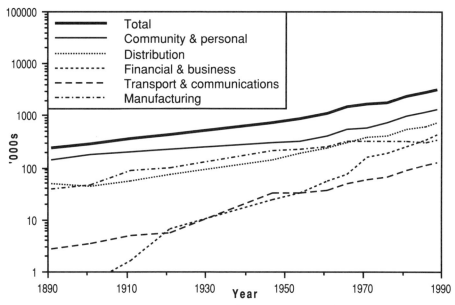

*Source*: Australia, *Census* (various), and ABS, *Labour statistics* (various).

**Figure 5.5 Relative shares in female market employment, Australia, 1891–1990**

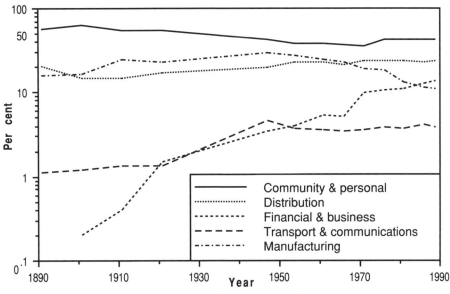

*Source*: Australia, *Census* (various), and ABS, *Labour statistics* (various).

tertiary sector, therefore, has been the main employer of female labour, and this sector has been supplemented by the manufacturing sector: together they have accounted for 89 to 98 per cent of female employment between 1891 and 1990. In other words the market employment opportunities for females, particularly before the Second World War, have been restricted to a very narrow range of industries.

## The changing structure of female employment

The contribution of these industries to total female employment has, as shown in Figure 5.5, changed in interesting ways over the last century.[34] In the decade before Federation, personal and community services employed about 60 per cent of the female workforce, with distribution—largely retail—employing about 18 per cent, and manufacturing a further 16 per cent. During the course of the next century the role of community and personal services gradually declined to 42 per cent (in 1990); distribution gradually increased to 23 per cent; manufacturing, which increased temporarily in the 1910s and the 1940s, actually declined to 11 per cent by 1990; and financial and business services, and transport and communication increased from insignificant levels in 1891 to 13 per cent and 4 per cent respectively in 1990.

Which of these sectors provided the most jobs for women during the course of the twentieth century? Clearly it was the tertiary sector, which provided a total of 2,414,300 new jobs for women out of a total of 2,913,000—82.9 per cent. Manufacturing provided a further 302,700 jobs, or 10.4 per cent of the total. Within the tertiary sector, the sub-group of community and personal services provided almost half the new jobs available to women this century, with distribution (28 per cent), and finance and business (17 per cent) providing much of the remainder.

## The 'feminization' of the market sector

To understand the fundamental changes taking place in the economy we need to examine, not only the changing pattern of female employment, but also the 'feminization' of the market sector. A dynamic picture of **economic feminization** over the past century is provided by Figure 5.6. Here we can see that the revolutionary change in the role of women in the Australian market economy occurred only after the 1950s. For the first fifty years of this period, female employment as a proportion of total employment in these categories hovered around 24 per cent—with a slight rise before the First World War and a decline until the 1940s—but then rose to 30 per cent in the mid 1960s, 37 per cent at the beginning of the 1980s, and 41 per cent at the beginning of the 1990s.

There are three leading sectors in this process of economic feminization: distribution, finance and business, and transport and communication. Femin-

**Figure 5.6 Economic 'feminization': female market employment as a proportion of total employment in various market sectors, Australia, 1891–1990**

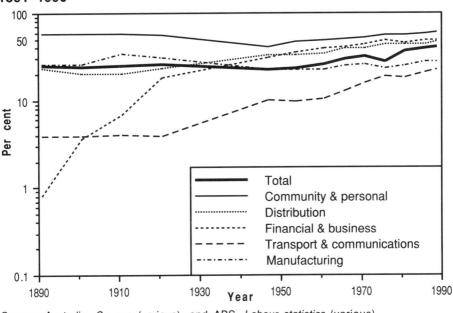

*Source*: Australia, *Census* (various), and ABS, *Labour statistics* (various).

ization throughout the past century doubled in distribution (23 to 46 per cent), increased by an impressive factor of six in transport and communication (4 to 22 per cent), and grew by a remarkable factor of 61 in finance and business (0.8 to 49 per cent)—largely after 1950 (do not be fooled by the log scale). Only in the more traditional sectors of female employment—manufacturing (26 to 28 per cent) and community and personal services (57 to 59 per cent)— did economic feminization change but modestly. Actually in these two traditional areas of female employment, peaks of feminization were achieved before the First World War, after which it declined until the 1930s or 1940s, and then recovered in the post–Second World War period. The general question that must be answered is, how do we account for the growing feminization of the market sector after the Second World War, and why did it occur later here than in the USA?

## The service industries

Female participation in the tertiary sector has changed radically throughout the past two centuries, but most of this change has been concentrated in the second half of the twentieth century. This contrasts with experience in the USA, where the feminization of the service sector began before the Great Depression.[35] Throughout the first 150 years of Australia's European history the great majority of females—largely unmarried—participating in paid

employment, used household and personal skills they learnt from their mothers
to seek employment as paid domestics and shop assistants. A much smaller
proportion worked as nurses and teachers. In 1891, for example, about two-
thirds of females employed in personal and community services, and one-third
of all female workers, were paid domestics. But this began to change gradually
after the First World War, and then rapidly after the Second World War. As
can be seen from Table 5.2, the number of female domestics continued to
increase until 1911 but, with the exception of an interesting expansion during
the Great Depression, fell rapidly thereafter, particularly from the 1940s. As
the traditional source of female employment in the tertiary sector declined
after the 1940s, the range of service activities open to females—particularly
in finance, business, the professions, transport, and communications—
increased rapidly.

While it is not the purpose of this study to explore female market
employment at the *occupational* level, it is necessary to focus more closely on
its *industrial* structure. Figure 5.7 provides a close-up of the group of industries
that have always dominated female employment in the tertiary sector—
community and personal services. In 1891 personal and recreational services
dominated (81 per cent of the total) this group; and in turn this category was
dominated (80 per cent) by domestic service. A very much smaller role (19 per

**Figure 5.7 Female employment in community and personal services,
Australia, 1891–1990**

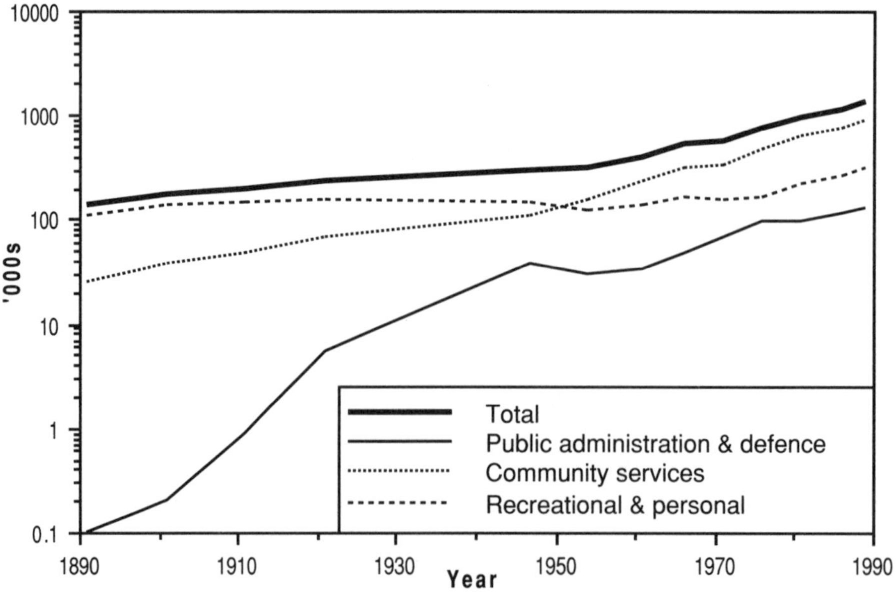

Source: Australia, *Census* (various), and ABS, *Labour statistics* (various).

cent of the total) was played by community services, which was dominated by nurses and teachers. At this time the public service employed very few women—only about 100 throughout the country! During the course of the following hundred years, the public sector emerged as a significant, but not an overwhelmingly important, employer of women—it only reached as high as 13 per cent of community and personal services, and, even that level, as late as the mid 1970s. It was left to the private sector, therefore, to provide most of the increase in jobs for women. This mainly occurred in community services, particularly after the Second World War when women moved in unprecedented numbers into the traditional areas of teaching, the arts, and nursing, but also into the professions that previously had been dominated by men. Community services was the major employer in this services group by 1990 when it contributed 67 per cent of the jobs. As community services increased, personal services declined—with the crossover point achieved about 1950—so that by 1990 it provided only 24 per cent of the jobs in this group.

What did these changes imply for the feminization of community and personal services? We saw from Figure 5.6 that, for the period as a whole, the relative contribution of females in this sector increased by only 4 per cent. But this aggregate figure masks considerable structural change. The most striking change shown in Figure 5.7 is the increase in economic feminization of the public service from a mere 0.6 per cent in 1891 to 39.1 per cent in 1990, and of community services from 41 to 65 per cent. On the other hand the relative contribution of females to personal services and recreation declined from 68 to 57 per cent. In part this was due to the decline in domestic service and the emergence of male dominated televised professional contact sport as a major form of entertainment. In view of a major theme in the chapter, this is an interesting development. While males with a comparative advantage in physical strength have been partially displaced (in relative terms) from industry owing to the growing capital intensity of the market economy, they have found an outlet for their investment in contact sport.

Service industries fall into two categories: those that are human-capital intensive, and those that are physical-capital intensive. The human-capital intensive group, which have become increasingly feminized, are public administration, and community and personal services. Those that are physical-capital intensive fall into two groups: one, where physical capital is substituted for human capital, as in finance and business (e.g. electronic machinery has replaced skills in banking and finance[36]); and two, where it is substituted for heavy labour, as in transport and storage, and in wholesale and retail services. The human-capital group have expanded with the growth of average living standards since 1950, which in turn has encouraged some women to invest in the required human capital. On the other hand the expansion of the physical-capital intensive group has enabled the employment of married women—a much larger category—by the substitution of capital for both labour skills and physical strength.

## Manufacturing

To explore further the thesis that widespread employment opportunities for women only opened up with the change in the market economy's technological base, we need to focus more closely on the manufacturing sector during the twentieth century.[37] Figure 5.8 shows the change in total, male, and female manufacturing employment throughout the twentieth century. Clearly, female employment in this sector kept pace with the growth of male employment. In 1901, females constituted 21.8 per cent of the factory workforce and in 1982 they made up a slightly higher 25.3 per cent,[38] although most of this change had occurred by the beginning of the First World War.

The changing structure of female employment in manufacturing is portrayed in Figure 5.9. It can be seen that the traditional avenues of female employment—clothing and textiles, food, and leather—increased very slowly after 1913, stagnated afer the 1940s, and began declining in absolute terms from the late 1960s (and particularly from the mid 1970s). This pattern is also reflected in traditional areas of male manufacturing employment. Increasingly from the 1940s, Australian manufacturers were unable to compete with producers located in low-wage third-world countries that were expanding production in these relatively labour-intensive manufacturing activities, particularly following the post-1968 rationalization of the tariff structure in Australia.[39] Had females continued to depend upon this traditional form of

**Figure 5.8 Manufacturing employment by gender, Australia, 1901–1982**

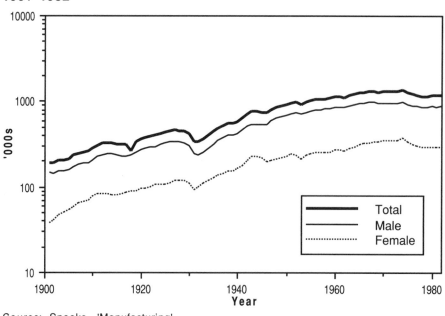

*Source*: Snooks, 'Manufacturing'.

employment, manufacturing would not have played a significant role in the shift of married women into the market workforce. The most dramatic increase in female employment occurred in the metals and engineering category, rising from 200 jobs in 1901 to 369,100 in 1974. Also there were healthy increases in female employment in the non-metal mining, chemical, and wood industries. As we shall see, these were industries in which an increase in the capital/labour ratio was essential if the degree of female participation was to increase.

A picture of the feminization of manufacturing employment is provided in Figure 5.10. This timescape shows those industries in which the employment of females was growing at the expense of male employment. To some, the results may appear surprising. A group of three industries stand out against the rest. In this picture, metals, wood, and non-metal mining have posed separately from the rest and have struck out diagonally across time. The rest are grouped together and reach out horizontally through the century. This family grouping may appear surprising, because metals, wood, and non-metal mining are heavy industries from which females have been traditionally excluded.

Part of the answer for the feminization of heavy industry can be found in their increasing capital/labour ratios, particularly after the Second World War. As shown in Figure 5.11, the industries with the fastest growing capital/labour ratios between 1950 and 1977, were metals, non-metal mining, leather, and possibly wood. Hence, there is some evidence at the aggregated level, although

**Figure 5.9 Female manufacturing employment by industry, Australia, 1901–1982**

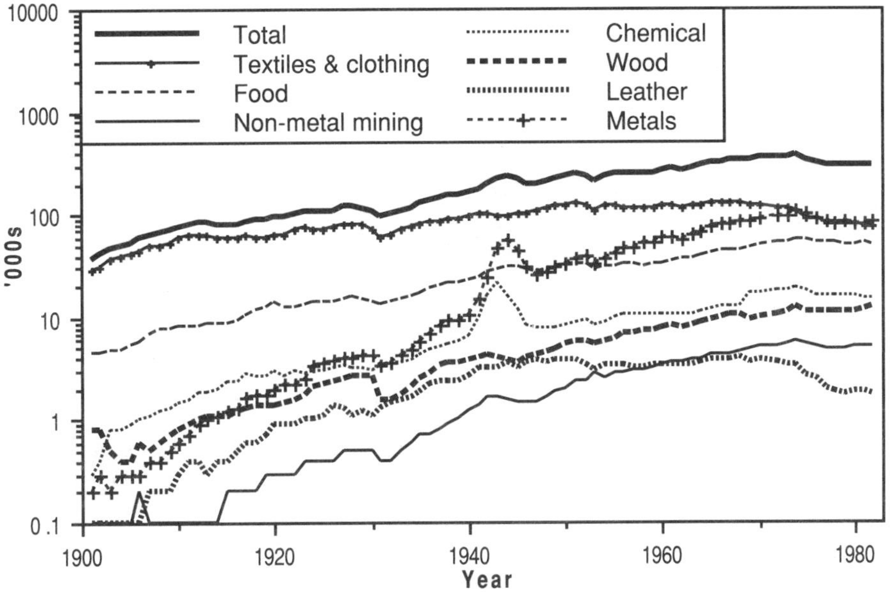

*Source*: Snooks, 'Manufacturing'.

**Figure 5.10 Female as a proportion of male manufacturing employment by industry, Australia, 1901–1982**

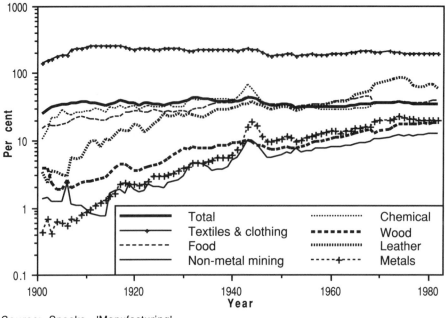

*Source*: Snooks, 'Manufacturing'.

**Figure 5.11 Manufacturing capitial/labour ratios by industry, Australia, 1950–1977**

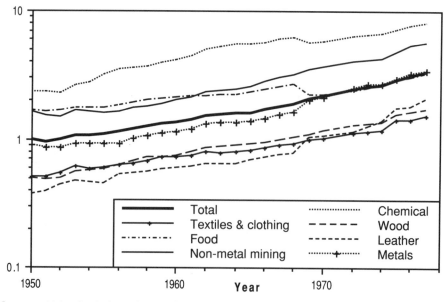

*Source*: Haig, *Capital stock* and Snooks, 'Manufacturing'.

it is not entirely clear-cut, to support the argument that heavy manufacturing industries that experienced the most rapid rates of growth of capital intensity, were also the industries that experienced the fastest rates of feminization. This analysis has been conducted at a highly aggregated level, and further exploration at the micro level should cast useful light on this issue.

An additional part of the answer lies in the growing sophistication of manufacturing technology that also enabled the substitution of automated, and particularly electronic, machinery for traditional labour skills. Married women, who have a comparative disadvantage in industries operated with traditional labour skills, had most to gain from technological change of this nature. In this changing industrial environment, males with these traditional industrial skills sought employment elsewhere.

By 1989, therefore, 48.4 per cent of all machine operators were female. Although equivalent information is not available for the interwar years, qualitative evidence suggests that this ratio was much lower at that time.[40] In contrast, it is interesting that female plant (both stationary and mobile) operators at the end of the 1980s only amounted to 1.2 per cent of the total. In part this can be explained by the greater degree of physical strength required by plant operators, and in part by the time and business experience needed by owner-operators in these occupations. Further, it is instructive that while 32.1 per cent of trades assistants and factory hands were female at the beginning of the 1990s, females comprised only 1.7 per cent of construction and mining labourers—who still relied heavily on hard physical labour and trade skills.[41]

# Conclusions

This chapter is concerned with the longrun dynamic relationship between the household and market sectors. The analysis is constructed on a general model of household–market interaction that involves forces on both the demand and supply sides. A central feature of the model, which integrates both the market and household sectors, is an extension of human capital theory to include investment in physical strength. The relationship between both sectors emerges from the interaction between market technological change and household human and physical capital. This is demonstrated by an examination of female employment in the service and manufacturing sectors during the past two centuries.

## Market change

The above evidence supports a central argument in the book, that Australia's market economy has undergone fundamental changes since the Second World War, changes which have increased the attractiveness (or in technical terms, increased the marginal product) of female labour to employers. This has involved a change in the technological foundations—or the production function—of the market economy.

The resulting increase in the marginal product of female labour—which has meant an outward shift of the demand schedule both absolutely and relatively to that of males—has come about for two main reasons. First, substitution of capital for heavy labour in manufacturing and more generally throughout the market economy, has increased the range of jobs that can be undertaken by 'light' labour. As light labour became available at lower wage rates than labour embodying investments in physical strength, employment opportunities for females have increased. The change in the gender structure of market demand for labour has increased both the real wage rate for females, and the female/male wage ratio. In turn this has resulted in married females working more hours in the market economy. Second, more sophisticated machinery, including electronic machinery and computers, has been substituted for traditional labour skills since 1950. This has led to a relative increase in the demand for (marginal products of) unskilled labour throughout the market economy but particularly in the service sector. Hence, females, who have traditionally had a comparative disadvantage in skilled market work (but a comparative advantage in skilled household work), have gained relatively more from this change. Once again, this change has increased female employment opportunities not only in manufacturing, but also in financial, property and business activities.

Accompanying the major post–Second World War change in the production function of the market economy has been a change in its sectoral structure. In our post-industrial society there has been a significant increase in the relative size of the tertiary, or services, sector. The effect of this structural change has been to increase the range of jobs available to females. When combined with other changes taking place in the market economy—changes that have been responsible for the structural change—the attractiveness of female labour to market employers has increased substantially, and has produced a major outward shift in the demand schedule for female labour, even on a part-time basis.

## Household response

Owing to the great change that has occurred in the gender structure of market demand for labour since 1950, there has been an increase in both the real wage rate for females and the female/male wage ratio. Faced with a change in the gender wage ratio, Australian households have had a strong incentive to supply more female labour time to the market sector because of the increased opportunity cost of restricting female labour services to the household. The increase in real female wages has occurred at a time when extra money income has been considered desirable—the marginal utility of money income being higher than the marginal utility of non-market activities—because of an unprecedented expansion in the amount and range of consumer durables. And what is more, this has occurred at a time when it has been possible to transfer a proportion of female labour to the market sector by substituting electrical household equipment for it. The fact that this transfer of married female labour from household to market, largely on a part-time basis, has been accompanied by an increase in real wage rates for females, reinforces the argument that this radical change has been demand led. Nevertheless, the rational household, which weighs up the costs and benefits of a changing market environment, has played an important role in this changing relationship between household and market economic activity.

In other words, the fundamental changes that have occurred in both the market and household sectors in the second half of the twentieth century have been the outcome of a mutually beneficial interreaction between the two. There can be little doubt that changes in the nature and structure of the household economy would not have taken place without a transformation of the market economy. Our examination of the lack of fundamental change in both sectors for the previous century, despite the surging feminist demand for change, is eloquent evidence of this. And it is equally true that the changes that have taken place in the market sector could not have occurred without a suitable— indeed rational—response from the household sector. There can be no doubt that the relationship between the household and the market is symbiotic. While I have said it before, I will say it again: the Total Economy is not a dual economy with different ruling principles and different, self-contained activities and outcomes. It is just not possible to fully understand one sector without taking into consideration the other. The Total Economy is one economy.

# 6

---

# *A new portrait of the*
# *Australian economy*

*W*hile this study has focused on the household within the Total Economy, much of the analysis goes beyond the economics of market–household dynamics. What emerges from these pages is a new portrait of the Australian economy. It is a portrait that includes three principal subjects—the household as well as the traditional private and public sectors—together with an integrated view of the driving force underlying the essential interaction between them. It is a portrait also, that spans the entire period of European–Asian settlement in Australia. To highlight the portrait developed earlier, this chapter provides an integrated discussion of the central features and processes of Australian economic development,[1] together with a more generalized account of the dynamics of longrun change in the Total Economy that should have a relevance beyond Australia.

## A dynamic view of the Total Economy

The longrun fortunes of the Total Economy are determined by the dynamic relationship between the market and household sectors. And the decision-making unit central to this interaction is the household. All economic activity had its beginning in the household. The market sector emerged from the household at the dawn of civilization, when it became clear that some economic activities could be undertaken more efficiently in a separate and specialized way. Once the household had contracted out a number of its former functions to the fledgling market sector, however, this sector gained a momentum of its own. Yet while the market economy has become largely self-referencing, the people making economic decisions in the market are the same people who are contributing to economic decision-making in the home. The common element between the two sectors—the linking mechanism—is the desire to maximize individual material returns. In the dynamic process of interaction within the Total Economy, the market sector provides the impetus for economic *growth*, while the household sector provides not only the driving force behind economic *expansion*, but also the integrating mechanisms within the Total Economy, and the ultimate purpose for economic activity.

The market sector is the source of longrun economic growth in the Total Economy. After separation from the household, the market—through the process of specialization and division of labour—was able to accumulate capital, introduce new techniques of production and organization, and achieve economies of scale. Consequently, the Total Economy generated not merely economic expansion (an increase in the number of households at a given average level of income) as in pre-market times, but economic growth (an increase in income per household). Indeed, economic growth, at least of a rapid and sustained kind, was not possible in the distant past until a market sector had emerged. As argued in Chapter 3, households cannot generate significant *growth* within their own sector, because their average size is severely limited (to about five people) by the difficulty of imposing efficient systems of supervision on family workers. Only organizations employing paid workers who are not related—or who, in the case of family firms, have surrendered their non-economic family rights for commercial returns—have been able to achieve increasing returns to scale. But while households are unable to achieve increasing returns through specialization, they are a source of economic *expansion* through the natural increase of population—provided additional natural resources are available—and they can enjoy the fruits of *growth* through an interaction with the market sector, which is why the market sector was initially established. Further, while a technologically determined dynamic process with its own internal logic has been nurtured within the market sector, it has depended on an intimate interaction with the household economy. The household can exist without the market, but the market cannot exist without the household. This obvious fact appears to have been forgotten by those economists who treat the market as if it were independent of the household.

Nevertheless, the market economy clearly plays an important role in the Total Economy. In modern economies it is not just a 'department' of the household. The market possesses the ability to generate forces that can radically change the economic environment within which household decision-making occurs. Through trade, capital accumulation, and the application of new ideas to economic organization and production, the market sector has played a central role in the transformation of European society during the past thousand years from feudalism to capitalism of the mercantile, industrial, and post-industrial varieties. Yet the market is not the driving force in human society, just the *proximate* source of economic growth. The ever-present driving force is economic man. And economic man operates in essentially the same way in both the market and the household, although his headquarters is the home. If there were any conflict of purpose and behaviour between economic man in the market and in the household (as suggested by Becker) it would lead to economic man being divided against himself—a logical impossibility, as market economic man cannot act independently of household economic man.

Throughout the last millennium, the household, which has remained largely unchanged in terms of size and function, has retained its controlling role. It has clung tenaciously down through the ages to a number of key economic functions—functions that it refuses to hand over to the market. These include a general control over household economic activity, and more specifically those private and highly personal economic activities that are essential to family care and individual regeneration. It is to the family that the highly competitive, even ruthless, market agents return, although not always successfully, for recreation and regeneration. If these key functions were taken over by the market the essential character of the household would be destroyed, and with it the ultimate meaning of economic life. The household, however, has continued to provide the Total Economy with its overall purpose—its rationale.

The household has also retained its role as an important source of economic *expansion* if not of economic *growth*. It was suggested in Chapter 3 that in early hunter–gatherer societies which did not develop market sectors—such as Aboriginal society prior to European settlement in 1788—economic expansion was achieved through a process of natural population increase that enabled an increasing exploitation of natural resources at a standard of living given by the state of their technologies. Once all natural resources had been utilized, this process of expansion came to an end. Only with the emergence of the market sector and new technologies—rather abruptly and disastrously in the case of traditional Australia—could economic expansion be resumed and rapid economic growth be achieved. But even with the emergence of the market and of rapid economic growth, the household economy retained the ability to generate economic expansion, albeit in concert with the market economy. With the emergence of the market economy, and of more rapid and systematic technological change, the process of economic expansion via natural population increase was released from dependence on the exploitation of *new* natural resources. The new constraint became the rate of growth of technological and organizational change in the market sector. Since the release of the forces of economic expansion from the constraints of natural resources (as long as technology can outpace population increase) the population of the world has increased exponentially. In Australia, population increased from about one million on the eve of European settlement in 1788—a level that had probably existed for many millennia—to seventeen million just two centuries later.

# A new model of very longrun development

From the empirical and analytical building blocks that have emerged in this study, it is possible to construct a new model to explain the process of

Australian—or indeed world—economic development over the last 60,000 years. This model has been constructed on two foundations. The first and most ancient foundation—as ancient as the human race itself—is the household economy, which is the source of economic *expansion*. The second, and much more recent foundation—as recent as the emergence of civilization some 6,000 years ago—is the market economy, which is the source of economic *growth*.

As dynamic economic processes are seldom discussed in the economic literature, there is limited consensus regarding the concepts necessary to analyse this issue. Economic growth is usually defined as an increase in real GDP per capita. Although this definition is somewhat limiting, and requires the definition of further dynamic concepts to fill the gaps, I have adopted it here with one important modification. I have defined economic growth as changes in real national income (however defined) per *household*, because the household is the central economic agency in my model of the Total Economy. Economic growth, however, is only part of the dynamic process of economic change. We need to consider change not encompassed by growth so defined, and to distinguish between dynamic processes that are based on 'extensive' resource use, and those that are based on 'intensive' resource use.

I have employed the term **economic expansion** to refer to economic change that is not encompassed by the concept of economic growth as defined above. And economic expansion has been defined here as an increase in the number of households without any increase in real household income. This can occur, either by bringing unutilized natural resources into the system of production, or by a more intensive use of existing resources through technological change (broadly envisaged). In societies where all natural resources are 'fully' utilized, economic growth and economic expansion can be regarded as component parts of a wider dynamic process of economic change. This process of economic change—which, in the absence of any other suitable term, I will call **technological dynamic change** (TDC)—is capable of generating either economic expansion (an increase in the number of households), or economic growth (an increase in real income per household), or both. The balance between these two outcomes will depend upon the nature of the aggregate production function in a particular society at a particular time, which in turn will be influenced by the internal dynamics (family fertility and consumption) of the household. But in societies where there are reserves of unutilized natural resources, it is possible to initiate a process of economic change—which I will call **environmental dynamic change** (EDC)—through an expansion of household numbers by the exploitation of those reserves without introducing technological change. This is the dynamic process that characterized pre-market economies—a dynamic process that has existed for millions of years.

## *The source of expansion—the household*

It was suggested earlier, that the source of economic expansion is, and has always been, the household. This is true for human beings, just as it is true for all animal species on this planet. The family is a centre not only of economic production, but also of reproduction of the species. Family reproduction underlies economic expansion. As households grow and mature, they give rise to further households in such a way that the frontier of human settlement on this planet expands. Settlement expansion occurs because each new household requires the same quantity and quality of natural resources if it is to enjoy a similar standard of living to the average of all other families, which is a prerequisite for household expansion. I have called this type of economic expansion, environmental dynamic change (EDC). And the standard of living achieved by each family—in terms of goods and services consumed—multiplied by the actual number of families, is the measure of the total income of a particular society. Economic expansion is, therefore, the increase in a society's real income that results from an increase in the number of households at a given standard of living. An increase in the number of households throughout the world can only occur through natural increase, but in a given region we must also consider the migration of individuals and family units from other regions in order to take advantage of unutilized or underutilized natural resources. This began in Australasia some 60,000 years ago.

But this is just a generalized account of what has happened. To construct a model to explain this process, we need to explain why households multiply, and what forces act to constrain this multiplication. These forces will determine a society's dynamic possibility curve—the upper limit to the rate and extent of economic change. The actual dynamic path will, of course, fluctuate within the boundaries of this curve, and will depend on the society's physical and disease environments.

## The driving force

Put quite simply, economic expansion is merely household multiplication. It was suggested in Chapter 3 that dynamic economic man is the driving force behind household multiplication. In a pre-market world, a family leader could maximize his material returns by increasing the size of the family group—either as an extended family or as a closely related group of family units—through procreation. This would increase the 'income' of the family group over which the leader exercises influence or control. In turn this expansion in economic power would increase the probability of the leader's survival in, and control over, the external world. Up to a point, therefore, a larger family group has greater economic resilience—greater power over survival. Economic resilience (as discussed in Chapter 2), rather than living standards, is the ultimate objective of human society. The maximization of economic resilience, however, must not be confused with the maximization of reproduction. To produce too many offspring would reduce a family's economic resilience by reducing the average consumption of its members to precarious levels. The number of offspring will increase only until the perceived benefit of an extra child (extra discounted economic support in old age) is balanced by the cost (in terms of forgone current consumption of all other family members) of producing and maintaining that child.

## *The constraining force*

The force constraining household multiplication, or economic expansion, in a pre-market society with a given state of technology (EDC), is the quantity and quality of accessible natural resources. With the pressure of population on natural resources, marginal (and average) consumption will decline, and population growth—and, with it, economic expansion—will slow, cease, and possibly even reverse itself until equilibrium—a balance between population and resources—is achieved. This has been the mechanism of economic expansion for almost the entirety of human experience. This is the ancient dynamic in human society, exercised through the household economy.

The age-old nexus between household multiplication and the supply of natural resources was irrevocably altered with the emergence of the market economy at the dawn of civilization some 6,000 years ago. With the emergence of the market economy it became possible to increase the output derived from a given input of natural resources and labour, through economies of scale and technological and organizational change. Economic production was released from the establishment-size limit imposed by the household. This occurred slowly at first, but accelerated with the accumulation of market infrastructure and embodied technology, and with the resulting institutional change.[2] These changes led to an increase in real GCI, which generated economic expansion even in those societies that had limited additional access to natural resources. Accordingly, economic expansion became liberated from natural resource constraints, and the world's stock of households and population increased exponentially. Of course there is an upper limit to this expansion—a limit imposed by the natural resources required to provide the world's population with unpolluted air, water, and food.

These two methods of economic expansion—EDC and TDC—have overlapped. In some regions in the past, where natural resources have approached full utilization with the existing state of technology, further expansion could only be achieved by growth in the market economy. At the same time there were other regions where, given the state of technology, natural resources were underutilized. Those regions with excess natural resources could accommodate rapid economic expansion if excess population were relocated there from regions with fully-utilized natural resources. This is what happened in Australia in 1788, and in the Americas in earlier centuries. Further, with each new round of major technological change, there is additional scope for economic expansion—or family multiplication—through the more *intensive* use of natural resources.

## *The source of growth—the market economy*

The source of economic growth is the market. In the market sector it is possible to produce goods and services more efficiently than in the household because it is possible to break through the establishment-size barrier in order to achieve economies of scale and to employ large-scale equipment embodying new techniques of process (labour and resource saving) and product. In this way it is possible to generate both an increase in real market income per household, and further economic expansion. But what is economic growth? How can it be recognized in the real world? And what part does it play in wider dynamic processes?

Unlike economic expansion, economic growth is difficult to recognize in the everyday world. We can *see* economic expansion taking place around us, even from day to day. Visit the fringes of any large city and you can actually see the roads being carved out of the bush or rural areas; the urban services being laid down; and the houses, shops, and offices being built. That is what economic expansion looks like. But how do we recognize economic growth? It *can* be seen, but usually only in retrospect, and only with a trained eye. It can be seen in the *new* economic activities that reflect structural change; in the new and 'better' goods in the shops; in the larger, better-quality houses being built; in the larger number of cars in the front driveways of suburbia; in the better-quality clothes that people are wearing; and the more frequent and more exotic holidays in which our neighbours indulge. Of course, all this is reflected more abstractly in the larger real wages and salaries that we bring home. But none of this occurs overnight, as does economic expansion. And it is difficult for the casual observer to know how representative these changes are of the entire community. This perceptual difficulty highlights an important, and often overlooked, characteristic of economic growth—its essential characteristic is qualitative, rather than quantitative as in the case of economic expansion.

Economic growth is essentially qualitative in nature and hence, elusive: not only to the eye, but also to the mind. What is economic growth? A few examples may help us go beyond the usual definition. Basically, economic growth means being able to do the old things—such as the production of basic commodities, for example food—in new ways, that involve less labour, and less natural resources; *and* being able to provide additional jobs in entirely new industries. These new industries are necessary to avoid unemployment emerging as old industries shed labour and as households multiply, thereby adding to potential labour supply. This is why structural change is an essential element in the process of economic growth. Further, economic growth is just part of a wider process of economic change that I earlier defined as technological dynamic change. TDC is a process fuelled by technological change which can give rise to economic expansion as well as economic growth.

## The driving force

What is the driving force behind economic growth and, more generally, TDC? As economics has expressed an interest in growth ever since Adam Smith's *Wealth of nations* in the late eighteenth century, we would expect a fairly clear and ready answer. But this is not the case. Economists are not really concerned with the driving force in the growth of economies, or the *process* by which growth is achieved. Instead they have focused on the initial conditions that are required to achieve a certain growth *outcome* (such as stagnation, or convergence or divergence from an equilibrium development path) or the likely outcomes from various initial conditions (such as increasing, decreasing, or constant returns). Economists are concerned with outcomes, not processes. The only mainstream economist to seriously concern himself with the driving force behind, and the process of, economic growth was Joseph Schumpeter. And, characteristically, he was interested in the wider dynamic process that transcended economic growth as narrowly defined. Schumpeter focused persuasively on the rent-seeking, risk-taking innovator, who introduced major new technologies in return for economic rents, and who was followed by a flock of imitators attempting to capture some of the rents for themselves. Schumpeterian economic change, therefore, proceeds via long cycles that involve processes of disequilibrium in the upswing and equilibrium in the downswing.[3]

Schumpeter provides an important insight, but is the driving force in society confined to rent-seeking innovators who inhabit the market sector? Does the household, which is intimately linked to the market, also play a role? While accepting that the market sector operates in a self-referencing way, it is important to realize that the household also plays a central role in the wider dynamic process (TDC). This role arises from the fact, made clear in this study, that the household, and the household alone, determines what use should be made of the fruits of economic change. Of course this decision is taken within the context of conditions prevailing in the Total Economy, and accordingly the nature of the decision will vary as those conditions vary.

What does technological dynamic change (TDC) mean to the household and, hence, to the Total Economy? The growth of employment opportunities and real market income per household, as a result of TDC, provides the average family with two basic choices. First, as with an increase in natural resources, it enables the production of children who, in a growing market sector, will find employment, will establish new households, and will add to the income of the extended family group. This is the traditional process of economic change. Second, an increase in real market income enables the average household to increase its consumption of goods and services through higher real wages (owing to an increase in the marginal product of market labour). This is a choice that was not available in the pre-market world, as an increase in natural resources—through settlement or invasion of neighbouring territory—could, with a given level of technology, only be used for household multiplication. Pre-market economies were unable to take advantage of the discovery of richer natural resources (such as more game or food per unit area) because there was no incentive to accumulate productive wealth through capital formation. Hence the only outcomes of a natural resource bonanza were more rapid household multiplication, or more leisure, or both.

Over the last century, and particularly since the 1940s, the balance between these two competing uses of the fruits of TDC, has shifted in favour of high consumption for the nuclear family. This has come about in an economic environment where the gender demand for labour has shifted in favour of female household workers, where it has been possible to substitute capital for labour in the household, and where the range of consumer goods available to the household has increased almost exponentially. Hence immediate consumption of material goods by nuclear families has been substituted for the longer term, and less materialistic, consumption by the extended family from the production of extra children. In the process, the size of the average family, as we have seen, has halved during this century. While this 'choice' is immediately determined by the nature of the aggregate production function for a given society at a particular time, these production relationships owe much to decisions made by households.

Hence, the motivation of the household as well as that of the market, must be taken into account when explaining TDC. The central role in decision-making is, as has always been the case, played by the household. Technological dynamic change merely provides the household with greater choice. In the pre-market world, the rational choice was between the stationary state—a static number of households at an average living standard determined by the existing technology—or economic expansion—household multiplication through natural settlement or invasion. In the post-market world, the range of household choice is much wider. Technological dynamic change makes it possible to achieve not only economic expansion, but also the substitution of material consumption for extra children. The importance of this point requires repetition: the choice between children and growing levels of consumption is only possible in an economy experiencing TDC. But it would seem that some household multiplication, or pure economic expansion, is still regarded as attractive to existing households—children are the ultimate indulgence.

This simple model can be extended by recognizing that modern economies are subject to outside influences; and that the market economy includes a public, as well as a private, sector. First, by relaxing the closed-economy assumption we can consider both external demand for local goods and services, and the external supply of goods, services, labour, and capital. Clearly the issue of external demand is important—extremely important for regions of recent European settlement. But, with the growing economic maturity of new regions, new sources of market growth have emerged in urban centres, and international trade in urban goods and services has grown more rapidly than that for rural, or natural resource, industries. The transition between these two sources of TDC—exploitation of natural resources and technological change in secondary and even tertiary activities—has not always been smooth, and this is reflected in the growth records of nations (such as in the interdepression period in Australia).

In an open economy, the supply of external resources must also be considered. Economic expansion is the result not only of natural population increase, but also of a net inflow of individuals and households from other economies where natural resources are more fully utilized. This inflow may result from the availability of underutilized natural resources in rural areas, or from higher real market incomes in urban areas. Immigration, therefore, has an obvious influence on economic expansion, but a less obvious influence on economic growth. The impact of immigration on economic growth will depend largely on the way it changes the balance of resources between rural and urban areas, and on the marginal product of labour in these areas. If, as was the case in interwar Australia, it leads to a relative shift of resources from high productivity rural activities to lower productivity urban activities (forced by a high tariff policy), the rate of economic growth will decelerate and may even become negative.

The role of the public sector will differ according to economic circumstances. In regions of recent European settlement, the public sector has assumed an active role in assisting immigration, particularly once natural resources have been fully utilized. This has been an important influence on the economic expansion of these regions by directly increasing the rate of household formation, but it has not necessarily stimulated economic growth. Partly in order to support these immigration programmes, governments have provided extensive infrastructure in the form of transport, communications, and urban facilities. Both types of public activities have stimulated the expansion of the household sector. And public tariff policies, often in support of immigration programmes after the region's natural resources have been fully utilized (at a given level of technology), have boosted the market sector. While these public activities have a positive influence on economic expansion, they may well act as a brake on economic growth. In effect there could be a trade-off between the number of households and the average living standards of households. But also there may be a threshold level, in terms of households and population, which, once surpassed, enables the achievement of significant economies of scale and greater efficiency in the use of labour, capital, and natural resources through large-scale technological change. (Such a threshold appears to have been reached in Australia during the 1940s.) Even so, this mechanism will be self-defeating in the longer term, as the process of expansion and growth through import replacement must eventually grind to a halt, generally at a level of productivity that precludes further growth through exports. (Such a position was reached in Australia by the late 1960s.)

## *The constraining force*
Economic growth comes to an end when the prevailing **technological paradigm** is exhausted and the pressure of population on natural resources causes a reduction in GCI per household. Population growth will decline, cease, and even reverse itself as a new equilibrium with natural resources is achieved. Hence, the age-old constraining force re-emerges. This dynamic economic sequence has occurred twice before in western Europe during the last millennium—in the late thirteenth century and in the second half of the seventeenth century—bringing the **great waves of economic change** to an end until new technological paradigms emerged in the sixteenth and eighteenth centuries.[4]

There are currently ominous signs that the technological paradigm ushered in by the Industrial Revolution more than two centuries ago is reaching exhaustion. The household multiplication and the rising levels of consumption per household that were made possible by the modern wave of technological dynamic change are placing seemingly unsustainable pressure on our physical environment. Our current state of technology is actually undermining the foundations on which modern growth is based. It may be the case that a completely new technology will be required if sustainable growth is to be achieved, and this may not emerge for a number of generations after a new equilibrium with natural resources is reached. Any future great wave of economic change, therefore, may require a change in technological paradigm comparable, in terms of economic and social impact, to that introduced by the Industrial Revolution.

As we shall see, this general model of economic development of the Total Economy has important implications for our interpretation of the Australian case over the past 60,000 years. It should also be relevant to the analysis of other regions or, indeed, the global economy.

# Australian economic development, 1788–1990

It is useful at this stage to bring together the essentials of what amounts to a new interpretation of Australian economic development over the last 200 years and beyond. This portrait of the dynamics of the Total Economy gives little emphasis to what we already know, such as the role of trade and the changing structure of the market sector, but instead focuses on the nature of the dynamic process of economic change, and in particular on the interactions of the market and household economies. The view presented here entails both new features and new processes.

## New features

The use of a social accounting framework for the Total Economy, as a basis for generating a comprehensive series of timescapes for Australia, has suggested a number of novel features concerning economic development.[5] In the first place, by using estimates of Gross Community Income (GCI) rather than GDP, the longrun profile of Australian economic development is significantly changed. We have seen that, on the one hand, GCI grew more rapidly than GDP from 1800 to 1860; that both variables increased at similar rates from 1861 to 1889; that GCI surged ahead during the interdepression period, 1889 to 1939; but that GDP resumed the leading role in the post–Second World War period. Accordingly we would be well advised to dispense with real GDP, that inconsistent hybrid proxy for total economic activity. GDP should— must—be replaced with GCI. This matter, however, is not the most important feature exposed by this study.

The second new feature of Australian economic development throughout the period 1860 to 1990, is the central dynamic process of interaction between three sectors of roughly equal size—the household, private, and public sectors. In other words the traditional two-sector (private and public) model that has been in vogue since Coghlan's work early in the century, and which received further development under Noel Butlin's influence during the late 1950s and early 1960s, provides only a partial view of the dynamics of the Australian economy. It served its purpose well for three-quarters of a century, but it is now time to move on.

The third new feature is the light cast on the stagnation debate concerning the period 1890 to 1939. This study shows very clearly that while the interdepression period experienced stagnation in market productivity (and a decline in the market capital/labour ratio), it actually suffered a decline in household productivity. Further, while GDP per capita suggests relative stagnation in average living standards during these years, both market and community income per *household*—which conceptually is a more appropriate measure of average living standards—shows an absolute decline. This decline in household living standards can be seen reflected clearly in the reduction in expenditure on household equipment in the interwar years. It should also be recalled that true performance within the interdepression period was even worse than recorded performance, as market rates for factors (used in the estimation of household activity) were generally above clearing rates. Further, it is in this period, in contrast to all other phases of development since the 1850s, that the private sector dropped into third place behind the public and household sectors. Economic growth gave way to economic expansion or household multiplication. This is a sure sign that the economy had fallen on hard times. Hence, there is no way that the interdepression period can be rehabilitated in relation to the long booms that preceded and succeeded it.

The fourth new issue that emerges from this study is the realization that income per capita, and income per household, are more than just indexes of average material standards of living. While they do have something to tell us about average living standards, they have much more to tell us about economic resilience—the power of economies to compete and survive in the fiercely competitive international environment. It may be true that changes in per capita income in a particular period underestimate changes in the quality of life, but it remains a good reflection of the control exercised by society over material resources and hence its control over survival. It is often argued that Aboriginal society before 1788 had a quality of life that compared favourably with that in England at the same time, even though its level of per capita income was considerably lower. But this misses the real point. The economic resilience of Aboriginal Australia was much lower than England's, and it was the lack of economic resilience that led to its collapse when these two societies confronted each other. It is also interesting to reflect that Australia, during the interdepression period, was losing economic resilience—losing the power to survive. Economic resilience, rather than average living standards, is the ultimate goal of the successful society, as the latter cannot be maintained without the former. Consequently we should not be misled by those who argue seductively that, as we have achieved a satisfactory level of per capita income, we should stop growing—that we should rest upon our economic laurels. Such advice weakens our power to survive in the longer term.

## New processes

### Longrun dynamics

Australian economic development over the last 60,000 years should be seen as the outcome of choices made by households in the Total Economy between the stationary state, economic expansion, and higher levels of household consumption. Viewed from this perspective, five phases of economic development can be identified for the past 60 millennia. The first phase, from the first Aboriginal migrations to European invasion in 1788, consisted of a gradual expansion of households until, at some unknown time in the distant past, all natural resources were fully utilized with the available hunter–gatherer state of technology, and *very* very longrun equilibrium (in effect, the stationary state) was achieved. The second phase, from 1788 to the 1850s was characterized by economic expansion—or household multiplication—as British settlers attempted to utilize Australia's natural resources by employing the technology of the Industrial Revolution. This process was made possible by exploiting the resources to produce and export commodities, such as wool and gold, that were demanded in Europe. The third phase, from the 1850s to the 1890s, was more complex, involving both the attempt to employ existing natural resources of eastern Australia more intensively (by applying a new capital-intensive technology in order to capture a rapidly growing industrial demand in Europe for raw materials) and the attempt to employ the fruits of this technological dynamic change to finance economic expansion— household multiplication—in urban areas, using a more labour-intensive technology. The fourth phase, from the 1890s to the 1940s, saw a high rate of household formation in a period of declining real market income per household, together with some limited opportunities for the more intensive use of natural resources through technological change. This took place against a background of a less expansive, and less certain, international economy. The final phase, from the 1940s to the 1990s, was one largely driven by high rates of growth of real market income per capita (at least until the mid 1970s) that were increasingly used to feed household consumption at the expense of household multiplication.

At a more detailed level, the dynamic process of economic change is interpreted as the outcome of an interaction between three sectors in the Total Economy—the household, private, and public sectors. In the longrun, the intimate interaction between these three sectors has generated a pattern of change in which each has traced out a broadly similar development path (see Figure 2.7, p. 31). On closer inspection, however, we notice three distinct phases of economic development in the past century-and-a half, each of which has been dominated by a different sector, and each of which corresponds with the phases of interaction between economic expansion and economic growth already discussed. In the rapid expansion and growth of the second half of the nineteenth century, the dominant if not the fastest growing sector, was the household; during the retarded development of the first half of the twentieth century, the public sector took the lead; and in the latter half of the twentieth century, the private sector triumphed.

The outcome of this dynamic process over the last 200 years is known in broad outline. Australian economic development has proceeded through four main longrun 'cycles' of forty to fifty years each: 1810s to 1840s; 1850s to 1890s; 1900s to 1930s; 1940s to 1990s. Within each of these 'cycles', a process of Schumpeterian disequilibrium in the upswing has been followed by a short-sharp depression (with the exception of the latest cycle when it has been replaced with an extended period of uncertain development and multiple recessions) during which the economy has attempted to reach an equilibrium growth path once more. Any apparent regularity in these cycles is largely fortuitous. In any case, it is the underlying dynamic process that is more interesting and important than the pattern of outcomes (although the two are clearly related).

## *60,000BP–1788AD*

From the early years of Aboriginal migration—about 60,000 years before the present—the number of family and kinship groups increased to take advantage of the vast natural resources of the ancient Australian continent.[6] At some indeterminate time in the distant past, all natural resources would have been fully utilized given the state of technology in this hunter–gatherer society. At this time the population of Australia may have been in the vicinity of one million people, as it probably was in 1788.[7] Once this equilibrium level had been achieved, population levels would have been carefully controlled in order to prevent any decline in average living standards. At this distant time, Aboriginal economy and population would have achieved a balance with the stock of natural resources, and would have entered into a *very* very longrun equilibrium, owing to the absence of outside pressure or competition. This equilibrium would have changed only gradually to accommodate slow changes in climate, disease, and technology. Aboriginal society is, therefore, an excellent example of the 'stationary state' that could be achieved in an isolated household economy.

In this hunter–gatherer economy the 'choice' initially facing Aboriginal family units was between the stationary state or economic expansion. But given the acquisitive nature of man, there was little choice here: the maximization of material returns, even in an isolated society, requires 'household' multi-plication for as long as underutilized natural resources exist. But, thereafter, expansion ceased because, in a closed society, the costs of developing a new technology exceeded the perceived benefits (see Chapter 3). Accordingly, once equilibrium between the number of households and the supply of natural resources had been achieved, the only real choice was the 'stationary state'.

## 1788–1850s

The second development phase was ushered in by the British invasion of 1788 and continued until the 1850s. To the European eye, conditioned by an entirely different technology, material standard of living, and experience of economic change (which had long included growth as well as expansion[8]), Australian natural resources were not just underutilized, they seemed completely unutilized. The seven decades that followed, was a period of very rapid economic expansion—the first such period on the Australian continent in tens of thousands of years—as the number of European households (Figure 3.2, p. 55) spread throughout the land to utilize Australian natural resources according to the knowledge generated by the Industrial Revolution, and to export the results of this exploitation (wool and gold) to European markets. By the end of this development phase, as Noel Butlin has recently shown, a European economic system had completely displaced the long-established Aboriginal system and the European population had just exceeded the pre-conquest level achieved by the Aboriginal population, of just over a million people.[9]

The main reason for viewing 1788 to 1860 as both the second phase of Australian, and the first phase of European, economic development, is that it was the result of a process of economic expansion based upon an 'extensive' use of natural resources, rather than of economic growth based upon an 'intensive' use of natural resources. Indeed, as shown in Table 2.1 (p. 24), the growth between 1800 and 1861 of income per household was actually negative, and it was not until after 1861 that it turned positive. This was a period of very rapid household multiplication (almost 12 per cent per annum), being twice as rapid as that for the entire two centuries, and greater than that in the second half of the nineteenth century by a factor of 3.7. The remarkable kink in the picture of household formation around 1860 (Figure 3.2, p. 55) is evidence of the change from 'extensive' to 'intensive' resource exploitation—the change from household-led economic expansion (EDC) to market-led economic growth and economic expansion (TDC). It is not surprising to find, therefore, that the household sector grew more rapidly than the market sector in this period. And while the household sector continued to expand throughout this phase of economic development, the emerging market sector experienced the well-known pattern of boom in the 1820s and 1830s, and bust in the 1840s.

## 1850s–1890s

This period saw the transition from 'extensive' to 'intensive' resource exploitation. The remarkable kink in the household-formation profile around 1860 attests to the drama of this transformation. Before 1860, household formation grew at the very rapid rate of 11.6 per cent per annum, whereas between 1860 and 1889 it fell to a mere 2.8 per cent per annum, which was only marginally greater than the rates achieved in subsequent booms. Nevertheless, the achievement in this period was considerable, and involved a large-scale application of a new rural, urban, transport, and communications technology to resources that had already been brought into the process of European production. Australia's resources were being employed more intensively through the process of technological dynamic change (TDC). This was a process that employed overseas capital and labour, and that generated large-scale exports of primary products. For the first time in Australian history—a history that extends back a 'century of millennia'—TDC, rather than extensive resource utilization or EDC, was the basis for economic expansion. Not only did economic expansion proceed rapidly but, for the first time, real GCI per household increased in a sustained fashion—at the rapid rate of 1.7 per cent per annum, a rate not exceeded until the post–Second World War period.

The dominating feature in the second half of the nineteenth century was the large inflow of population and capital from Europe, largely the UK, which, combined with a new technology, greatly increased the intensity of natural resource use in Australia. During this period, population, which increased by a factor of eight, fuelled the rapid expansion of Australian cities. Indeed the great economic achievement of this half-century was Australia's ability not only to retain the goldrush population after the alluvial gold had been worked out, but also to absorb a large annual inflow during the three decades prior to the depression of the 1890s, and to house them at a relatively high standard. This achievement was based on the ability of the Total Economy to generate a level of per capita income, a distribution of that income, a range of urban employment, a standard of public utilities, and a quality of residential living that made Australia attractive—despite the economic and social costs of global isolation—to a growing number of European families that were shedding the restrictions of traditional economy and society. It was based, in other words, on the ability to make a successful transition between the extensive and intensive forms of natural resource exploitation.

It is not surprising, in these circumstances, that the largest sector in the Australian economy during these forty years should be the household economy, nor that this sector should have a powerful impact on the market economy. The household was at the very centre of the dominant process of economic expansion (or household multiplication), and its impact was felt through a considerable demand for the goods and services supplied by the private and public sectors rather than as an aggressive source of labour supply for the market. As we have seen, market demand for labour was predominantly for males and, to a much lesser degree, for single females[10] (owing to the structure and labour-intensive nature of market work discussed in Chapter 5) which was largely met through immigration, while the household sector itself exerted a very strong demand for married (or potentially marriageable) females owing to the gender imbalance that prevailed throughout the nineteenth century (also discussed in Chapter 5). The goods and services in great demand were housing, household equipment, material inputs for household production, domestic and personal service, transport, and a range of publicly supplied utilities. This outcome, if not the process by which it was achieved, has been examined by Noel Butlin in *Investment in Australian economic development*.

In the period framed by the 1850s and 1890s, therefore, the household sector clearly responded to buoyant market conditions, but it interacted more closely with the public than the private sector. This phase of intensive natural resource exploitation was closely associated with waves of immigration that in turn were accompanied by heavy public investment of borrowed funds in infrastructure, particularly in urban areas. It was to this public investment in towns, especially capital cities, that the household sector responded most closely. To ignore the household sector is to underestimate the role of urbanization in Australian economic development. A paramount need of this period was not only to provide housing in the rapidly growing urban areas, but to create a household structure that would support and sustain the European settlement of this vast land. Naturally, in turn, the rapid rate of family formation generated an equally rapid growth in the demand for both private and public goods and services. There can be little doubt that the economic dynamics of Australian settlement involved an intimate interaction between these three sectors.

### 1890s–1940s

The fourth phase of development occurred between the 1890s and the 1940s, and was marked by a technologically, and sometimes publicly, led transfer of land resources from pastoral to arable farming (particularly in the West)— 'intensive' rather than 'extensive' use of natural resources—but primarily by a high rate of household formation (2.2 per cent per annum) despite a negative rate of growth of real income per household (−0.2 per cent per annum). Clearly this was a period when the internal dynamics of the household economy— mainly the breakup of the traditional extended family—carried the increase in total population further than would be predicted from the more intensive use of natural resources made possible by technological change and the decline in real income per household. During these years, Australia's population went from 3.2 to 7.6 million and the number of households increased from 0.59 million to 1.87 million, even at the expense of household living standards.

The retarded market development in this period was largely an outcome of a transition between two means of generating economic growth—the traditional reliance upon the export of commodities produced from the increasingly intensive exploitation of natural resources, and a growing gamble (through tariff protection) with the production and consumption of urban goods and services in the metropolitan areas. Australia's problem in this period was twofold. First, foreign demand for primary products did not grow as rapidly after the 1890s as it had done before, and indeed in the 1930s it actually collapsed. Second, the scale of the Australian economy was not great enough until the 1940s, for the generation of self-sustained economic growth in the larger urban areas.

Immigration, while still important at times during the interdepression period (in the 1900s, 1910s, and first half of the 1920s), did not play its former starring role, despite being publicly assisted. Population increased by a factor of only 2.4. The market economy, particularly the private part, was unable to provide the opportunities for a continuous and rapid inflow of population during a period in which sound natural resource boundaries (given the state of technology) had been exceeded;[11] in which foreign trade was no longer an effective engine of growth owing to the precariousness of the world economy;[12] and in which economic expansion was badly punctuated by a series of major wars, depressions, recessions, and droughts. And as the market sector was unable to provide opportunities for a much larger population, the feed-back effects from the household economy to the private sector—especially via residential construction—were much less than in the second half of the nineteenth century. Nevertheless, the household sector did expand more rapidly than the private sector owing to its own internal dynamics and to its close association with the public sector (particularly assisted immigration and urban infrastructure), and it did act to dampen the effects of severe downturn in private enterprise.

In addition to the economic performance of the private sector we need to consider its nature and structure. Both public and private demand for labour, initiated by various shortrun bursts of investment was, as in the nineteenth century, low on skill and high on physical strength. The government sector, for example, undertook basic, unsophisticated public works projects,[13] while the private sector was engaged in heavy industry and basic construction using second-best technology from the UK.[14] Hence the gender division of labour in the household, according to comparative advantage (see Chapter 3), meant that 'married' women specialized in housework and their men specialized in market work. Accordingly the female/male wage ratio changed only marginally during this period—increasing by only 12.2 per cent, from 0.49 just prior to the First World War to 0.55 in the late 1930s. Hence, fundamental economic forces rather than institutional arrangements (e.g. the Arbitration Commission) determined what Claudia Goldin in another context has called the 'gender gap'. Quite clearly, Australian institutions were sensitive to market forces.

The labour supply response to these market conditions involved both a reduction in unemployment, where the unemployed were deemed suitable, and an increase in male immigration. 'Married' women remained in the home, and there was no need for the substitution of capital for labour in the household. Indeed the real value of net additions to equipment per household fell from $41.3 in the decade before the First World War, to $29.3 in the 1920s, and $29.3 in the second half of the 1930s. And all this at a time when a new technology was actually available for electrical household equipment, and when the relative price of equipment to labour fell by 21.4 per cent. Hence the nature of market labour demand in Australia was responsible for the recognized fact that internationally available consumer durables were slow to make inroads into the Australian household economy in the 1920s.[15] And it may even be part of the reason for the weaker direct relationship between the household and private sectors in comparison with the post–Second World War years.

The fourth period, therefore, was one of less certain development. A less buoyant, and potentially vulnerable, international economy dampened the driving force in the private sector. By default, the public sector took the leading role in a process of economic change that was lacking in confidence and direction, and that was punctuated by economic and political crises. The public sector took responsibility for encouraging immigration, and hence the inflow of capital, through the stimulation of both rural (particularly in Western Australia and Victoria)[16] and urban development,[17] by the provision of infrastructure, financial grants, subsidies, and tariffs. Once again it was this direct and indirect public activity that the household sector responded to and, in turn, stimulated. But at the same time, the internal dynamics of the household sector—the decision to procreate and change the structure of family organization—created a rate of economic expansion that defied an uncertain market economy.

## 1940s–1990s

The final phase of development, from the 1940s to the close of the twentieth century, was driven largely by an unprecedentedly high rate of growth of real market income per household (at least until 1974). This was the outcome of both a dramatic recovery of the international economy after the Second World War, which regenerated demand for the products of Australia's natural resources (wheat, wool, animal products, and minerals); and a rapid growth of urban industries, fed on a rich diet of import quotas, tariffs, improved technology, and increasing returns to scale. Despite the occasional discovery of new mineral resources, it became clear in this period that further economic expansion, in terms of household multiplication, would depend predominantly on technological dynamic change rather than on resource exploitation. Also during these years there was a marked change in the way households employed the fruits of TDC. Owing to fundamental changes in the Total Economy, the balance in the use of household income shifted dramatically away from procreation to the consumption of market goods and services.

One of the central events of this period was the rush of female household workers to join the market workforce. This phenomenon, which constitutes nothing less than an economic and social revolution—a revolution shared with the rest of the Western World—saw the proportion of female household workers who also had market jobs rise from 8.0 per cent in 1947 to 36.5 per cent in 1990. This amounted to almost a five-fold increase after a period of fifty years during which this ratio had stagnated at a much lower level of 5 to 7 per cent. One implication is that, although immigration was an important source of male labour (1.56 million) in this period,[18] it was actually surpassed by the household sector which supplied 2.11 million 'married' women. While this event is common knowledge, the forces responsible are less clearly understood. Many commentators see this change as a result of socio-political forces—the assertion by women of their rights, or the change in social attitudes forged by concerned social leaders. In fact this change was a result of economic forces affecting both the demand for, and supply of, female labour, and of the resulting change in the economic aspirations of households. This was an economic response by households (not just female householders) to a transformation of the economic forces underlying Australian—indeed Western—society. It was a response to the new economic revolution.

On the demand side there was a major change in the structure of the market sector, both private and public. Fundamental technological change involving the substitution of capital for labour on a large scale, which began in the recovery from the Great Depression, accelerated during the Second World War, and spread out widely through the economy in the post-war period. As shown in Chapter 5, this was associated with the changing relative factor prices of capital and labour and to changing patterns of consumer demand. Because of these fundamental changes, developed economies, including Australia, generated a wider range of market occupations that suited the physical capabilities and technical training of female household workers. And as a result of this outward shift in the demand for female labour, the relative wage rate of females to males increased by 69 per cent (from 0.55 to 0.93) between the late 1930s (or 1920s) and the 1970s. This shift of market demand for female labour, for the first time since the Industrial Revolution, enabled women to escape from the low-level wage trap that resulted, not from widespread social discrimination, but from the restricted range of employment categories in which females could effectively compete with males. There is no good evidence here for the basically non-economic argument about segmented or dual markets, which requires an elaborate conspiracy between different groups of males that possess conflicting economic interests (such as trade unions and employers) and which cut across the interests of powerful economic groups.[19] Indeed it is possible to explain 98 per cent of the increase in female participation since the Second World War by reference solely to economic forces. This leaves little room for conspiracy theories. It was largely a question of the changing gender structure of market demand for labour, rather than changing social attitudes, that brought about the transformation in the employment of 'married' women. The evidence in this study strongly suggests that social rationalization follows economic imperatives, and not the other way round.

The fact that women seeking to enter the market prior to the 1940s experienced limited employment opportunities and relatively low wages was a reflection of the nature of industry that underpinned the market demand for labour; of the restricted investment undertaken by women in human capital owing to the perceived length of time they expected to spend in the workforce; and to the nature of the market economy's technological base which required a range of physical strength that exceeded the capabilities of the average Australian female. The end result was an excessive supply of females in a restricted number of occupations, and hence the generation of lower wage rates for females than enjoyed by males. Even accurate claims of household and institutional discrimination against females acquiring human capital must be balanced against considerations of expected rates of return on that investment. Obviously discrimination against females on the supply side has always existed, but once again only within narrow limits in what is basically an open economy. Once households and institutions realize that expected rates of return have risen, their attitudes will change, as indeed they did after the 1950s. While the desire to discriminate—and not only against women—may be present in those who are keen to maintain their economic advantages, the question is: how widespread and profound is it? Discrimination is always most noticeable during periods of rapid change because of the attempt of vested interests to maintain their existing advantage. But in an open society, discrimination will only exist within narrow limits, and then only in the shortrun. Discrimination does not drive the economic system, and certainly not in the longrun. The dramatic longrun changes observed in this study can be explained entirely in economic terms, without recourse to spurious non-economic arguments. It is not correct, as some (Gregory *et al.*) have claimed, that the central feature of this period must be regarded as exogenous (institutionally determined) to any economic explanation.

Fundamental technological change in the market sector is only part of a complex economic explanation of changing female market participation. Also on the demand side we must consider the alternative employer of female labour—the household. It has already been suggested that, in the nineteenth century, the gender imbalance in favour of males generated an unusually high demand for marriageable women to establish and maintain households. And during the period before the Great Depression, when large families were the norm, there was an additional demand for single females to assist married women with the running of large and highly labour-intensive households (Figure 4.2 on p. 84 shows that until 1961 there were more full-time female household workers than there were households). Both these aspects of household labour demand had run their course by the Second World War.

Then there is the supply side. A range of new labour-saving household equipment, particularly that powered by electricity, was becoming increasingly available in industrial economies after the First World War. But despite the modest decline in relative factor prices before the Second World War, the real value of equipment per household actually *declined*. Clearly there was no widespread demand for these new consumer durables because the structure of market demand for labour had yet to change. Forces on the demand side were demonstrably more important that those on the supply side. One could anticipate, therefore, that only once the structure of market demand for labour changed sufficiently to include the work skills possessed by the average female household worker, that new electrical household equipment would be adopted on a widespread scale. Only then would this equipment be required as a substitute for female household labour attracted to the market place, and only then would household money incomes be sufficiently high to allow their purchase. Needless to say the picture is even more complex than this. These structural changes also took place against a secular rise in average market incomes at an unprecedented rate (3 per cent per annum), which provided the necessary basis for mass purchases of an endless variety of consumer durables. Added to this was an accelerated decline in the relative factor prices of capital compared with labour: between the second half of the 1930s and the 1970s relative factor prices (capital to labour) declined by 72.7 per cent. This was the nature of supply side determinants underlying the new economic revolution.

Finally we need to briefly consider the behavioural responses of Australian households to these changing market conditions. There are two closely related issues, one concerning the question of opportunity cost, and the other concerning the use that can be made of higher disposable cash incomes—increased consumption of goods and services, or procreation—by the household. The first of these involves the very process of household economic decision-making. As argued above, households will allocate labour between market work, household work, and leisure in such a way that wage rates and shadow prices (reflecting the utility derived from housework and leisure) are equated at the margin. If this equilibrium is disrupted by an increase in the real market wage rate then, on average, households will reallocate their labour between these three basic activities until equilibrium is again achieved. In this case the average household will increase time worked in the market sector and will reduce time devoted to household work and leisure. This brings the second issue into contention. The transfer of household labour to the market economy presupposes that the substitution of market goods and services for household goods, services, and leisure is, on average, considered attractive by households. In turn this requires a critical choice between procreation—the source of household multiplication or economic expansion—and the increased consumption by existing households of market goods and services—the source of further economic growth. The evidence clearly suggests that Australian households, and households throughout the Western World, chose to increase their consumption. What has been substituted for family time is a bewildering array of consumer durables, fast foods, domestic service, cars, larger homes, restaurants, entertainment, exotic holidays, travel, holiday houses, hobby farms, motor launches, yachts, four-wheel drive vehicles, together with expensive clothing and a vast range of personal goods.[20] There appears to be no limit to human inventiveness when it comes to spending money. It would seem that diminishing returns in consumption can be indefinitely postponed by merely creating new and novel consumer goods and services. And in the process, economic growth becomes more important to households than economic expansion.

Yet, the process is even more complex than this suggests. The balance between procreation and consumption is determined by an interaction between the economic interests of households and the nature of the aggregate production function—after all, children will only be produced if families believe their offspring will find market employment, and production systems will only be introduced that meet the aspirations of households, at least in the longrun. This of course does not deny the possibility of decision-making error. Indeed the June 1992 high rate of youth unemployment—about one-third of those looking for work—suggests that households did not shift far enough from procreation to consumption in the early 1970s. As a consequence, while the average worker is currently experiencing a severe recession (over 11 per cent unemployment), our youth are experiencing a depression as severe as the Great Depression!

But returning to the main theme: as we saw in Chapter 4, the effect of all these changes upon the structure of the household in this period was profound. The marked and rapid increase in market participation by female household-workers—which more than doubled from 6.4 in the late 1930s to 15.3 in 1960, and doubled again to 31.5 in 1975 after which it increased slowly to 36.5 in 1990—was accompanied by an equally rapid increase in the substitution of equipment for female labour in the household. This substitution is reflected in the increase in real equipment expenditures per household by a factor of 3.4 from the late 1930s to the 1950s, at a time when relative factor prices (equipment/female wages) declined by a factor of only 1.7. This suggests a major role for forces underlying the market demand for labour. Between the 1950s and 1970s real household equipment expenditure only increased by a factor of 1.6 at a time when relative factor prices declined by a multiple as large as 2.3. In other words real equipment expenditure was not highly responsive to changing relative factor prices.

These profound changes in household structure and expenditure patterns had a further important impact on the private sector, which expanded to meet these new demands for goods and services. Little wonder that the interaction between these two sectors increased during the second half of the twentieth century. An important conclusion, therefore, is that while the growth of the household sector owed much to the buoyant market conditions and the changing structure of market labour requirements in the post–Second World War period, this buoyancy also owed much to the demand for market goods and services generated within the household economy. The strong interaction between all three sectors must be recognized as an important element in the economic development of the Australian economy in the second half of the twentieth century.

The fifth period (at least prior to 1974), therefore, saw the emergence of the private market economy as a leading sector for the first time in Australian history. This was largely due to the unusual buoyancy of an international economy released from the steely grip of depression and war. These were the years of fundamental technological and structural change in the private sector, which dominated the fortunes of the Total Economy and led to a uniquely rapid rate of technological dynamic change (TDC). While the public sector was content to play less of a direct role in this new economic climate, it was still substantially involved in the development process through its protectionist and immigration policies. But the private sector led the way, and the household sector followed. And in following, the household further stimulated the other two sectors. Indeed it is probably the case that all three sectors interacted more closely during the second half of the twentieth century, than in earlier periods.

## Overview

The household, therefore, has played a central role in Australian economic development. This role has been acted out at a number of levels. At the most fundamental level, the household has generated the economic expansion that we see occurring all around us, by making a choice about the use of both natural resources and the fruits of technological dynamic change. The elusive gains from TDC are translated into tangible forms—into more households and/or more complex consumer goods—by the household. This is a choice conditioned by the nature of the aggregate production function of this period. In addition, at a less fundamental, but still essential level, the household has played a mediating and integrating role in the Total Economy. It has responded to, even orchestrated, changing economic forces, both in terms of its demand for market goods and services and in terms of resources—both labour and capital—that it has directed to the market sector. All this in an attempt to maximize its material returns.

The market sector, on the other hand, through its specialized productive activities, is the dynamic source of TDC which provides the resources for the household to pursue its rational objectives. And the analysis of the market sector within the context of the Australian Total Economy, raises an important question about the relative importance of physical and human capital in the dynamic process of economic change. As a force for change, there seems little doubt that physical capital has been far more important than human capital. It was shown in Chapter 4 that there was little advance in human capital per capita in Australia, apart from that imported through immigration, between the 1860s and the 1940s. In contrast, there was a significant increase in the physical capital/labour ratio (see Figure 4.3, p. 87), mainly in the second half of the nineteenth century. Only after the Second World War did Australian society begin to increase its human capital stock through general and technical schooling, and to change its gender distribution of skills. The question is: what direct impact did this increase in human capital have on the development process in the second half of the twentieth century? It is difficult to provide a quantitatively-based answer, but it would seem that the increase in per capita levels, and change in gender distribution, of human capital probably helped to *facilitate* the changing technological foundations of the economy, but only in a passive way, by supplying the new labour skills required by a post-industrial society. There is even an element of deskilling here. We have seen how the changing technological foundations of the market sector in these years enabled the substitution of relatively unskilled female household workers for skilled and semi-skilled male workers in many service and manufacturing industries.

There can be little doubt, however, that the changing foundations of the economy depended on the rapidly changing *physical* capital/labour ratio. Physical capital was the vehicle of economic change in the post–Second World War years, and human capital helped to pave its way. Further, there is a paradox associated with the increase in human capital per capita achieved during these years. A significant increase in human capital per capita should, according to human capital theory, raise the price of labour relative to the price of capital (*ceteris paribus*), which in turn will encourage an even greater substitution of physical capital for labour than would otherwise have been the case. Indeed this was the basis for the shift of largely unskilled female labour from the household to the market in the post–Second World War period. Can this, therefore, be the dynamic role of human capital—to enhance the contribution of physical capital? This is indeed a paradox. But it is a paradox that places human capital theory in a more realistic context than its followers have been prepared to do.

## Shortrun fluctuations

So far we have been considering longrun growth and expansion. But the analysis in this study also has something new to say about shortrun economic fluctuations. We have noticed a general inverse relationship between the household and market sectors throughout the entire period. During booms the market sector tends to outstrip the household sector, whereas during depressions the household economy expands to absorb those workers being shed by the market sector. In effect, the Total Economy possesses an automatic countercyclical mechanism. During a boom, underemployed household labour is attracted to the market sector and market goods and services are substituted for those produced in the household, whereas, during a sharp recession or depression, market workers are absorbed back into the household, and household goods and services are substituted for those produced in the market. The complex countercyclical pattern in both the past and present, is discussed in detail in Chapter 2.

The failure to recognize this countercyclical mechanism in any formal or systematic way in economics and economic history, has led to an overevaluation of the impact of booms and, particularly, depressions, on average living standards, particularly of households in contrast to individuals. The common response during a depression is to assume that the reduction in average living standards is equal to the reduction in *per capita* market income, and that unemployment is equal to the number of people that are forced to relinquish *market* employment. Any discussion or analysis that ignores the household sector as a source of employment, production, and 'income', is not only inadequate, it is also highly misleading.

# A complex dynamic process

While a number of significant new insights concerning the dynamic process of Australian economic development have emerged from this study, which primarily attempts to place the household sector back within the context of the Total Economy, there remains much work to be done before this new picture is complete. In particular, greater concentration needs to be given to microeconomic processes based on detailed data relating to individual house-holds.[21] And there is much qualitative evidence that still needs to be brought to bear on this subject. But the broad outlines of the longrun dynamic processes of change in the Australian Total Economy have been exposed, and a more comprehensive and complex system of explanation has been proposed. Not only have we begun to remember the forgotten economy, but we have begun to see what the existential model of total Australian economic change really looks like. Unlike in some recent studies, Australian economic development is viewed here as an internally generated dynamic process, which is occasionally disturbed by external shocks. The driving force comes from within rather than without. This study attempts to provide a challenging picture of the complex dynamic process that is transporting the Australian Total Economy out of the past and into the future.

# Part Two

---

## Accounting for the Total Economy

# 7

## A new approach to historical social accounting

### The statistical foundations for the forgotten economy

The pioneering international work on modern official national accounts took place in colonial New South Wales exactly one hundred years ago. Timothy Coghlan, the Colony's Statistician between 1886 and 1905, was responsible for drawing the crucial distinction between the proportions of the population engaged in market and non-market activities—a distinction between 'bread-winners' and 'dependents'. This distinction not only formed the basis for Coghlan's Australian national income estimates, but was to become the foundation for modern national accounts throughout the world. While the division of economic activity into market and non-market was an essential step in the early development of national accounts—largely because economic theory at that time had not resolved the problem of shadow prices—it became the basis for the forgotten economy.

That the household economy, and hence the Total Economy, has been forgotten for so long is the fault not of Coghlan, whose work was without peer in his own time and was not surpassed until after the Second World War, but of less adventurous official statisticians throughout the world since his time. Official caution is difficult to understand in view of the exploratory work undertaken by individual economists in the USA and Europe since the late 1970s.[1]

It is as a pioneer of national accounting that Coghlan is best known.[2] Considerable claims can and have been made for the quality of Coghlan's national income estimates of Australasia. If nothing else, they were the first *official* estimates of national income to be produced anywhere in the world. This was an outstanding achievement. As Australia experienced very rapid development in the second half of the nineteenth century (with real Gross

Community Income (GCI) increasing by 5 per cent per annum), not surprisingly, it attracted the attention of the quantifiers. The first attempts were made by W.C. Wentworth (the famous son of convict parents), who estimated the gross value of physical output in New South Wales and Tasmania for 1819 and 1821,[3] and M.G. Mulhall, who provided crude income estimates in his *Dictionary of Statistics* from 1882.[4] Mulhall's lead was followed up by the statisticians of both New South Wales (T.A. Coghlan)[5] and Victoria (H.H. Hayter).[6] While Hayter's 1891 estimate was a direct copy of Mulhall's, Coghlan's 1887 calculation took a more independent path which continued to develop in an innovative way until the early years of the twentieth century.

Mulhall may have been the first great popularizer of aggregative statistics, including national income, but it was Coghlan who transformed a crude value added approach into a modern system of national accounts (in gross terms) involving estimates of income received (from 1886), value added (from 1888) and expenditure (from 1888), and who explored the difference between domestic and national product.[7] Coghlan was the first national accountant to do so. In addition to improving his methods, Coghlan was able, as Government Statistician, to improve the nature and quality of the raw data. His estimates for 1891 were made more reliable using data from the population census of that year, which was radically restructured through his personal intervention. By the late 1890s, Coghlan had developed his own original system of national accounting, using tax data (first collected in New South Wales in 1897) as well as population, production, and retail data.[8] At this stage he was acknowledged as a world leader in national income accounting, and the quality and sophistication of his estimates were superior to anything published in Australia—by J.T. Sutcliffe (1926), F.C. Benham (1928), Colin Clark and J.G. Crawford (1938)—or elsewhere—Simon Kuznets (1937–40) in the USA and Colin Clark in the UK (1932 and 1937)—prior to the official estimates developed during and after the Second World War.[9] Much intellectual capital could have been saved had Coghlan's achievements been used as a foundation for the revival of interest in national income from the 1930s.

There are two reasons why Coghlan's pioneering work was overlooked. First, there is Coghlan's decision to refuse the new post of Federal Statistician offered to him in 1906, which, given the lack of interest in economic aggregates of those finally appointed, prevented national accounts from becoming an integral part of Australian official publications until the 1940s. Australia narrowly missed out, thereby, on having a continuous series of *official* national accounts stretching back to the 1880s. Second, Coghlan was a generation or so before his time. Orthodox economics expressed little interest in macroeconomic questions between the work of the classical economists and the *General Theory* of J.M. Keynes. It was the *General Theory* that brought the work of national accountants like Colin Clark and Simon Kuznets into international prominence. Third, it is an unfortunate fact that economic ideas, like other ideas, make little international headway until they are 'reinvented' by the superpowers. Finally, this is an outstanding example of the loss of collective memory that is inevitable in a discipline like economics, which has little or no interest in the past, even its own past.

Coghlan was no less creative in his role as census taker. The modern system of occupation classification, which draws a distinction between 'breadwinners' and 'dependents', is largely his work.[10] At the Census Conference held in Hobart in March 1890, convened by the various colonies in an attempt to forge a common approach to the forthcoming 1891 population census, the Victorian representatives wanted all colonies to adopt the British method (developed by Dr William Farr, Deputy Registrar-General of England) which classified occupations according to a non-economic criterion—the 'material which workers employed in their trades'. Coghlan, who wanted to provide an economic structure for the census, recalled: 'The proposal was strenuously opposed by the author, and, as it fortunately happened by Mr. R.M. Johnston, of Tasmania', because of the anomalies created by the 'British system'—no distinction was made between 'producer and dealer', and the 'domestic' occupation category included 'wives and widows, sons, daughters, relatives, and visitors, university students, children attending school, beer and wine sellers, and persons engaged in the supply of board and lodging, and in rendering personal service for which remuneration is paid'.[11] Coghlan and Johnston proposed the 'Australian method' which began by dividing the population into two groups—'breadwinners' and 'dependents'—on the basis of whether they were 'engaged in pursuits for which remuneration is paid'. Coghlan explained:

> In dealing with the subject of *occupations*, as for every other branch of the Census enumeration, *it was necessary to account for the whole population*, though it is obvious that a large proportion had not what is technically termed an occupation . . . In order, then, to account for the whole population, it has been necessary to show it in two divisions, viz., breadwinners, and dependents or non-breadwinners.[12]

When discussing the detailed occupation categories, Coghlan says of his 'Class II, Domestic' category that it no longer includes wives, widows, children, relatives, visitors, scholars and students 'nor does it cover any persons engaged at home in any domestic duty for which no remuneration is paid, nor dependent relatives or children, *not because they do not perform a specific service, but because they are not direct breadwinners*'.[13] The receipt of market income became, for the first time in official accounts, the great measure of distinction between 'independent' and 'dependent' economic activity—between, in effect, the market and household sectors.[14] Coghlan, however, was not entirely happy with the word 'dependent' in this context. As he said: 'The term "dependent" is not altogether a happy one, seeing that under this designation are included married women and others who perform domestic duties [which he regarded as a productive service]; nevertheless it is justified on the ground that for such services no money-wages are paid'.[15] Coghlan needed to make this distinction, therefore, not because he thought that unpaid household work was 'unproductive' (how could it be, if paid housework was productive?) as some have claimed, but because it was central to his attempt, begun some six years previously, to estimate the value of national income. Coghlan's role as census taker was subordinated to his role as national income estimator.

The implications of this 'Australian method' are enormous, and are with us still. It is not only the foundation on which modern census occupational categories world-wide are based, it is also the cornerstone of current official national income estimates. It is the cornerstone of the forgotten economy. Ironically, Coghlan's distinction between 'breadwinner' and 'dependent'—a distinction between market and household employment—is essential for a wider analysis of total economic activity. But Coghlan was unable to resolve the problem of how to measure the contribution of household economic activity, and his own estimates of national income—like those of Colin Clark and Simon Kuznets who followed after him and helped to determine the nature of official national accounts throughout the world—are estimates of market income rather than total income. Coghlan appears to have taken the position that, even if it were possible to measure the value of household activity, there was little point in doing so because of some sort of longrun balance between the household and market sectors. In a section entitled 'The employment of women' in the 1891 Census Report,[16] he appears to argue that a flow of female labour from the home to the workplace will merely cause the wages of males to decline, such that national income will remain unchanged and household activities will remain unaffected owing to underemployment in the home. Presumably in such a situation, estimates of market income will always be a good proxy for total income. This is a curiously static view of the Total Economy. Coghlan did not take into account the dynamic nature of the economy, nor did he foresee the changing gender structure of labour demand, which is responsible for fluctuations in the balance between the market and household sectors. It has been the purpose of this work to examine the dynamic relationship in the Total Economy denied by Coghlan.

Only in the last decade or so have scholars given serious consideration to estimating non-market income,[17] and official statistical bureaus around the world have done little more than flirt cautiously with the idea.[18] In Australia, apart from the very tentative experiment in 1990 to estimate household labour services for the single year 1986–87, the Australian Bureau of Statistics has not managed to take up the pioneering mantle relinquished by Timothy Coghlan when he left Australia for London in 1905.

# A new system of national accounts

The dilemma of whether or not to include non-market goods and services in the national accounts has long concerned those compiling and using these estimates.[19] While the conceptual and empirical difficulties involved in defining and measuring non-market economic activities have discouraged those who construct official estimates of National Income, considerable attention has been devoted to this issue by applied economists over the last decade or so.[20] This recent interest has arisen from a number of developments, including the theoretical advances made concerning the allocation of time, and the economics of the household; the growing availability of survey data on household activities; and a concern that the dramatically changing workforce participation rates of females is seriously impairing the usefulness of official GDP estimates.[21]

The *a priori* reasons for including the value of housework in a more comprehensive measure of economic activity, which has been called **Gross Community Income** (GCI) in this book, appear quite compelling. First, as European and American studies have demonstrated that the value of household labour services is large in relation to official estimates of GDP (ranging from 33 to 57 per cent),[22] any analysis of the economy which fails to take this sector into account, is, at best, incomplete. A recent (1990) study by the Australian Bureau of Statistics has attempted to estimate the value of household labour services by employing a 1987 pilot time-use survey of 1,000 Sydney households. While there are a number of reasons for believing that this official calculation is an overestimate—discussed in detail in Chapter 8—it confirms that, in the Australian context, the household sector makes a significant contribution (47–62 per cent of GDP) to total economic activity.

The second reason for estimating Gross Community Income is that the different mix of market and non-market economic activities in different countries (regions) makes international (inter-regional) comparisons difficult to evaluate. Third, a considerable proportion of non-reported income, which has been a growing problem in the last decade or so, would be accounted for if a value was assigned to housework. Fourth, some have argued that the failure to measure household 'income' renders incomplete and unreliable any discussion of income distribution and poverty, because two families with the same measured income will have entirely different standards of living if in one, both adults, and in the other only one adult, are employed outside the home.[23] For similar reasons an income tax which does not discriminate between the different allocation of time between employed work and housework, will be biased in favour of families with non-working spouses. Fifth, as shown in Chapter 5, any study of unemployment, or the market participation of married women, that ignores the household sector will be seriously flawed.

Finally, there are good reasons for expecting that the use of existing GDP estimates for measuring growth rates may produce misleading results. As shown in Part One (particularly Figure 2.7, p. 31), there has been considerable ebb and flow between the household and market sectors over the last two centuries. This possibility was discussed by Studenski in 1958,[24] and more recently by Weinrobe who suggests that, owing to marked changes in workforce participation rates of females since the 1950s,[25] it is highly likely that the relationship between recorded production and actual production has changed. In fact, the real-world processes which have produced a significant increase in female market participation are more complex than Weinrobe appears to realize, involving the substitution of other forms of labour and household equipment for female labour in the household. As shown in Chapter 2 the end result cannot be predicted in advance.

# Alternative conceptual approaches to measuring housework

It is necessary to clarify what is meant by non-market economic activities, how they can be measured in physical terms, and how these quantities should be valued. To isolate the non-market sector of economic activity, a workable definition of total economic activity is required. Economic activities are usually defined as those undertaken primarily to generate income, or at least goods and services *which could be marketed*, rather than activities in which the act of production cannot be separated from the act of consumption, such as social and leisure-time pursuits.[26] By applying this general distinction to household activities, it is possible to define household production as the 'non-market uses of household time that result in the production of a good or service that could be purchased [and sold] in the market'.[27] The type of household activities that are normally considered to lie within the boundaries of this definition include: the preparation of meals and the associated clearing away and dishwashing, laundry, house cleaning, child-care and informal education, the production of clothing and furnishings, garden care, house repairs, and other activities such as shopping, record keeping, and payment of household accounts. Volunteer and community work (care of the sick, frail, and disabled, together with other good works) are also often included in the definition of household activities. This broad definition of household work has been adopted in this study.

Ideally, we wish to measure the value added by these various household activities. There are two methods of estimating value added: first by subtracting the value of material inputs from the value of output; and second by estimating the value paid to the various factors of production. Despite some recent experimental survey work, particularly in Finland since 1979, aimed at collecting data on the quantities of some types of household output, this approach is unlikely to be successful owing to the very considerable burdens that it places on the long-suffering respondent.[28] Fortunately, it is more feasible to attempt an estimate of factor returns. While most published attempts to measure factor returns have focused on valuing household labour, it is also possible to estimate the value both of household capital stock and of residential land. These estimates can be used as a basis for measuring the return to all household factors of production. It will be clear that, because of the growing capital input into household production during this century, the estimates of labour services in any longrun study will constitute a declining proportion of household production over time. Accordingly, in this study an attempt has been made to estimate both the value of household labour services (Chapter 8) and the value of services from household capital and land (Chapter 9).

While early attempts to measure the value of household services focused on the number of households as the basic physical input,[29] more recent work has employed time-use surveys to arrive at estimates of hours of housework undertaken by various family members.[30] Those studying household services in the USA are particularly fortunate in this respect, because time-use surveys extend as far back as 1917, and have been undertaken on a reasonably regular basis since 1924.[31] As only three small regional time-use surveys have been undertaken in Australia—in 1974, 1976 and 1987—it has been necessary in this study to use census data on household numbers and household workers. The procedure employed here, however, has two important advantages over that of employing time-use surveys: it is possible to calculate *annual* rather than merely periodic (coinciding with a score of surveys in the USA) estimates of household services; and the data employed are more objective than those arising from questionnaires about how long and how hard people work. As will be discussed later, the responses to survey questions of this type are difficult to interpret with any degree of precision.

Three main approaches have been employed in the literature to value physical labour inputs: the first involves using market wage rates of general domestic workers in conjunction with total hours of housework per week; the second involves the application of market rates of various domestic specialists to hours devoted to separate household tasks; and the third involves estimating the opportunity cost of those actually engaged in household production. The first of these approaches, which employs the market wages of general domestics, is based on the assumption that a single employee is capable of undertaking all types of household activity. While this approach has its enthusiastic supporters,[32] there are some duties (such as child-care, record keeping and house and car maintenance) that require greater skills than those normally possessed by general domestic workers. Some have argued that the use of general domestic worker wage rates will tend to 'undervalue' the contribution of household services. They claim that the alternative, and second approach, which involves substituting specialist market services for the various household duties, will overcome the above defect, particularly as it is not unusual for households to employ the part-time services of a housecleaner, a gardener, and a child-care agency. Yet this approach should not be pursued too far because, today at least, housework is undertaken by generalists rather than specialists. Also there are practical problems about the choice of appropriate wage rates.[33]

The third approach involves the opportunity cost principle, which is based on the assumption that rational individuals will allocate their time between housework and paid work so that the marginal value of an hour of housework will be equated with the forgone net return to a marginal hour of paid work. Those who favour this method employ market wage rates, either plus or minus tax, or minus both tax and other work-related costs (including travel and increased costs of food and clothing), the latter being the closest approximation to the theoretical variable.[34] This method, it is claimed, suffers from a number of conceptual and empirical problems. In the first place, as opportunity cost is an equilibrium concept, it will not be appropriate to the extent that individuals are unable to work the number of hours they consider desirable, or are involuntarily unemployed. Second, the opportunity cost of those who are voluntarily unemployed is not known. Third, the available average wage rates are not really appropriate because they do not include net non-pecuniary benefits of paid work. And finally it is rather difficult to obtain data on the appropriate tax rates and job-related expenses that must be subtracted from wage rates to estimate net returns.

The first two theoretical points should not be considered a serious problem in advanced market economies, other than during depressions, and even then only if the focus is on shortrun fluctuations. The existence of involuntary unemployment suggests that the market rate for factor prices is too high to clear factor markets. Hence during a depression the market rate overvalues resources employed in *both* the market and household sectors. While this should not affect longrun comparisons made between years of peak economic activity, as has been done throughout Chapters 2 to 6, it will *overstate* economic performance during depressions. In other words *within* the depression period, true performance will be even worse than recorded performance, irrespective of whether GDP or GCI is employed. The main implication here is that it reinforces my conclusion that the interdepression years from the 1890s to the 1930s was a period of relative and absolute stagnation and decline. The third problem is less important for all workers than for relatively small numbers of professional and managerial groups; but the fourth point poses a difficult problem, particularly in the case of historical estimates.

The arguments for and against competing measurement alternatives fall into place when we consider the theoretical proposition that, for all households treated together, the opportunity cost of labour, as measured by the general market wage rate, is the basis of decisions made by the household as to whether labour time should be reallocated between market work, household work, or leisure. As Becker has shown, single-person households will attempt to maximize their utility by allocating their time between competing uses so that in equilibrium the marginal utility of all uses of time will be equal to each other and to the market wage rate (expressed in 'real' terms).[35] Any change in this real-wage rate will result in a shift of labour time from one use to another until, once again, marginal utilities are equated. He also shows that if all time were spent in the household sector 'the value of time would not be measured by the wage rate but by a shadow price equal to the marginal product of time in the household sector'; but if 'time is [also] spent working in the marketplace, the wage rate has to equal the shadow price of household time . . . otherwise, the marginal value of working time would be less than the marginal value of household time'.[36]

In formal terms, the single-person household receives income from time spent working in the market place, and receives utility from time spent on household activities. (This analysis, in contrast to that of Becker, emphasizes that household utility arises in two ways—indirectly from the production of goods and services that are substitutes for those produced in the market place, and directly from involvement in leisure activities that cannot be marketed.) The utility function is:

$$U = U(x_1, \ldots, x_n, t_{h_1}, \ldots, t_{h_r}) \tag{1}$$

subject to: a budget constraint $\Sigma p_i x_i = I$, where $p_i$ is the price of the $i$th good $x_i$, and $I$ is the household's money income; and a time-budget constraint:

$$\sum_{j=1}^{r} t_{h_j} + t_w = t \tag{2}$$

where $t$ is the total time available during a given time period; $t_{h_j}$ is the time spent on the $j$th activity; and $t_w$ is the time spent in paid employment.

The goods and time-budget constraints are interdependent, and can be combined into one overall constraint:

$$\Sigma p_i x_i + w \Sigma t_{h_j} = wt + v = S \tag{3}$$

where $w$ is the earnings per hour of paid work, $v$ is property income, and $S$ is 'full' or potential income (or the money income when all time is allocated to the market sector).

The equilibrium conditions from maximizing the utility function (1), subject to the full-income constraint in (3) include:

$$MU_{t_{h_k}}/MU_{t_{h_j}} = 1, \text{ and } MU_{t_{h_j}}/MU_{x_i} = w/p_i \tag{4}$$

where $MU$ is the marginal utility of time in various uses, and $p_i$ is the price of market commodities.

The general market wage rate is, therefore, the appropriate theoretical measure of the household shadow price for labour. As McCloskey argues in a different, but relevant, context:[37]

That shadow wages are hard to measure is not much of an objection to including all the income of the nation [including non-market income] in a measure of national income. All things are valued at their marginal values. The super housewife with a high shadow wage earns so to speak a consumer's surplus from consuming housemaking, but so does a pizza lover with a total valuation of pizza higher than its price. The exclusion of consumer's surplus from national income is not a flaw if you believe that national income pretends only to measure the nation's budget constraint, not its happiness.

Happiness, of course, is beyond quantification. Also, as I am concerned to analyse the interaction between the household and market sectors over time (i.e. the shift in labour time between paid and unpaid work), the general market wage rate (i.e. the opportunity cost of household labour viewed as a whole) is the only analytically meaningful measure of the value of household labour services.

The allocation of time between market and non-market activities (including leisure) for an individual can be graphically illustrated by Figure 7.1 (adapted from McCloskey[38]), which is based upon consumption theory. The figure shows that equilibrium is achieved by the tangency between an indifference curve for market goods and non-market time, and the budget line fixed on the horizontal axis at the 24-hour point but free to rotate according to the level of the market wage earned. The slope of the budget line is determined by the money wage divided by the price of market goods. As the market wage increases, the budget line rotates upwards, and the amount of time that the individual

**Figure 7.1 The supply of market and non-market (including leisure) labour**

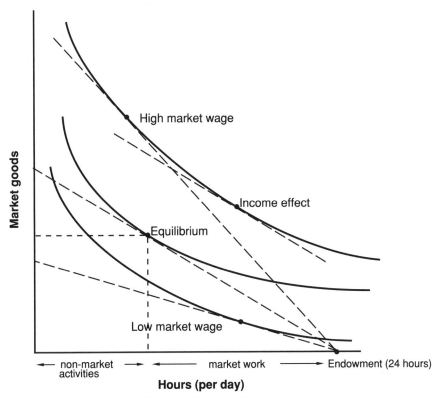

*Source*: Adapted from McCloskey, *Applied theory*.

is prepared to work in the market place will increase, unless the income effect (as in Figure 7.1) outweighs the substitution effect. This determines the supply curve for both market and non-market activities. If however, the income effect is overwhelming at higher wage levels, the market supply curve will be backward bending.

# Methods and sources

A clear working definition of what we are attempting to measure is essential. Household production is treated as the non-market use of household time (including volunteer work) employed in conjunction with non-market capital and land, to produce goods and services that could be, but are not, marketed. Accordingly, it is necessary to identify those people who undertake unpaid and non-marketed work in the household. The data must *not* include paid labour recruited in the marketplace—such as household domestics, house cleaners, window cleaners, gardeners etc.—even though they are engaged in the production of goods and services that are directly consumed by the household employing them. Paid labour of this nature involves market incursions into the household sector—incursions that have undergone considerable fluctuation over the last few hundred years. The definition underlying the statistical work in this book, therefore, is based, not on all economic activities actually undertaken in the household, but rather on those household activities undertaken by unpaid household labour. The definition has a functional rather than a locational base. As we shall see in Chapter 8, a variety of data sources and statistical techniques have been used to estimate the physical quantities of labour employed in unpaid labour in the home. A similar approach, discussed fully in Chapter 9, has been taken to non-labour factors of production.

Briefly, a pragmatic attempt has been made in this book to develop a conceptual framework that utilizes available Australian data over the past two centuries to the best advantage. This approach employs a variety of statistical sources to estimate the annual numbers of males and females working in the household sector, and the value of stocks of private dwellings (including land) and household equipment. These quantities have been valued by employing the opportunity cost approach. The value of household labour services is estimated as the sum of the value of 'primary' household labour (largely female) and the value of 'secondary' household labour (largely male). More precisely, primary household labour consists of full-time household workers (largely females and retired males) together with females who work in both the market and the household sectors, valued by the general market wage rate for adult females. Secondary household labour services comprise the part-time work done in the household sector by males (net of those who have retired) and single people, valued by the market wage rate for adult males. The value of household capital and land services is estimated using an historical discount rate.

# Total social accounts for Australia, 1788–1990

The following tables—7.1 to 7.11—present the first set of total social accounts for Australia over the first two centuries of European–Asian settlement. These accounts, which provide an outline of Australian total economic activity in the longrun, are presented on a household and market basis, and include Gross Community Income (GCI) and Gross Community Capital Formation (GCCF) in both nominal and real terms. As no attempt has been made to deduct either depreciation or net investment income due to non-residents, the estimates are both 'gross' and 'domestic'. The detailed tables underlying these summary estimates are presented and discussed in Chapters 8 and 9.

While it is always possible to make marginal improvements to any set of national accounts, it is my judgement (based on more than twenty-five years practical experience in estimating historical national accounts in Australia[39]) that the estimates presented in Chapters 7, 8, and 9 are on a par with other nonofficial estimates of Australian GDP. More specifically, they are as reliable as estimates of factor income for the service sector made by Butlin (1962), Snooks (1972), and Sinclair (1984),[40] and more reliable than estimates of value added in the manufacturing, agricultural, pastoral, and construction sectors by the same authors, as they are based on the population census which is more reliable, particularly in the nineteenth century, than the various production censuses. The aim in this study has been to make the best use of Australian statistical sources throughout these two centuries. Also, I hope it is not too far from the mark to claim that the Total Economy estimates are on a par, as far as reliability is concerned, with the market estimates of Simon Kuznets in the USA, and Charles Feinstein in the UK.[41]

**Table 7.1　Gross Community Income (current prices), Australia, 1788–1990** ($m)

| Year ending 31st Dec. | Household sector | Market sector | Total economy | Year ending 31st Dec. | Household sector | Market sector | Total economy |
|---|---|---|---|---|---|---|---|
| 1788 | 0.01 | 0.04 | 0.05 | 1843 | 6.43 | 9.50 | 15.93 |
| 1789 | 0.01 | 0.03 | 0.04 | 1844 | 6.82 | 9.75 | 16.57 |
| 1790 | 0.03 | 0.04 | 0.07 | 1845 | 8.27 | 11.23 | 19.50 |
| 1791 | 0.04 | 0.06 | 0.10 | 1846 | 9.33 | 12.94 | 22.27 |
| 1792 | 0.05 | 0.08 | 0.13 | 1847 | 10.50 | 13.83 | 24.33 |
| 1793 | 0.06 | 0.10 | 0.16 | 1848 | 11.11 | 18.55 | 29.66 |
| 1794 | 0.07 | 0.14 | 0.21 | 1849 | 11.01 | 16.39 | 27.40 |
| 1795 | 0.07 | 0.17 | 0.24 | 1850 | 12.57 | 19.21 | 31.78 |
| 1796 | 0.07 | 0.19 | 0.26 | 1851 | 14.48 | 23.19 | 37.67 |
| 1797 | 0.07 | 0.21 | 0.28 | 1852 | 20.29 | 54.20 | 74.49 |
| 1798 | 0.08 | 0.24 | 0.32 | 1853 | 34.48 | 74.41 | 108.89 |
| 1799 | 0.08 | 0.27 | 0.35 | 1854 | 58.79 | 82.46 | 141.25 |
| 1800 | 0.08 | 0.30 | 0.38 | 1855 | 49.89 | 88.39 | 138.28 |
| 1801 | 0.10 | 0.36 | 0.46 | 1856 | 46.52 | 93.42 | 139.94 |
| 1802 | 0.11 | 0.35 | 0.46 | 1857 | 49.96 | 99.03 | 148.99 |
| 1803 | 0.11 | 0.38 | 0.49 | 1858 | 56.66 | 101.15 | 157.81 |
| 1804 | 0.13 | 0.44 | 0.57 | 1859 | 55.34 | 108.12 | 163.46 |
| 1805 | 0.13 | 0.47 | 0.60 | 1860 | 60.81 | 112.54 | 173.35 |
| 1806 | 0.14 | 0.51 | 0.65 | 1861 | 64.7 | 113.2 | 177.9 |
| 1807 | 0.15 | 0.54 | 0.69 | 1862 | 68.6 | 113.2 | 181.8 |
| 1808 | 0.18 | 0.52 | 0.70 | 1863 | 69.9 | 111.4 | 181.3 |
| 1809 | 0.22 | 0.56 | 0.78 | 1864 | 73.9 | 115.2 | 189.1 |
| 1810 | 0.23 | 0.79 | 1.02 | 1865 | 68.7 | 115.4 | 184.1 |
| 1811 | 0.24 | 0.73 | 0.97 | 1866 | 79.0 | 124.2 | 203.2 |
| 1812 | 0.27 | 0.74 | 1.01 | 1867 | 78.9 | 126.6 | 205.5 |
| 1813 | 0.30 | 0.76 | 1.06 | 1868 | 84.6 | 136.2 | 220.8 |
| 1814 | 0.32 | 0.78 | 1.10 | 1869 | 83.5 | 137.2 | 220.7 |
| 1815 | 0.35 | 0.95 | 1.30 | 1870 | 89.1 | 143.8 | 232.9 |
| 1816 | 0.41 | 0.87 | 1.28 | 1871 | 88.1 | 135.4 | 223.5 |
| 1817 | 0.49 | 0.96 | 1.45 | 1872 | 97.4 | 162.4 | 259.8 |
| 1818 | 0.58 | 1.11 | 1.69 | 1873 | 103.3 | 190.6 | 293.9 |
| 1819 | 0.67 | 1.22 | 1.89 | 1874 | 101.6 | 197.8 | 299.4 |
| 1820 | 0.73 | 1.32 | 2.05 | 1875 | 111.3 | 214.2 | 325.5 |
| 1821 | 0.78 | 1.67 | 2.45 | 1876 | 122.1 | 209.4 | 331.5 |
| 1822 | 0.84 | 1.89 | 2.73 | 1877 | 127.9 | 213.8 | 341.7 |
| 1823 | 0.91 | 1.98 | 2.89 | 1878 | 128.8 | 226.8 | 355.6 |
| 1824 | 1.05 | 2.21 | 3.26 | 1879 | 136.7 | 225.2 | 361.9 |
| 1825 | 1.13 | 2.40 | 3.53 | 1880 | 136.4 | 232.0 | 368.4 |
| 1826 | 1.18 | 2.51 | 3.69 | 1881 | 144.9 | 247.0 | 391.9 |
| 1827 | 1.25 | 2.75 | 4.00 | 1882 | 153.7 | 256.2 | 409.9 |
| 1828 | 1.29 | 3.09 | 4.38 | 1883 | 160.2 | 287.4 | 447.6 |
| 1829 | 1.42 | 3.39 | 4.81 | 1884 | 167.2 | 277.8 | 445.0 |
| 1830 | 1.62 | 3.88 | 5.50 | 1885 | 172.4 | 298.0 | 470.4 |
| 1831 | 1.78 | 4.01 | 5.79 | 1886 | 177.1 | 295.8 | 472.9 |
| 1832 | 2.01 | 4.21 | 6.22 | 1887 | 191.3 | 326.0 | 517.3 |
| 1833 | 2.30 | 5.00 | 7.30 | 1888 | 183.9 | 333.4 | 517.3 |
| 1834 | 2.63 | 6.90 | 9.53 | 1889 | 193.0 | 368.2 | 561.2 |
| 1835 | 3.06 | 9.21 | 12.27 | 1890 | 208.9 | 353.4 | 562.3 |
| 1836 | 3.46 | 9.45 | 12.91 | 1891 | 196.5 | 361.8 | 558.3 |
| 1837 | 4.20 | 9.64 | 13.84 | 1892 | 174.8 | 297.8 | 472.6 |
| 1838 | 4.88 | 9.98 | 14.86 | 1893 | 167.5 | 266.6 | 434.1 |
| 1839 | 5.88 | 11.81 | 17.69 | 1894 | 170.6 | 257.0 | 427.6 |
| 1840 | 6.91 | 14.73 | 21.64 | 1895 | 180.0 | 243.8 | 423.8 |
| 1841 | 6.79 | 11.82 | 18.61 | 1896 | 173.6 | 284.4 | 458.0 |
| 1842 | 6.62 | 10.31 | 16.93 | 1897 | 171.7 | 272.4 | 444.1 |

**Table 7.1**   continued

| Year ending 31st Dec. | Household sector | Market sector | Total economy | Year ending 30th June | Household sector | Market sector | Total economy |
|---|---|---|---|---|---|---|---|
| **1898** | 175.0 | 316.6 | 491.6 | **1944** | 1401 | 2802 | 4203 |
| **1899** | 176.9 | 323.2 | 500.1 | **1945** | 1424 | 2727 | 4151 |
| **1900** | 175.2 | 338.0 | 513.2 | **1946** | 1542 | 2826 | 4368 |
| 30th June | | | | **1947** | 1655 | 3050 | 4705 |
| **1901** | 192.0 | 341.2 | 533.2 | **1948** | 1934 | 3786 | 5720 |
| **1902** | 193.4 | 361.6 | 555.0 | **1949** | 2139 | 4349 | 6488 |
| **1903** | 189.3 | 354.2 | 543.5 | **1950** | 2733 | 5149 | 7882 |
| **1904** | 174.8 | 406.0 | 580.8 | **1951** | 3382 | 6867 | 10249 |
| **1905** | 207.7 | 409.4 | 617.1 | **1952** | 3927 | 7425 | 11352 |
| **1906** | 213.8 | 440.4 | 654.2 | **1953** | 4161 | 8408 | 12569 |
| **1907** | 224.5 | 500.0 | 724.5 | **1954** | 4319 | 9169 | 13488 |
| **1908** | 234.7 | 505.2 | 739.9 | **1955** | 4635 | 9745 | 14380 |
| **1909** | 251.1 | 517.6 | 768.7 | **1956** | 4977 | 10547 | 15524 |
| **1910** | 271.4 | 581.4 | 852.8 | **1957** | 5185 | 11474 | 16659 |
| **1911** | 298.1 | 612.6 | 910.7 | **1958** | 5408 | 11708 | 17116 |
| **1912** | 326.4 | 640.6 | 967.0 | **1959** | 5919 | 12553 | 18472 |
| **1913** | 355.2 | 693.4 | 1048.6 | **1960** | 6309 | 13853 | 20162 |
| **1914** | 369.0 | 760.0 | 1129.0 | **1961** | 6766 | 14672 | 21438 |
| **1915** | 379.2 | 680.4 | 1059.6 | **1962** | 6945 | 14974 | 21919 |
| **1916** | 402.0 | 765.0 | 1167.0 | **1963** | 7260 | 16136 | 23396 |
| **1917** | 429.7 | 885.8 | 1315.5 | **1964** | 7836 | 17924 | 25760 |
| **1918** | 451.3 | 917.2 | 1368.5 | **1965** | 8313 | 19722 | 28035 |
| **1919** | 523.2 | 985.8 | 1509.0 | **1966** | 8995 | 20693 | 29688 |
| **1920** | 631.0 | 1075.6 | 1706.6 | **1967** | 9865 | 22787 | 32652 |
| **1921** | 665.6 | 1284.4 | 1950.0 | **1968** | 10967 | 24304 | 35271 |
| **1922** | 706.3 | 1226.2 | 1932.5 | **1969** | 12180 | 27385 | 39565 |
| **1923** | 750.5 | 1300.6 | 2051.1 | **1970** | 13436 | 30278 | 43714 |
| **1924** | 781.0 | 1345.2 | 2126.2 | **1971** | 16276 | 33293 | 49569 |
| **1925** | 822.6 | 1531.2 | 2353.8 | **1972** | 18237 | 37185 | 55422 |
| **1926** | 866.0 | 1440.0 | 2306.0 | **1973** | 22533 | 42355 | 64888 |
| **1927** | 912.8 | 1390.6 | 2303.4 | **1974** | 31800 | 50743 | 82543 |
| **1928** | 948.5 | 1463.4 | 2411.9 | **1975** | 38333 | 61186 | 99519 |
| **1929** | 973.9 | 1449.8 | 2423.7 | **1976** | 45213 | 72079 | 117292 |
| **1930** | 968.5 | 1301.4 | 2269.9 | **1977** | 51655 | 82019 | 133674 |
| **1931** | 873.4 | 1068.8 | 1942.2 | **1978** | 56858 | 88498 | 145356 |
| **1932** | 812.8 | 983.8 | 1796.6 | **1979** | 60686 | 100956 | 161642 |
| **1933** | 809.3 | 1027.0 | 1836.3 | **1980** | 70285 | 114256 | 184541 |
| **1934** | 837.3 | 1107.2 | 1944.5 | **1981** | 81592 | 130152 | 211744 |
| **1935** | 858.6 | 1172.8 | 2031.4 | **1982** | 93160 | 146527 | 239687 |
| **1936** | 897.1 | 1290.0 | 2187.1 | **1983** | 99535 | 158485 | 258020 |
| **1937** | 969.3 | 1436.6 | 2405.9 | **1984** | 106525 | 180007 | 286532 |
| **1938** | 1014.4 | 1557.8 | 2572.2 | **1985** | 115406 | 200044 | 315450 |
| **1939** | 1055.4 | 1537.0 | 2592.4 | **1986** | 123895 | 221962 | 345857 |
| **1940** | 1099 | 1861 | 2960 | **1987** | 130232 | 244541 | 374773 |
| **1941** | 1173 | 1994 | 3167 | **1988** | 147347 | 276343 | 423690 |
| **1942** | 1291 | 2362 | 3653 | **1989** | 160125 | 314141 | 474266 |
| **1943** | 1353 | 2749 | 4102 | **1990** | 175643 | 342523 | 518166 |

**Table 7.2   Household and market shares in Gross Community Income, Australia, 1788–1990** (per cent)

| Year ending 31st Dec. | Household sector | Market sector | Total economy | Year ending 31st Dec. | Household sector | Market sector | Total economy |
|---|---|---|---|---|---|---|---|
| 1788 | 20.0 | 80.0 | 100.0 | 1843 | 40.4 | 59.6 | 100.0 |
| 1789 | 25.0 | 75.0 | 100.0 | 1844 | 41.2 | 58.8 | 100.0 |
| 1790 | 42.9 | 57.1 | 100.0 | 1845 | 42.4 | 57.6 | 100.0 |
| 1791 | 40.0 | 60.0 | 100.0 | 1846 | 41.9 | 58.1 | 100.0 |
| 1792 | 38.5 | 61.5 | 100.0 | 1847 | 43.2 | 56.8 | 100.0 |
| 1793 | 37.5 | 62.5 | 100.0 | 1848 | 37.5 | 62.5 | 100.0 |
| 1794 | 33.3 | 66.7 | 100.0 | 1849 | 40.2 | 59.8 | 100.0 |
| 1795 | 29.2 | 70.8 | 100.0 | 1850 | 39.6 | 60.4 | 100.0 |
| 1796 | 26.9 | 73.1 | 100.0 | 1851 | 38.4 | 61.6 | 100.0 |
| 1797 | 25.0 | 75.0 | 100.0 | 1852 | 27.2 | 72.8 | 100.0 |
| 1798 | 25.0 | 75.0 | 100.0 | 1853 | 31.7 | 68.3 | 100.0 |
| 1799 | 22.9 | 77.1 | 100.0 | 1854 | 41.6 | 58.4 | 100.0 |
| 1800 | 21.1 | 78.9 | 100.0 | 1855 | 36.1 | 63.9 | 100.0 |
| 1801 | 21.7 | 78.3 | 100.0 | 1856 | 33.2 | 66.8 | 100.0 |
| 1802 | 23.9 | 76.1 | 100.0 | 1857 | 33.5 | 66.5 | 100.0 |
| 1803 | 22.4 | 77.6 | 100.0 | 1858 | 35.9 | 64.1 | 100.0 |
| 1804 | 22.8 | 77.2 | 100.0 | 1859 | 33.9 | 66.1 | 100.0 |
| 1805 | 21.7 | 78.3 | 100.0 | 1860 | 35.1 | 64.9 | 100.0 |
| 1806 | 21.5 | 78.5 | 100.0 | 1861 | 36.4 | 63.6 | 100.0 |
| 1807 | 21.7 | 78.3 | 100.0 | 1862 | 37.7 | 62.3 | 100.0 |
| 1808 | 25.7 | 74.3 | 100.0 | 1863 | 38.6 | 61.4 | 100.0 |
| 1809 | 28.2 | 71.8 | 100.0 | 1864 | 39.1 | 60.9 | 100.0 |
| 1810 | 22.5 | 77.5 | 100.0 | 1865 | 37.3 | 62.7 | 100.0 |
| 1811 | 24.7 | 75.3 | 100.0 | 1866 | 38.9 | 61.1 | 100.0 |
| 1812 | 26.7 | 73.3 | 100.0 | 1867 | 38.4 | 61.6 | 100.0 |
| 1813 | 28.3 | 71.7 | 100.0 | 1868 | 38.3 | 61.7 | 100.0 |
| 1814 | 29.1 | 70.9 | 100.0 | 1869 | 37.8 | 62.2 | 100.0 |
| 1815 | 26.9 | 73.1 | 100.0 | 1870 | 38.3 | 61.7 | 100.0 |
| 1816 | 32.0 | 68.0 | 100.0 | 1871 | 39.4 | 60.6 | 100.0 |
| 1817 | 33.8 | 66.2 | 100.0 | 1872 | 37.5 | 62.5 | 100.0 |
| 1818 | 34.3 | 65.7 | 100.0 | 1873 | 35.1 | 64.9 | 100.0 |
| 1819 | 35.4 | 64.6 | 100.0 | 1874 | 33.9 | 66.1 | 100.0 |
| 1820 | 35.6 | 64.4 | 100.0 | 1875 | 34.2 | 65.8 | 100.0 |
| 1821 | 31.8 | 68.2 | 100.0 | 1876 | 36.8 | 63.2 | 100.0 |
| 1822 | 30.8 | 69.2 | 100.0 | 1877 | 37.4 | 62.6 | 100.0 |
| 1823 | 31.5 | 68.5 | 100.0 | 1878 | 36.2 | 63.8 | 100.0 |
| 1824 | 32.2 | 67.8 | 100.0 | 1879 | 37.8 | 62.2 | 100.0 |
| 1825 | 32.0 | 68.0 | 100.0 | 1880 | 37.0 | 63.0 | 100.0 |
| 1826 | 32.0 | 68.0 | 100.0 | 1881 | 37.0 | 63.0 | 100.0 |
| 1827 | 31.3 | 68.8 | 100.0 | 1882 | 37.5 | 62.5 | 100.0 |
| 1828 | 29.5 | 70.5 | 100.0 | 1883 | 35.8 | 64.2 | 100.0 |
| 1829 | 29.5 | 70.5 | 100.0 | 1884 | 37.6 | 62.4 | 100.0 |
| 1830 | 29.5 | 70.5 | 100.0 | 1885 | 36.6 | 63.4 | 100.0 |
| 1831 | 30.7 | 69.3 | 100.0 | 1886 | 37.4 | 62.6 | 100.0 |
| 1832 | 32.3 | 67.7 | 100.0 | 1887 | 37.0 | 63.0 | 100.0 |
| 1833 | 31.5 | 68.5 | 100.0 | 1888 | 35.5 | 64.5 | 100.0 |
| 1834 | 27.6 | 72.4 | 100.0 | 1889 | 34.4 | 65.6 | 100.0 |
| 1835 | 24.9 | 75.1 | 100.0 | 1890 | 37.2 | 62.8 | 100.0 |
| 1836 | 26.8 | 73.2 | 100.0 | 1891 | 35.2 | 64.8 | 100.0 |
| 1837 | 30.3 | 69.7 | 100.0 | 1892 | 37.0 | 63.0 | 100.0 |
| 1838 | 32.8 | 67.2 | 100.0 | 1893 | 38.6 | 61.4 | 100.0 |
| 1839 | 33.2 | 66.8 | 100.0 | 1894 | 39.9 | 60.1 | 100.0 |
| 1840 | 31.9 | 68.1 | 100.0 | 1895 | 42.5 | 57.5 | 100.0 |
| 1841 | 36.5 | 63.5 | 100.0 | 1896 | 37.9 | 62.1 | 100.0 |
| 1842 | 39.1 | 60.9 | 100.0 | 1897 | 38.7 | 61.3 | 100.0 |

**Table 7.2**  continued

| Year ending 31st Dec. | Household sector | Market sector | Total economy | Year ending 30th June | Household sector | Market sector | Total economy |
|---|---|---|---|---|---|---|---|
| **1898** | 35.6 | 64.4 | 100.0 | **1944** | 33.3 | 66.7 | 100.0 |
| **1899** | 35.4 | 64.6 | 100.0 | **1945** | 34.3 | 65.7 | 100.0 |
| **1900** | 34.1 | 65.9 | 100.0 | **1946** | 35.3 | 64.7 | 100.0 |
| 30th June | | | | **1947** | 35.2 | 64.8 | 100.0 |
| **1901** | 36.0 | 64.0 | 100.0 | **1948** | 33.8 | 66.2 | 100.0 |
| **1902** | 34.8 | 65.2 | 100.0 | **1949** | 33.0 | 67.0 | 100.0 |
| **1903** | 34.8 | 65.2 | 100.0 | **1950** | 34.7 | 65.3 | 100.0 |
| **1904** | 30.1 | 69.9 | 100.0 | **1951** | 33.0 | 67.0 | 100.0 |
| **1905** | 33.7 | 66.3 | 100.0 | **1952** | 34.6 | 65.4 | 100.0 |
| **1906** | 32.7 | 67.3 | 100.0 | **1953** | 33.1 | 66.9 | 100.0 |
| **1907** | 31.0 | 69.0 | 100.0 | **1954** | 32.0 | 68.0 | 100.0 |
| **1908** | 31.7 | 68.3 | 100.0 | **1955** | 32.2 | 67.8 | 100.0 |
| **1909** | 32.7 | 67.3 | 100.0 | **1956** | 32.1 | 67.9 | 100.0 |
| **1910** | 31.8 | 68.2 | 100.0 | **1957** | 31.1 | 68.9 | 100.0 |
| **1911** | 32.7 | 67.3 | 100.0 | **1958** | 31.6 | 68.4 | 100.0 |
| **1912** | 33.8 | 66.2 | 100.0 | **1959** | 32.0 | 68.0 | 100.0 |
| **1913** | 33.9 | 66.1 | 100.0 | **1960** | 31.3 | 68.7 | 100.0 |
| **1914** | 32.7 | 67.3 | 100.0 | **1961** | 31.6 | 68.4 | 100.0 |
| **1915** | 35.8 | 64.2 | 100.0 | **1962** | 31.7 | 68.3 | 100.0 |
| **1916** | 34.4 | 65.6 | 100.0 | **1963** | 31.0 | 69.0 | 100.0 |
| **1917** | 32.7 | 67.3 | 100.0 | **1964** | 30.4 | 69.6 | 100.0 |
| **1918** | 33.0 | 67.0 | 100.0 | **1965** | 29.7 | 70.3 | 100.0 |
| **1919** | 34.7 | 65.3 | 100.0 | **1966** | 30.3 | 69.7 | 100.0 |
| **1920** | 37.0 | 63.0 | 100.0 | **1967** | 30.2 | 69.8 | 100.0 |
| **1921** | 34.1 | 65.9 | 100.0 | **1968** | 31.1 | 68.9 | 100.0 |
| **1922** | 36.5 | 63.5 | 100.0 | **1969** | 30.8 | 69.2 | 100.0 |
| **1923** | 36.6 | 63.4 | 100.0 | **1970** | 30.7 | 69.3 | 100.0 |
| **1924** | 36.7 | 63.3 | 100.0 | **1971** | 32.8 | 67.2 | 100.0 |
| **1925** | 34.9 | 65.1 | 100.0 | **1972** | 32.9 | 67.1 | 100.0 |
| **1926** | 37.6 | 62.4 | 100.0 | **1973** | 34.7 | 65.3 | 100.0 |
| **1927** | 39.6 | 60.4 | 100.0 | **1974** | 38.5 | 61.5 | 100.0 |
| **1928** | 39.3 | 60.7 | 100.0 | **1975** | 38.5 | 61.5 | 100.0 |
| **1929** | 40.2 | 59.8 | 100.0 | **1976** | 38.5 | 61.5 | 100.0 |
| **1930** | 42.7 | 57.3 | 100.0 | **1977** | 38.6 | 61.4 | 100.0 |
| **1931** | 45.0 | 55.0 | 100.0 | **1978** | 39.1 | 60.9 | 100.0 |
| **1932** | 45.2 | 54.8 | 100.0 | **1979** | 37.5 | 62.5 | 100.0 |
| **1933** | 44.1 | 55.9 | 100.0 | **1980** | 38.1 | 61.9 | 100.0 |
| **1934** | 43.1 | 56.9 | 100.0 | **1981** | 38.5 | 61.5 | 100.0 |
| **1935** | 42.3 | 57.7 | 100.0 | **1982** | 38.9 | 61.1 | 100.0 |
| **1936** | 41.0 | 59.0 | 100.0 | **1983** | 38.6 | 61.4 | 100.0 |
| **1937** | 40.3 | 59.7 | 100.0 | **1984** | 37.2 | 62.8 | 100.0 |
| **1938** | 39.4 | 60.6 | 100.0 | **1985** | 36.6 | 63.4 | 100.0 |
| **1939** | 40.7 | 59.3 | 100.0 | **1986** | 35.8 | 64.2 | 100.0 |
| **1940** | 37.1 | 62.9 | 100.0 | **1987** | 34.7 | 65.3 | 100.0 |
| **1941** | 37.0 | 63.0 | 100.0 | **1988** | 34.8 | 65.2 | 100.0 |
| **1942** | 35.3 | 64.7 | 100.0 | **1989** | 33.8 | 66.2 | 100.0 |
| **1943** | 33.0 | 67.0 | 100.0 | **1990** | 33.9 | 66.1 | 100.0 |

**Table 7.3    Real Gross Community Income (GDP deflator, 1966/67 prices), Australia, 1800–1990 ($m)**

| Year ending 31st Dec. | Household sector | Market sector | Total economy | Year ending 31st Dec. | Household sector | Market sector | Total economy |
|---|---|---|---|---|---|---|---|
| 1800 | 1 | 2 | 3 | 1855 | 231 | 409 | 640 |
| 1801 | 1 | 3 | 4 | 1856 | 282 | 566 | 848 |
| 1802 | 1 | 3 | 4 | 1857 | 274 | 543 | 817 |
| 1803 | 1 | 3 | 4 | 1858 | 274 | 490 | 764 |
| 1804 | 1 | 3 | 4 | 1859 | 333 | 651 | 984 |
| 1805 | 1 | 3 | 4 | 1860 | 356 | 659 | 1015 |
| 1806 | 1 | 4 | 5 | 1861 | 373 | 653 | 1026 |
| 1807 | 1 | 4 | 5 | 1862 | 393 | 648 | 1041 |
| 1808 | 1 | 4 | 5 | 1863 | 420 | 669 | 1089 |
| 1809 | 2 | 4 | 6 | 1864 | 478 | 746 | 1224 |
| 1810 | 2 | 6 | 8 | 1865 | 440 | 739 | 1179 |
| 1811 | 2 | 5 | 7 | 1866 | 495 | 779 | 1274 |
| 1812 | 2 | 5 | 7 | 1867 | 548 | 880 | 1428 |
| 1813 | 2 | 5 | 7 | 1868 | 580 | 934 | 1514 |
| 1814 | 2 | 6 | 8 | 1869 | 579 | 951 | 1530 |
| 1815 | 3 | 7 | 10 | 1870 | 620 | 1000 | 1620 |
| 1816 | 3 | 6 | 9 | 1871 | 615 | 945 | 1560 |
| 1817 | 4 | 7 | 11 | 1872 | 631 | 1051 | 1682 |
| 1818 | 4 | 8 | 12 | 1873 | 636 | 1173 | 1809 |
| 1819 | 5 | 9 | 14 | 1874 | 640 | 1246 | 1886 |
| 1820 | 5 | 9 | 14 | 1875 | 718 | 1381 | 2099 |
| 1821 | 6 | 12 | 18 | 1876 | 792 | 1358 | 2150 |
| 1822 | 6 | 14 | 20 | 1877 | 844 | 1411 | 2255 |
| 1823 | 6 | 13 | 19 | 1878 | 889 | 1565 | 2454 |
| 1824 | 7 | 14 | 21 | 1879 | 941 | 1550 | 2491 |
| 1825 | 7 | 15 | 22 | 1880 | 949 | 1613 | 2562 |
| 1826 | 7 | 16 | 23 | 1881 | 1016 | 1732 | 2748 |
| 1827 | 8 | 17 | 25 | 1882 | 1029 | 1715 | 2744 |
| 1828 | 8 | 19 | 27 | 1883 | 1038 | 1863 | 2901 |
| 1829 | 9 | 22 | 31 | 1884 | 1114 | 1851 | 2965 |
| 1830 | 13 | 31 | 44 | 1885 | 1160 | 2005 | 3165 |
| 1831 | 15 | 33 | 48 | 1886 | 1207 | 2016 | 3223 |
| 1832 | 17 | 35 | 52 | 1887 | 1345 | 2293 | 3638 |
| 1833 | 17 | 38 | 55 | 1888 | 1281 | 2323 | 3604 |
| 1834 | 16 | 42 | 58 | 1889 | 1301 | 2483 | 3784 |
| 1835 | 19 | 56 | 75 | 1890 | 1394 | 2359 | 3753 |
| 1836 | 20 | 56 | 76 | 1891 | 1370 | 2523 | 3893 |
| 1837 | 25 | 58 | 83 | 1892 | 1302 | 2217 | 3519 |
| 1838 | 30 | 61 | 91 | 1893 | 1305 | 2078 | 3383 |
| 1839 | 29 | 58 | 87 | 1894 | 1411 | 2126 | 3537 |
| 1840 | 38 | 82 | 120 | 1895 | 1537 | 2082 | 3619 |
| 1841 | 41 | 72 | 113 | 1896 | 1437 | 2354 | 3791 |
| 1842 | 43 | 66 | 109 | 1897 | 1373 | 2179 | 3552 |
| 1843 | 53 | 79 | 132 | 1898 | 1385 | 2505 | 3890 |
| 1844 | 64 | 92 | 156 | 1899 | 1383 | 2527 | 3910 |
| 1845 | 72 | 98 | 170 | 1900 | 1368 | 3029 | 4397 |
| 1846 | 83 | 115 | 198 | 30th June | | | |
| 1847 | 106 | 139 | 245 | 1901 | 1443 | 2565 | 4008 |
| 1848 | 115 | 192 | 307 | 1902 | 1509 | 2823 | 4332 |
| 1849 | 121 | 181 | 302 | 1903 | 1434 | 2683 | 4117 |
| 1850 | 118 | 181 | 299 | 1904 | 1410 | 3274 | 4684 |
| 1851 | 149 | 238 | 387 | 1905 | 1662 | 3275 | 4937 |
| 1852 | 124 | 332 | 456 | 1906 | 1656 | 3411 | 5067 |
| 1853 | 180 | 388 | 568 | 1907 | 1768 | 3937 | 5705 |
| 1854 | 255 | 358 | 613 | 1908 | 1713 | 3688 | 5401 |

**Table 7.3** continued

| Year ending 30th June | Household sector | Market sector | Total economy | Year ending 30th June | Household sector | Market sector | Total economy |
|---|---|---|---|---|---|---|---|
| **1909** | 1781 | 3671 | 5452 | **1950** | 5827 | 10979 | 16806 |
| **1910** | 1872 | 4010 | 5882 | **1951** | 5742 | 11659 | 17401 |
| **1911** | 2042 | 4196 | 6238 | **1952** | 6395 | 12091 | 18486 |
| **1912** | 2053 | 4029 | 6082 | **1953** | 5927 | 11977 | 17904 |
| **1913** | 2248 | 4389 | 6637 | **1954** | 5982 | 12699 | 18681 |
| **1914** | 2182 | 4494 | 6676 | **1955** | 6383 | 13421 | 19804 |
| **1915** | 2039 | 3658 | 5697 | **1956** | 6645 | 14081 | 20726 |
| **1916** | 2083 | 3964 | 6047 | **1957** | 6480 | 14341 | 20821 |
| **1917** | 2046 | 4218 | 6264 | **1958** | 6752 | 14617 | 21369 |
| **1918** | 2032 | 4130 | 6162 | **1959** | 7386 | 15672 | 23058 |
| **1919** | 2235 | 4211 | 6446 | **1960** | 7528 | 16529 | 24057 |
| **1920** | 2328 | 3969 | 6297 | **1961** | 7839 | 16999 | 24838 |
| **1921** | 2531 | 4884 | 7415 | **1962** | 7946 | 17133 | 25079 |
| **1922** | 2835 | 4923 | 7758 | **1963** | 8221 | 18272 | 26493 |
| **1923** | 2843 | 4927 | 7770 | **1964** | 8554 | 19566 | 28120 |
| **1924** | 2958 | 5095 | 8053 | **1965** | 8844 | 20981 | 29825 |
| **1925** | 3024 | 5629 | 8653 | **1966** | 9292 | 21377 | 30669 |
| **1926** | 3208 | 5333 | 8541 | **1967** | 9865 | 22787 | 32652 |
| **1927** | 3381 | 5150 | 8531 | **1968** | 10668 | 23642 | 34310 |
| **1928** | 3460 | 5339 | 8799 | **1969** | 11467 | 25781 | 37248 |
| **1929** | 3540 | 5270 | 8810 | **1970** | 12103 | 27275 | 39378 |
| **1930** | 3904 | 5245 | 9149 | **1971** | 14012 | 28661 | 42673 |
| **1931** | 3882 | 4750 | 8632 | **1972** | 14775 | 30126 | 44901 |
| **1932** | 3906 | 4728 | 8634 | **1973** | 16691 | 31374 | 48065 |
| **1933** | 3948 | 5010 | 8958 | **1974** | 20478 | 32676 | 53154 |
| **1934** | 3950 | 5223 | 9173 | **1975** | 20891 | 33346 | 54237 |
| **1935** | 3921 | 5355 | 9276 | **1976** | 21388 | 34098 | 55486 |
| **1936** | 3916 | 5631 | 9547 | **1977** | 22004 | 34939 | 56943 |
| **1937** | 4004 | 5934 | 9938 | **1978** | 22479 | 34988 | 57467 |
| **1938** | 4123 | 6333 | 10456 | **1979** | 22233 | 36986 | 59219 |
| **1939** | 4205 | 6124 | 10329 | **1980** | 23209 | 37729 | 60938 |
| **1940** | 4243 | 7185 | 11428 | **1981** | 24423 | 38958 | 63381 |
| **1941** | 4493 | 7637 | 12130 | **1982** | 25310 | 39808 | 65118 |
| **1942** | 4872 | 8913 | 13785 | **1983** | 24475 | 38970 | 63445 |
| **1943** | 4849 | 9853 | 14702 | **1984** | 24479 | 41365 | 65844 |
| **1944** | 4880 | 9760 | 14640 | **1985** | 25114 | 43532 | 68646 |
| **1945** | 4779 | 9151 | 13930 | **1986** | 25245 | 45226 | 70471 |
| **1946** | 4802 | 8801 | 13603 | **1987** | 25921 | 46395 | 72316 |
| **1947** | 4702 | 8665 | 13367 | **1988** | 25879 | 48536 | 74415 |
| **1948** | 4946 | 9683 | 14629 | **1989** | 25678 | 50377 | 76055 |
| **1949** | 4974 | 10114 | 15088 | **1990** | 26710 | 52088 | 78798 |

**Table 7.4   Alternative real Gross Community Income (FC/GDP deflators, 1966/67 prices), Australia, 1861–1990 ($m)**

| Year ending 31st Dec. | Household sector | Market sector | Total economy | Year ending 31st Dec. | Household sector | Market sector | Total economy |
|---|---|---|---|---|---|---|---|
| 1861 | 329 | 653 | 982 | 1894 | 1422 | 2126 | 3548 |
| 1862 | 367 | 648 | 1015 | 1895 | 1487 | 2082 | 3569 |
| 1863 | 380 | 670 | 1050 | 1896 | 1336 | 2354 | 3690 |
| 1864 | 417 | 746 | 1163 | 1897 | 1244 | 2179 | 3423 |
| 1865 | 335 | 739 | 1074 | 1898 | 1232 | 2505 | 3737 |
| 1866 | 416 | 779 | 1195 | 1899 | 1282 | 2527 | 3809 |
| 1867 | 512 | 880 | 1392 | 1900 | 1308 | 3029 | 4337 |
| 1868 | 525 | 934 | 1459 | *30th June* | | | |
| 1869 | 568 | 952 | 1520 | 1901 | 1352 | 2565 | 3917 |
| 1870 | 619 | 1000 | 1619 | 1902 | 1432 | 2823 | 4255 |
| 1871 | 591 | 945 | 1536 | 1903 | 1392 | 2683 | 4075 |
| 1872 | 677 | 1051 | 1728 | 1904 | 1410 | 3274 | 4684 |
| 1873 | 658 | 1173 | 1831 | 1905 | 1689 | 3275 | 4964 |
| 1874 | 601 | 1246 | 1847 | 1906 | 1670 | 3411 | 5081 |
| 1875 | 687 | 1381 | 2068 | 1907 | 1840 | 3937 | 5777 |
| 1876 | 731 | 1358 | 2089 | 1908 | 1726 | 3688 | 5414 |
| 1877 | 780 | 1411 | 2191 | 1909 | 1756 | 3671 | 5427 |
| 1878 | 837 | 1565 | 2402 | 1910 | 1834 | 4010 | 5844 |
| 1879 | 942 | 1550 | 2492 | 1911 | 1987 | 4196 | 6183 |
| 1880 | 982 | 1613 | 2595 | 1912 | 1978 | 4029 | 6007 |
| 1881 | 1057 | 1732 | 2789 | 1913 | 2206 | 4389 | 6595 |
| 1882 | 955 | 1715 | 2670 | 1914 | 2073 | 4494 | 6567 |
| 1883 | 1001 | 1863 | 2864 | 1915 | 1850 | 3658 | 5508 |
| 1884 | 1079 | 1851 | 2930 | 1916 | 1755 | 3964 | 5719 |
| 1885 | 1084 | 2005 | 3089 | 1917 | 1580 | 4218 | 5798 |
| 1886 | 1054 | 2016 | 3070 | 1918 | 1589 | 4130 | 5719 |
| 1887 | 1259 | 2293 | 3552 | 1919 | 1804 | 4211 | 6015 |
| 1888 | 1210 | 2323 | 3533 | 1920 | 2132 | 3969 | 6101 |
| 1889 | 1199 | 2483 | 3682 | 1921 | 2249 | 4884 | 7133 |
| 1890 | 1289 | 2359 | 3648 | 1922 | 2597 | 4923 | 7520 |
| 1891 | 1284 | 2523 | 3807 | 1923 | 2661 | 4927 | 7588 |
| 1892 | 1197 | 2217 | 3414 | 1924 | 2947 | 5096 | 8043 |
| 1893 | 1196 | 2078 | 3274 | 1925 | 3152 | 5629 | 8781 |

Note: FC = final consumption price index used to deflate household sector.

**Table 7.4** continued

| Year ending 30th June | Household sector | Market sector | Total economy | Year ending 30th June | Household sector | Market sector | Total economy |
|---|---|---|---|---|---|---|---|
| 1926 | 3138 | 5333 | 8471 | 1959 | 7232 | 15672 | 22904 |
| 1927 | 3319 | 5150 | 8469 | 1960 | 7502 | 16529 | 24031 |
| 1928 | 3474 | 5339 | 8813 | 1961 | 7715 | 16999 | 24714 |
| 1929 | 3491 | 5270 | 8761 | 1962 | 7874 | 17133 | 25007 |
| 1930 | 3739 | 5246 | 8985 | 1963 | 8148 | 18272 | 26420 |
| 1931 | 3580 | 4750 | 8330 | 1964 | 8659 | 19566 | 28225 |
| 1932 | 3596 | 4728 | 8324 | 1965 | 8881 | 20981 | 29862 |
| 1933 | 3629 | 5010 | 8639 | 1966 | 9292 | 21377 | 30669 |
| 1934 | 3823 | 5223 | 9046 | 1967 | 9865 | 22787 | 32652 |
| 1935 | 3563 | 5355 | 8918 | 1968 | 10627 | 23642 | 34269 |
| 1936 | 3722 | 5631 | 9353 | 1969 | 11501 | 25781 | 37282 |
| 1937 | 3940 | 5934 | 9874 | 1970 | 12215 | 27275 | 39490 |
| 1938 | 3917 | 6333 | 10250 | 1971 | 13935 | 28661 | 42596 |
| 1939 | 3665 | 6124 | 9789 | 1972 | 14636 | 30126 | 44762 |
| 1940 | 3580 | 7185 | 10765 | 1973 | 17032 | 31374 | 48406 |
| 1941 | 3654 | 7637 | 11291 | 1974 | 21457 | 32676 | 54133 |
| 1942 | 3865 | 8913 | 12778 | 1975 | 21682 | 33346 | 55028 |
| 1943 | 3748 | 9853 | 13601 | 1976 | 22098 | 34098 | 56196 |
| 1944 | 3881 | 9760 | 13641 | 1977 | 22636 | 34939 | 57575 |
| 1945 | 4045 | 9151 | 13196 | 1978 | 22825 | 34988 | 57813 |
| 1946 | 4112 | 8801 | 12913 | 1979 | 22327 | 36986 | 59313 |
| 1947 | 4402 | 8665 | 13067 | 1980 | 23460 | 37729 | 61189 |
| 1948 | 4835 | 9683 | 14518 | 1981 | 24792 | 38958 | 63750 |
| 1949 | 5009 | 10114 | 15123 | 1982 | 25878 | 39808 | 65686 |
| 1950 | 5890 | 10979 | 16869 | 1983 | 24940 | 38970 | 63910 |
| 1951 | 6467 | 11659 | 18126 | 1984 | 24854 | 41365 | 66219 |
| 1952 | 6214 | 12091 | 18305 | 1985 | 25386 | 43532 | 68918 |
| 1953 | 6101 | 11977 | 18078 | 1986 | 25167 | 45226 | 70393 |
| 1954 | 6126 | 12699 | 18825 | 1987 | 25537 | 46395 | 71932 |
| 1955 | 6455 | 13421 | 19876 | 1988 | 25688 | 48536 | 74224 |
| 1956 | 6672 | 14081 | 20753 | 1989 | 26092 | 50377 | 76469 |
| 1957 | 6555 | 14341 | 20896 | 1990 | 26890 | 52088 | 78978 |
| 1958 | 6718 | 14617 | 21335 | | | | |

**Table 7.5    Real Gross Community Income (GCI) per capita and per household (1966/67 prices), Australia, 1800–1990**

| Year ending 31st Dec. | GCI per capita ($) | GCI per household ($'000) | Year ending 31st Dec. | GCI per capita ($) | GCI per household ($'000) |
|---|---|---|---|---|---|
| 1800 | 551 | 5.9 | 1848 | 749 | 4.7 |
| 1801 | 644 | 6.9 | 1849 | 641 | 3.9 |
| 1802 | 546 | 5.9 | 1850 | 593 | 3.5 |
| 1803 | 529 | 5.7 | 1851 | 729 | 5.0 |
| 1804 | 504 | 5.3 | 1852 | 766 | 5.2 |
| 1805 | 497 | 5.2 | 1853 | 776 | 5.2 |
| 1806 | 605 | 6.3 | 1854 | 701 | 4.5 |
| 1807 | 544 | 5.7 | 1855 | 675 | 4.1 |
| 1808 | 466 | 4.8 | 1856 | 833 | 4.9 |
| 1809 | 414 | 4.3 | 1857 | 733 | 4.0 |
| 1810 | 580 | 6.0 | 1858 | 624 | 3.3 |
| 1811 | 484 | 5.0 | 1859 | 770 | 3.9 |
| 1812 | 455 | 4.7 | 1860 | 760 | 3.7 |
| 1813 | 480 | 5.0 | 1861 | 841 | 4.0 |
| 1814 | 544 | 5.6 | 1862 | 841 | 4.1 |
| 1815 | 572 | 5.9 | 1863 | 833 | 4.1 |
| 1816 | 436 | 4.5 | 1864 | 878 | 4.3 |
| 1817 | 407 | 4.2 | 1865 | 773 | 3.8 |
| 1818 | 407 | 4.2 | 1866 | 828 | 4.1 |
| 1819 | 365 | 3.7 | 1867 | 938 | 4.7 |
| 1820 | 371 | 3.8 | 1868 | 947 | 4.7 |
| 1821 | 432 | 4.4 | 1869 | 954 | 4.8 |
| 1822 | 461 | 4.6 | 1870 | 983 | 5.0 |
| 1823 | 401 | 4.0 | 1871 | 903 | 4.6 |
| 1824 | 378 | 3.8 | 1872 | 992 | 5.1 |
| 1825 | 365 | 3.6 | 1873 | 1020 | 5.3 |
| 1826 | 373 | 3.7 | 1874 | 998 | 5.3 |
| 1827 | 374 | 3.7 | 1875 | 1089 | 5.8 |
| 1828 | 395 | 3.9 | 1876 | 1067 | 5.7 |
| 1829 | 433 | 4.2 | 1877 | 1079 | 5.9 |
| 1830 | 547 | 5.2 | 1878 | 1148 | 6.3 |
| 1831 | 542 | 5.1 | 1879 | 1152 | 6.4 |
| 1832 | 525 | 4.9 | 1880 | 1163 | 6.5 |
| 1833 | 478 | 4.5 | 1881 | 1209 | 6.8 |
| 1834 | 472 | 4.4 | 1882 | 1118 | 6.2 |
| 1835 | 574 | 5.3 | 1883 | 1143 | 6.5 |
| 1836 | 520 | 4.8 | 1884 | 1124 | 6.3 |
| 1837 | 513 | 4.6 | 1885 | 1147 | 6.4 |
| 1838 | 485 | 4.3 | 1886 | 1101 | 6.2 |
| 1839 | 417 | 3.6 | 1887 | 1233 | 6.9 |
| 1840 | 523 | 4.4 | 1888 | 1185 | 6.6 |
| 1841 | 416 | 3.4 | 1889 | 1202 | 6.7 |
| 1842 | 362 | 2.9 | 1890 | 1158 | 6.4 |
| 1843 | 412 | 3.2 | 1891 | 1175 | 6.5 |
| 1844 | 453 | 3.4 | 1892 | 1033 | 5.6 |
| 1845 | 470 | 3.3 | 1893 | 974 | 5.3 |
| 1846 | 529 | 3.6 | 1894 | 1035 | 5.6 |
| 1847 | 629 | 4.1 | 1895 | 1022 | 5.5 |

**Table 7.5**   continued

| Year ending 31st Dec. | GCI per capita ($) | GCI per household ($'000) | Year ending 30th June | GCI per capita ($) | GCI per household ($'000) |
|---|---|---|---|---|---|
| **1896** | 1039 | 5.6 | **1943** | 1871 | 7.6 |
| **1897** | 946 | 5.1 | **1944** | 1857 | 7.6 |
| **1898** | 1020 | 5.5 | **1945** | 1776 | 7.3 |
| **1899** | 1025 | 5.5 | **1946** | 1718 | 7.1 |
| **1900** | 1152 | 6.2 | **1947** | 1711 | 7.0 |
| 30th June | | | **1948** | 1863 | 7.6 |
| **1901** | 1024 | 5.5 | **1949** | 1880 | 7.7 |
| **1902** | 1098 | 5.9 | **1950** | 2031 | 8.3 |
| **1903** | 1041 | 5.6 | **1951** | 2125 | 8.6 |
| **1904** | 1179 | 6.3 | **1952** | 2094 | 8.4 |
| **1905** | 1231 | 6.6 | **1953** | 2031 | 8.0 |
| **1906** | 1242 | 6.6 | **1954** | 2071 | 8.0 |
| **1907** | 1388 | 7.3 | **1955** | 2134 | 8.3 |
| **1908** | 1279 | 6.6 | **1956** | 2177 | 8.4 |
| **1909** | 1255 | 6.4 | **1957** | 2144 | 8.3 |
| **1910** | 1321 | 6.7 | **1958** | 2145 | 8.3 |
| **1911** | 1352 | 6.9 | **1959** | 2254 | 8.7 |
| **1912** | 1266 | 6.5 | **1960** | 2312 | 8.9 |
| **1913** | 1348 | 6.9 | **1961** | 2331 | 8.9 |
| **1914** | 1321 | 6.7 | **1962** | 2313 | 8.8 |
| **1915** | 1108 | 5.5 | **1963** | 2397 | 9.1 |
| **1916** | 1163 | 5.6 | **1964** | 2509 | 9.5 |
| **1917** | 1164 | 5.6 | **1965** | 2602 | 9.7 |
| **1918** | 1126 | 5.5 | **1966** | 2644 | 9.8 |
| **1919** | 1134 | 5.7 | **1967** | 2769 | 10.2 |
| **1920** | 1127 | 5.6 | **1968** | 2856 | 10.4 |
| **1921** | 1294 | 6.4 | **1969** | 3044 | 11.0 |
| **1922** | 1334 | 6.6 | **1970** | 3163 | 11.3 |
| **1923** | 1318 | 6.4 | **1971** | 3293 | 11.7 |
| **1924** | 1367 | 6.6 | **1972** | 3393 | 12.0 |
| **1925** | 1463 | 6.9 | **1973** | 3611 | 12.6 |
| **1926** | 1383 | 6.4 | **1974** | 3977 | 13.8 |
| **1927** | 1355 | 6.2 | **1975** | 3982 | 13.6 |
| **1928** | 1387 | 6.2 | **1976** | 4024 | 13.6 |
| **1929** | 1361 | 6.1 | **1977** | 4080 | 13.6 |
| **1930** | 1382 | 6.1 | **1978** | 4048 | 13.4 |
| **1931** | 1271 | 5.6 | **1979** | 4109 | 13.5 |
| **1932** | 1260 | 5.6 | **1980** | 4191 | 13.6 |
| **1933** | 1298 | 5.7 | **1981** | 4305 | 13.9 |
| **1934** | 1349 | 5.9 | **1982** | 4364 | 14.0 |
| **1935** | 1320 | 5.7 | **1983** | 4179 | 13.3 |
| **1936** | 1373 | 5.8 | **1984** | 4276 | 13.5 |
| **1937** | 1437 | 6.0 | **1985** | 4395 | 13.8 |
| **1938** | 1478 | 6.1 | **1986** | 4427 | 13.8 |
| **1939** | 1397 | 5.7 | **1987** | 4457 | 13.8 |
| **1940** | 1521 | 6.2 | **1988** | 4525 | 14.1 |
| **1941** | 1581 | 6.4 | **1989** | 4580 | 14.1 |
| **1942** | 1774 | 7.2 | **1990** | 4657 | 14.2 |

**Table 7.6   Gross Community Capital Formation (current prices), Australia, 1861–1990 ($m)**

| Year ending 31st Dec. | Household sector | Market sector Private | Market sector Public* | Market sector Total | Total economy |
|---|---|---|---|---|---|
| 1861 | 6.17 | 3.74 | 5.78 | 9.52 | 15.69 |
| 1862 | 6.11 | 2.26 | 5.63 | 7.89 | 14.00 |
| 1863 | 6.84 | 7.28 | 5.10 | 12.38 | 19.22 |
| 1864 | 8.65 | 4.26 | 4.48 | 8.74 | 17.39 |
| 1865 | 8.48 | 5.39 | 4.02 | 9.41 | 17.89 |
| 1866 | 7.42 | 4.77 | 4.48 | 9.25 | 16.67 |
| 1867 | 8.34 | 3.29 | 6.33 | 9.62 | 17.96 |
| 1868 | 7.33 | 8.65 | 5.45 | 14.10 | 21.43 |
| 1869 | 8.75 | 6.78 | 4.75 | 11.53 | 20.28 |
| 1870 | 8.47 | 5.60 | 4.40 | 10.00 | 18.47 |
| 1871 | 7.57 | 4.48 | 4.88 | 9.36 | 16.93 |
| 1872 | 10.37 | 9.95 | 4.88 | 14.83 | 25.20 |
| 1873 | 10.78 | 11.00 | 6.43 | 17.43 | 28.21 |
| 1874 | 10.96 | 12.69 | 8.57 | 21.26 | 32.22 |
| 1875 | 11.42 | 17.38 | 10.74 | 28.12 | 39.54 |
| 1876 | 15.05 | 16.38 | 9.74 | 26.12 | 41.17 |
| 1877 | 12.13 | 29.19 | 10.90 | 40.09 | 52.22 |
| 1878 | 11.52 | 21.04 | 14.32 | 35.36 | 46.88 |
| 1879 | 11.96 | 13.53 | 16.74 | 30.27 | 42.23 |
| 1880 | 10.78 | 21.45 | 15.19 | 36.64 | 47.42 |
| 1881 | 16.63 | 28.03 | 16.91 | 44.94 | 61.57 |
| 1882 | 17.75 | 16.64 | 20.41 | 37.05 | 54.80 |
| 1883 | 26.97 | 13.55 | 23.90 | 37.45 | 64.42 |
| 1884 | 26.95 | 17.31 | 24.75 | 42.06 | 69.01 |
| 1885 | 25.06 | 17.30 | 25.75 | 43.05 | 68.11 |
| 1886 | 22.04 | 28.07 | 26.59 | 54.66 | 76.70 |
| 1887 | 26.76 | 28.32 | 23.22 | 51.54 | 78.30 |
| 1888 | 29.22 | 31.84 | 23.21 | 55.05 | 84.27 |
| 1889 | 21.25 | 32.84 | 26.44 | 59.28 | 80.53 |
| 1890 | 23.64 | 21.05 | 24.88 | 45.93 | 69.57 |
| 1891 | 18.18 | 32.92 | 26.97 | 59.89 | 78.07 |
| 1892 | 15.06 | 10.69 | 19.26 | 29.95 | 45.01 |
| 1893 | 10.90 | 6.04 | 15.31 | 21.35 | 32.25 |
| 1894 | 11.78 | 10.36 | 12.16 | 22.52 | 34.30 |
| 1895 | 9.83 | 4.94 | 13.15 | 18.09 | 27.92 |
| 1896 | 10.22 | 13.76 | 15.38 | 29.14 | 39.36 |
| 1897 | 5.91 | 4.23 | 17.81 | 22.04 | 27.95 |
| 1898 | 10.72 | 14.12 | 17.72 | 31.84 | 42.56 |
| 1899 | 6.26 | 16.63 | 20.29 | 36.92 | 43.18 |
| 1900 | 5.93 | 14.46 | 21.35 | 35.81 | 41.74 |
| *30th June* | | | | | |
| 1901 | 14 | 18 | 27 | 45 | 59 |
| 1902 | 23 | 23 | 37 | 60 | 83 |
| 1903 | 18 | 22 | 33 | 55 | 73 |
| 1904 | 16 | 18 | 22 | 40 | 56 |
| 1905 | 17 | 17 | 17 | 34 | 51 |
| 1906 | 19 | 20 | 20 | 40 | 59 |
| 1907 | 22 | 29 | 23 | 52 | 74 |
| 1908 | 22 | 26 | 29 | 55 | 77 |
| 1909 | 20 | 25 | 36 | 61 | 81 |
| 1910 | 22 | 27 | 39 | 66 | 88 |
| 1911 | 26 | 32 | 49 | 81 | 107 |
| 1912 | 33 | 37 | 61 | 98 | 131 |
| 1913 | 41 | 40 | 69 | 109 | 150 |
| 1914 | 44 | 43 | 71 | 114 | 158 |
| 1915 | 40 | 24 | 73 | 97 | 137 |
| 1916 | 33 | 26 | 71 | 97 | 130 |
| 1917 | 29 | 39 | 61 | 100 | 129 |
| 1918 | 28 | 36 | 51 | 87 | 115 |
| 1919 | 37 | 51 | 59 | 110 | 147 |
| 1920 | 60 | 69 | 92 | 161 | 221 |
| 1921 | 72 | 80 | 116 | 196 | 268 |
| 1922 | 64 | 89 | 117 | 206 | 270 |
| 1923 | 81 | 87 | 118 | 205 | 286 |
| 1924 | 90 | 90 | 125 | 215 | 305 |
| 1925 | 88 | 86 | 140 | 226 | 314 |

*Note:* * excludes defence.

**Table 7.6** continued

| Year ending 30th June | Household sector | Market sector Private | Market sector Public* | Market sector Total | Total economy | Year ending 30th June | Household sector | Market sector Private | Market sector Public* | Market sector Total | Total economy |
|---|---|---|---|---|---|---|---|---|---|---|---|
| 1926 | 88 | 82 | 146 | 228 | 316 | 1959 | 914 | 1452 | 931 | 2383 | 3297 |
| 1927 | 99 | 79 | 157 | 236 | 335 | 1960 | 1025 | 1660 | 1034 | 2694 | 3719 |
| 1928 | 100 | 75 | 160 | 235 | 335 | 1961 | 1141 | 1836 | 1066 | 2902 | 4043 |
| 1929 | 90 | 77 | 149 | 226 | 316 | 1962 | 1089 | 1804 | 1261 | 3065 | 4154 |
| 1930 | 66 | 49 | 130 | 179 | 245 | 1963 | 1175 | 2021 | 1275 | 3296 | 4471 |
| 1931 | 35 | 47 | 96 | 143 | 178 | 1964 | 1330 | 2279 | 1422 | 3701 | 5031 |
| 1932 | 23 | 35 | 67 | 102 | 125 | 1965 | 1502 | 2636 | 1667 | 4303 | 5805 |
| 1933 | 31 | 34 | 70 | 104 | 135 | 1966 | 1551 | 2885 | 1813 | 4698 | 6249 |
| 1934 | 41 | 48 | 72 | 120 | 161 | 1967 | 1678 | 3005 | 1915 | 4920 | 6598 |
| 1935 | 49 | 66 | 94 | 160 | 209 | 1968 | 1847 | 3206 | 2076 | 5282 | 7129 |
| 1936 | 63 | 70 | 102 | 172 | 235 | 1969 | 2094 | 3732 | 2229 | 5961 | 8055 |
| 1937 | 70 | 76 | 108 | 184 | 254 | 1970 | 2376 | 3965 | 2435 | 6400 | 8776 |
| 1938 | 83 | 101 | 125 | 226 | 309 | 1971 | 2504 | 4612 | 2604 | 7216 | 9720 |
| 1939 | 86 | 97 | 119 | 216 | 302 | 1972 | 2831 | 4874 | 3044 | 7918 | 10749 |
| 1940 | 82 | 114 | 108 | 222 | 304 | 1973 | 3292 | 5229 | 3179 | 8408 | 11700 |
| 1941 | 75 | 96 | 100 | 196 | 271 | 1974 | 4060 | 6054 | 3682 | 9736 | 13796 |
| 1942 | 53 | 82 | 92 | 174 | 227 | 1975 | 4404 | 6628 | 5198 | 11826 | 16230 |
| 1943 | 30 | 70 | 89 | 159 | 189 | 1976 | 5785 | 7934 | 5974 | 13908 | 19693 |
| 1944 | 28 | 80 | 110 | 190 | 218 | 1977 | 7042 | 9049 | 6339 | 15388 | 22430 |
| 1945 | 37 | 102 | 113 | 215 | 252 | 1978 | 6963 | 10220 | 6848 | 17068 | 24031 |
| 1946 | 70 | 168 | 127 | 295 | 365 | 1979 | 7359 | 12844 | 7372 | 20216 | 27575 |
| 1947 | 137 | 220 | 212 | 432 | 569 | 1980 | 8498 | 13858 | 8232 | 22090 | 30588 |
| 1948 | 203 | 272 | 257 | 529 | 732 | 1981 | 10394 | 17655 | 9047 | 26702 | 37096 |
| 1949 | 290 | 375 | 230 | 605 | 895 | 1982 | 11661 | 21129 | 10954 | 32083 | 43744 |
| 1950 | 404 | 484 | 332 | 816 | 1220 | 1983 | 10619 | 20268 | 12608 | 32876 | 43495 |
| 1951 | 533 | 691 | 487 | 1178 | 1711 | 1984 | 12108 | 21466 | 13377 | 34843 | 46951 |
| 1952 | 682 | 830 | 652 | 1482 | 2164 | 1985 | 14269 | 25500 | 14255 | 39755 | 54024 |
| 1953 | 617 | 822 | 657 | 1479 | 2096 | 1986 | 15752 | 30016 | 16978 | 46994 | 62746 |
| 1954 | 716 | 993 | 654 | 1647 | 2363 | 1987 | 15751 | 34106 | 18026 | 52132 | 67883 |
| 1955 | 771 | 1122 | 715 | 1837 | 2608 | 1988 | 17467 | 41303 | 16372 | 57675 | 75142 |
| 1956 | 789 | 1265 | 768 | 2033 | 2822 | 1989 | 22570 | 49037 | 17210 | 66247 | 88817 |
| 1957 | 755 | 1337 | 804 | 2141 | 2896 | 1990 | 30412 | 48748 | 20201 | 68949 | 99361 |
| 1958 | 798 | 1429 | 849 | 2278 | 3076 | | | | | | |

*Note:* * excludes defence.

**Table 7.7  Shares of Gross Community Capital Formation, Australia, 1861–1990 (per cent)**

| Year ending 31st Dec. | Household sector | Market sector Private | Market sector Public* | Market sector Total | Total economy |
|---|---|---|---|---|---|
| 1861 | 39.3 | 23.8 | 36.8 | 60.6 | 100.0 |
| 1862 | 43.6 | 16.1 | 40.2 | 56.3 | 100.0 |
| 1863 | 35.6 | 37.9 | 26.5 | 64.4 | 100.0 |
| 1864 | 49.7 | 24.5 | 25.8 | 50.3 | 100.0 |
| 1865 | 47.4 | 30.1 | 22.5 | 52.6 | 100.0 |
| 1866 | 44.5 | 28.6 | 26.9 | 55.5 | 100.0 |
| 1867 | 46.4 | 18.3 | 35.2 | 53.5 | 100.0 |
| 1868 | 34.2 | 40.4 | 25.4 | 65.8 | 100.0 |
| 1869 | 43.2 | 33.4 | 23.4 | 56.8 | 100.0 |
| 1870 | 45.9 | 30.3 | 23.8 | 54.1 | 100.0 |
| 1871 | 44.7 | 26.5 | 28.8 | 55.3 | 100.0 |
| 1872 | 41.2 | 39.5 | 19.4 | 58.9 | 100.0 |
| 1873 | 38.2 | 39.0 | 22.8 | 61.8 | 100.0 |
| 1874 | 34.0 | 39.4 | 26.6 | 66.0 | 100.0 |
| 1875 | 28.9 | 44.0 | 27.2 | 71.2 | 100.0 |
| 1876 | 36.6 | 39.8 | 23.7 | 63.5 | 100.0 |
| 1877 | 23.2 | 55.9 | 20.9 | 76.8 | 100.0 |
| 1878 | 24.6 | 44.9 | 30.6 | 75.5 | 100.0 |
| 1879 | 28.3 | 32.0 | 39.6 | 71.6 | 100.0 |
| 1880 | 22.7 | 45.2 | 32.0 | 77.2 | 100.0 |
| 1881 | 27.0 | 45.5 | 27.5 | 73.0 | 100.0 |
| 1882 | 32.4 | 30.4 | 37.2 | 67.6 | 100.0 |
| 1883 | 41.9 | 21.0 | 37.1 | 58.1 | 100.0 |
| 1884 | 39.1 | 25.1 | 35.9 | 61.0 | 100.0 |
| 1885 | 36.8 | 25.4 | 37.8 | 63.2 | 100.0 |
| 1886 | 28.7 | 36.6 | 34.7 | 71.3 | 100.0 |
| 1887 | 34.2 | 36.2 | 29.7 | 65.9 | 100.0 |
| 1888 | 34.7 | 37.8 | 27.5 | 65.3 | 100.0 |
| 1889 | 26.4 | 40.8 | 32.8 | 73.6 | 100.0 |
| 1890 | 34.0 | 30.3 | 35.8 | 66.1 | 100.0 |
| 1891 | 23.3 | 42.2 | 34.6 | 76.8 | 100.0 |
| 1892 | 33.5 | 23.8 | 42.8 | 66.6 | 100.0 |
| 1893 | 33.8 | 18.7 | 47.5 | 66.2 | 100.0 |
| 1894 | 34.3 | 30.2 | 35.5 | 65.7 | 100.0 |
| 1895 | 35.2 | 17.7 | 47.1 | 64.8 | 100.0 |
| 1896 | 26.0 | 35.0 | 39.1 | 74.1 | 100.0 |
| 1897 | 21.1 | 15.1 | 63.7 | 78.8 | 100.0 |
| 1898 | 25.2 | 33.2 | 41.6 | 74.8 | 100.0 |
| 1899 | 14.5 | 38.5 | 47.0 | 85.5 | 100.0 |
| 1900 | 14.2 | 34.6 | 51.2 | 85.8 | 100.0 |
| 30th June | | | | | |
| 1901 | 24 | 31 | 46 | 77 | 100 |
| 1902 | 28 | 28 | 45 | 73 | 100 |
| 1903 | 25 | 30 | 45 | 75 | 100 |
| 1904 | 29 | 32 | 39 | 71 | 100 |
| 1905 | 33 | 33 | 33 | 66 | 100 |
| 1906 | 32 | 34 | 34 | 68 | 100 |
| 1907 | 30 | 39 | 31 | 70 | 100 |
| 1908 | 29 | 34 | 38 | 72 | 100 |
| 1909 | 25 | 31 | 44 | 75 | 100 |
| 1910 | 25 | 31 | 44 | 75 | 100 |
| 1911 | 24 | 30 | 46 | 76 | 100 |
| 1912 | 25 | 28 | 47 | 75 | 100 |
| 1913 | 27 | 27 | 46 | 73 | 100 |
| 1914 | 28 | 27 | 45 | 72 | 100 |
| 1915 | 29 | 18 | 53 | 71 | 100 |
| 1916 | 25 | 20 | 55 | 75 | 100 |
| 1917 | 22 | 30 | 47 | 77 | 100 |
| 1918 | 24 | 31 | 44 | 75 | 100 |
| 1919 | 25 | 35 | 40 | 75 | 100 |
| 1920 | 27 | 31 | 42 | 73 | 100 |
| 1921 | 27 | 30 | 43 | 73 | 100 |
| 1922 | 24 | 33 | 43 | 76 | 100 |
| 1923 | 28 | 30 | 41 | 71 | 100 |
| 1924 | 30 | 30 | 41 | 71 | 100 |
| 1925 | 28 | 27 | 45 | 72 | 100 |

*Note:* * excludes defence.

**Table 7.7** continued

| Year ending 30th June | Household sector | Market sector | | | Total economy |
|---|---|---|---|---|---|
| | | Private | Public* | Total | |
| 1926 | 28 | 26 | 46 | 72 | 100 |
| 1927 | 30 | 24 | 47 | 71 | 100 |
| 1928 | 30 | 22 | 48 | 70 | 100 |
| 1929 | 28 | 24 | 47 | 71 | 100 |
| 1930 | 27 | 20 | 53 | 73 | 100 |
| 1931 | 20 | 26 | 54 | 80 | 100 |
| 1932 | 18 | 28 | 54 | 82 | 100 |
| 1933 | 23 | 25 | 52 | 77 | 100 |
| 1934 | 25 | 30 | 45 | 75 | 100 |
| 1935 | 23 | 32 | 45 | 77 | 100 |
| 1936 | 27 | 30 | 43 | 73 | 100 |
| 1937 | 28 | 30 | 43 | 73 | 100 |
| 1938 | 27 | 33 | 40 | 73 | 100 |
| 1939 | 28 | 32 | 39 | 71 | 100 |
| 1940 | 27 | 38 | 36 | 74 | 100 |
| 1941 | 28 | 35 | 37 | 72 | 100 |
| 1942 | 23 | 36 | 41 | 77 | 100 |
| 1943 | 16 | 37 | 47 | 84 | 100 |
| 1944 | 13 | 37 | 50 | 87 | 100 |
| 1945 | 15 | 40 | 45 | 85 | 100 |
| 1946 | 19 | 46 | 35 | 81 | 100 |
| 1947 | 24 | 39 | 37 | 76 | 100 |
| 1948 | 28 | 37 | 35 | 72 | 100 |
| 1949 | 32 | 42 | 26 | 68 | 100 |
| 1950 | 33 | 40 | 27 | 67 | 100 |
| 1951 | 31 | 40 | 28 | 68 | 100 |
| 1952 | 32 | 38 | 30 | 68 | 100 |
| 1953 | 29 | 39 | 31 | 70 | 100 |
| 1954 | 30 | 42 | 28 | 70 | 100 |
| 1955 | 30 | 43 | 27 | 70 | 100 |
| 1956 | 28 | 45 | 27 | 72 | 100 |
| 1957 | 26 | 46 | 28 | 74 | 100 |
| 1958 | 26 | 46 | 28 | 74 | 100 |

| Year ending 30th June | Household sector | Market sector | | | Total economy |
|---|---|---|---|---|---|
| | | Private | Public* | Total | |
| 1959 | 28 | 44 | 28 | 72 | 100 |
| 1960 | 28 | 45 | 28 | 73 | 100 |
| 1961 | 28 | 45 | 26 | 71 | 100 |
| 1962 | 26 | 43 | 30 | 73 | 100 |
| 1963 | 26 | 45 | 29 | 74 | 100 |
| 1964 | 26 | 45 | 28 | 73 | 100 |
| 1965 | 26 | 45 | 29 | 74 | 100 |
| 1966 | 25 | 46 | 29 | 75 | 100 |
| 1967 | 25 | 46 | 29 | 75 | 100 |
| 1968 | 26 | 45 | 29 | 74 | 100 |
| 1969 | 26 | 46 | 28 | 74 | 100 |
| 1970 | 27 | 45 | 28 | 73 | 100 |
| 1971 | 26 | 47 | 27 | 74 | 100 |
| 1972 | 26 | 45 | 28 | 73 | 100 |
| 1973 | 28 | 45 | 27 | 72 | 100 |
| 1974 | 29 | 44 | 27 | 71 | 100 |
| 1975 | 27 | 41 | 32 | 73 | 100 |
| 1976 | 29 | 40 | 30 | 70 | 100 |
| 1977 | 31 | 40 | 28 | 68 | 100 |
| 1978 | 29 | 43 | 28 | 71 | 100 |
| 1979 | 27 | 47 | 27 | 74 | 100 |
| 1980 | 28 | 45 | 27 | 72 | 100 |
| 1981 | 28 | 48 | 24 | 72 | 100 |
| 1982 | 27 | 48 | 25 | 73 | 100 |
| 1983 | 24 | 47 | 29 | 76 | 100 |
| 1984 | 26 | 46 | 28 | 74 | 100 |
| 1985 | 26 | 47 | 26 | 73 | 100 |
| 1986 | 25 | 48 | 27 | 75 | 100 |
| 1987 | 23 | 50 | 27 | 77 | 100 |
| 1988 | 23 | 55 | 22 | 77 | 100 |
| 1989 | 25 | 55 | 19 | 74 | 100 |
| 1990 | 31 | 49 | 20 | 69 | 100 |

*Note:* * excludes defence.

**Table 7.8   Real Gross Community Capital Formation (1966/67 prices), Australia, 1861–1990 ($m)**

| Year ending 31st Dec. | Household sector | Market sector Private | Market sector Public* | Market sector Total | Total economy |
|---|---|---|---|---|---|
| 1861 | 46.2 | 23.1 | 53.4 | 76.5 | 122.7 |
| 1862 | 48.6 | 14.4 | 49.9 | 64.3 | 112.9 |
| 1863 | 56.7 | 44.1 | 45.9 | 90.0 | 146.7 |
| 1864 | 79.9 | 26.9 | 41.7 | 68.6 | 148.5 |
| 1865 | 72.6 | 36.1 | 36.2 | 72.3 | 144.9 |
| 1866 | 61.4 | 33.3 | 40.8 | 74.1 | 135.5 |
| 1867 | 75.5 | 25.1 | 58.1 | 83.2 | 158.7 |
| 1868 | 65.7 | 59.4 | 51.3 | 110.7 | 176.4 |
| 1869 | 86.3 | 53.2 | 44.8 | 98.0 | 184.3 |
| 1870 | 72.1 | 36.9 | 41.5 | 78.4 | 150.5 |
| 1871 | 67.7 | 35.9 | 50.1 | 86.0 | 153.7 |
| 1872 | 91.7 | 57.6 | 42.4 | 100.0 | 191.7 |
| 1873 | 82.1 | 61.0 | 49.0 | 110.0 | 192.1 |
| 1874 | 87.4 | 64.4 | 68.4 | 132.8 | 220.2 |
| 1875 | 100.8 | 95.5 | 90.6 | 186.1 | 286.9 |
| 1876 | 130.9 | 94.7 | 83.4 | 178.1 | 309.0 |
| 1877 | 106.7 | 183.9 | 98.7 | 282.6 | 389.3 |
| 1878 | 100.0 | 139.9 | 131.1 | 271.0 | 371.0 |
| 1879 | 107.7 | 92.4 | 154.1 | 246.5 | 354.2 |
| 1880 | 97.8 | 148.0 | 132.4 | 280.4 | 378.2 |
| 1881 | 145.3 | 189.0 | 155.7 | 344.7 | 490.0 |
| 1882 | 153.7 | 122.5 | 184.7 | 307.2 | 460.9 |
| 1883 | 237.2 | 94.6 | 217.1 | 311.7 | 548.9 |
| 1884 | 240.7 | 127.2 | 225.4 | 352.6 | 593.3 |
| 1885 | 205.1 | 132.2 | 237.8 | 370.0 | 575.1 |
| 1886 | 185.9 | 230.3 | 257.2 | 487.5 | 673.4 |
| 1887 | 238.8 | 238.8 | 226.3 | 465.1 | 703.9 |
| 1888 | 259.7 | 261.2 | 226.4 | 487.6 | 747.3 |
| 1889 | 171.7 | 261.3 | 253.3 | 514.6 | 686.3 |
| 1890 | 196.3 | 158.7 | 225.6 | 384.3 | 580.6 |
| 1891 | 151.5 | 253.6 | 245.0 | 498.6 | 650.1 |
| 1892 | 147.1 | 90.4 | 180.7 | 271.1 | 418.2 |
| 1893 | 114.2 | 55.1 | 149.7 | 204.8 | 319.0 |

| Year ending 31st Dec. | Household sector | Market sector Private | Market sector Public* | Market sector Total | Total economy |
|---|---|---|---|---|---|
| 1894 | 138.6 | 102.0 | 124.1 | 226.1 | 364.7 |
| 1895 | 112.4 | 50.3 | 126.9 | 177.2 | 289.6 |
| 1896 | 117.1 | 136.8 | 148.5 | 285.3 | 402.4 |
| 1897 | 63.9 | 43.2 | 169.8 | 213.0 | 276.9 |
| 1898 | 114.9 | 132.3 | 173.9 | 306.2 | 421.1 |
| 1899 | 59.1 | 143.6 | 186.0 | 329.6 | 388.7 |
| 1900 | 54.6 | 112.9 | 175.4 | 288.3 | 342.9 |
| 30th June | | | | | |
| 1901 | 117.1 | 151.3 | 226.9 | 378.2 | 495.3 |
| 1902 | 205.3 | 200.0 | 330.4 | 530.4 | 735.7 |
| 1903 | 160.3 | 194.7 | 294.6 | 489.3 | 649.6 |
| 1904 | 146.5 | 162.2 | 194.7 | 356.9 | 503.4 |
| 1905 | 159.0 | 153.2 | 151.8 | 305.0 | 464.0 |
| 1906 | 174.5 | 170.9 | 177.0 | 347.9 | 522.4 |
| 1907 | 203.8 | 243.7 | 188.5 | 432.2 | 636.0 |
| 1908 | 186.0 | 216.7 | 233.9 | 450.6 | 636.6 |
| 1909 | 171.2 | 206.6 | 285.7 | 492.3 | 663.5 |
| 1910 | 183.1 | 214.3 | 309.5 | 523.8 | 706.9 |
| 1911 | 208.2 | 244.3 | 374.0 | 618.3 | 826.5 |
| 1912 | 233.6 | 264.3 | 426.6 | 690.9 | 924.5 |
| 1913 | 283.8 | 274.0 | 469.4 | 743.4 | 1027.2 |
| 1914 | 303.2 | 288.6 | 479.7 | 768.3 | 1071.5 |
| 1915 | 260.5 | 146.3 | 447.9 | 594.2 | 854.7 |
| 1916 | 197.4 | 130.7 | 344.7 | 475.4 | 672.8 |
| 1917 | 157.9 | 174.9 | 258.5 | 433.4 | 591.3 |
| 1918 | 140.6 | 146.3 | 197.7 | 344.0 | 484.6 |
| 1919 | 179.6 | 226.7 | 229.6 | 456.3 | 635.9 |
| 1920 | 262.3 | 267.4 | 310.8 | 578.2 | 840.5 |
| 1921 | 302.2 | 305.3 | 361.4 | 666.7 | 968.9 |
| 1922 | 271.4 | 347.7 | 434.9 | 782.6 | 1054.0 |
| 1923 | 343.1 | 339.8 | 462.7 | 802.5 | 1145.6 |
| 1924 | 386.3 | 351.6 | 500.0 | 851.6 | 1237.9 |
| 1925 | 366.4 | 337.3 | 549.0 | 886.3 | 1252.7 |

*Note: * excludes defence.*

**Table 7.8**  continued

| Year ending 30th June | Household sector | Market sector Private | Market sector Public* | Market sector Total | Total economy |
|---|---|---|---|---|---|
| 1926 | 366.0 | 319.1 | 557.3 | 876.4 | 1242.4 |
| 1927 | 409.5 | 306.2 | 597.0 | 903.2 | 1312.7 |
| 1928 | 416.3 | 290.7 | 603.8 | 894.5 | 1310.8 |
| 1929 | 370.3 | 297.3 | 568.7 | 866.0 | 1236.3 |
| 1930 | 272.4 | 200.0 | 562.8 | 762.8 | 1035.2 |
| 1931 | 145.9 | 191.8 | 408.5 | 600.3 | 746.2 |
| 1932 | 100.5 | 142.9 | 314.6 | 457.5 | 558.0 |
| 1933 | 138.0 | 145.3 | 346.5 | 491.8 | 629.8 |
| 1934 | 187.4 | 206.0 | 354.7 | 560.7 | 748.1 |
| 1935 | 220.1 | 285.7 | 465.3 | 751.0 | 971.1 |
| 1936 | 280.7 | 304.3 | 500.0 | 804.3 | 1085.0 |
| 1937 | 301.5 | 312.8 | 504.7 | 817.5 | 1119.0 |
| 1938 | 345.3 | 405.6 | 568.2 | 973.8 | 1319.1 |
| 1939 | 340.1 | 468.6 | 531.3 | 999.9 | 1340.0 |
| 1940 | 297.1 | 522.9 | 471.6 | 994.5 | 1291.6 |
| 1941 | 245.6 | 405.1 | 392.2 | 797.3 | 1042.9 |
| 1942 | 161.9 | 285.7 | 338.2 | 623.9 | 785.8 |
| 1943 | 75.9 | 243.1 | 279.0 | 522.1 | 598.0 |
| 1944 | 66.4 | 273.0 | 333.3 | 606.3 | 672.7 |
| 1945 | 91.9 | 348.1 | 345.6 | 693.7 | 785.6 |
| 1946 | 173.7 | 571.4 | 375.7 | 947.1 | 1120.8 |
| 1947 | 345.1 | 707.4 | 605.7 | 1313.1 | 1658.2 |
| 1948 | 486.3 | 770.5 | 671.0 | 1441.5 | 1927.8 |
| 1949 | 627.0 | 961.5 | 556.9 | 1518.4 | 2145.4 |
| 1950 | 783.4 | 1133.5 | 741.1 | 1874.6 | 2658.0 |
| 1951 | 872.0 | 1326.3 | 954.9 | 2281.2 | 3153.2 |
| 1952 | 994.0 | 1298.9 | 1090.3 | 2389.2 | 3383.2 |
| 1953 | 812.3 | 1184.4 | 988.0 | 2172.4 | 2984.7 |
| 1954 | 926.0 | 1384.9 | 946.5 | 2331.4 | 3257.4 |
| 1955 | 961.1 | 1508.1 | 997.2 | 2505.3 | 3466.4 |
| 1956 | 940.1 | 1601.3 | 1028.1 | 2629.4 | 3569.5 |
| 1957 | 879.5 | 1626.5 | 1033.4 | 2659.9 | 3539.4 |
| 1958 | 917.1 | 1683.2 | 1082.9 | 2766.1 | 3683.2 |
| 1959 | 1045.6 | 1690.3 | 1165.2 | 2855.5 | 3901.1 |
| 1960 | 1155.2 | 1943.8 | 1261.0 | 3204.8 | 4360.0 |
| 1961 | 1249.7 | 2093.5 | 1261.5 | 3355.0 | 4604.7 |
| 1962 | 1186.4 | 2027.0 | 1456.1 | 3483.1 | 4669.5 |
| 1963 | 1281.6 | 2245.6 | 1455.5 | 3701.1 | 4982.7 |
| 1964 | 1433.9 | 2507.2 | 1585.3 | 4092.5 | 5526.4 |
| 1965 | 1582.1 | 2774.7 | 1786.7 | 4561.4 | 6143.5 |
| 1966 | 1590.2 | 2980.4 | 1890.5 | 4870.9 | 6461.1 |
| 1967 | 1678.4 | 3005.0 | 1915.0 | 4920.0 | 6598.4 |
| 1968 | 1799.5 | 3149.3 | 2003.9 | 5153.2 | 6952.7 |
| 1969 | 1987.6 | 3478.1 | 2079.3 | 5557.4 | 7545.0 |
| 1970 | 2188.5 | 3601.3 | 2166.4 | 5767.7 | 7956.2 |
| 1971 | 2207.1 | 3993.1 | 2186.4 | 6179.5 | 8386.6 |
| 1972 | 2330.8 | 3940.2 | 2381.8 | 6322.0 | 8652.8 |
| 1973 | 2494.8 | 3976.4 | 2302.0 | 6278.4 | 8773.2 |
| 1974 | 2608.0 | 4155.1 | 2364.8 | 6519.9 | 9127.9 |
| 1975 | 2350.6 | 3684.3 | 2682.1 | 6366.4 | 8717.0 |
| 1976 | 2624.9 | 3794.4 | 2670.5 | 6464.9 | 9089.8 |
| 1977 | 2861.3 | 3878.7 | 2540.7 | 6419.4 | 9280.7 |
| 1978 | 2648.4 | 3939.9 | 2540.1 | 6480.0 | 9128.4 |
| 1979 | 2697.3 | 4486.2 | 2558.8 | 7045.0 | 9742.3 |
| 1980 | 2895.7 | 4379.9 | 2426.9 | 6806.8 | 9702.5 |
| 1981 | 3149.0 | 5047.2 | 2511.0 | 7558.2 | 10707.2 |
| 1982 | 3176.3 | 5541.3 | 2707.4 | 8248.7 | 11425.0 |
| 1983 | 2636.0 | 4840.7 | 2736.1 | 7576.8 | 10212.8 |
| 1984 | 2846.5 | 4907.6 | 2737.3 | 7644.9 | 10491.4 |
| 1985 | 3136.8 | 5584.8 | 2765.3 | 8350.1 | 11486.9 |
| 1986 | 3195.3 | 5832.9 | 3041.0 | 8873.9 | 12069.2 |
| 1987 | 3016.4 | 6033.3 | 3004.3 | 9037.6 | 12054.0 |
| 1988 | 3131.0 | 6958.1 | 2573.8 | 9531.9 | 12662.9 |
| 1989 | 3511.2 | 8013.9 | 2554.5 | 10568.4 | 14079.6 |
| 1990 | 3463.2 | 7809.7 | 2837.6 | 10647.3 | 14110.5 |

*Note: * excludes defence.*

**Table 7.9    Real GDP and GDP per capita (GDP deflator, 1966/67 prices),
Australia, 1800–1990**

| Year ending 31st Dec. | Real GDP ($m) | Population ('000) | Real GDP per capita ($) | Year ending 31st Dec. | Real GDP ($m) | Population ('000) | Real GDP per capita ($) |
|---|---|---|---|---|---|---|---|
| **1800** | 2.15 | 5.2 | 413 | **1848** | 230.26 | 332.3 | 693 |
| **1801** | 2.58 | 6.0 | 430 | **1849** | 222.71 | 373.4 | 596 |
| **1802** | 2.58 | 7.0 | 369 | **1850** | 220.43 | 405.4 | 544 |
| **1803** | 2.72 | 7.2 | 378 | **1851** | 281.13 | 437.7 | 642 |
| **1804** | 3.15 | 7.6 | 414 | **1852** | 370.51 | 513.8 | 721 |
| **1805** | 3.44 | 7.7 | 447 | **1853** | 457.97 | 601.0 | 762 |
| **1806** | 3.72 | 7.9 | 471 | **1854** | 447.18 | 694.9 | 644 |
| **1807** | 4.01 | 8.8 | 456 | **1855** | 471.23 | 793.3 | 594 |
| **1808** | 3.94 | 10.3 | 383 | **1856** | 628.24 | 876.7 | 717 |
| **1809** | 4.23 | 11.6 | 365 | **1857** | 601.21 | 970.3 | 620 |
| **1810** | 6.02 | 11.6 | 519 | **1858** | 546.49 | 1050.8 | 520 |
| **1811** | 5.59 | 11.9 | 470 | **1859** | 735.60 | 1097.3 | 670 |
| **1812** | 5.73 | 12.6 | 455 | **1860** | 744.79 | 1145.6 | 650 |
| **1813** | 6.02 | 14.0 | 430 | **1861** | 744.37 | 1168.2 | 637 |
| **1814** | 6.23 | 14.1 | 442 | **1862** | 734.97 | 1206.9 | 609 |
| **1815** | 7.59 | 15.1 | 503 | **1863** | 758.41 | 1259.3 | 602 |
| **1816** | 7.09 | 17.6 | 403 | **1864** | 841.97 | 1325.2 | 635 |
| **1817** | 7.95 | 21.2 | 375 | **1865** | 839.21 | 1390.0 | 604 |
| **1818** | 9.10 | 25.9 | 351 | **1866** | 892.10 | 1444.0 | 618 |
| **1819** | 9.96 | 31.5 | 316 | **1867** | 997.92 | 1483.9 | 673 |
| **1820** | 10.82 | 33.5 | 323 | **1868** | 1048.66 | 1539.6 | 681 |
| **1821** | 13.54 | 35.5 | 381 | **1869** | 1059.64 | 1592.2 | 666 |
| **1822** | 15.19 | 37.4 | 406 | **1870** | 1136.30 | 1647.8 | 690 |
| **1823** | 14.19 | 40.6 | 350 | **1871** | 1094.21 | 1700.9 | 643 |
| **1824** | 15.85 | 48.1 | 330 | **1872** | 1211.65 | 1742.9 | 695 |
| **1825** | 17.12 | 52.5 | 326 | **1873** | 1337.85 | 1794.5 | 746 |
| **1826** | 17.83 | 53.9 | 331 | **1874** | 1381.61 | 1849.4 | 747 |
| **1827** | 19.47 | 56.3 | 346 | **1875** | 1531.91 | 1898.2 | 807 |
| **1828** | 21.55 | 58.2 | 370 | **1876** | 1527.89 | 1958.7 | 780 |
| **1829** | 24.25 | 61.9 | 392 | **1877** | 1590.76 | 2031.1 | 783 |
| **1830** | 34.78 | 70.0 | 497 | **1878** | 1741.89 | 2092.2 | 833 |
| **1831** | 37.40 | 76.0 | 492 | **1879** | 1774.26 | 2162.3 | 821 |
| **1832** | 39.80 | 83.9 | 474 | **1880** | 1860.92 | 2231.5 | 834 |
| **1833** | 42.34 | 98.1 | 432 | **1881** | 1997.19 | 2306.7 | 866 |
| **1834** | 46.56 | 105.6 | 441 | **1882** | 1982.60 | 2388.1 | 830 |
| **1835** | 61.73 | 113.4 | 544 | **1883** | 2139.99 | 2505.7 | 854 |
| **1836** | 62.58 | 125.1 | 500 | **1884** | 2158.56 | 2605.7 | 828 |
| **1837** | 67.94 | 134.5 | 505 | **1885** | 2332.44 | 2694.5 | 866 |
| **1838** | 72.23 | 151.9 | 476 | **1886** | 2320.38 | 2788.1 | 832 |
| **1839** | 68.33 | 169.9 | 402 | **1887** | 2645.57 | 2881.4 | 918 |
| **1840** | 95.77 | 190.4 | 503 | **1888** | 2692.68 | 2981.7 | 903 |
| **1841** | 85.86 | 221.0 | 389 | **1889** | 2865.81 | 3062.5 | 936 |
| **1842** | 80.57 | 241.0 | 334 | **1890** | 2754.34 | 3151.4 | 874 |
| **1843** | 98.42 | 250.9 | 392 | **1891** | 2828.45 | 3241.0 | 873 |
| **1844** | 117.04 | 264.3 | 443 | **1892** | 2545.05 | 3305.8 | 770 |
| **1845** | 124.83 | 279.2 | 447 | **1893** | 2385.04 | 3361.9 | 709 |
| **1846** | 143.22 | 293.3 | 488 | **1894** | 2453.27 | 3426.8 | 716 |
| **1847** | 172.94 | 308.8 | 560 | **1895** | 2401.37 | 3491.6 | 688 |

**Table 7.9** continued

| Year ending 31st Dec. | Real GDP ($m) | Population ('000) | Real GDP per capita ($) | Year ending 30th June | Real GDP ($m) | Population ('000) | Real GDP per capita ($) |
|---|---|---|---|---|---|---|---|
| 1896 | 2644.04 | 3553.1 | 744 | 1943 | 11073.92 | 7269.7 | 1523 |
| 1897 | 2454.40 | 3617.8 | 678 | 1944 | 11091.70 | 7347.0 | 1510 |
| 1898 | 2818.04 | 3664.7 | 769 | 1945 | 10261.65 | 7430.2 | 1381 |
| 1899 | 2838.15 | 3716.0 | 764 | 1946 | 10306.17 | 7518.0 | 1371 |
| 1900 | 2952.38 | 3765.3 | 784 | 1947 | 10682.21 | 7638.0 | 1399 |
| 30th June | | | | 1948 | 12227.65 | 7792.5 | 1569 |
| 1901 | 2854.14 | 3824.9 | 746 | 1949 | 12769.89 | 8045.6 | 1587 |
| 1902 | 3113.19 | 3875.3 | 803 | 1950 | 13552.43 | 8307.5 | 1631 |
| 1903 | 2966.67 | 3916.6 | 757 | 1951 | 16344.19 | 8527.9 | 1917 |
| 1904 | 3466.04 | 3974.2 | 872 | 1952 | 16174.84 | 8739.6 | 1851 |
| 1905 | 3395.45 | 4033.0 | 842 | 1953 | 14590.83 | 8902.7 | 1639 |
| 1906 | 3866.13 | 4091.5 | 945 | 1954 | 15285.78 | 9089.9 | 1682 |
| 1907 | 4305.60 | 4161.7 | 1035 | 1955 | 14246.44 | 9311.8 | 1530 |
| 1908 | 4224.63 | 4232.3 | 998 | 1956 | 14998.61 | 9530.9 | 1574 |
| 1909 | 4409.45 | 4324.0 | 1020 | 1957 | 16233.30 | 9744.1 | 1666 |
| 1910 | 4575.18 | 4425.1 | 1034 | 1958 | 16101.47 | 9947.4 | 1619 |
| 1911 | 4692.20 | 4573.8 | 1026 | 1959 | 16190.48 | 10161.0 | 1593 |
| 1912 | 4790.34 | 4746.6 | 1009 | 1960 | 17862.67 | 10391.9 | 1719 |
| 1913 | 5157.53 | 4893.7 | 1054 | 1961 | 18987.52 | 10603.9 | 1791 |
| 1914 | 5183.65 | 4971.8 | 1043 | 1962 | 18595.63 | 10810.4 | 1720 |
| 1915 | 4713.92 | 4969.5 | 949 | 1963 | 19507.59 | 11022.8 | 1770 |
| 1916 | 4897.69 | 4918.0 | 996 | 1964 | 21399.31 | 11250.7 | 1902 |
| 1917 | 5108.60 | 4982.1 | 1025 | 1965 | 23303.14 | 11478.7 | 2030 |
| 1918 | 5097.41 | 5080.9 | 1003 | 1966 | 23609.87 | 11599.5 | 2035 |
| 1919 | 5033.33 | 5303.6 | 949 | 1967 | 25368.09 | 11793.6 | 2151 |
| 1920 | 5194.96 | 5411.3 | 960 | 1968 | 26337.81 | 11997.8 | 2195 |
| 1921 | 5850.49 | 5510.9 | 1062 | 1969 | 28725.00 | 12246.7 | 2346 |
| 1922 | 4863.47 | 5637.3 | 863 | 1970 | 30955.25 | 12485.6 | 2479 |
| 1923 | 5321.67 | 5756.0 | 925 | 1971 | 33059.69 | 12937.2 | 2555 |
| 1924 | 5831.39 | 5882.0 | 991 | 1972 | 35395.91 | 13192.2 | 2683 |
| 1925 | 6229.55 | 6003.0 | 1038 | 1973 | 38553.72 | 13406.6 | 2876 |
| 1926 | 5911.36 | 6124.0 | 965 | 1974 | 43414.89 | 13612.0 | 3189 |
| 1927 | 5585.29 | 6251.0 | 894 | 1975 | 47902.96 | 13818.2 | 3467 |
| 1928 | 5914.81 | 6355.8 | 931 | 1976 | 49354.76 | 13965.8 | 3534 |
| 1929 | 5888.15 | 6436.2 | 915 | 1977 | 47759.55 | 14110.8 | 3385 |
| 1930 | 5257.21 | 6500.8 | 809 | 1978 | 45079.71 | 14280.2 | 3157 |
| 1931 | 4354.05 | 6552.6 | 664 | 1979 | 46204.47 | 14436.4 | 3201 |
| 1932 | 4461.10 | 6603.8 | 676 | 1980 | 48601.64 | 14601.8 | 3328 |
| 1933 | 5128.89 | 6656.7 | 770 | 1981 | 51350.38 | 14809.8 | 3467 |
| 1934 | 5949.06 | 6707.3 | 887 | 1982 | 52216.43 | 15051.5 | 3469 |
| 1935 | 6365.85 | 6755.7 | 942 | 1983 | 51375.42 | 15291.5 | 3360 |
| 1936 | 6725.47 | 6810.4 | 988 | 1984 | 52873.29 | 15485.2 | 3414 |
| 1937 | 7201.83 | 6871.5 | 1048 | 1985 | 53127.77 | 15681.9 | 3388 |
| 1938 | 7421.21 | 6935.9 | 1070 | 1986 | 55175.45 | 15901.0 | 3470 |
| 1939 | 6943.41 | 7004.9 | 991 | 1987 | 57696.78 | 16139.9 | 3575 |
| 1940 | 8166.26 | 7077.6 | 1154 | 1988 | 61082.97 | 16402.0 | 3724 |
| 1941 | 8524.70 | 7143.6 | 1193 | 1989 | 64655.46 | 16696.7 | 3872 |
| 1942 | 9683.01 | 7201.1 | 1345 | 1990 | 65366.73 | 16958.6 | 3854 |

**Table 7.10　Gross Community Income price indexes—GDP deflator and final consumption (FC) deflator, Australia, 1800–1990** (1966/67 = 1000)

| Year ending 31st Dec. | GDP deflator | FC deflator | Year ending 31st Dec. | GDP deflator | FC deflator | Year ending 31st Dec. | GDP deflator | FC deflator |
|---|---|---|---|---|---|---|---|---|
| 1800 | 139.6 | | 1832 | 120.6 | | 1864 | 154.4 | 177 |
| 1801 | 139.6 | | 1833 | 133.2 | | 1865 | 156.1 | 205 |
| 1802 | 139.6 | | 1834 | 164.1 | | 1866 | 159.4 | 190 |
| 1803 | 139.6 | | 1835 | 164.1 | | 1867 | 143.9 | 154 |
| 1804 | 139.6 | | 1836 | 168.9 | | 1868 | 145.9 | 161 |
| 1805 | 139.6 | | 1837 | 165.0 | | 1869 | 144.2 | 147 |
| 1806 | 139.6 | | 1838 | 163.1 | | 1870 | 143.8 | 144 |
| 1807 | 139.6 | | 1839 | 204.6 | | 1871 | 143.3 | 149 |
| 1808 | 139.6 | | 1840 | 179.5 | | 1872 | 154.5 | 144 |
| 1809 | 139.6 | | 1841 | 164.1 | | 1873 | 162.5 | 157 |
| 1810 | 139.6 | | 1842 | 155.4 | | 1874 | 158.8 | 169 |
| 1811 | 139.6 | | 1843 | 120.6 | | 1875 | 155.1 | 162 |
| 1812 | 139.6 | | 1844 | 106.2 | | 1876 | 154.2 | 167 |
| 1813 | 139.6 | | 1845 | 114.8 | | 1877 | 151.5 | 164 |
| 1814 | 139.6 | | 1846 | 112.9 | | 1878 | 144.9 | 154 |
| 1815 | 139.6 | | 1847 | 99.4 | | 1879 | 145.3 | 145 |
| 1816 | 139.6 | | 1848 | 96.5 | | 1880 | 143.8 | 139 |
| 1817 | 139.6 | | 1849 | 90.7 | | 1881 | 142.6 | 137 |
| 1818 | 139.6 | | 1850 | 106.2 | | 1882 | 149.4 | 161 |
| 1819 | 139.6 | | 1851 | 97.5 | | 1883 | 154.3 | 160 |
| 1820 | 139.6 | | 1852 | 163.1 | | 1884 | 150.1 | 155 |
| 1821 | 139.6 | | 1853 | 192.0 | | 1885 | 148.6 | 159 |
| 1822 | 139.6 | | 1854 | 230.6 | | 1886 | 146.7 | 168 |
| 1823 | 157.1 | | 1855 | 216.2 | | 1887 | 142.2 | 152 |
| 1824 | 157.1 | | 1856 | 165.0 | | 1888 | 143.5 | 152 |
| 1825 | 157.1 | | 1857 | 182.4 | | 1889 | 148.3 | 161 |
| 1826 | 158.2 | | 1858 | 206.5 | | 1890 | 149.8 | 162 |
| 1827 | 158.2 | | 1859 | 166.0 | | 1891 | 143.4 | 153 |
| 1828 | 159.2 | | 1860 | 170.8 | | 1892 | 134.3 | 146 |
| 1829 | 156.3 | | 1861 | 173.3 | 197 | 1893 | 128.3 | 140 |
| 1830 | 124.5 | | 1862 | 174.7 | 187 | 1894 | 120.9 | 120 |
| 1831 | 120.6 | | 1863 | 166.4 | 184 | 1895 | 117.1 | 121 |

**Table 7.10**  continued

| Year ending 31st Dec. | GDP deflator | FC deflator | Year ending 30th June | GDP deflator | FC deflator | Year ending 30th June | GDP deflator | FC deflator |
|---|---|---|---|---|---|---|---|---|
| 1896 | 120.8 | 130 | 1927 | 270.0 | 275 | 1959 | 801.0 | 818 |
| 1897 | 125.0 | 138 | 1928 | 274.1 | 273 | 1960 | 838.1 | 841 |
| 1898 | 126.4 | 142 | 1929 | 275.1 | 279 | 1961 | 863.1 | 877 |
| 1899 | 127.9 | 138 | 1930 | 248.1 | 259 | 1962 | 874.0 | 882 |
| 1900 | 128.1 | 134 | 1931 | 225.0 | 244 | 1963 | 883.1 | 891 |
| 30th June | | | 1932 | 208.1 | 226 | 1964 | 916.1 | 905 |
| 1901 | 133.0 | 142 | 1933 | 205.0 | 223 | 1965 | 940.0 | 936 |
| 1902 | 128.1 | 135 | 1934 | 212.0 | 219 | 1966 | 968.0 | 968 |
| 1903 | 132.0 | 136 | 1935 | 219.0 | 241 | 1967 | 1000.0 | 1000 |
| 1904 | 124.0 | 124 | 1936 | 229.1 | 241 | 1968 | 1028.0 | 1032 |
| 1905 | 125.0 | 123 | 1937 | 242.1 | 246 | 1969 | 1062.2 | 1059 |
| 1906 | 129.1 | 128 | 1938 | 246.0 | 259 | 1970 | 1110.1 | 1100 |
| 1907 | 127.0 | 122 | 1939 | 251.0 | 288 | 1971 | 1161.6 | 1168 |
| 1908 | 137.0 | 136 | 1940 | 259.0 | 307 | 1972 | 1234.3 | 1246 |
| 1909 | 141.0 | 143 | 1941 | 261.1 | 321 | 1973 | 1350.0 | 1323 |
| 1910 | 145.0 | 148 | 1942 | 265.0 | 334 | 1974 | 1552.9 | 1482 |
| 1911 | 146.0 | 150 | 1943 | 279.0 | 361 | 1975 | 1834.9 | 1768 |
| 1912 | 159.0 | 165 | 1944 | 287.1 | 361 | 1976 | 2113.9 | 2046 |
| 1913 | 158.0 | 161 | 1945 | 298.0 | 352 | 1977 | 2347.5 | 2282 |
| 1914 | 169.1 | 178 | 1946 | 321.1 | 375 | 1978 | 2529.4 | 2491 |
| 1915 | 186.0 | 205 | 1947 | 352.0 | 376 | 1979 | 2729.6 | 2718 |
| 1916 | 193.0 | 229 | 1948 | 391.0 | 400 | 1980 | 3028.3 | 2996 |
| 1917 | 210.0 | 272 | 1949 | 430.0 | 427 | 1981 | 3340.8 | 3291 |
| 1918 | 222.1 | 284 | 1950 | 469.0 | 464 | 1982 | 3680.8 | 3600 |
| 1919 | 234.1 | 290 | 1951 | 589.0 | 523 | 1983 | 4066.8 | 3991 |
| 1920 | 271.0 | 296 | 1952 | 614.1 | 632 | 1984 | 4351.7 | 4286 |
| 1921 | 263.0 | 296 | 1953 | 702.0 | 682 | 1985 | 4595.3 | 4546 |
| 1922 | 249.1 | 272 | 1954 | 722.0 | 705 | 1986 | 4907.8 | 4923 |
| 1923 | 264.0 | 282 | 1955 | 726.1 | 718 | 1987 | 5270.8 | 5350 |
| 1924 | 264.0 | 265 | 1956 | 749.0 | 746 | 1988 | 5693.6 | 5736 |
| 1925 | 272.0 | 261 | 1957 | 800.1 | 791 | 1989 | 6235.8 | 6137 |
| 1926 | 270.0 | 276 | 1958 | 801.0 | 805 | 1990 | 6575.9 | 6532 |

**Table 7.11   Gross Community Capital Formation price indexes, Australia, 1861–1990 (1966/67 = 1000)**

| Year ending 31st Dec. | Household buildings | Household equipment | Private non-dwelling | Public non-dwelling |
|---|---|---|---|---|
| 1861 | 110.6 | 266.5 | 161.6 | 108.3 |
| 1862 | 104.7 | 243.2 | 157.2 | 112.9 |
| 1863 | 100.8 | 252.2 | 165.1 | 111.2 |
| 1864 | 91.8 | 233.4 | 158.5 | 107.4 |
| 1865 | 96.8 | 241.8 | 149.4 | 110.9 |
| 1866 | 98.8 | 223.8 | 143.2 | 109.8 |
| 1867 | 95.2 | 185.9 | 131.2 | 109.0 |
| 1868 | 93.4 | 202.6 | 145.7 | 106.2 |
| 1869 | 87.6 | 173.9 | 127.4 | 106.0 |
| 1870 | 103.0 | 180.7 | 151.7 | 106.0 |
| 1871 | 95.4 | 177.0 | 124.9 | 97.5 |
| 1872 | 102.6 | 161.8 | 172.8 | 115.1 |
| 1873 | 119.8 | 178.0 | 180.4 | 131.1 |
| 1874 | 109.3 | 193.4 | 196.9 | 125.3 |
| 1875 | 96.5 | 199.7 | 182.0 | 118.6 |
| 1876 | 101.4 | 192.8 | 173.0 | 116.8 |
| 1877 | 94.8 | 200.5 | 158.7 | 110.4 |
| 1878 | 96.5 | 190.9 | 150.4 | 109.2 |
| 1879 | 97.5 | 170.5 | 146.4 | 108.6 |
| 1880 | 97.5 | 169.7 | 144.9 | 114.7 |
| 1881 | 103.6 | 171.0 | 148.3 | 108.6 |
| 1882 | 99.7 | 209.1 | 135.8 | 110.5 |
| 1883 | 99.9 | 204.9 | 143.3 | 110.1 |
| 1884 | 96.6 | 194.3 | 136.1 | 109.8 |
| 1885 | 103.6 | 199.7 | 130.9 | 108.3 |
| 1886 | 98.2 | 208.9 | 121.9 | 103.4 |
| 1887 | 97.2 | 193.9 | 118.6 | 102.6 |
| 1888 | 97.8 | 193.2 | 121.9 | 102.5 |
| 1889 | 103.6 | 190.7 | 125.7 | 104.4 |
| 1890 | 103.9 | 190.7 | 132.6 | 110.3 |
| 1891 | 102.5 | 187.2 | 129.8 | 110.1 |
| 1892 | 82.3 | 184.9 | 118.3 | 106.6 |
| 1893 | 75.0 | 180.1 | 109.7 | 102.3 |

| Year ending 31st Dec. | Household buildings | Household equipment | Private non-dwelling | Public non-dwelling |
|---|---|---|---|---|
| 1894 | 71.3 | 158.1 | 101.6 | 98.0 |
| 1895 | 73.1 | 155.8 | 98.2 | 103.6 |
| 1896 | 73.2 | 158.3 | 100.6 | 103.6 |
| 1897 | 72.1 | 156.4 | 98.0 | 104.9 |
| 1898 | 82.8 | 155.5 | 106.7 | 101.9 |
| 1899 | 88.4 | 169.7 | 115.8 | 109.1 |
| 1900 | 91.1 | 160.8 | 128.1 | 121.7 |
| 30th June | | | | |
| 1901 | 102 | 187 | 119 | 119 |
| 1902 | 101 | 178 | 115 | 112 |
| 1903 | 97 | 179 | 113 | 112 |
| 1904 | 95 | 163 | 111 | 113 |
| 1905 | 91 | 162 | 111 | 112 |
| 1906 | 98 | 169 | 117 | 113 |
| 1907 | 97 | 161 | 119 | 122 |
| 1908 | 105 | 179 | 120 | 124 |
| 1909 | 102 | 188 | 121 | 126 |
| 1910 | 105 | 195 | 126 | 126 |
| 1911 | 112 | 198 | 131 | 131 |
| 1912 | 125 | 217 | 140 | 143 |
| 1913 | 134 | 212 | 146 | 147 |
| 1914 | 135 | 235 | 149 | 148 |
| 1915 | 137 | 270 | 164 | 163 |
| 1916 | 144 | 302 | 199 | 206 |
| 1917 | 150 | 358 | 223 | 236 |
| 1918 | 164 | 374 | 246 | 258 |
| 1919 | 174 | 382 | 225 | 257 |
| 1920 | 211 | 390 | 258 | 296 |
| 1921 | 218 | 390 | 262 | 321 |
| 1922 | 218 | 358 | 256 | 269 |
| 1923 | 221 | 372 | 256 | 255 |
| 1924 | 221 | 349 | 256 | 250 |
| 1925 | 227 | 344 | 255 | 255 |

**Table 7.11** continued

| Year ending 30th June | Household buildings | Household equipment | Private non-dwelling | Public non-dwelling |
|---|---|---|---|---|
| 1926 | 225 | 364 | 257 | 262 |
| 1927 | 227 | 362 | 258 | 263 |
| 1928 | 226 | 360 | 258 | 265 |
| 1929 | 227 | 368 | 259 | 262 |
| 1930 | 226 | 341 | 245 | 231 |
| 1931 | 217 | 322 | 245 | 235 |
| 1932 | 205 | 298 | 245 | 213 |
| 1933 | 207 | 294 | 234 | 202 |
| 1934 | 204 | 289 | 233 | 203 |
| 1935 | 204 | 318 | 231 | 202 |
| 1936 | 206 | 318 | 230 | 204 |
| 1937 | 217 | 324 | 243 | 214 |
| 1938 | 222 | 341 | 249 | 220 |
| 1939 | 230 | 380 | 207 | 224 |
| 1940 | 245 | 405 | 218 | 229 |
| 1941 | 279 | 423 | 237 | 255 |
| 1942 | 290 | 440 | 287 | 272 |
| 1943 | 340 | 476 | 288 | 319 |
| 1944 | 355 | 476 | 293 | 330 |
| 1945 | 357 | 464 | 293 | 327 |
| 1946 | 368 | 494 | 294 | 338 |
| 1947 | 367 | 496 | 311 | 350 |
| 1948 | 375 | 527 | 353 | 383 |
| 1949 | 428 | 563 | 390 | 413 |
| 1950 | 476 | 618 | 427 | 448 |
| 1951 | 587 | 678 | 521 | 510 |
| 1952 | 644 | 807 | 639 | 598 |
| 1953 | 731 | 869 | 694 | 665 |
| 1954 | 736 | 883 | 717 | 691 |
| 1955 | 774 | 881 | 744 | 717 |
| 1956 | 822 | 883 | 790 | 747 |
| 1957 | 837 | 920 | 822 | 778 |
| 1958 | 851 | 934 | 849 | 784 |
| 1959 | 851 | 944 | 859 | 799 |
| 1960 | 865 | 954 | 854 | 820 |
| 1961 | 894 | 966 | 877 | 845 |
| 1962 | 894 | 979 | 890 | 866 |
| 1963 | 894 | 977 | 900 | 876 |
| 1964 | 914 | 964 | 909 | 897 |
| 1965 | 942 | 972 | 950 | 933 |
| 1966 | 971 | 989 | 968 | 959 |
| 1967 | 1000 | 1000 | 1000 | 1000 |
| 1968 | 1029 | 1019 | 1018 | 1036 |
| 1969 | 1058 | 1040 | 1073 | 1072 |
| 1970 | 1096 | 1053 | 1101 | 1124 |
| 1971 | 1149 | 1090 | 1155 | 1191 |
| 1972 | 1236 | 1146 | 1237 | 1278 |
| 1973 | 1361 | 1187 | 1315 | 1381 |
| 1974 | 1654 | 1296 | 1457 | 1557 |
| 1975 | 2019 | 1538 | 1799 | 1938 |
| 1976 | 2361 | 1783 | 2091 | 2237 |
| 1977 | 2635 | 1963 | 2333 | 2495 |
| 1978 | 2803 | 2126 | 2594 | 2696 |
| 1979 | 2894 | 2259 | 2863 | 2881 |
| 1980 | 3096 | 2442 | 3164 | 3392 |
| 1981 | 3466 | 2713 | 3498 | 3603 |
| 1982 | 3880 | 3001 | 3813 | 4046 |
| 1983 | 4274 | 3359 | 4187 | 4608 |
| 1984 | 4481 | 3597 | 4374 | 4887 |
| 1985 | 4808 | 3768 | 4566 | 5155 |
| 1986 | 5236 | 4075 | 5146 | 5583 |
| 1987 | 5577 | 4373 | 5653 | 6000 |
| 1988 | 5923 | 4677 | 5936 | 6361 |
| 1989 | 6880 | 4943 | 6119 | 6737 |
| 1990 | 7639 | 5214 | 6242 | 7119 |

# 8

# *Households and household workers*

*T*his chapter provides the building blocks—numbers of households and household workers—for the estimates of household income and, ultimately, of Gross Community Income. As far as historical social accounts are concerned, these buildings blocks are relatively sound and can bear the weight of interpretation that has been erected upon them in earlier chapters. Annual estimates of households and household workers are based on reliable colonial and national census counts together with local authority data used to determine rates and taxes. These sources are generally regarded as a more reliable foundation than the equivalent sources employed by N. G. Butlin (1962), G. D. Snooks (1972) and W. A. Sinclair (1984) to estimate sectoral production in the market economy over the same period.[1]

## Household formation

Households are the basic unit of production in the household economy, just as firms are the basic unit of production in the market sector. But there is an important difference. Firms exist only to organize the various factors of production so as to produce goods and services for sale and, hopefully, for profit. Households on the other hand are units not only for the production of goods and services, but also for the employment of market and household goods and services, together with household time, to produce higher 'commodities' of children, 'happiness', and recreation.[2] In view of the central importance of households in the Total Economy, it is hard to explain why they have not received greater attention in mainstream economics.

### Methods

Accurate estimates of households are essential to this study. Fortunately, reliable data on numbers of households, which officially are defined as 'private occupied dwellings', are available for each of the census years between 1841 and 1986. It is also possible to interpolate between the census years with a reasonable degree of accuracy by using data concerning changes in the annual stock of occupied private dwellings recorded by local authorities in each colony/state. The annual data are particularly reliable after the Second World War; they are generally good from Federation to the Second World War; and are 'fair' during the nineteenth century. For comparative purposes, the reliability of the data before the Second World War, owing to the similarity of data sources and techniques, is closely comparable with the reliability of Noel Butlin's estimates of housing stock changes.[3]

## The census data

The census definition of a household is a private occupied dwelling. The distinction between private and non-private dwellings is the distinction between self-contained houses, flats, and apartments on the one hand, and hotels and boarding houses on the other—a distinction, in other words, between the household and the market in the matter of accommodation. This distinction is clearly made in all censuses from 1901, and the ratio does not change significantly. Earlier census data, therefore, can be deflated by the ratio of private to total occupied dwellings in the 1901 census (i.e. 0.9565). As our concern is to identify households rather than residential structures, we wish to exclude unoccupied dwellings, but to include tents and other temporary dwellings. This contrasts with the approach of Butlin who, wishing to estimate investment in dwellings, included unoccupied dwellings and excluded tents and other temporary dwellings. The census data, therefore, provide a series of regular and consistent benchmarks over the last 200 years.

## Inter-censal data

Annual data on dwellings have been assiduously collected by local authorities from the mid nineteenth century because of the need to collect rates and taxes from the occupants. The quality of the record is generally good for all states after the early 1900s, but varies considerably in the nineteenth century. Each colony/state has been dealt with separately (various *Statistical registers*) until 1947/48 after which national data—provided in the ABS *Building and construction bulletin*—have been used.

Butlin provides a good discussion of the nature of the local authority returns published in the *Statistical register* for each colony/state.[4] These returns begin in 1882 in Victoria, 1885 in New South Wales, 1867 in Queensland, 1908 in South Australia (except for the city of Adelaide, for which data are available from 1881–1901), 1907 in Western Australia, and incompletely in Tasmania after 1901. In order to employ a consistent technique, the variety of different sources used by Butlin in the construction of his housing stock estimates has *not* been followed. Instead, gaps in the earlier years have been filled by calculating the ratio between population and dwellings in each colony for census years (or at either end of the data gap); assuming that these ratios change by a constant annual amount between censuses; and applying the resulting annual series of ratios to an annual series of population data. This technique, which has been applied consistently throughout, produces reasonably reliable estimates, although it will tend to smooth out any inter-censal fluctuations in the relationship between population and dwellings. This is not a problem in a study of the longrun and, even in the shortrun, the regularity of censuses in nineteenth-century Australia means that it is not a major cause for concern.

It should be realized, however, that in the early years of each colony, data on a family basis are inadequate. Accordingly, the estimated numbers of households in the colonial foundation period are nominal, in the sense that they represent households that would have existed if the household/population ratio of the nearest census year had applied. But, as the institutional arrangements in the early years of each colony differed from those prevailing in later years, the initial household numbers should not be taken too literally. While this information does not affect the reliability of the income estimates (in millions of dollars), it should be taken into account by those with more specific interests.

Table 8.2 presents estimates of the number of Australian households from 1788 to 1990. Before 1901 these estimates are provided for each colony and after Federation for the nation as a whole.

# Household workers

## *Primary household workers*

Household workers consist of primary household workers (largely female) who are responsible for the bulk of activities undertaken in the household sector, and secondary household workers (largely male) who make a contribution to household work, largely outside the home. The first of these categories, primary household workers, includes full-time household workers (females and retired males) and females who are employed part-time or full-time in the market sector but who also undertake the bulk of the work in their households. Typically these market/household workers are married or 'once married' females who, in addition to their market work, are engaged in household work for thirty or more hours per week.[5] The basic approach taken in this chapter, which values all the activities of primary household workers, will capture unpaid volunteer and community work, as well as work within the household.

## *Full-time household workers*
The aim is to estimate the total number of females and males involved in full-time housework for which no direct payment is made. Detailed data are available in the regular colonial/state censuses between 1833 and 1901,

together with the national censuses between 1911 and 1986. These censuses provide data in the following categories.

- All adult females engaged in 'unpaid home duties' or classified as 'not in workforce' (usually classified as the wives, widows, and mothers of household heads)—this is the dominant category.
- All daughters and sons of household heads who are not employed in the market and who are not students, scholars, or small children. This category is important until the Second World War.
- All wives and daughters 'assisting' on farms and stations, on the grounds that: while they may assist their husbands and fathers, they are mainly responsible for all work within the house, and that this is necessary for consistency over time with other occupational categories (classified by main activity). The numbers in this category are not large (zero for some colonies), except for the 1881 census, when the earlier British practice of allocating the wives and daughters to their husbands' occupations in rural areas was briefly adopted (but rejected by Coghlan).
- Others who, although not recorded as being engaged in 'home duties', reasonably can be expected to be involved in house duties, gardening, and particularly child-minding. This group includes 'pensioners', 'annuitants' and 'retired' people (both males and females), and other 'unoccupied' (but not 'unemployed') relatives.

The resulting estimates for each census year provide the total number of people who are not designated as part of the market labour force (either 'employed' or 'unemployed'), but who can reasonably be expected to be part of, what I will call, the full-time household labour force.

To obtain an *annual* series of full-time household workers it is necessary to employ an appropriate annual index for the purposes of extrapolation. The best available index is the number of Australian households, 1788 to 1990, presented in Table 8.2. As we have seen, annual household numbers can be reliably estimated using census data together with annual data on completed *occupied* dwellings that have been carefully collected by local authorities in each colony/state. The interpolation method employed was as follows: for each census year the ratio of full-time household workers to households was calculated; it was assumed that this *ratio* changed between each census by a constant annual amount; the resulting annual ratios were applied to the annual household series. Considerable confidence in this procedure is provided by the remarkable stability of these census ratios before the Second World War.

The only official Australian time use survey (ABS 1987) *suggests* (because it was only a pilot study) that in 1987 married women not employed in the market worked an average of 48.5 hours per week on 'domestic', 'childcare', and shopping activities. This has been treated as a standard working week equivalent to that in the market sector on the grounds that some of these self-nominated hours inevitably include leisure activities and were not worked under a regime of market discipline. To value each self-nominated hour of household work by full-time household workers as equivalent to an hour worked in the market place would lead to an overvaluation of household activities.[6] This has been overlooked by the ABS in its recent (1990) 'experimental' estimate of the value of unpaid household work for the single year 1986–87. This is a serious limitation of estimates based solely on survey responses.

The numbers of full-time household workers, on a colonial basis before 1901 and a national basis thereafter, are presented in Tables 8.3 to 8.10.

## Market/household workers

Market/household workers are typically women employed in the market sector, but who are still responsible for managing homes and families despite their 'outside' work—women who are either 'married' or 'once married' (separated, divorced, and widowed). The 1987 time-use survey *suggests* that employed married women worked an average of 34.1 hours per week in the home, as well as 30.3 hours per week in the market. As housework by this group was done under a strong time constraint (a total working week of 64.4 hours), which must be regarded at least as effective as market place discipline, it is reasonable to treat an hour of housework as equivalent to an hour of market work. Taking the 1987 survey data at face value, this means that employed married women worked in the household the equivalent of 0.922 of a standard market working week.

This raises the question of whether we should adjust the number of workers in this category by 0.922 to arrive at an estimate of full-time equivalents. This is a complex issue. There is evidence to suggest that the main reason for employed married women working fewer hours in the household than married women who are not employed, is that their spouses and families do more household work than their counterparts in families where the wife does not work in the market. But this appears to be a recent development. A generation ago married women who worked in the market received very little support from their families in the home. A persuasive argument is that although employed married women today work 0.922 of a market week in the home, a generation ago (say the mid 1960s) they worked a full (1.0) week in the home in addition to their market work.

On the face of it, this suggests that a graduated ratio increasing from 0.92 in 1990 to 1.0 in, say, 1965 should be applied to the number of people in the market/household category. But there are in fact a number of good arguments as to why this should not be done. The first is that over the same period of time the ratio between *de facto* and *de jure* married women has risen, which will help to offset the effect of any decline in hours worked. Second, as shown below, the method employed in estimating the number of males involved in housework does not pick up the increase in hours worked by the families of employed married women. And finally, the adjustment of 0.922 is relatively insignificant in the household sector as a whole—it would only reduce the 1987 estimate of household income by 1.7 per cent. In this study, therefore, the housework done by employed married women is regarded as equivalent to the standard market working week for females.

An annual series of market/household workers from 1788 to 1990 can be estimated by using census data between 1911 and 1986 on 'married' and 'once married' females employed in the market sector, and by interpolating between and extrapolating beyond these census benchmarks by employing an annual series of total female market workers. For this purpose it has been assumed, as elsewhere, that census *ratios* change by a constant annual amount between benchmarks, and that ratios are constant beyond benchmarks (i.e. before 1841 and after 1986). The total female market workforce was estimated by using the censuses between 1841 and 1986 to provide reliable benchmarks at regular intervals over the 150 year period. To interpolate between, and extrapolate beyond, these benchmarks the following annual data on female market workers were employed:

- 1961–1991: the ABS *Labour force survey*.
- 1911–1961: Keating, 'Australian workforce', Series B.
- 1861–1901: a weighted index of women employed in 'manufacturing' (42.2 per cent) and 'domestic and personal service' (57.8 per cent)—the weights are from Keating, 'Australian workforce', p. 160; the manufacturing data from Linge, *Industrial awakening*, pp. 741 and 746, and Snooks, 'Manufacturing', p. 292; and services data from Butlin, *Australian domestic product*, pp. 226 and 229.
- 1788–1861: annual female population estimates (Clio, Economic History Timeseries Database, RSSS, ANU).

The numbers of market/household workers, together with total primary household workers, are presented in Tables 8.3 to 8.10.

It has been suggested that, in the nineteenth century, censuses in the English-speaking world were not always a reliable guide to female participation in the market, because some married women may have failed to declare that they were undertaking paid work outside the home.[7] This, it has been argued, will lead to an underestimate of market activities. This argument, however, is not correct in the case of Australia. First, with the exception of the 1881 census, Australian Government statisticians went to great pains to carefully record the *main* economic activity of women. And, as discussed elsewhere in this volume, I have attempted to sort out the problems in the 1881 census. Second, while part-time market work by married women may have been overlooked, this does not pose a problem because the objective has been to classify female work by *main* activity. Part-time female work has been estimated in a different way. Third, even if the estimate of household/market workers is too low (and I do not think this is the case), this would not lead to an underestimate of market activity, because market activity has been estimated by Noel Butlin from different sources using different methods. At worst it would lead to an underestimate of household activity, which would imply that my conclusions about the importance of the household sector are particularly robust.

## Secondary household workers

A major popular misconception about household work is that it is, and always has been, undertaken virtually entirely by married women. In fact, males play a secondary but, nonetheless, important role in the household sector. Surveys of how Australian households use time—undertaken in 1974, 1976, and 1987— suggest that, on average, males are responsible for approximately 30 per cent of all unpaid household work.[8] This involves 14.4 hours of unpaid work per week compared with 36 hours of unpaid work by women. And to place this in a wider context of *all* work—both market and household—the 1987 time-use survey suggested that the average number of hours worked per day on all activities was very similar for both men (7.27 hours) and women (7.13 hours). Women, in their turn, were responsible for only 32.3 per cent of all market work.

The nature of household work differs between the two categories of primary and secondary household workers. As discussed above, the typical primary household worker is the married female who, assisted by males and females in both the older and younger generations, is largely engaged in household duties such as cooking, cleaning, washing, shopping, child-minding etc. The typical secondary household worker, on the other hand, is the married male, who is engaged in outdoor activities such as gardening, home construction and maintenance, car repairs, shopping and travel. In 1987, for example, approximately 59 per cent of male household work was undertaken on these activities. But the picture is more complex than many realize: cooking occupied 20 per cent of the time males devoted to household work, cleaning 8 per cent, laundry 3 per cent, and childcare 10 per cent.

Unfortunately the normally valuable population census tells us nothing about the contribution made to the household economy by males, whose main economic role is played out in the market sector. Nor are we provided with any information about single males and females living on their own or in shared private accommodation. Only time-use surveys can tell us anything about the household activities of these two important groups, and this information is only available for Australia since the mid 1970s, and even then the samples used are very small and regionally specific. But we can approach this subject indirectly.

Time-use surveys in Australia for 1974, 1976, and 1987 tell us two important things about secondary household workers. First, the average married male between 25 and 50 years of age undertakes between 13 to 15 hours of household work per week, compared with about 42 to 45 hours of market work per week. In other words, the amount of household work undertaken by the average secondary household worker amounts to about one-third of the work he does in the market sector. We also know from time-use data, both over long periods of time (since 1917 in USA) and between households at a point in time, that the hours worked in the household by males has changed in parallel fashion with the length of the market working week, and is little affected by variation in the number of market hours worked by their wives. The second important piece of information disclosed by time-use surveys is that the hours of household work done by single males and females living alone or sharing accommodation is, when averaged, similar to the number of hours worked by married men.[9]

These two vital pieces of information can be used, together with the annual estimates of household numbers presented in Table 8.2, to construct an annual series of secondary household workers over the last 200 years. First, the annual series of Australian households must be adjusted by subtracting the number of households presided over by retired heads of households (obtained from census records), as they have been included in the calculation of primary household workers. This leaves the number of households occupied by married men and single males and females. Second, as we know (from time-use surveys in USA since 1917 and in Australia since 1974) that, on average, each of these households possesses one-third of a secondary household worker, we can estimate the total number of these workers in full-time equivalents. It could be argued that the main problem with this approximate method is that there *may* have been a marginal increase in hours worked by males in the household since the early 1960s owing to changing lifestyles for both males and females. But this is unlikely to have been very marked in Australia before 1987, as the ABS time-use survey for that year shows that the male contribution to housework did not vary significantly across the sample despite a wide variation in hours of market work undertaken by the respondents' wives.[10] While this method is not as satisfactory as that used to estimate the number of primary household workers, it will not be far from the mark, particularly when aggregated with the number of primary household workers which, as suggested above, probably contains an upward bias since the mid–1960s.

Considerable confidence can be had in the trend of the time-series presented in Tables 8.13 and 8.14, and even in the fluctuations, which are correctly dominated by the changing number of households rather than the changing hours of secondary household work.

# Valuing household work

In Chapter 7 two main methods of valuation—wage rates for domestics and opportunity cost—were discussed and reasons were given for adopting the opportunity cost approach. This approach has been used to value primary and secondary household labour. Market wage rates, rather than average earnings, should be used to value household labour services because, as demonstrated theoretically in Chapter 7 and econometrically in Chapter 4 (Table 4.1, p. 86), it is the change in market wage rates that motivates households to change their allocation of time between paid work, household work, and leisure. Average earnings, on the other hand, reflect hours worked (in the form of overtime) as well as the market weekly wage rate. A further and pragmatic consideration is that data on wage rates are more readily available in the past than average earnings. We have already noted, in Chapter 7, that during periods of involuntary unemployment the market wage rate will be higher than the clearing wage rate, and therefore will lead to an overvaluation not only of household activity but also market activity. While relativities between the sectors remain substantially unaffected, those who wish to employ my estimates should realize that the most meaningful comparisons are between years with similar rates of unemployment, and that the true performance during depressions is actually *worse* than the recorded performance. Although not generally recognized, the same is true for market estimates.

An issue that must be squarely faced is the implication for the opportunity-cost principle of the involvement of the Arbitration Commission in Australian wage determinations from the 1910s. The general view taken in this study (see Chapters 4 and 6) is that Arbitration decisions on gender wage relativities reflected market conditions rather than being an exogenous determinant of them. There is strong evidence for this view. First, the econometric results in Table 4.1, p. 86, suggest that the major determinant of female market participation has been the market capital/labour ratio which reflects the underlying technological conditions of the Australian economy. Second, Figure 4.3, p. 87, shows that there is strong correlation between the market capital/labour ratio and the gender wage ratio. In other words, relative market job opportunities and remuneration for females were determined by fundamental economic forces rather than arbitrary institutional arrangements. Hence, in my dynamic model of the total Australian economy, wage rates for males and females are endogenously determined.

## *Secondary household services*

As the male wage rate data are more abundant and reliable, secondary household services will be dealt with first. The general market rate for adult male workers has been used to value work done in this category, because the vast majority of secondary workers consist of working-age males. This is the marginal rate at which decisions are made either to work an extra hour in the market place, to work an extra hour in the household (gardening, labouring, painting etc.), or to devote an extra hour to leisure activities. The weekly award wage rate for adult males from 1906 to 1973 can be found in the *Labour report*, from 1974 to 1985 in *Labour statistics, Australia*, and since 1985 in ABS *Award rates of pay indexes, Australia*. Because nineteenth century wage-rate data can be employed as an index of annual rates of change, but not of the absolute level of the average wage, owing to a less representative range of occupations and to unknown deductions for board and lodging, the 1906 wage level was extrapolated back to 1861 by employing the extensive wage data for New South Wales, Victoria, and Queensland in Butlin, *Australian domestic product*; and beyond 1861 to 1823 with wage data for bricklayers, carpenters, masons, smiths, and wheelwrights in Coghlan's *Wealth and progress*. These wage rate data were used to construct weighted (by relative employment) indexes for this early period. Government wages reported in Butlin, 'Public sector wage rates', suggest that between 1788 and the 1820s, wage rates, in what was essentially a command economy, did not change significantly and can be assumed constant.

These weekly wage rates were converted to an annual basis and were used to value numbers of secondary household workers. The annual wage rates are presented in Table 8.16, and the value of secondary household labour services in Table 8.15.

## Primary household services

Primary household workers are mainly female, both married and single, but also include a relatively small number of retired males. All these categories possess a similar opportunity cost, as retired males who attempt to obtain market employment would, on average, compete with females for lighter and less skilled jobs such as cleaning, caretaking, gardening, childminding etc. Accordingly, the appropriate measure of opportunity cost for this group as a whole is the general adult female market wage rate. For reasons discussed above, the working week for primary household workers is treated as equivalent, for valuation purposes, to a standard working week in the market sector.

Market weekly award wage rates for adult females can be found in the *Labour report* for 1914 to 1973, *Labour statistics, Australia* for 1974 to 1985, and *Award rates of pay indexes, Australia* after 1985. The wage data for females before 1914 is both meagre and misleading. It is possible to extract data from Coghlan, *Wealth and progress* (and from succeeding volumes) for a small group of occupations in New South Wales including cooks, dairywomen, housemaids, laundresses, nursemaids, and servants (both farm and general), and to construct a combined wage-rate series weighted by the relative importance of each occupational category for the period 1843 to 1914. But there are two major problems that prevent us from adopting this series as it stands. First, as these data are not representative of the average female wage earner, and as it excludes certain allowances such as board and lodging, the series cannot be used to represent absolute wage levels. Second, as the ratio between the value of money wages (known) and allowances (largely unknown) appears to have changed between the 1840s and the turn of the century, this series cannot be used even to extrapolate the 1914 level back to 1843 (which was possible in the case of male wage rates because of the absence of this problem owing to a wider range of wage-rate data). Yet while the trend in this series is highly suspect, there is every reason to believe that the short-term (or annual) fluctuations are, in fact, a reflection of short-term changes in market demand and supply for female labour.

**Figure 8.1 Estimating female/male wage ratios, New South Wales, 1843–1902**

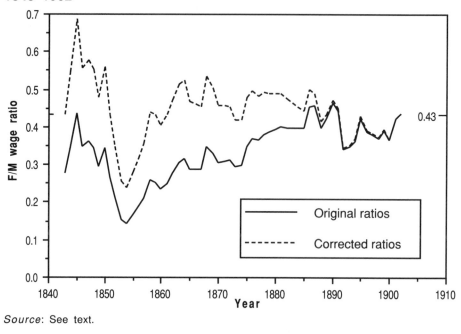

*Source*: See text.

Fortunately it is possible to correct for the misleading trend while retaining the pattern of annual fluctuations. Although we cannot successfully calculate the changing ratio between the monetized and non-monetized components of female wage rates over the second half of the nineteenth century, it is possible to resolve this problem. Two pieces of information enable us to do so. First, we start with the annual ratio between female (high degree of non-monetized income) and male (absence of non-monetized income) wage rates in New South Wales from 1843 to 1906—represented by the solid line in Figure 8.1—which almost doubled from an unbelievably low 0.249 in 1861 to a more reasonable 0.462 in 1890. Second, it is possible to compare this highly suspect trend with the results of a small sample of male and female workers engaged in the same occupation—that of domestic service—in which we could expect a similar ratio to exist between monetized and non-monetized components of wages for both sexes. The small sample suggests that the female/male wage ratio was much the same in the mid–1840s, in 1861, and in 1889 as it was in 1902, yet with fluctuations in between.

It was possible, using a computer program, to correct the trend, while retaining the pattern of annual fluctuations. This was achieved by constraining the solid line in Figure 8.1 to conform to the supplementary evidence that the female/male wage ratios in 1843, 1861, and 1889 were all equal to that in 1902 i.e. 0.43. This corresponds with other evidence on gender wage relativities, together with their fluctuation before and during the goldrush period.[11] The estimated series of gender ratios is represented by the dotted line in Figure 8.1. This set of ratios was then applied to the earlier estimated series of male wage rates between 1843 and 1914. For the period 1788 to 1842, the 1843 ratio was applied to the male wage rate series. Needless to say the estimates before the 1840s are not to be taken too seriously—but certainly as seriously as the existing GDP estimates (by Butlin) for these early years. The female wage rate series is presented in Table 8.16 and the value of female labour services in Table 8.15.

# The ABS estimate of 'unpaid household work' for 1986–87

In 1990 the Australian Bureau of Statistics (ABS) published an 'experimental' estimate of 'unpaid household work' for the single year 1986–87. This was seven years after my own 'preliminary' estimates of the value of Australian household labour services for the period 1891–1981.[12] This estimate was based on the time-use data obtained from a sample of 1,000 Sydney households for the period 23 May to 4 June 1987—a rather narrow base for such an important estimate. Nevertheless, this experimental estimate by ABS is most welcome.

The ABS opportunity cost (using award wage rates) estimate for unpaid household work in Australia in 1986–87 is $151,513 million, or 58 per cent of GDP, which is higher than estimates for other countries (see Table 8.1). While we would not expect two very different methods of estimating household labour services to produce the same result—certainly this has not been achieved elsewhere—a comparison of this estimate with my own for the same year will be the occasion to examine our respective approaches. My opportunity cost estimate of household labour services for 1986–87 (Table 8.15) is $111,237 million or 43 per cent of GDP (while my estimate of total household income is $130,232 million, or 50 per cent of GDP, or 53 per cent of market income). My estimate is, therefore, 73.4 per cent of the ABS figure. The ABS authors have attempted to rationalize their high estimate relative to other countries by making passing reference to 'methodological differences', 'cultural factors'—for example, 'a high level of home ownership in Australia and the predominance of detached housing with gardens' (which ignores the garden allotments in European countries); 'the later reference period'; and to 'reservations regarding the time-use data'. But no analysis is made of these issues.

There can be little doubt that the ABS figure is an overestimate, a conclusion that was obviously suggested to its authors by an international comparison with similar estimates undertaken elsewhere. Table 8.1 shows my estimate to be in line with those for Canada, France, and Finland. Only the estimates reported by Murphy for USA[13] are higher and comparable with the ABS estimate. But even here there is an inconsistency. The US opportunity cost estimate does not bear the same relationship with the replacement costs estimates, that it does in other countries including Australia (ABS). If the US replacement cost ratios are correct (32 per cent), then the US opportunity cost ratio is far too high. Or, in other words, if the ABS replacement cost (47 per cent) ratio was the same as that in the US (32 per cent) then the Australian opportunity cost ratio would be, *ceteris paribus*, in the vicinity of 40 per cent, which is slightly lower than my estimate.

But my main reasons for thinking that the ABS opportunity cost measure is an overestimate arise from the precariousness of their statistical base (a very small and regionally specific time-use survey), and from the methods they have employed. The first issue about methods concerns their measure of labour input, which is based on the number of hours that survey respondents *claimed* to have worked during a two-week period. No objective check was, nor could be, made on the veracity of the responses. A wider geographical sample might, however, indicate different regional responses that could be useful in adjusting the raw data. My very strong reservations about this subjective labour input data are as follows:

- Respondents are likely to overstate the number of hours they claim to work in the household to give the impression that, as useful citizens, they are more than pulling their weight. Indeed it is highly likely that there will be intra and inter-household competition in this.
- Household work by full-time household workers is not done under market workplace discipline and, therefore, is highly likely to occur at a more leisurely pace. In other words, the output from an hour's input of labour will differ between the household and the market. This poses a significant problem when valuing housework hours with a market wage rate. As discussed earlier in this chapter, I have deliberately reduced my labour input estimate (by about 22 per cent) to take account of this obvious source of inflation. The ABS has not attempted to adjust for this important factor. This is probably the main reason for the difference in our estimates for 1986–87.
- Household work and leisure activities are highly intertwined, and difficult for even the most scrupulous respondent to unravel. For example, what proportion of hours spent in the garden by the householder should be regarded as leisure? (The test, which was not applied by the ABS, is whether they would be prepared to employ someone else to undertake the same number of hours of gardening if they had the funds.) They do, however, recognize this problem (p. 7).

The second doubt I have about the ABS method, concerns the rates of pay employed. Their wage rates are higher than those I have used, owing to the fact that they are 'person's rates' ('because it was assumed that a market replacement could be either male or female') rather than female rates. This

**Table 8.1   International comparisons of estimates of household labour services** (per cent of GDP)

| Country | Year | Method of valuation | | |
|---|---|---|---|---|
| | | Housekeeper replacement | Individual function replacement | Opportunity cost |
| France | 1975 | 31* | | 44* |
| Canada | 1971 | 33 | 40 | |
| | 1981 | | 35 | 40 |
| USA | 1976 | 32* | 44* | 51–60* |
| Finland | 1980 | 32* | | |
| Australia (ABS) | 1986–87 | 47 | 52–57 | 58–62 |
| Australia (Snooks) | 1986–87 | | | 43 |

*Sources*:  ABS, 'Measuring unpaid household work', p. 17 (using award rates); Snooks, Table 8.14.
*Notes*:    * GNP rather than GDP, which inflates the value.
          *Household replacement*: housekeeper wage rate used for valuation.
          *Individual function replacement*: composite wage rate, consisting of weighted wage rates
          for individual activities, used for valuation.

overestimates the value of work that is done by a group of workers who are predominantly women, because it includes allowances for human capital that the average married woman does not possess.

The ABS estimate appears, therefore, to be inflated. But even if it was not, the analysis in Part One based upon my estimates in Part Two would remain unaffected, because I am concerned with longrun changes in these variables rather than with absolute levels. Indeed no set of national accounts should be used uncritically to examine *absolute* levels of income.

**Table 8.2   Number of households, Australia, 1788–1990**

| Year ending 31st Dec. | New South Wales | Victoria | Queensland | South Australia | Western Australia | Tasmania | Australia |
|---|---|---|---|---|---|---|---|
| **1788** | 80 | | | | | | 80 |
| **1789** | 60 | | | | | | 60 |
| **1790** | 191 | | | | | | 191 |
| **1791** | 267 | | | | | | 267 |
| **1792** | 303 | | | | | | 303 |
| **1793** | 326 | | | | | | 326 |
| **1794** | 332 | | | | | | 332 |
| **1795** | 322 | | | | | | 322 |
| **1796** | 381 | | | | | | 381 |
| **1797** | 403 | | | | | | 403 |
| **1798** | 426 | | | | | | 426 |
| **1799** | 472 | | | | | | 472 |
| **1800** | 484 | | | | | | 484 |
| **1801** | 552 | | | | | | 552 |
| **1802** | 651 | | | | | | 651 |
| **1803** | 656 | | | | | 22 | 678 |
| **1804** | 654 | | | | | 69 | 723 |
| **1805** | 645 | | | | | 94 | 739 |
| **1806** | 665 | | | | | 93 | 758 |
| **1807** | 738 | | | | | 105 | 843 |
| **1808** | 846 | | | | | 144 | 989 |
| **1809** | 953 | | | | | 161 | 1114 |
| **1810** | 938 | | | | | 182 | 1120 |
| **1811** | 955 | | | | | 197 | 1152 |
| **1812** | 1016 | | | | | 210 | 1226 |
| **1813** | 1129 | | | | | 223 | 1352 |
| **1814** | 1131 | | | | | 236 | 1367 |
| **1815** | 1218 | | | | | 241 | 1459 |
| **1816** | 1441 | | | | | 252 | 1693 |
| **1817** | 1657 | | | | | 415 | 2072 |
| **1818** | 2084 | | | | | 424 | 2508 |
| **1819** | 2420 | | | | | 671 | 3091 |
| **1820** | 2602 | | | | | 684 | 3287 |
| **1821** | 2755 | | | | | 722 | 3477 |
| **1822** | 2756 | | | | | 953 | 3709 |
| **1823** | 2844 | | | | | 1241 | 4085 |
| **1824** | 3322 | | | | | 1525 | 4847 |
| **1825** | 3558 | | | | | 1759 | 5317 |
| **1826** | 3612 | | | | | 1859 | 5470 |
| **1827** | 3665 | | | | | 2087 | 5752 |
| **1828** | 3721 | | | | | 2247 | 5968 |
| **1829** | 3831 | | | | 143 | 2481 | 6455 |
| **1830** | 4209 | | | | 167 | 3010 | 7386 |
| **1831** | 4569 | | | | 191 | 3303 | 8062 |
| **1832** | 5136 | | | | 215 | 3583 | 8934 |
| **1833** | 6008 | | | | 235 | 4256 | 10499 |
| **1834** | 6441 | | | | 256 | 4672 | 11370 |
| **1835** | 7007 | | | | 267 | 4980 | 12254 |
| **1836** | 7817 | 16 | | 97 | 278 | 5416 | 13625 |

*Note*: Victorian data separated from New South Wales total in 1836.

**Table 8.2**   continued

| Year ending 31st Dec. | New South Wales | Victoria | Queensland | South Australia | Western Australia | Tasmania | Australia |
|---|---|---|---|---|---|---|---|
| **1837** | 8632 | 91 | | 584 | 289 | 5293 | 14889 |
| **1838** | 9875 | 252 | | 1071 | 274 | 5674 | 17145 |
| **1839** | 11497 | 418 | | 1841 | 306 | 5459 | 19521 |
| **1840** | 13018 | 738 | | 2611 | 329 | 5703 | 22399 |
| **1841** | 14951 | 1465 | | 2764 | 393 | 7119 | 26691 |
| **1842** | 17411 | 1996 | | 2916 | 494 | 7296 | 30114 |
| **1843** | 18882 | 2313 | | 3069 | 548 | 7678 | 32490 |
| **1844** | 20703 | 2889 | | 3391 | 619 | 8069 | 35670 |
| **1845** | 22622 | 3759 | | 3816 | 637 | 8470 | 39302 |
| **1846** | 24539 | 5070 | | 4176 | 647 | 8880 | 43311 |
| **1847** | 26428 | 5500 | | 5146 | 671 | 9299 | 47044 |
| **1848** | 29382 | 6369 | | 6539 | 657 | 9519 | 52466 |
| **1849** | 33931 | 7932 | | 9153 | 661 | 10090 | 61766 |
| **1850** | 37736 | 8806 | | 11271 | 837 | 10665 | 69314 |
| **1851** | 28711 | 10866 | | 12033 | 1022 | 11245 | 63877 |
| **1852** | 29480 | 21574 | | 12291 | 1239 | 10392 | 74975 |
| **1853** | 31976 | 32228 | | 13987 | 1327 | 10886 | 90404 |
| **1854** | 34107 | 45884 | | 16227 | 1670 | 10789 | 108677 |
| **1855** | 37119 | 61928 | | 16897 | 1793 | 11723 | 129460 |
| **1856** | 39807 | 76134 | | 19016 | 1871 | 12989 | 149817 |
| **1857** | 44934 | 96662 | | 19677 | 1901 | 14273 | 177447 |
| **1858** | 52113 | 108478 | | 21570 | 2068 | 15080 | 199309 |
| **1859** | 53582 | 117526 | 4214 | 22648 | 2110 | 16022 | 216102 |
| **1860** | 60006 | 125113 | 5027 | 23519 | 2178 | 16981 | 232824 |
| **1861** | 64571 | 129196 | 6158 | 24859 | 2258 | 17566 | 244608 |
| **1862** | 66173 | 129906 | 7863 | 26132 | 2499 | 17442 | 250014 |
| **1863** | 68182 | 131664 | 10429 | 27510 | 2740 | 17377 | 257902 |
| **1864** | 70584 | 136394 | 12134 | 29244 | 2868 | 17518 | 268743 |
| **1865** | 73916 | 138586 | 15838 | 31537 | 3006 | 17671 | 280554 |
| **1866** | 77500 | 139752 | 18957 | 33210 | 3139 | 17857 | 290416 |
| **1867** | 80405 | 140558 | 21404 | 34218 | 3242 | 17838 | 297666 |
| **1868** | 83779 | 143027 | 24839 | 35182 | 3396 | 18025 | 308248 |
| **1869** | 87116 | 145828 | 25086 | 36425 | 3440 | 17926 | 315821 |
| **1870** | 90266 | 148793 | 25995 | 37257 | 3500 | 18048 | 323859 |
| **1871** | 93690 | 150618 | 26931 | 38333 | 3608 | 18217 | 331397 |
| **1872** | 96074 | 151962 | 27899 | 38361 | 3732 | 18407 | 336434 |
| **1873** | 98612 | 153541 | 29802 | 38894 | 3812 | 18622 | 343282 |
| **1874** | 101537 | 154662 | 32238 | 39526 | 3953 | 18600 | 350515 |
| **1875** | 104092 | 155064 | 34625 | 39976 | 4103 | 18494 | 356355 |
| **1876** | 106683 | 155759 | 36554 | 42007 | 4275 | 18803 | 364082 |
| **1877** | 110877 | 156997 | 39045 | 43782 | 4435 | 19077 | 374212 |
| **1878** | 114755 | 157710 | 39733 | 45531 | 4566 | 19568 | 381863 |
| **1879** | 120141 | 158547 | 40421 | 47016 | 4724 | 20001 | 390849 |
| **1880** | 124554 | 160279 | 41309 | 48135 | 4867 | 20392 | 399537 |
| **1881** | 129439 | 161680 | 43153 | 48880 | 5042 | 20907 | 409102 |
| **1882** | 134381 | 170566 | 47255 | 49962 | 5213 | 21194 | 428571 |
| **1883** | 141334 | 172526 | 51219 | 51622 | 5251 | 21482 | 443434 |
| **1884** | 147890 | 177437 | 57720 | 52862 | 5699 | 22020 | 463629 |
| **1885** | 154584 | 183407 | 62314 | 53067 | 6125 | 22768 | 482266 |

**Table 8.2**   continued

| Year ending 31st Dec. | New South Wales | Victoria | Queensland | South Australia | Western Australia | Tasmania | Australia |
|---|---|---|---|---|---|---|---|
| **1886** | 160554 | 190313 | 65562 | 52800 | 6911 | 22943 | 499084 |
| **1887** | 165206 | 195965 | 69556 | 53471 | 7484 | 23637 | 515319 |
| **1888** | 169708 | 204506 | 74324 | 53530 | 7548 | 24108 | 533724 |
| **1889** | 180066 | 207450 | 76869 | 54494 | 7928 | 24865 | 551672 |
| **1890** | 191534 | 211163 | 80080 | 55340 | 8466 | 25325 | 571909 |
| **1891** | 206797 | 214276 | 75017 | 57231 | 9776 | 26805 | 589903 |
| **1892** | 212020 | 222519 | 78738 | 59248 | 11035 | 26750 | 610309 |
| **1893** | 214530 | 225500 | 79766 | 61057 | 12557 | 27076 | 620486 |
| **1894** | 217549 | 229151 | 82675 | 61827 | 16217 | 27896 | 635315 |
| **1895** | 221568 | 231935 | 82848 | 62475 | 20504 | 28767 | 648098 |
| **1896** | 224182 | 233417 | 84444 | 62541 | 28665 | 30020 | 663268 |
| **1897** | 227596 | 229832 | 87410 | 62651 | 34517 | 30366 | 672373 |
| **1898** | 230587 | 229660 | 89786 | 63168 | 36716 | 31096 | 681014 |
| **1899** | 233397 | 229412 | 91242 | 64059 | 38333 | 32005 | 688448 |
| **1900** | 239546 | 231346 | 94106 | 63742 | 41597 | 32259 | 702596 |

| Year ending 30th June | Australia | Year ending 30th June | Australia | Year ending 30th June | Australia |
|---|---|---|---|---|---|
| **1901** | 712518 | **1931** | 1476073 | **1961** | 2781945 |
| **1902** | 718156 | **1932** | 1486354 | **1962** | 2846271 |
| **1903** | 729312 | **1933** | 1509671 | **1963** | 2911709 |
| **1904** | 743183 | **1934** | 1540574 | **1964** | 2983843 |
| **1905** | 756005 | **1935** | 1572309 | **1965** | 3067847 |
| **1906** | 771398 | **1936** | 1602133 | **1966** | 3151926 |
| **1907** | 793531 | **1937** | 1634401 | **1967** | 3241708 |
| **1908** | 824957 | **1938** | 1669977 | **1968** | 3338132 |
| **1909** | 852697 | **1939** | 1705541 | **1969** | 3442995 |
| **1910** | 871718 | **1940** | 1738021 | **1970** | 3557106 |
| **1911** | 894389 | **1941** | 1768229 | **1971** | 3670553 |
| **1912** | 923288 | **1942** | 1785093 | **1972** | 3762358 |
| **1913** | 954046 | **1943** | 1789278 | **1973** | 3859209 |
| **1914** | 982298 | **1944** | 1794949 | **1974** | 3957925 |
| **1915** | 1005168 | **1945** | 1806273 | **1975** | 4052268 |
| **1916** | 1019372 | **1946** | 1831798 | **1976** | 4140521 |
| **1917** | 1030668 | **1947** | 1873623 | **1977** | 4257143 |
| **1918** | 1045275 | **1948** | 1918731 | **1978** | 4360988 |
| **1919** | 1063170 | **1949** | 1972411 | **1979** | 4455328 |
| **1920** | 1086477 | **1950** | 2030475 | **1980** | 4559440 |
| **1921** | 1107010 | **1951** | 2101082 | **1981** | 4668909 |
| **1922** | 1137234 | **1952** | 2182715 | **1982** | 4777469 |
| **1923** | 1181695 | **1953** | 2264395 | **1983** | 4868250 |
| **1924** | 1227363 | **1954** | 2343421 | **1984** | 4965397 |
| **1925** | 1272763 | **1955** | 2406342 | **1985** | 5077143 |
| **1926** | 1321809 | **1956** | 2466500 | **1986** | 5187422 |
| **1927** | 1370478 | **1957** | 2518943 | **1987** | 5281429 |
| **1928** | 1412710 | **1958** | 2576097 | **1988** | 5374377 |
| **1929** | 1447841 | **1959** | 2640587 | **1989** | 5492379 |
| **1930** | 1468625 | **1960** | 2709570 | **1990** | 5617971 |

**Table 8.3 Total primary household workers, Australian colonies, 1788–1840**

| Year ending 31st Dec. | New South Wales | Victoria | South Australia | Western Australia | Tasmania | Australia |
|---|---|---|---|---|---|---|
| 1788 | 144 | | | | | 144 |
| 1789 | 108 | | | | | 108 |
| 1790 | 345 | | | | | 345 |
| 1791 | 481 | | | | | 481 |
| 1792 | 547 | | | | | 547 |
| 1793 | 588 | | | | | 588 |
| 1794 | 600 | | | | | 600 |
| 1795 | 581 | | | | | 581 |
| 1796 | 687 | | | | | 687 |
| 1797 | 726 | | | | | 726 |
| 1798 | 766 | | | | | 766 |
| 1799 | 846 | | | | | 846 |
| 1800 | 873 | | | | | 873 |
| 1801 | 992 | | | | | 992 |
| 1802 | 1169 | | | | | 1169 |
| 1803 | 1184 | | | | 25 | 1209 |
| 1804 | 1187 | | | | 78 | 1265 |
| 1805 | 1172 | | | | 107 | 1279 |
| 1806 | 1212 | | | | 106 | 1318 |
| 1807 | 1346 | | | | 120 | 1466 |
| 1808 | 1543 | | | | 168 | 1711 |
| 1809 | 1740 | | | | 190 | 1930 |
| 1810 | 1713 | | | | 214 | 1927 |
| 1811 | 1749 | | | | 232 | 1981 |
| 1812 | 1861 | | | | 247 | 2108 |
| 1813 | 2065 | | | | 262 | 2327 |
| 1814 | 2066 | | | | 277 | 2343 |
| 1815 | 2227 | | | | 284 | 2511 |
| 1816 | 2628 | | | | 296 | 2924 |
| 1817 | 3025 | | | | 483 | 3508 |
| 1818 | 3803 | | | | 493 | 4296 |
| 1819 | 4413 | | | | 775 | 5188 |
| 1820 | 4712 | | | | 789 | 5501 |
| 1821 | 4960 | | | | 824 | 5784 |
| 1822 | 4962 | | | | 1081 | 6043 |
| 1823 | 5112 | | | | 1424 | 6536 |
| 1824 | 5931 | | | | 1751 | 7682 |
| 1825 | 6353 | | | | 2019 | 8372 |
| 1826 | 6447 | | | | 2137 | 8584 |
| 1827 | 6542 | | | | 2402 | 8944 |
| 1828 | 6642 | | | | 2578 | 9220 |
| 1829 | 6848 | | | 187 | 2858 | 9893 |
| 1830 | 7518 | | | 219 | 3475 | 11212 |
| 1831 | 8165 | | | 252 | 3816 | 12233 |
| 1832 | 9189 | | | 284 | 4149 | 13622 |
| 1833 | 10778 | | | 312 | 4932 | 16022 |
| 1834 | 11562 | | | 340 | 5430 | 17332 |
| 1835 | 12569 | | | 356 | 5788 | 18713 |
| 1836 | 14045 | 18 | 162 | 372 | 6297 | 20894 |
| 1837 | 15524 | 104 | 977 | 388 | 6161 | 23154 |
| 1838 | 17788 | 288 | 1792 | 369 | 6621 | 26858 |
| 1839 | 20775 | 479 | 3079 | 412 | 6362 | 31107 |
| 1840 | 23562 | 845 | 4367 | 440 | 6656 | 35870 |

*Note:* Victorian data separated from New South Wales total in 1836.

**Table 8.4   Total primary household workers, New South Wales, 1841–1900**

| Year ending 31st Dec. | Full-time household workers | Market/household workers | Total | Year ending 31st Dec. | Full-time household workers | Market/household workers | Total |
|---|---|---|---|---|---|---|---|
| 1841 | 25356 | 1814 | 27170 | 1871 | 121128 | 6955 | 128083 |
| 1842 | 28529 | 2129 | 30658 | 1872 | 124325 | 7160 | 131485 |
| 1843 | 29854 | 2221 | 32075 | 1873 | 127726 | 7390 | 135116 |
| 1844 | 31545 | 2395 | 33940 | 1874 | 131636 | 7629 | 139265 |
| 1845 | 33169 | 2525 | 35694 | 1875 | 135072 | 7850 | 142922 |
| 1846 | 34572 | 2621 | 37193 | 1876 | 138561 | 8077 | 146638 |
| 1847 | 36832 | 2727 | 39559 | 1877 | 144140 | 8394 | 152534 |
| 1848 | 40504 | 2984 | 43488 | 1878 | 149318 | 8712 | 158030 |
| 1849 | 46260 | 3419 | 49679 | 1879 | 156469 | 9121 | 165590 |
| 1850 | 50876 | 3737 | 54613 | 1880 | 162365 | 9464 | 171829 |
| 1851 | 38273 | 2802 | 41075 | 1881 | 168888 | 9797 | 178685 |
| 1852 | 39343 | 3011 | 42354 | 1882 | 174686 | 10347 | 185033 |
| 1853 | 42724 | 3389 | 46113 | 1883 | 183041 | 11041 | 194082 |
| 1854 | 45622 | 3669 | 49291 | 1884 | 190817 | 11747 | 202564 |
| 1855 | 49709 | 4402 | 54111 | 1885 | 198707 | 12484 | 211191 |
| 1856 | 53369 | 5040 | 58409 | 1886 | 205605 | 13223 | 218828 |
| 1857 | 57350 | 5355 | 62705 | 1887 | 210764 | 13866 | 224630 |
| 1858 | 63159 | 5648 | 68807 | 1888 | 215687 | 14464 | 230151 |
| 1859 | 61490 | 5485 | 66975 | 1889 | 227981 | 15107 | 243088 |
| 1860 | 64999 | 5691 | 70690 | 1890 | 241575 | 15865 | 257440 |
| 1861 | 65788 | 5806 | 71594 | 1891 | 259826 | 16671 | 276497 |
| 1862 | 69233 | 5911 | 75144 | 1892 | 269410 | 17502 | 286912 |
| 1863 | 73204 | 6061 | 79265 | 1893 | 275659 | 18243 | 293902 |
| 1864 | 77717 | 6190 | 83907 | 1894 | 282639 | 19025 | 301664 |
| 1865 | 83410 | 6343 | 89753 | 1895 | 291019 | 19831 | 310850 |
| 1866 | 89579 | 6464 | 96043 | 1896 | 297647 | 20492 | 318139 |
| 1867 | 95140 | 6576 | 101716 | 1897 | 305426 | 21231 | 326657 |
| 1868 | 101427 | 6667 | 108094 | 1898 | 312727 | 22008 | 334735 |
| 1869 | 107854 | 6771 | 114625 | 1899 | 319864 | 22827 | 342691 |
| 1870 | 114227 | 6867 | 121094 | 1900 | 331707 | 23647 | 355354 |

**Table 8.5  Total primary household workers, Victoria, 1841–1900**

| Year ending 31st Dec. | Full-time household workers | Market/household workers | Total | Year ending 31st Dec. | Full-time household workers | Market/household workers | Total |
|---|---|---|---|---|---|---|---|
| 1841 | | | 1677 | 1871 | 141059 | 9787 | 150846 |
| 1842 | | | 2285 | 1872 | 147395 | 10204 | 157599 |
| 1843 | | | 2649 | 1873 | 154057 | 10600 | 164657 |
| 1844 | | | 3307 | 1874 | 160350 | 10979 | 171329 |
| 1845 | | | 4304 | 1875 | 165948 | 11301 | 177249 |
| 1846 | | | 5805 | 1876 | 171897 | 11651 | 183548 |
| 1847 | | | 6297 | 1877 | 178509 | 12051 | 190560 |
| 1848 | | | 7292 | 1878 | 184589 | 12417 | 197006 |
| 1849 | | | 9082 | 1879 | 190867 | 12806 | 203673 |
| 1850 | | | 10083 | 1880 | 198307 | 13257 | 211564 |
| 1851 | 11484 | 957 | 12441 | 1881 | 205443 | 13688 | 219131 |
| 1852 | 22801 | 1472 | 24273 | 1882 | 217223 | 13886 | 231109 |
| 1853 | 34060 | 2037 | 36097 | 1883 | 220214 | 14046 | 234260 |
| 1854 | 48493 | 2766 | 51259 | 1884 | 226992 | 14263 | 241255 |
| 1855 | 60186 | 3782 | 63968 | 1885 | 235155 | 14457 | 249612 |
| 1856 | 67521 | 4805 | 72326 | 1886 | 244555 | 14768 | 259323 |
| 1857 | 77511 | 5575 | 83086 | 1887 | 252380 | 15079 | 267459 |
| 1858 | 87238 | 5983 | 93221 | 1888 | 263967 | 15659 | 279626 |
| 1859 | 94788 | 6314 | 101102 | 1889 | 268362 | 15957 | 284319 |
| 1860 | 101199 | 6544 | 107743 | 1890 | 273770 | 16287 | 290057 |
| 1861 | 104802 | 6720 | 111522 | 1891 | 278421 | 16543 | 294964 |
| 1862 | 107006 | 6992 | 113998 | 1892 | 289964 | 17290 | 307254 |
| 1863 | 110105 | 7378 | 117483 | 1893 | 294692 | 18004 | 312696 |
| 1864 | 115770 | 7748 | 123518 | 1894 | 300321 | 18713 | 319034 |
| 1865 | 119368 | 8066 | 127434 | 1895 | 304837 | 19395 | 324232 |
| 1866 | 122124 | 8308 | 130432 | 1896 | 307658 | 20005 | 327663 |
| 1867 | 124590 | 8534 | 133124 | 1897 | 303792 | 20603 | 324395 |
| 1868 | 128571 | 8837 | 137408 | 1898 | 304424 | 21181 | 325605 |
| 1869 | 132917 | 9158 | 142075 | 1899 | 304954 | 21886 | 326840 |
| 1870 | 137485 | 9496 | 146981 | 1900 | 308390 | 22631 | 331021 |

**Table 8.6  Total primary household workers, Queensland, 1859–1900**

| Year ending 31st Dec. | Full-time household workers | Market/household workers | Total |
|---|---|---|---|
| 1859 | | | 783 |
| 1860 | | | 925 |
| 1861 | 793 | 336 | 1129 |
| 1862 | 3426 | 462 | 3888 |
| 1863 | 7746 | 646 | 8392 |
| 1864 | 12737 | 786 | 13523 |
| 1865 | 16134 | 975 | 17109 |
| 1866 | 18724 | 1133 | 19857 |
| 1867 | 20477 | 1209 | 21686 |
| 1868 | 22993 | 1315 | 24308 |
| 1869 | 22909 | 1432 | 24341 |
| 1870 | 23414 | 1579 | 24993 |
| 1871 | 23921 | 1739 | 25660 |
| 1872 | 24862 | 1834 | 26696 |
| 1873 | 26644 | 2002 | 28646 |
| 1874 | 28916 | 2182 | 31098 |
| 1875 | 31158 | 2296 | 33454 |
| 1876 | 33000 | 2416 | 35416 |
| 1877 | 39046 | 2547 | 41593 |
| 1878 | 39734 | 2663 | 42397 |
| 1879 | 40422 | 2753 | 43175 |
| 1880 | 41310 | 2871 | 44181 |
| 1881 | 45299 | 3004 | 48303 |
| 1882 | 49496 | 3280 | 52776 |
| 1883 | 53530 | 3761 | 57291 |
| 1884 | 60191 | 4073 | 64264 |
| 1885 | 64838 | 4311 | 69149 |
| 1886 | 68066 | 4584 | 72650 |
| 1887 | 72052 | 4918 | 76970 |
| 1888 | 76820 | 5205 | 82025 |
| 1889 | 79273 | 5483 | 84756 |
| 1890 | 82400 | 5708 | 88108 |
| 1891 | 77017 | 5889 | 82906 |
| 1892 | 81663 | 6064 | 87727 |
| 1893 | 83566 | 6227 | 89793 |
| 1894 | 87481 | 6408 | 93889 |
| 1895 | 88534 | 6627 | 95161 |
| 1896 | 91125 | 6822 | 97947 |
| 1897 | 95243 | 7004 | 102247 |
| 1898 | 98774 | 7171 | 105945 |
| 1899 | 101333 | 7361 | 108694 |
| 1900 | 105501 | 7535 | 113036 |

**Table 8.7  Total primary household workers, South Australia, 1841–1900**

| Year ending 31st Dec. | Full-time household workers | Market/household workers | Total | Year ending 31st Dec. | Full-time household workers | Market/household workers | Total |
|---|---|---|---|---|---|---|---|
| **1841** | 4472 | 151 | 4623 | **1871** | 58040 | 1438 | 59478 |
| **1842** | 4718 | 159 | 4877 | **1872** | 57883 | 1499 | 59382 |
| **1843** | 4965 | 170 | 5135 | **1873** | 58485 | 1578 | 60063 |
| **1844** | 5486 | 182 | 5668 | **1874** | 59230 | 1666 | 60896 |
| **1845** | 6201 | 211 | 6412 | **1875** | 59697 | 1746 | 61443 |
| **1846** | 6817 | 242 | 7059 | **1876** | 62512 | 1895 | 64407 |
| **1847** | 8640 | 314 | 8954 | **1877** | 66721 | 2033 | 68754 |
| **1848** | 11284 | 418 | 11702 | **1878** | 71017 | 2179 | 73196 |
| **1849** | 16222 | 607 | 16829 | **1879** | 75016 | 2332 | 77348 |
| **1850** | 20501 | 754 | 21255 | **1880** | 78525 | 2466 | 80991 |
| **1851** | 22448 | 833 | 23281 | **1881** | 81491 | 2604 | 84095 |
| **1852** | 22501 | 856 | 23357 | **1882** | 82372 | 2718 | 85090 |
| **1853** | 25119 | 867 | 25986 | **1883** | 84155 | 2865 | 87020 |
| **1854** | 28576 | 939 | 29515 | **1884** | 85200 | 2978 | 88178 |
| **1855** | 29167 | 1133 | 30300 | **1885** | 84550 | 3049 | 87599 |
| **1856** | 32115 | 1257 | 33372 | **1886** | 83150 | 3074 | 86224 |
| **1857** | 32497 | 1335 | 33832 | **1887** | 83219 | 3157 | 86376 |
| **1858** | 34818 | 1444 | 36262 | **1888** | 82322 | 3232 | 85554 |
| **1859** | 35713 | 1523 | 37236 | **1889** | 82798 | 3312 | 86110 |
| **1860** | 36209 | 1562 | 37771 | **1890** | 83061 | 3412 | 86473 |
| **1861** | 37344 | 1635 | 38979 | **1891** | 84842 | 3528 | 88370 |
| **1862** | 39774 | 1637 | 41411 | **1892** | 87149 | 3699 | 90848 |
| **1863** | 42416 | 1639 | 44055 | **1893** | 89105 | 3871 | 92976 |
| **1864** | 45669 | 1648 | 47317 | **1894** | 89515 | 4022 | 93537 |
| **1865** | 49875 | 1680 | 51555 | **1895** | 89733 | 4167 | 93900 |
| **1866** | 53179 | 1678 | 54857 | **1896** | 89106 | 4272 | 93378 |
| **1867** | 54196 | 1639 | 55835 | **1897** | 88540 | 4366 | 92906 |
| **1868** | 55110 | 1598 | 56708 | **1898** | 88542 | 4463 | 93005 |
| **1869** | 56422 | 1556 | 57978 | **1899** | 89052 | 4568 | 93620 |
| **1870** | 57061 | 1498 | 58559 | **1900** | 87876 | 4659 | 92535 |

**Table 8.8  Total primary household workers, Western Australia, 1841–1900**

| Year ending 31st Dec. | Full-time household workers | Market/household workers | Total | Year ending 31st Dec. | Full-time household workers | Market/household workers | Total |
|---|---|---|---|---|---|---|---|
| 1841 | | | 526 | 1871 | 4577 | 192 | 4769 |
| 1842 | | | 663 | 1872 | 4734 | 219 | 4953 |
| 1843 | | | 736 | 1873 | 4835 | 244 | 5079 |
| 1844 | | | 831 | 1874 | 5014 | 274 | 5288 |
| 1845 | | | 855 | 1875 | 5205 | 306 | 5511 |
| 1846 | 820 | 48 | 868 | 1876 | 5424 | 341 | 5765 |
| 1847 | 851 | 61 | 912 | 1877 | 5626 | 377 | 6003 |
| 1848 | 834 | 69 | 903 | 1878 | 5792 | 411 | 6203 |
| 1849 | 838 | 87 | 925 | 1879 | 5993 | 447 | 6440 |
| 1850 | 1062 | 116 | 1178 | 1880 | 6175 | 490 | 6665 |
| 1851 | 1296 | 144 | 1440 | 1881 | 6396 | 528 | 6924 |
| 1852 | 1572 | 152 | 1724 | 1882 | 6495 | 527 | 7022 |
| 1853 | 1684 | 155 | 1839 | 1883 | 6421 | 528 | 6949 |
| 1854 | 2119 | 144 | 2263 | 1884 | 6839 | 533 | 7372 |
| 1855 | 2274 | 148 | 2422 | 1885 | 7210 | 544 | 7754 |
| 1856 | 2374 | 144 | 2518 | 1886 | 7977 | 570 | 8547 |
| 1857 | 2412 | 155 | 2567 | 1887 | 8466 | 585 | 9051 |
| 1858 | 2624 | 172 | 2796 | 1888 | 8366 | 567 | 8933 |
| 1859 | 2677 | 198 | 2875 | 1889 | 8606 | 566 | 9172 |
| 1860 | 2763 | 223 | 2986 | 1890 | 8996 | 566 | 9562 |
| 1861 | 2864 | 240 | 3104 | 1891 | 10165 | 576 | 10741 |
| 1862 | 3171 | 248 | 3419 | 1892 | 11159 | 652 | 11811 |
| 1863 | 3476 | 256 | 3732 | 1893 | 12341 | 730 | 13071 |
| 1864 | 3639 | 254 | 3893 | 1894 | 15476 | 850 | 16326 |
| 1865 | 3814 | 250 | 4064 | 1895 | 18982 | 1033 | 20015 |
| 1866 | 3982 | 243 | 4225 | 1896 | 25721 | 1398 | 27119 |
| 1867 | 4113 | 236 | 4349 | 1897 | 29989 | 1936 | 31925 |
| 1868 | 4308 | 231 | 4539 | 1898 | 30854 | 2263 | 33117 |
| 1869 | 4363 | 221 | 4584 | 1899 | 31120 | 2519 | 33639 |
| 1870 | 4440 | 208 | 4648 | 1900 | 32585 | 2882 | 35467 |

**Table 8.9  Total primary household workers, Tasmania, 1841–1900**

| Year ending 31st Dec. | Full-time household workers | Market/household workers | Total | Year ending 31st Dec. | Full-time household workers | Market/household workers | Total |
|---|---|---|---|---|---|---|---|
| 1841 | 7761 | 561 | 8322 | 1871 | 20083 | 1549 | 21632 |
| 1842 | 7954 | 591 | 8545 | 1872 | 20811 | 1575 | 22386 |
| 1843 | 8533 | 639 | 9172 | 1873 | 21578 | 1593 | 23171 |
| 1844 | 9139 | 688 | 9827 | 1874 | 22077 | 1605 | 23682 |
| 1845 | 9773 | 740 | 10513 | 1875 | 22472 | 1611 | 24083 |
| 1846 | 10434 | 794 | 11228 | 1876 | 23377 | 1644 | 25021 |
| 1847 | 11124 | 820 | 11944 | 1877 | 24255 | 1675 | 25930 |
| 1848 | 11589 | 853 | 12442 | 1878 | 25430 | 1726 | 27156 |
| 1849 | 11688 | 885 | 12573 | 1879 | 26556 | 1769 | 28325 |
| 1850 | 11724 | 917 | 12641 | 1880 | 27650 | 1816 | 29466 |
| 1851 | 11697 | 949 | 12646 | 1881 | 28937 | 1858 | 30795 |
| 1852 | 10953 | 978 | 11931 | 1882 | 29413 | 1897 | 31310 |
| 1853 | 11623 | 967 | 12590 | 1883 | 29893 | 1941 | 31834 |
| 1854 | 11668 | 968 | 12636 | 1884 | 30723 | 1994 | 32717 |
| 1855 | 12839 | 1144 | 13983 | 1885 | 31852 | 2018 | 33870 |
| 1856 | 14404 | 1355 | 15759 | 1886 | 32182 | 2034 | 34216 |
| 1857 | 16024 | 1412 | 17436 | 1887 | 33243 | 2091 | 35334 |
| 1858 | 16439 | 1417 | 17856 | 1888 | 33996 | 2128 | 36124 |
| 1859 | 16945 | 1423 | 18368 | 1889 | 35156 | 2183 | 37339 |
| 1860 | 17406 | 1434 | 18840 | 1890 | 35900 | 2202 | 38102 |
| 1861 | 17434 | 1413 | 18847 | 1891 | 38098 | 2284 | 40382 |
| 1862 | 17469 | 1425 | 18894 | 1892 | 37830 | 2274 | 40104 |
| 1863 | 17562 | 1430 | 18992 | 1893 | 38098 | 2325 | 40423 |
| 1864 | 17864 | 1445 | 19309 | 1894 | 39054 | 2391 | 41445 |
| 1865 | 18180 | 1462 | 19642 | 1895 | 40069 | 2444 | 42513 |
| 1866 | 18534 | 1482 | 20016 | 1896 | 41601 | 2531 | 44132 |
| 1867 | 18676 | 1488 | 20164 | 1897 | 41864 | 2618 | 44482 |
| 1868 | 19036 | 1516 | 20552 | 1898 | 42650 | 2682 | 45332 |
| 1869 | 19094 | 1519 | 20613 | 1899 | 43669 | 2757 | 46426 |
| 1870 | 19388 | 1541 | 20929 | 1900 | 43786 | 2810 | 46596 |

**Table 8.10    Primary household workers, Australia, 1788–1990**

| Year ending 31st Dec. | Full-time household workers | Market/ household workers | Total | Year ending 31st Dec. | Full-time household workers | Market/ household workers | Total |
|---|---|---|---|---|---|---|---|
| 1788 | | | 144 | 1839 | | | 31107 |
| 1789 | | | 108 | 1840 | | | 35870 |
| 1790 | | | 345 | 1841 | 37589 | 2526 | 40115 |
| 1791 | | | 481 | 1842 | 41201 | 2879 | 44080 |
| 1792 | | | 547 | 1843 | 43352 | 3030 | 46382 |
| 1793 | | | 588 | 1844 | 46170 | 3265 | 49435 |
| 1794 | | | 600 | 1845 | 49143 | 3476 | 52619 |
| 1795 | | | 581 | 1846 | 52643 | 3705 | 56348 |
| 1796 | | | 687 | 1847 | 57447 | 3922 | 61369 |
| 1797 | | | 726 | 1848 | 64211 | 4324 | 68535 |
| 1798 | | | 766 | 1849 | 75008 | 4998 | 80006 |
| 1799 | | | 846 | 1850 | 84163 | 5524 | 89687 |
| 1800 | | | 873 | 1851 | 85198 | 5685 | 90883 |
| 1801 | | | 992 | 1852 | 97170 | 6469 | 103639 |
| 1802 | | | 1169 | 1853 | 115210 | 7415 | 122625 |
| 1803 | | | 1209 | 1854 | 136478 | 8486 | 144964 |
| 1804 | | | 1265 | 1855 | 154175 | 10609 | 164784 |
| 1805 | | | 1279 | 1856 | 169783 | 12601 | 182384 |
| 1806 | | | 1318 | 1857 | 185794 | 13832 | 199626 |
| 1807 | | | 1466 | 1858 | 204278 | 14664 | 218942 |
| 1808 | | | 1711 | 1859 | 211613 | 14943 | 226556 |
| 1809 | | | 1930 | 1860 | 222576 | 15454 | 238030 |
| 1810 | | | 1927 | 1861 | 229025 | 16150 | 245175 |
| 1811 | | | 1981 | 1862 | 240079 | 16675 | 256754 |
| 1812 | | | 2108 | 1863 | 254509 | 17410 | 271919 |
| 1813 | | | 2327 | 1864 | 273396 | 18071 | 291467 |
| 1814 | | | 2343 | 1865 | 290781 | 18776 | 309557 |
| 1815 | | | 2511 | 1866 | 306122 | 19308 | 325430 |
| 1816 | | | 2924 | 1867 | 317192 | 19682 | 336874 |
| 1817 | | | 3508 | 1868 | 331445 | 20164 | 351609 |
| 1818 | | | 4296 | 1869 | 343559 | 20657 | 364216 |
| 1819 | | | 5188 | 1870 | 356015 | 21189 | 377204 |
| 1820 | | | 5501 | 1871 | 368808 | 21660 | 390468 |
| 1821 | | | 5784 | 1872 | 380010 | 22491 | 402501 |
| 1822 | | | 6043 | 1873 | 393325 | 23407 | 416732 |
| 1823 | | | 6536 | 1874 | 407223 | 24335 | 431558 |
| 1824 | | | 7682 | 1875 | 419552 | 25110 | 444662 |
| 1825 | | | 8372 | 1876 | 434771 | 26024 | 460795 |
| 1826 | | | 8584 | 1877 | 458297 | 27077 | 485374 |
| 1827 | | | 8944 | 1878 | 475880 | 28108 | 503988 |
| 1828 | | | 9220 | 1879 | 495323 | 29228 | 524551 |
| 1829 | | | 9893 | 1880 | 514332 | 30364 | 544696 |
| 1830 | | | 11212 | 1881 | 536454 | 31479 | 567933 |
| 1831 | | | 12233 | 1882 | 559685 | 32655 | 592340 |
| 1832 | | | 13622 | 1883 | 577254 | 34182 | 611436 |
| 1833 | | | 16022 | 1884 | 600762 | 35588 | 636350 |
| 1834 | | | 17332 | 1885 | 622312 | 36863 | 659175 |
| 1835 | | | 18713 | 1886 | 641535 | 38253 | 679788 |
| 1836 | | | 20894 | 1887 | 660124 | 39696 | 699820 |
| 1837 | | | 23154 | 1888 | 681158 | 41255 | 722413 |
| 1838 | | | 26858 | 1889 | 702176 | 42608 | 744784 |

**Table 8.10**  continued

| Year ending 31st Dec. | Full-time household workers | Market/ household workers | Total | Year ending 30th June | Full-time household workers | Market/ household workers | Total |
|---|---|---|---|---|---|---|---|
| **1890** | 725702 | 44040 | 769742 | **1940** | 2189733 | 161372 | 2351105 |
| **1891** | 748369 | 45491 | 793860 | **1941** | 2215556 | 168746 | 2384302 |
| **1892** | 777175 | 47481 | 824656 | **1942** | 2224333 | 184360 | 2408693 |
| **1893** | 793461 | 49400 | 842861 | **1943** | 2217166 | 206815 | 2423981 |
| **1894** | 814486 | 51409 | 865895 | **1944** | 2211772 | 220115 | 2431887 |
| **1895** | 833174 | 53497 | 886671 | **1945** | 2213226 | 220381 | 2433607 |
| **1896** | 852858 | 55520 | 908378 | **1946** | 2231826 | 205593 | 2437419 |
| **1897** | 864854 | 57758 | 922612 | **1947** | 2269820 | 197611 | 2467431 |
| **1898** | 877971 | 59768 | 937739 | **1948** | 2288701 | 216241 | 2504942 |
| **1899** | 889992 | 61918 | 951910 | **1949** | 2315946 | 242971 | 2558917 |
| **1900** | 909845 | 64164 | 974009 | **1950** | 2346275 | 268115 | 2614390 |
| 30th June | | | | **1951** | 2388678 | 299795 | 2688473 |
| **1901** | 923032 | 66469 | 989501 | **1952** | 2440799 | 323603 | 2764402 |
| **1902** | 932217 | 65903 | 998120 | **1953** | 2489906 | 331394 | 2821300 |
| **1903** | 948609 | 67602 | 1016211 | **1954** | 2533117 | 362043 | 2895160 |
| **1904** | 968598 | 68924 | 1037522 | **1955** | 2572644 | 384555 | 2957199 |
| **1905** | 987290 | 69302 | 1056592 | **1956** | 2607781 | 409055 | 3016836 |
| **1906** | 1009421 | 69302 | 1078723 | **1957** | 2633404 | 427380 | 3060784 |
| **1907** | 1040462 | 70435 | 1110897 | **1958** | 2662680 | 447042 | 3109722 |
| **1908** | 1083829 | 70057 | 1153886 | **1959** | 2698073 | 465711 | 3163784 |
| **1909** | 1122507 | 70246 | 1192753 | **1960** | 2736395 | 496000 | 3232395 |
| **1910** | 1149831 | 70246 | 1220077 | **1961** | 2776647 | 528130 | 3304777 |
| **1911** | 1182074 | 70435 | 1252509 | **1962** | 2767230 | 579392 | 3346622 |
| **1912** | 1225933 | 71810 | 1297743 | **1963** | 2755496 | 619511 | 3375007 |
| **1913** | 1272611 | 72609 | 1345220 | **1964** | 2746568 | 675121 | 3421689 |
| **1914** | 1316319 | 72839 | 1389158 | **1965** | 2744496 | 754706 | 3499202 |
| **1915** | 1353117 | 72878 | 1425995 | **1966** | 2738179 | 826103 | 3564282 |
| **1916** | 1378487 | 74944 | 1453431 | **1967** | 2813414 | 888172 | 3701586 |
| **1917** | 1400080 | 76253 | 1476333 | **1968** | 2894261 | 940209 | 3834470 |
| **1918** | 1426320 | 77730 | 1504050 | **1969** | 2982253 | 984316 | 3966569 |
| **1919** | 1457255 | 77734 | 1534989 | **1970** | 3078071 | 1059684 | 4137755 |
| **1920** | 1495851 | 79002 | 1574853 | **1971** | 3173120 | 1119104 | 4292224 |
| **1921** | 1530906 | 78993 | 1609899 | **1972** | 3186379 | 1154419 | 4340798 |
| **1922** | 1565641 | 82404 | 1648045 | **1973** | 3200596 | 1240928 | 4441524 |
| **1923** | 1619501 | 85295 | 1704796 | **1974** | 3212964 | 1341486 | 4554450 |
| **1924** | 1674467 | 88024 | 1762491 | **1975** | 3218352 | 1482127 | 4700479 |
| **1925** | 1728489 | 91140 | 1819629 | **1976** | 3215681 | 1566226 | 4781907 |
| **1926** | 1786887 | 94831 | 1881718 | **1977** | 3289324 | 1608677 | 4898001 |
| **1927** | 1844156 | 99289 | 1943445 | **1978** | 3352248 | 1613226 | 4965474 |
| **1928** | 1892212 | 101738 | 1993950 | **1979** | 3407034 | 1604050 | 5011084 |
| **1929** | 1930262 | 105322 | 2035584 | **1980** | 3468548 | 1683769 | 5152317 |
| **1930** | 1948851 | 106312 | 2055163 | **1981** | 3533249 | 1705578 | 5238827 |
| **1931** | 1949553 | 103171 | 2052724 | **1982** | 3576318 | 1717162 | 5293480 |
| **1932** | 1953902 | 105474 | 2059376 | **1983** | 3604404 | 1734742 | 5339146 |
| **1933** | 1975159 | 111202 | 2086361 | **1984** | 3635713 | 1779127 | 5414840 |
| **1934** | 2004934 | 116966 | 2121900 | **1985** | 3675953 | 1805837 | 5481790 |
| **1935** | 2035354 | 123471 | 2158825 | **1986** | 3713349 | 1897344 | 5610693 |
| **1936** | 2062874 | 131188 | 2194062 | **1987** | 3780658 | 2043294 | 5823952 |
| **1937** | 2093112 | 139139 | 2232251 | **1988** | 3847194 | 2118277 | 5965471 |
| **1938** | 2127117 | 149306 | 2276423 | **1989** | 3931665 | 2206650 | 6138315 |
| **1939** | 2160613 | 157327 | 2317940 | **1990** | 4021568 | 2310421 | 6331989 |

**Table 8.11    Female workforce by colony, Australia, 1796–1900**

| Year ending 31st Dec. | New South Wales | Victoria | Queensland | South Australia | Western Australia | Tasmania | Australia |
|---|---|---|---|---|---|---|---|
| **1796** | 202 | | | | | | 202 |
| **1797** | 208 | | | | | | 208 |
| **1798** | 215 | | | | | | 215 |
| **1799** | 226 | | | | | | 226 |
| **1800** | 253 | | | | | | 253 |
| **1801** | 276 | | | | | | 276 |
| **1802** | 317 | | | | | | 317 |
| **1803** | 357 | | | | | 3 | 360 |
| **1804** | 385 | | | | | 16 | 401 |
| **1805** | 380 | | | | | 24 | 404 |
| **1806** | 417 | | | | | 25 | 442 |
| **1807** | 466 | | | | | 33 | 499 |
| **1808** | 541 | | | | | 59 | 600 |
| **1809** | 617 | | | | | 70 | 687 |
| **1810** | 612 | | | | | 81 | 693 |
| **1811** | 640 | | | | | 87 | 727 |
| **1812** | 690 | | | | | 93 | 783 |
| **1813** | 746 | | | | | 99 | 845 |
| **1814** | 729 | | | | | 104 | 833 |
| **1815** | 801 | | | | | 107 | 908 |
| **1816** | 912 | | | | | 110 | 1022 |
| **1817** | 1061 | | | | | 159 | 1220 |
| **1818** | 1334 | | | | | 160 | 1494 |
| **1819** | 1534 | | | | | 223 | 1757 |
| **1820** | 1476 | | | | | 221 | 1697 |
| **1821** | 1427 | | | | | 193 | 1620 |
| **1822** | 1428 | | | | | 215 | 1643 |
| **1823** | 1434 | | | | | 368 | 1802 |
| **1824** | 1478 | | | | | 453 | 1931 |
| **1825** | 1582 | | | | | 522 | 2104 |
| **1826** | 1600 | | | | | 567 | 2167 |
| **1827** | 1617 | | | | | 657 | 2274 |
| **1828** | 1641 | | | | | 663 | 2304 |
| **1829** | 1737 | | | | 26 | 791 | 2554 |
| **1830** | 1878 | | | | 33 | 1002 | 2913 |
| **1831** | 2066 | | | | 40 | 1108 | 3214 |
| **1832** | 2375 | | | | 48 | 1256 | 3679 |
| **1833** | 2920 | | | | 56 | 1511 | 4487 |
| **1834** | 3164 | | | | 65 | 1739 | 4968 |
| **1835** | 3402 | | | | 71 | 1855 | 5328 |
| **1836** | 3911 | | | 35 | 78 | 2030 | 6054 |
| **1837** | 4390 | | | 211 | 86 | 2019 | 6706 |
| **1838** | 5164 | | | 388 | 86 | 2246 | 7884 |
| **1839** | 6337 | | | 666 | 94 | 2121 | 9218 |
| **1840** | 7365 | | | 945 | 97 | 2266 | 10673 |
| **1841** | 9000 | | | 1000 | 116 | 2900 | 13016 |
| **1842** | 10560 | | | 1047 | 150 | 3051 | 14808 |
| **1843** | 11017 | | | 1123 | 171 | 3298 | 15609 |
| **1844** | 11881 | | | 1201 | 190 | 3556 | 16828 |
| **1845** | 12526 | | | 1391 | 197 | 3823 | 17937 |
| **1846** | 13000 | | | 1600 | 200 | 4100 | 18900 |
| **1847** | 13528 | | | 2072 | 256 | 4238 | 20094 |
| **1848** | 14803 | | | 2762 | 289 | 4405 | 22259 |

**Table 8.11**   continued

| Year ending 31st Dec. | New South Wales | Victoria | Queensland | South Australia | Western Australia | Tasmania | Australia |
|---|---|---|---|---|---|---|---|
| **1849** | 16959 | | | 4007 | 363 | 4571 | 25900 |
| **1850** | 18539 | | | 4982 | 485 | 4736 | 28742 |
| **1851** | 13900 | 5400 | | 5500 | 600 | 4900 | 30300 |
| **1852** | 14936 | 8302 | | 5651 | 635 | 5054 | 34578 |
| **1853** | 16813 | 11491 | | 5726 | 646 | 4996 | 39672 |
| **1854** | 18200 | 15600 | | 6200 | 600 | 5000 | 45600 |
| **1855** | 21837 | 21328 | | 7483 | 617 | 5911 | 57176 |
| **1856** | 25000 | 27100 | | 8300 | 600 | 7000 | 68000 |
| **1857** | 26567 | 31443 | | 8815 | 646 | 7294 | 74765 |
| **1858** | 28016 | 33746 | | 9538 | 715 | 7318 | 79333 |
| **1859** | 27210 | 35611 | 1212 | 10059 | 824 | 7352 | 82268 |
| **1860** | 28231 | 36910 | 1409 | 10315 | 928 | 7407 | 85200 |
| **1861** | 28800 | 37900 | 1700 | 10800 | 1000 | 7300 | 87500 |
| **1862** | 29323 | 39434 | 2339 | 10812 | 1034 | 7363 | 90305 |
| **1863** | 30068 | 41610 | 3272 | 10825 | 1066 | 7389 | 94230 |
| **1864** | 30706 | 43695 | 3981 | 10885 | 1057 | 7464 | 97788 |
| **1865** | 31468 | 45490 | 4935 | 11095 | 1040 | 7551 | 101579 |
| **1866** | 32068 | 46856 | 5735 | 11082 | 1013 | 7655 | 104409 |
| **1867** | 32623 | 48132 | 6119 | 10827 | 985 | 7686 | 106372 |
| **1868** | 33075 | 49840 | 6652 | 10553 | 962 | 7829 | 108911 |
| **1869** | 33587 | 51650 | 7244 | 10279 | 922 | 7844 | 111526 |
| **1870** | 34068 | 53559 | 7988 | 9893 | 868 | 7961 | 114337 |
| **1871** | 34500 | 55200 | 8800 | 9500 | 800 | 8000 | 116800 |
| **1872** | 35518 | 57547 | 9282 | 9902 | 912 | 8138 | 121299 |
| **1873** | 36659 | 59782 | 10129 | 10421 | 1018 | 8227 | 126236 |
| **1874** | 37847 | 61921 | 11039 | 11001 | 1143 | 8291 | 131242 |
| **1875** | 38941 | 63735 | 11617 | 11530 | 1276 | 8321 | 135420 |
| **1876** | 40066 | 65707 | 12221 | 12516 | 1420 | 8494 | 140424 |
| **1877** | 41640 | 67967 | 12885 | 13426 | 1570 | 8653 | 146141 |
| **1878** | 43218 | 70031 | 13475 | 14389 | 1711 | 8914 | 151738 |
| **1879** | 45249 | 72221 | 13934 | 15399 | 1862 | 9140 | 157805 |
| **1880** | 46948 | 74770 | 14529 | 16288 | 2042 | 9380 | 163957 |
| **1881** | 48600 | 77200 | 15200 | 17200 | 2200 | 9600 | 170000 |
| **1882** | 51328 | 78315 | 16597 | 17954 | 2197 | 9798 | 176189 |
| **1883** | 54772 | 79218 | 19030 | 18921 | 2199 | 10029 | 184169 |
| **1884** | 58276 | 80439 | 20612 | 19669 | 2221 | 10300 | 191517 |
| **1885** | 61931 | 81536 | 21813 | 20135 | 2268 | 10425 | 198108 |
| **1886** | 65598 | 83287 | 23197 | 20300 | 2374 | 10508 | 205264 |
| **1887** | 68784 | 85044 | 24887 | 20851 | 2438 | 10801 | 212805 |
| **1888** | 71755 | 88316 | 26338 | 21346 | 2363 | 10993 | 221111 |
| **1889** | 74942 | 89998 | 27744 | 21876 | 2359 | 11279 | 228198 |
| **1890** | 78702 | 91859 | 28880 | 22537 | 2357 | 11378 | 235713 |
| **1891** | 82700 | 93300 | 29800 | 23300 | 2400 | 11800 | 243300 |
| **1892** | 86824 | 97513 | 30683 | 24429 | 2718 | 11745 | 253912 |
| **1893** | 90501 | 101537 | 31505 | 25568 | 3043 | 12009 | 264163 |
| **1894** | 94377 | 105539 | 32426 | 26564 | 3541 | 12350 | 274797 |
| **1895** | 98375 | 109388 | 33531 | 27522 | 4306 | 12624 | 285746 |
| **1896** | 101657 | 112828 | 34514 | 28215 | 5825 | 13073 | 296112 |
| **1897** | 105323 | 116200 | 35438 | 28833 | 8068 | 13526 | 307388 |
| **1898** | 109176 | 119456 | 36287 | 29477 | 9432 | 13853 | 317681 |
| **1899** | 113241 | 123433 | 37245 | 30166 | 10499 | 14240 | 328824 |
| **1900** | 117306 | 127638 | 38125 | 30768 | 12012 | 14516 | 340365 |

**Table 8.12    Female workforce, Australia, 1901–1990**

| Year ending 30th June | Female work-force ('000) | Year ending 30th June | Female work-force ('000) | Year ending 30th June | Female work-force ('000) |
|---|---|---|---|---|---|
| 1901 | 352 | 1931 | 549 | 1961 | 1059 |
| 1902 | 349 | 1932 | 559 | 1962 | 1127 |
| 1903 | 358 | 1933 | 587 | 1963 | 1170 |
| 1904 | 365 | 1934 | 598 | 1964 | 1239 |
| 1905 | 367 | 1935 | 612 | 1965 | 1347 |
| 1906 | 367 | 1936 | 631 | 1966 | 1435 |
| 1907 | 373 | 1937 | 650 | 1967 | 1498 |
| 1908 | 371 | 1938 | 678 | 1968 | 1541 |
| 1909 | 372 | 1939 | 695 | 1969 | 1569 |
| 1910 | 372 | 1940 | 694 | 1970 | 1644 |
| 1911 | 373 | 1941 | 707 | 1971 | 1691 |
| 1912 | 382 | 1942 | 753 | 1972 | 1715 |
| 1913 | 388 | 1943 | 824 | 1973 | 1813 |
| 1914 | 391 | 1944 | 856 | 1974 | 1928 |
| 1915 | 393 | 1945 | 837 | 1975 | 2096 |
| 1916 | 406 | 1946 | 763 | 1976 | 2180 |
| 1917 | 415 | 1947 | 717 | 1977 | 2265 |
| 1918 | 425 | 1948 | 727 | 1978 | 2298 |
| 1919 | 427 | 1949 | 761 | 1979 | 2312 |
| 1920 | 436 | 1950 | 786 | 1980 | 2456 |
| 1921 | 438 | 1951 | 826 | 1981 | 2518 |
| 1922 | 455 | 1952 | 841 | 1982 | 2541 |
| 1923 | 469 | 1953 | 815 | 1983 | 2573 |
| 1924 | 482 | 1954 | 845 | 1984 | 2645 |
| 1925 | 497 | 1955 | 877 | 1985 | 2691 |
| 1926 | 515 | 1956 | 912 | 1986 | 2834 |
| 1927 | 537 | 1957 | 932 | 1987 | 3052 |
| 1928 | 548 | 1958 | 954 | 1988 | 3164 |
| 1929 | 565 | 1959 | 973 | 1989 | 3296 |
| 1930 | 568 | 1960 | 1015 | 1990 | 3451 |

**Table 8.13   Secondary household workers, Australia, 1788–1990**

| Year ending 31st Dec. | Number of households with secondary workers | Number of secondary household workers (full-time equivalents) | Year ending 31st Dec. | Number of households with secondary workers | Number of secondary household workers (full-time equivalents) |
|---|---|---|---|---|---|
| 1788 | 86 | 29 | 1839 | 18945 | 6315 |
| 1789 | 65 | 22 | 1840 | 21391 | 7130 |
| 1790 | 208 | 69 | 1841 | 24799 | 8267 |
| 1791 | 290 | 97 | 1842 | 27631 | 9210 |
| 1792 | 329 | 110 | 1843 | 29654 | 9884 |
| 1793 | 355 | 118 | 1844 | 32212 | 10737 |
| 1794 | 360 | 120 | 1845 | 34927 | 11642 |
| 1795 | 350 | 117 | 1846 | 37579 | 12525 |
| 1796 | 413 | 138 | 1847 | 40833 | 13611 |
| 1797 | 438 | 146 | 1848 | 45318 | 15106 |
| 1798 | 462 | 154 | 1849 | 52948 | 17650 |
| 1799 | 513 | 171 | 1850 | 59524 | 19841 |
| 1800 | 526 | 175 | 1851 | 62942 | 20980 |
| 1801 | 599 | 200 | 1852 | 73912 | 24638 |
| 1802 | 707 | 236 | 1853 | 89158 | 29720 |
| 1803 | 734 | 244 | 1854 | 107222 | 35740 |
| 1804 | 777 | 259 | 1855 | 127917 | 42639 |
| 1805 | 793 | 264 | 1856 | 148283 | 49428 |
| 1806 | 814 | 272 | 1857 | 175935 | 58645 |
| 1807 | 905 | 302 | 1858 | 197614 | 65873 |
| 1808 | 1060 | 353 | 1859 | 214355 | 71451 |
| 1809 | 1193 | 398 | 1860 | 230931 | 76977 |
| 1810 | 1197 | 399 | 1861 | 242619 | 80873 |
| 1811 | 1230 | 410 | 1862 | 247977 | 82659 |
| 1812 | 1309 | 436 | 1863 | 255802 | 85268 |
| 1813 | 1445 | 481 | 1864 | 266567 | 88855 |
| 1814 | 1461 | 487 | 1865 | 278287 | 92762 |
| 1815 | 1560 | 520 | 1866 | 288055 | 96018 |
| 1816 | 1812 | 604 | 1867 | 295205 | 98403 |
| 1817 | 2207 | 735 | 1868 | 305666 | 101889 |
| 1818 | 2680 | 893 | 1869 | 313123 | 104375 |
| 1819 | 3288 | 1096 | 1870 | 321045 | 107014 |
| 1820 | 3499 | 1167 | 1871 | 328460 | 109486 |
| 1821 | 3702 | 1234 | 1872 | 333422 | 111141 |
| 1822 | 3932 | 1310 | 1873 | 340186 | 113395 |
| 1823 | 4310 | 1437 | 1874 | 347328 | 115776 |
| 1824 | 5108 | 1703 | 1875 | 353087 | 117696 |
| 1825 | 5595 | 1865 | 1876 | 360720 | 120240 |
| 1826 | 5753 | 1918 | 1877 | 370670 | 123555 |
| 1827 | 6036 | 2012 | 1878 | 378142 | 126047 |
| 1828 | 6254 | 2084 | 1879 | 386910 | 128970 |
| 1829 | 6707 | 2236 | 1880 | 395397 | 131798 |
| 1830 | 7623 | 2541 | 1881 | 404744 | 134915 |
| 1831 | 8278 | 2759 | 1882 | 419923 | 139974 |
| 1832 | 9133 | 3044 | 1883 | 441678 | 147225 |
| 1833 | 10682 | 3561 | 1884 | 460170 | 153390 |
| 1834 | 11511 | 3837 | 1885 | 476704 | 158902 |
| 1835 | 12354 | 4119 | 1886 | 494274 | 164757 |
| 1836 | 13659 | 4553 | 1887 | 511953 | 170651 |
| 1837 | 14795 | 4932 | 1888 | 531034 | 177011 |
| 1838 | 16820 | 5607 | 1889 | 546500 | 182167 |

**Table 8.13**  continued

| Year ending 31st Dec. | Number of households with secondary workers | Number of secondary household workers (full-time equivalents) | Year ending 30th June | Number of households with secondary workers | Number of secondary household workers (full-time equivalents) |
|---|---|---|---|---|---|
| **1890** | 563405 | 187802 | **1940** | 1546000 | 515000 |
| **1891** | 580481 | 193494 | **1941** | 1571000 | 524000 |
| **1892** | 592790 | 197597 | **1942** | 1584000 | 528000 |
| **1893** | 603651 | 201217 | **1943** | 1585000 | 528000 |
| **1894** | 616346 | 205448 | **1944** | 1589000 | 530000 |
| **1895** | 629294 | 209765 | **1945** | 1597000 | 532000 |
| **1896** | 642341 | 214114 | **1946** | 1618000 | 539000 |
| **1897** | 655924 | 218641 | **1947** | 1653000 | 551000 |
| **1898** | 665872 | 221957 | **1948** | 1693000 | 564000 |
| **1899** | 676564 | 225521 | **1949** | 1740000 | 580000 |
| **1900** | 687254 | 229085 | **1950** | 1793000 | 598000 |
| 30th June | | | **1951** | 1855000 | 618000 |
| **1901** | 700000 | 233000 | **1952** | 1928000 | 643000 |
| **1902** | 706000 | 235000 | **1953** | 2000000 | 667000 |
| **1903** | 717000 | 239000 | **1954** | 2070000 | 690000 |
| **1904** | 731000 | 244000 | **1955** | 2124000 | 708000 |
| **1905** | 744000 | 248000 | **1956** | 2177000 | 726000 |
| **1906** | 759000 | 253000 | **1957** | 2221000 | 740000 |
| **1907** | 782000 | 261000 | **1958** | 2270000 | 757000 |
| **1908** | 812000 | 271000 | **1959** | 2326000 | 775000 |
| **1909** | 840000 | 280000 | **1960** | 2385000 | 795000 |
| **1910** | 859000 | 286000 | **1961** | 2447000 | 816000 |
| **1911** | 881000 | 294000 | **1962** | 2509000 | 836000 |
| **1912** | 909000 | 303000 | **1963** | 2573000 | 858000 |
| **1913** | 939000 | 313000 | **1964** | 2643000 | 881000 |
| **1914** | 966000 | 322000 | **1965** | 2724000 | 908000 |
| **1915** | 988000 | 329000 | **1966** | 2805000 | 935000 |
| **1916** | 1001000 | 334000 | **1967** | 2877000 | 959000 |
| **1917** | 1012000 | 337000 | **1968** | 2955000 | 985000 |
| **1918** | 1025000 | 342000 | **1969** | 3040000 | 1013000 |
| **1919** | 1042000 | 347000 | **1970** | 3132000 | 1044000 |
| **1920** | 1065000 | 355000 | **1971** | 3224000 | 1075000 |
| **1921** | 1084000 | 361000 | **1972** | 3319000 | 1106000 |
| **1922** | 1106000 | 369000 | **1973** | 3420000 | 1140000 |
| **1923** | 1141000 | 380000 | **1974** | 3523000 | 1174000 |
| **1924** | 1176000 | 392000 | **1975** | 3623000 | 1208000 |
| **1925** | 1211000 | 404000 | **1976** | 3719000 | 1240000 |
| **1926** | 1249000 | 416000 | **1977** | 3814000 | 1271000 |
| **1927** | 1286000 | 429000 | **1978** | 3897000 | 1299000 |
| **1928** | 1316000 | 439000 | **1979** | 3972000 | 1324000 |
| **1929** | 1338000 | 446000 | **1980** | 4054000 | 1351000 |
| **1930** | 1347000 | 449000 | **1981** | 4142000 | 1381000 |
| **1931** | 1344000 | 448000 | **1982** | 4232000 | 1411000 |
| **1932** | 1343000 | 448000 | **1983** | 4306000 | 1435000 |
| **1933** | 1354000 | 451000 | **1984** | 4385000 | 1462000 |
| **1934** | 1380000 | 460000 | **1985** | 4478000 | 1493000 |
| **1935** | 1406000 | 469000 | **1986** | 4568000 | 1523000 |
| **1936** | 1431000 | 477000 | **1987** | 4651000 | 1550000 |
| **1937** | 1458000 | 486000 | **1988** | 4733000 | 1578000 |
| **1938** | 1489000 | 496000 | **1989** | 4837000 | 1612000 |
| **1939** | 1519000 | 506000 | **1990** | 4947000 | 1649000 |

**Table 8.14    Total household workers, Australia, 1788–1990**

| Year ending 31st Dec. | Primary household workers | Secondary household workers | Total household workers | Year ending 31st Dec. | Primary household workers | Secondary household workers | Total household workers |
|---|---|---|---|---|---|---|---|
| **1788** | 144 | 29 | 173 | **1839** | 31107 | 6315 | 37422 |
| **1789** | 108 | 22 | 130 | **1840** | 35870 | 7130 | 43000 |
| **1790** | 345 | 69 | 414 | **1841** | 40115 | 8267 | 48382 |
| **1791** | 481 | 97 | 578 | **1842** | 44080 | 9210 | 53290 |
| **1792** | 547 | 110 | 657 | **1843** | 46382 | 9884 | 56266 |
| **1793** | 588 | 118 | 706 | **1844** | 49435 | 10737 | 60172 |
| **1794** | 600 | 120 | 720 | **1845** | 52619 | 11642 | 64261 |
| **1795** | 581 | 117 | 698 | **1846** | 56348 | 12525 | 68873 |
| **1796** | 687 | 138 | 825 | **1847** | 61369 | 13611 | 74980 |
| **1797** | 726 | 146 | 872 | **1848** | 68535 | 15106 | 83641 |
| **1798** | 766 | 154 | 920 | **1849** | 80006 | 17650 | 97656 |
| **1799** | 846 | 171 | 1017 | **1850** | 89687 | 19841 | 109528 |
| **1800** | 873 | 175 | 1048 | **1851** | 90883 | 20980 | 111863 |
| **1801** | 992 | 200 | 1192 | **1852** | 103639 | 24638 | 128277 |
| **1802** | 1169 | 236 | 1405 | **1853** | 122625 | 29720 | 152345 |
| **1803** | 1209 | 244 | 1453 | **1854** | 144964 | 35740 | 180704 |
| **1804** | 1265 | 259 | 1524 | **1855** | 164784 | 42639 | 207423 |
| **1805** | 1279 | 264 | 1543 | **1856** | 182384 | 49428 | 231812 |
| **1806** | 1318 | 272 | 1590 | **1857** | 199626 | 58645 | 258271 |
| **1807** | 1466 | 302 | 1768 | **1858** | 218942 | 65873 | 284815 |
| **1808** | 1711 | 353 | 2064 | **1859** | 226556 | 71451 | 298007 |
| **1809** | 1930 | 398 | 2328 | **1860** | 238030 | 76977 | 315007 |
| **1810** | 1927 | 399 | 2326 | **1861** | 245175 | 80873 | 326048 |
| **1811** | 1981 | 410 | 2391 | **1862** | 256754 | 82659 | 339413 |
| **1812** | 2108 | 436 | 2544 | **1863** | 271919 | 85268 | 357187 |
| **1813** | 2327 | 481 | 2808 | **1864** | 291467 | 88855 | 380322 |
| **1814** | 2343 | 487 | 2830 | **1865** | 309557 | 92762 | 402319 |
| **1815** | 2511 | 520 | 3031 | **1866** | 325430 | 96018 | 421448 |
| **1816** | 2924 | 604 | 3528 | **1867** | 336874 | 98403 | 435277 |
| **1817** | 3508 | 735 | 4243 | **1868** | 351609 | 101889 | 453498 |
| **1818** | 4296 | 893 | 5189 | **1869** | 364216 | 104375 | 468591 |
| **1819** | 5188 | 1096 | 6284 | **1870** | 377204 | 107014 | 484218 |
| **1820** | 5501 | 1167 | 6668 | **1871** | 390468 | 109486 | 499954 |
| **1821** | 5784 | 1234 | 7018 | **1872** | 402501 | 111141 | 513642 |
| **1822** | 6043 | 1310 | 7353 | **1873** | 416732 | 113395 | 530127 |
| **1823** | 6536 | 1437 | 7973 | **1874** | 431558 | 115776 | 547334 |
| **1824** | 7682 | 1703 | 9385 | **1875** | 444662 | 117696 | 562358 |
| **1825** | 8372 | 1865 | 10237 | **1876** | 460795 | 120240 | 581035 |
| **1826** | 8584 | 1918 | 10502 | **1877** | 485374 | 123555 | 608929 |
| **1827** | 8944 | 2012 | 10956 | **1878** | 503988 | 126047 | 630035 |
| **1828** | 9220 | 2084 | 11304 | **1879** | 524551 | 128970 | 653521 |
| **1829** | 9893 | 2236 | 12129 | **1880** | 544696 | 131798 | 676494 |
| **1830** | 11212 | 2541 | 13753 | **1881** | 567933 | 134915 | 702848 |
| **1831** | 12233 | 2759 | 14992 | **1882** | 592340 | 139974 | 732314 |
| **1832** | 13622 | 3044 | 16666 | **1883** | 611436 | 147225 | 758661 |
| **1833** | 16022 | 3561 | 19583 | **1884** | 636350 | 153390 | 789740 |
| **1834** | 17332 | 3837 | 21169 | **1885** | 659175 | 158902 | 818077 |
| **1835** | 18713 | 4119 | 22832 | **1886** | 679788 | 164757 | 844545 |
| **1836** | 20894 | 4553 | 25447 | **1887** | 699820 | 170651 | 870471 |
| **1837** | 23154 | 4932 | 28086 | **1888** | 722413 | 177011 | 899424 |
| **1838** | 26858 | 5607 | 32465 | **1889** | 744784 | 182167 | 926951 |

**Table 8.14**   continued

| Year ending 31st Dec. | Primary household workers | Secondary household workers | Total household workers | Year ending 30th June | Primary household workers | Secondary household workers | Total household workers |
|---|---|---|---|---|---|---|---|
| **1890** | 769742 | 187802 | 957544 | **1940** | 2351105 | 515000 | 2866105 |
| **1891** | 793860 | 193494 | 987354 | **1941** | 2384302 | 524000 | 2908302 |
| **1892** | 824656 | 197597 | 1022253 | **1942** | 2408693 | 528000 | 2936693 |
| **1893** | 842861 | 201217 | 1044078 | **1943** | 2423981 | 528000 | 2951981 |
| **1894** | 865895 | 205448 | 1071343 | **1944** | 2431887 | 530000 | 2961887 |
| **1895** | 886671 | 209765 | 1096436 | **1945** | 2433607 | 532000 | 2965607 |
| **1896** | 908378 | 214114 | 1122492 | **1946** | 2437419 | 539000 | 2976419 |
| **1897** | 922612 | 218641 | 1141253 | **1947** | 2467431 | 551000 | 3018431 |
| **1898** | 937739 | 221957 | 1159696 | **1948** | 2504942 | 564000 | 3068942 |
| **1899** | 951910 | 225521 | 1177431 | **1949** | 2558917 | 580000 | 3138917 |
| **1900** | 974009 | 229085 | 1203094 | **1950** | 2614390 | 598000 | 3212390 |
| 30th June | | | | **1951** | 2688473 | 618000 | 3306473 |
| **1901** | 989501 | 233000 | 1222501 | **1952** | 2764402 | 643000 | 3407402 |
| **1902** | 998120 | 235000 | 1233120 | **1953** | 2821300 | 667000 | 3488300 |
| **1903** | 1016211 | 239000 | 1255211 | **1954** | 2895160 | 690000 | 3585160 |
| **1904** | 1037522 | 244000 | 1281522 | **1955** | 2957199 | 708000 | 3665199 |
| **1905** | 1056592 | 248000 | 1304592 | **1956** | 3016836 | 726000 | 3742836 |
| **1906** | 1078723 | 253000 | 1331723 | **1957** | 3060784 | 740000 | 3800784 |
| **1907** | 1110897 | 261000 | 1371897 | **1958** | 3109722 | 757000 | 3866722 |
| **1908** | 1153886 | 271000 | 1424886 | **1959** | 3163784 | 775000 | 3938784 |
| **1909** | 1192753 | 280000 | 1472753 | **1960** | 3232395 | 795000 | 4027395 |
| **1910** | 1220077 | 286000 | 1506077 | **1961** | 3304777 | 816000 | 4120777 |
| **1911** | 1252509 | 294000 | 1546509 | **1962** | 3346622 | 836000 | 4182622 |
| **1912** | 1297743 | 303000 | 1600743 | **1963** | 3375007 | 858000 | 4233007 |
| **1913** | 1345220 | 313000 | 1658220 | **1964** | 3421689 | 881000 | 4302689 |
| **1914** | 1389158 | 322000 | 1711158 | **1965** | 3499202 | 908000 | 4407202 |
| **1915** | 1425995 | 329000 | 1754995 | **1966** | 3564282 | 935000 | 4499282 |
| **1916** | 1453431 | 334000 | 1787431 | **1967** | 3701586 | 959000 | 4660586 |
| **1917** | 1476333 | 337000 | 1813333 | **1968** | 3834470 | 985000 | 4819470 |
| **1918** | 1504050 | 342000 | 1846050 | **1969** | 3966569 | 1013000 | 4979569 |
| **1919** | 1534989 | 347000 | 1881989 | **1970** | 4137755 | 1044000 | 5181755 |
| **1920** | 1574853 | 355000 | 1929853 | **1971** | 4292224 | 1075000 | 5367224 |
| **1921** | 1609989 | 361000 | 1970899 | **1972** | 4340798 | 1106000 | 5446798 |
| **1922** | 1648045 | 369000 | 2017045 | **1973** | 4441524 | 1140000 | 5581524 |
| **1923** | 1704796 | 380000 | 2084796 | **1974** | 4554450 | 1174000 | 5728450 |
| **1924** | 1762491 | 392000 | 2154491 | **1975** | 4700479 | 1208000 | 5908479 |
| **1925** | 1819629 | 404000 | 2223629 | **1976** | 4781907 | 1240000 | 6021907 |
| **1926** | 1881718 | 416000 | 2297718 | **1977** | 4898001 | 1271000 | 6169001 |
| **1927** | 1943445 | 429000 | 2372445 | **1978** | 4965474 | 1299000 | 6264474 |
| **1928** | 1993950 | 439000 | 2432950 | **1979** | 5011084 | 1324000 | 6335084 |
| **1929** | 2035584 | 446000 | 2481584 | **1980** | 5152317 | 1351000 | 6503317 |
| **1930** | 2055163 | 449000 | 2504163 | **1981** | 5238827 | 1381000 | 6619827 |
| **1931** | 2052724 | 448000 | 2500724 | **1982** | 5293480 | 1411000 | 6704480 |
| **1932** | 2059376 | 448000 | 2507376 | **1983** | 5339146 | 1435000 | 6774146 |
| **1933** | 2086361 | 451000 | 2537361 | **1984** | 5414840 | 1462000 | 6876840 |
| **1934** | 2121900 | 460000 | 2581900 | **1985** | 5481790 | 1493000 | 6974790 |
| **1935** | 2158825 | 469000 | 2627825 | **1986** | 5610693 | 1523000 | 7133693 |
| **1936** | 2194062 | 477000 | 2671062 | **1987** | 5823952 | 1550000 | 7373952 |
| **1937** | 2232251 | 486000 | 2718251 | **1988** | 5965471 | 1578000 | 7543471 |
| **1938** | 2276423 | 496000 | 2772423 | **1989** | 6138315 | 1612000 | 7750315 |
| **1939** | 2317940 | 506000 | 2823940 | **1990** | 6331989 | 1649000 | 7980989 |

**Table 8.15   Value of total household labour services, Australia, 1788-1990** ($m)

| Year ending 31st Dec. | Primary | Secondary | Total | Year ending 31st Dec. | Primary | Secondary | Total |
|---|---|---|---|---|---|---|---|
| 1788 | 0.01 | 0.00 | 0.01 | 1839 | 2.20 | 1.04 | 3.24 |
| 1789 | 0.01 | 0.00 | 0.01 | 1840 | 2.67 | 1.23 | 3.90 |
| 1790 | 0.02 | 0.01 | 0.03 | 1841 | 2.66 | 1.28 | 3.94 |
| 1791 | 0.03 | 0.01 | 0.04 | 1842 | 2.57 | 1.25 | 3.82 |
| 1792 | 0.03 | 0.02 | 0.05 | 1843 | 2.33 | 1.15 | 3.48 |
| 1793 | 0.04 | 0.02 | 0.06 | 1844 | 2.52 | 1.01 | 3.53 |
| 1794 | 0.04 | 0.02 | 0.06 | 1845 | 3.39 | 1.09 | 4.48 |
| 1795 | 0.04 | 0.02 | 0.06 | 1846 | 3.81 | 1.53 | 5.34 |
| 1796 | 0.04 | 0.02 | 0.06 | 1847 | 4.57 | 1.75 | 6.32 |
| 1797 | 0.04 | 0.02 | 0.06 | 1848 | 4.70 | 1.88 | 6.58 |
| 1798 | 0.05 | 0.02 | 0.07 | 1849 | 4.30 | 1.99 | 6.29 |
| 1799 | 0.05 | 0.02 | 0.07 | 1850 | 5.30 | 2.09 | 7.39 |
| 1800 | 0.05 | 0.02 | 0.07 | 1851 | 6.02 | 3.21 | 9.23 |
| 1801 | 0.06 | 0.03 | 0.09 | 1852 | 7.62 | 5.21 | 12.83 |
| 1802 | 0.07 | 0.03 | 0.10 | 1853 | 9.68 | 9.26 | 18.94 |
| 1803 | 0.07 | 0.03 | 0.10 | 1854 | 17.01 | 17.71 | 34.72 |
| 1804 | 0.08 | 0.04 | 0.12 | 1855 | 16.83 | 15.55 | 32.38 |
| 1805 | 0.08 | 0.04 | 0.12 | 1856 | 17.47 | 15.07 | 32.54 |
| 1806 | 0.08 | 0.04 | 0.12 | 1857 | 19.93 | 16.50 | 36.43 |
| 1807 | 0.09 | 0.04 | 0.13 | 1858 | 23.94 | 16.38 | 40.32 |
| 1808 | 0.10 | 0.05 | 0.15 | 1859 | 22.08 | 16.20 | 38.28 |
| 1809 | 0.12 | 0.06 | 0.18 | 1860 | 23.66 | 19.07 | 42.73 |
| 1810 | 0.12 | 0.06 | 0.18 | 1861 | 25.43 | 19.49 | 44.92 |
| 1811 | 0.12 | 0.06 | 0.18 | 1862 | 29.29 | 20.10 | 49.39 |
| 1812 | 0.13 | 0.06 | 0.19 | 1863 | 31.02 | 18.98 | 50.00 |
| 1813 | 0.14 | 0.07 | 0.21 | 1864 | 33.29 | 19.46 | 52.75 |
| 1814 | 0.14 | 0.07 | 0.21 | 1865 | 27.92 | 17.94 | 45.86 |
| 1815 | 0.15 | 0.07 | 0.22 | 1866 | 32.43 | 20.85 | 53.28 |
| 1816 | 0.18 | 0.08 | 0.26 | 1867 | 33.50 | 21.66 | 55.16 |
| 1817 | 0.21 | 0.10 | 0.31 | 1868 | 40.97 | 22.19 | 63.16 |
| 1818 | 0.26 | 0.13 | 0.39 | 1869 | 39.67 | 22.69 | 62.36 |
| 1819 | 0.31 | 0.15 | 0.46 | 1870 | 39.27 | 24.47 | 63.74 |
| 1820 | 0.33 | 0.16 | 0.49 | 1871 | 37.73 | 23.17 | 60.90 |
| 1821 | 0.35 | 0.17 | 0.52 | 1872 | 41.44 | 25.38 | 66.82 |
| 1822 | 0.37 | 0.18 | 0.55 | 1873 | 42.69 | 27.91 | 70.60 |
| 1823 | 0.40 | 0.20 | 0.60 | 1874 | 45.09 | 28.97 | 74.06 |
| 1824 | 0.47 | 0.24 | 0.71 | 1875 | 52.72 | 29.29 | 82.01 |
| 1825 | 0.51 | 0.26 | 0.77 | 1876 | 58.71 | 30.86 | 89.57 |
| 1826 | 0.52 | 0.27 | 0.79 | 1877 | 61.71 | 32.65 | 94.36 |
| 1827 | 0.55 | 0.29 | 0.84 | 1878 | 64.24 | 32.70 | 96.94 |
| 1828 | 0.57 | 0.30 | 0.87 | 1879 | 64.79 | 32.57 | 97.36 |
| 1829 | 0.61 | 0.32 | 0.93 | 1880 | 62.93 | 31.10 | 94.03 |
| 1830 | 0.69 | 0.37 | 1.06 | 1881 | 67.71 | 32.95 | 100.66 |
| 1831 | 0.76 | 0.40 | 1.16 | 1882 | 71.79 | 35.83 | 107.62 |
| 1832 | 0.85 | 0.44 | 1.29 | 1883 | 72.93 | 37.89 | 110.82 |
| 1833 | 1.00 | 0.52 | 1.52 | 1884 | 74.19 | 39.44 | 113.63 |
| 1834 | 1.14 | 0.58 | 1.72 | 1885 | 75.29 | 40.93 | 116.22 |
| 1835 | 1.28 | 0.66 | 1.94 | 1886 | 83.78 | 40.81 | 124.59 |
| 1836 | 1.40 | 0.71 | 2.11 | 1887 | 88.70 | 44.23 | 132.93 |
| 1837 | 1.55 | 0.77 | 2.32 | 1888 | 77.30 | 45.76 | 123.06 |
| 1838 | 1.81 | 0.88 | 2.69 | 1889 | 82.06 | 46.63 | 128.69 |

**Table 8.15**  continued

| Year ending 31st Dec. | Primary | Secondary | Total | Year ending 30th June | Primary | Secondary | Total |
|---|---|---|---|---|---|---|---|
| 1890 | 93.50 | 48.46 | 141.96 | 1940 | 663.01 | 262.65 | 925.66 |
| 1891 | 93.79 | 50.73 | 144.52 | 1941 | 722.44 | 284.01 | 1006.45 |
| 1892 | 71.62 | 49.99 | 121.61 | 1942 | 804.50 | 317.86 | 1122.36 |
| 1893 | 70.67 | 48.08 | 118.75 | 1943 | 860.51 | 327.36 | 1187.87 |
| 1894 | 73.98 | 47.96 | 121.94 | 1944 | 909.53 | 329.13 | 1238.66 |
| 1895 | 86.27 | 47.81 | 134.08 | 1945 | 929.64 | 333.03 | 1262.67 |
| 1896 | 80.88 | 49.15 | 130.03 | 1946 | 1023.72 | 360.05 | 1383.77 |
| 1897 | 80.13 | 49.73 | 129.86 | 1947 | 1100.47 | 395.07 | 1495.54 |
| 1898 | 77.89 | 49.82 | 127.71 | 1948 | 1307.58 | 458.53 | 1766.11 |
| 1899 | 80.66 | 48.86 | 129.52 | 1949 | 1450.91 | 511.56 | 1962.47 |
| 1900 | 77.34 | 49.79 | 127.13 | 1950 | 1908.50 | 639.26 | 2547.76 |
| 30th June | | | | 1951 | 2381.99 | 799.07 | 3181.06 |
| 1901 | 93.01 | 51.96 | 144.97 | 1952 | 2780.99 | 930.42 | 3711.41 |
| 1902 | 94.82 | 51.23 | 146.05 | 1953 | 2903.12 | 997.83 | 3900.95 |
| 1903 | 90.44 | 52.10 | 142.54 | 1954 | 2979.12 | 1040.52 | 4019.64 |
| 1904 | 74.70 | 51.73 | 126.43 | 1955 | 3181.95 | 1104.48 | 4286.43 |
| 1905 | 102.49 | 55.30 | 157.79 | 1956 | 3409.02 | 1181.93 | 4590.95 |
| 1906 | 106.79 | 58.19 | 164.98 | 1957 | 3522.96 | 1221.74 | 4744.70 |
| 1907 | 114.42 | 62.12 | 176.54 | 1958 | 3650.81 | 1271.00 | 4921.81 |
| 1908 | 118.85 | 65.04 | 183.89 | 1959 | 3983.20 | 1388.80 | 5372.00 |
| 1909 | 128.82 | 68.88 | 197.70 | 1960 | 4231.21 | 1467.57 | 5698.78 |
| 1910 | 141.53 | 72.64 | 214.17 | 1961 | 4487.89 | 1552.03 | 6039.92 |
| 1911 | 159.07 | 78.50 | 237.57 | 1962 | 4551.41 | 1593.42 | 6144.83 |
| 1912 | 175.20 | 84.84 | 260.04 | 1963 | 4684.51 | 1675.67 | 6360.18 |
| 1913 | 189.68 | 89.83 | 279.51 | 1964 | 5043.57 | 1816.62 | 6860.19 |
| 1914 | 197.26 | 93.06 | 290.32 | 1965 | 5294.29 | 1924.96 | 7219.25 |
| 1915 | 202.49 | 96.73 | 299.22 | 1966 | 5688.59 | 2093.47 | 7782.06 |
| 1916 | 215.11 | 105.54 | 320.65 | 1967 | 6270.49 | 2244.06 | 8514.55 |
| 1917 | 233.26 | 112.56 | 345.82 | 1968 | 6948.06 | 2508.80 | 9456.86 |
| 1918 | 248.17 | 117.99 | 366.16 | 1969 | 7774.48 | 2732.06 | 10506.54 |
| 1919 | 296.25 | 135.33 | 431.58 | 1970 | 8536.19 | 2941.99 | 11478.18 |
| 1920 | 363.79 | 165.79 | 529.58 | 1971 | 10503.07 | 3441.08 | 13944.15 |
| 1921 | 373.50 | 177.25 | 550.75 | 1972 | 11746.20 | 3894.23 | 15640.43 |
| 1922 | 410.36 | 175.64 | 586.00 | 1973 | 15012.35 | 4599.90 | 19612.25 |
| 1923 | 438.13 | 186.20 | 624.33 | 1974 | 21697.40 | 6445.26 | 28142.66 |
| 1924 | 454.72 | 192.08 | 646.80 | 1975 | 26534.20 | 7408.66 | 33942.86 |
| 1925 | 478.56 | 203.21 | 681.77 | 1976 | 31125.43 | 8708.52 | 39833.95 |
| 1926 | 506.18 | 214.66 | 720.84 | 1977 | 35358.67 | 9799.41 | 45158.08 |
| 1927 | 534.45 | 223.51 | 757.96 | 1978 | 38442.70 | 10783.00 | 49225.70 |
| 1928 | 558.31 | 229.16 | 787.47 | 1979 | 40158.83 | 11575.73 | 51734.56 |
| 1929 | 572.00 | 234.60 | 806.60 | 1980 | 46571.79 | 13168.20 | 59739.99 |
| 1930 | 573.39 | 225.85 | 799.24 | 1981 | 53792.28 | 15497.58 | 69289.86 |
| 1931 | 507.02 | 202.05 | 709.07 | 1982 | 60763.86 | 17617.75 | 78381.61 |
| 1932 | 473.66 | 190.40 | 664.06 | 1983 | 64427.47 | 18814.29 | 83241.76 |
| 1933 | 471.52 | 188.97 | 660.49 | 1984 | 68275.72 | 20010.39 | 88286.11 |
| 1934 | 490.16 | 195.96 | 686.12 | 1985 | 73724.59 | 21745.55 | 95470.14 |
| 1935 | 505.17 | 202.14 | 707.31 | 1986 | 78628.25 | 23023.19 | 101651.44 |
| 1936 | 528.77 | 210.36 | 739.13 | 1987 | 86474.04 | 24762.80 | 111236.84 |
| 1937 | 575.92 | 228.42 | 804.34 | 1988 | 92667.63 | 26382.58 | 119050.21 |
| 1938 | 607.80 | 241.06 | 848.86 | 1989 | 100220.27 | 27890.82 | 128111.09 |
| 1939 | 635.12 | 250.98 | 886.10 | 1990 | 109347.12 | 30211.33 | 139558.45 |

**Table 8.16  Market (award) wages for females and males, Australia, 1788–1990 ($)**

| Year ending 31st Dec. | Female | Male | Year ending 31st Dec. | Female | Male | Year ending 31st Dec. | Female | Male |
|---|---|---|---|---|---|---|---|---|
| 1788 | 60.48 | 140.53 | 1823 | 60.48 | 140.53 | 1858 | 109.35 | 248.63 |
| 1789 | 60.48 | 140.53 | 1824 | 60.78 | 141.22 | 1859 | 97.45 | 226.78 |
| 1790 | 60.48 | 140.53 | 1825 | 60.98 | 141.68 | 1860 | 99.41 | 247.71 |
| 1791 | 60.48 | 140.53 | 1826 | 61.08 | 141.91 | 1861 | 103.74 | 241.04 |
| 1792 | 60.48 | 140.53 | 1827 | 61.28 | 142.37 | 1862 | 114.09 | 243.11 |
| 1793 | 60.48 | 140.53 | 1828 | 61.47 | 142.83 | 1863 | 114.06 | 222.64 |
| 1794 | 60.48 | 140.53 | 1829 | 61.67 | 143.29 | 1864 | 114.21 | 218.96 |
| 1795 | 60.48 | 140.53 | 1830 | 61.87 | 143.75 | 1865 | 90.20 | 193.43 |
| 1796 | 60.48 | 140.53 | 1831 | 62.07 | 144.21 | 1866 | 99.66 | 217.12 |
| 1797 | 60.48 | 140.53 | 1832 | 62.27 | 144.67 | 1867 | 99.45 | 220.11 |
| 1798 | 60.48 | 140.53 | 1833 | 62.46 | 145.13 | 1868 | 116.53 | 217.81 |
| 1799 | 60.48 | 140.53 | 1834 | 65.53 | 152.26 | 1869 | 108.91 | 217.35 |
| 1800 | 60.48 | 140.53 | 1835 | 68.60 | 159.39 | 1870 | 104.11 | 228.62 |
| 1801 | 60.48 | 140.53 | 1836 | 67.02 | 155.71 | 1871 | 96.62 | 211.60 |
| 1802 | 60.48 | 140.53 | 1837 | 67.12 | 155.94 | 1872 | 102.96 | 228.39 |
| 1803 | 60.48 | 140.53 | 1838 | 67.22 | 156.17 | 1873 | 102.45 | 246.10 |
| 1804 | 60.48 | 140.53 | 1839 | 70.88 | 164.68 | 1874 | 104.48 | 250.24 |
| 1805 | 60.48 | 140.53 | 1840 | 74.54 | 173.19 | 1875 | 118.56 | 248.86 |
| 1806 | 60.48 | 140.53 | 1841 | 66.42 | 154.33 | 1876 | 127.42 | 256.68 |
| 1807 | 60.48 | 140.53 | 1842 | 58.41 | 135.70 | 1877 | 127.14 | 264.27 |
| 1808 | 60.48 | 140.53 | 1843 | 50.19 | 116.61 | 1878 | 127.46 | 259.44 |
| 1809 | 60.48 | 140.53 | 1844 | 50.88 | 93.61 | 1879 | 123.52 | 252.54 |
| 1810 | 60.48 | 140.53 | 1845 | 64.37 | 93.61 | 1880 | 115.54 | 235.98 |
| 1811 | 60.48 | 140.53 | 1846 | 67.59 | 121.90 | 1881 | 119.22 | 244.26 |
| 1812 | 60.48 | 140.53 | 1847 | 74.41 | 128.80 | 1882 | 121.19 | 255.99 |
| 1813 | 60.48 | 140.53 | 1848 | 68.61 | 124.43 | 1883 | 119.27 | 257.37 |
| 1814 | 60.48 | 140.53 | 1849 | 53.69 | 112.70 | 1884 | 116.59 | 257.14 |
| 1815 | 60.48 | 140.53 | 1850 | 59.09 | 105.57 | 1885 | 114.22 | 257.60 |
| 1816 | 60.48 | 140.53 | 1851 | 66.20 | 153.18 | 1886 | 123.24 | 247.71 |
| 1817 | 60.48 | 140.53 | 1852 | 73.55 | 211.60 | 1887 | 126.75 | 259.21 |
| 1818 | 60.48 | 140.53 | 1853 | 78.94 | 311.65 | 1888 | 107.00 | 258.52 |
| 1819 | 60.48 | 140.53 | 1854 | 117.32 | 495.65 | 1889 | 110.18 | 255.99 |
| 1820 | 60.48 | 140.53 | 1855 | 102.14 | 364.78 | 1890 | 121.47 | 258.06 |
| 1821 | 60.48 | 140.53 | 1856 | 95.76 | 304.98 | 1891 | 118.15 | 262.20 |
| 1822 | 60.48 | 140.53 | 1857 | 99.86 | 281.29 | 1892 | 86.85 | 253.00 |

**Table 8.16**  continued

| Year ending 31st Dec. | Female | Male | Year ending 30th June | Female | Male | Year ending 30th June | Female | Male |
|---|---|---|---|---|---|---|---|---|
| 1893 | 83.85 | 238.97 | 1925 | 263 | 503 | 1958 | 1174 | 1679 |
| 1894 | 85.44 | 233.45 | 1926 | 269 | 516 | 1959 | 1259 | 1792 |
| 1895 | 97.30 | 227.93 | 1927 | 275 | 521 | 1960 | 1309 | 1846 |
| 1896 | 89.04 | 229.54 | 1928 | 280 | 522 | 1961 | 1358 | 1902 |
| 1897 | 86.85 | 227.47 | 1929 | 281 | 526 | 1962 | 1360 | 1906 |
| 1898 | 83.06 | 224.48 | 1930 | 279 | 503 | 1963 | 1388 | 1953 |
| 1899 | 84.74 | 216.66 | 1931 | 247 | 451 | 1964 | 1474 | 2062 |
| 1900 | 79.40 | 217.35 | 1932 | 230 | 425 | 1965 | 1513 | 2120 |
| 30th June | | | 1933 | 226 | 419 | 1966 | 1596 | 2239 |
| 1901 | 94 | 223 | 1934 | 231 | 426 | 1967 | 1694 | 2340 |
| 1902 | 95 | 218 | 1935 | 234 | 431 | 1968 | 1812 | 2547 |
| 1903 | 89 | 218 | 1936 | 241 | 441 | 1969 | 1960 | 2697 |
| 1904 | 72 | 212 | 1937 | 258 | 470 | 1970 | 2063 | 2818 |
| 1905 | 97 | 223 | 1938 | 267 | 486 | 1971 | 2447 | 3201 |
| 1906 | 99 | 230 | 1939 | 274 | 496 | 1972 | 2706 | 3521 |
| 1907 | 99 | 238 | 1940 | 282 | 510 | 1973 | 3380 | 4035 |
| 1908 | 103 | 240 | 1941 | 303 | 542 | 1974 | 4764 | 5490 |
| 1909 | 103 | 246 | 1942 | 334 | 602 | 1975 | 5645 | 6133 |
| 1910 | 108 | 254 | 1943 | 355 | 620 | 1976 | 6509 | 7023 |
| 1911 | 116 | 267 | 1944 | 374 | 621 | 1977 | 7219 | 7710 |
| 1912 | 127 | 280 | 1945 | 382 | 626 | 1978 | 7742 | 8301 |
| 1913 | 135 | 287 | 1946 | 420 | 668 | 1979 | 8014 | 8743 |
| 1914 | 141 | 289 | 1947 | 446 | 717 | 1980 | 9039 | 9747 |
| 1915 | 142 | 294 | 1948 | 522 | 813 | 1981 | 10268 | 11222 |
| 1916 | 142 | 316 | 1949 | 567 | 882 | 1982 | 11479 | 12486 |
| 1917 | 148 | 334 | 1950 | 730 | 1069 | 1983 | 12067 | 13111 |
| 1918 | 158 | 345 | 1951 | 886 | 1293 | 1984 | 12609 | 13687 |
| 1919 | 165 | 390 | 1952 | 1006 | 1447 | 1985 | 13449 | 14565 |
| 1920 | 193 | 467 | 1953 | 1029 | 1496 | 1986 | 14014 | 15117 |
| 1921 | 231 | 491 | 1954 | 1029 | 1508 | 1987 | 14848 | 15976 |
| 1922 | 232 | 476 | 1955 | 1076 | 1560 | 1988 | 15534 | 16719 |
| 1923 | 249 | 490 | 1956 | 1130 | 1628 | 1989 | 16327 | 17302 |
| 1924 | 257 | 490 | 1957 | 1151 | 1651 | 1990 | 17269 | 18321 |

*Note:*  These wages are the equivalent of what would be paid if labour were employed for a full year with all non-pecuniary benefits (board, lodging etc.) monetarized.

# 9

# Capital, land, and income in the Total Economy

*W*hile labour services are the most important part of the household story, they are not the whole story. Value added in the household sector is the combined product of labour, capital, and land. In contrast to the firm, enterprise is not considered to be important in determining value added in the household, largely because output is not competitively marketed. Land, however, has always been an important input in the Australian household economy, because the 'Australian dream' has always revolved around the idea of a detached house on a quarter-acre block that could be used to grow vegetables and raise poultry. And Australia appeared, at least until the mid-1970s, to have enough land to meet this ideal—an ideal that has long been a central part of political folk lore, and that has led to the high cost of urbanization in this country. Capital has also played an important role in the household economy, as it has in the market economy. Indeed, residential construction, a major input in the household sector, has always been actively involved in the fluctuating fortunes of the market sector. And the mass exodus of married women from the home to the market after the mid 1950s was facilitated (but not caused) by the rapid and widespread adoption of sophisticated household appliances, which in turn stimulated the growth of the market sector. Clearly all factors of production must be taken into account when, as has been done later in this chapter, estimating household income and, finally, total income.

## Household capital

### Investment

Household capital includes both the stock of housing and the value of household equipment installed. As we already have adequate estimates of investment in dwellings,[1] the task here—and it has been a time-consuming task—has been to collect and present data on household equipment. It is interesting that considerable effort has been devoted to the estimation of housing investment by those working on national accounts for the market sector—it is interesting because the nation's housing stock should be regarded as an input of the household sector, not of the market sector. This, together with imputed rents for owner-occupied dwellings, is a curious inconsistency in the existing national accounts, and probably can be explained by the perceived importance of housing to the market economy. Summary estimates (both values and shares) of new gross household capital formation, for both equipment and buildings, are presented in Tables 9.2 to 9.5 in both current and constant prices. And the value of household capital stock (1966/67 prices) can be found in Table 9.7.

The method employed here to estimate new gross expenditure on household equipment between 1900 and 1985, is that referred to by Roland Wilson in his famous 1939 Australian and New Zealand Association for the Advancement of Science (ANZAAS) paper on 'Public and private investment in Australia' as the 'flow-of-goods' approach. This method, which is the alternative to the 'change-in-stock' approach, has been used regularly since the 1930s to estimate Australian capital expenditures, most notably by Noel Butlin and Bryan Haig.[2] Briefly, this method involves the summation of finished household equipment produced locally, and net imports (including customs duties), together with the addition of mark-ups for distribution and sales taxes. As with similar estimates of market investment it does not include the sale of used equipment. However, this and depreciation are taken into account when estimating capital stock. The annual data were collected laboriously according to the detailed categories listed in Table 9.1, including equipment used in food preparation; cooking; food storage; house cleaning; clothes washing; water heating; clothes making; space heating and cooling; and gardening and house maintenance. The tests for inclusion in these categories are: did they contribute to economic production (in contrast to leisure activities) and did they have a life of more than one year?

A useful test of the reliability of the data generated in this way is provided by the 1984 ABS *Household expenditure survey*. In the volume entitled *Detailed expenditure items*, Table 1, average weekly household expenditure incorporates (amongst a host of other items) appliances, kitchenware, and garden and household tools. The weekly total amounts to $10.66, and the annual total to $554.32, per household. By applying the average annual sum to the number of households for 1984 (an average of 1983/84 and 1984/85) we obtain a total expenditure figure for all Australian households of $2,783.2 million. This official estimate is only 0.2 per cent lower than my estimate of $2,788.9 million for the same year. Clearly the difference is not significant, a fact which provides a high level of confidence in the methods employed in this study for estimating capital expenditure.

## Table 9.1   Categories of Australian household economic equipment

1. Food preparation
   1.1  kitchenware
   1.2  electrical goods
   1.3  kitchen knives etc.
   1.4  total

2. Cooking
   2.1  solid fuel cookers
   2.2  gas cookers
   2.3  electric cookers
   2.4  other
   2.5  total

3. Food storage and cooling
   3.1  foodsafes, icechests etc.
   3.2  refrigerators
   3.3  total

4. House cleaning
   4.1  vacuum cleaners
   4.2  floor polishers
   4.3  dishwashers
   4.4  other
   4.5  total

5. Clothes washing
   5.1  washing machines
   5.2  laundry boilers
   5.3  drying machines
   5.4  ironing machines
   5.5  other
   5.6  total

6. Water heating
   6.1  hot water systems
   6.2  other
   6.3  total

7. Clothes making (sewing machines)

8. Space heating and cooling
   8.1  space heating: solid, electric, gas, other
   8.2  space cooling: fans, airconditioners
   8.3  total

9. Gardening and house maintenance
   9.1  lawn mowers
   9.2  household tools
   9.3  other
   9.4  total

Estimates of capital expenditures using data from the ABS *Household expenditure survey* have been made for 1984/85 onwards. This approach has been adopted not only because of the growing difficulties in employing previous data sources, but also because of growing confidence in the survey results. In the early 1980s the ABS made a decision not to publish the former detail for trade and production, which was becoming increasingly complex, but to provide it on microfiche on request. As the microfiche data is not indexed, an already complex task was made even more difficult owing to problems in tracking down extremely detailed items. Given that estimates based on the survey data for 1984 were almost identical with estimates based on the production and trade data, it was decided to utilize the former after the mid 1980s.

The ABS surveys provide data on household equipment expenditure per household for 1984 and 1988/89. These average household data were converted to 1984/85 prices (by using the ABS price index for private equipment), were assumed to change between the two bench years by a constant annual amount, were converted to current prices, and were applied to the number of households between 1985/86 and 1989/90.

## Detailed methods and sources

Annual data on the value (factory-door) of locally manufactured *finished* household equipment for the period between 1900 and 1985 can be found in the various ABS publications that present Australian manufacturing data. These publications include the *Statistical register* of the various states and colonies, the *Production bulletin*, the *Secondary industries bulletin*, and the *Principal articles produced bulletin*. Between 1900 and 1937 the data are reliable but are only available in a highly aggregated form (i.e. by types of goods in the various categories in Table 9.1 rather than by individual items), whereas since 1937 the data are very detailed, being recorded on an individual item basis. While the increased detail after 1937 makes it possible to allocate items more easily between the various categories in Table 9.1, it also makes the task far more time-consuming.

Data on the value (at port) of *cleared* imports (plus duties) of finished household equipment are available in the *Overseas trade bulletin* in the early years, and later can be found in the *Imports cleared for home consumption bulletin*, and more recently on microfiche from the ABS (unfortunately without an index). It is important to realize that the data collected relates to imports 'cleared' for sale rather than imports 'off-loaded' because, while they are generally similar, from time to time they diverge markedly. Also, as the official data before 1947 are valued at c.i.f. (actually f.o.b. plus 10 per cent), and after 1947 at f.o.b., an adjustment (by adding a mark-up for insurance and freight ranging from 10 per cent in the 1940s to 20 per cent in the 1980s) for consistency needs to be made. The trade data, both for exports and imports, are provided on a very detailed basis throughout the twentieth century, thereby allowing identification of individual items on a consistent basis. The high proportion of household equipment imported before the Second World War compensates for the less detailed local production recorded before 1937. Finally, the value of exports of finished household equipment are also to be found in the *Overseas trade bulletin*.

As household equipment is valued at the port (c.i.f.) and at the factory door, the raw data must be revalued to include distribution costs and sales taxes. The distribution mark-up (50 per cent) employed is based upon evidence in Butlin, *Australian domestic product* (Chapter 13, particularly pp. 215–7). While it would be desirable to have annual data on distribution margins, this information is just not available. This makes my household investment series comparable in reliability to Butlin's market investment series over the same period. The annual rate of sales tax introduced in 1930/31 can be found in the annual *Report of the Commissioner of Taxation*—these rates ranged from 5 per cent in the 1930s to 20 per cent in the 1980s. If anything, the calculations underestimate total annual expenditure on household equipment because some of the smaller items of household capital may have escaped notice. But, owing to the detailed official nature of the data, the degree of measurement error from these sources should be regarded as very small. Finally, it should be realized that investment in private motor vehicles has not been included, because of a number of conceptual and practical problems. On the one hand, it is not possible to determine the proportion of total mileage devoted to household economic activities (as opposed to leisure, and travel to work); and, on the other hand, the data on motor vehicle imports and construction are so detailed (down to spark plugs) as to defy reconstruction (leading to the eventual rejection of a great deal of data that had been collected for this task).

It should also be noted that a distinction has been made between productive capital and leisure capital. Often both are lumped together under the name 'consumer durables'. Clearly this is not valid, as washing machines, vacuum cleaners, lawn mowers etc. are *not* inputs into consumption—ask any house person! On the other hand, television sets, video recorders, sound systems, radios, furniture, sporting goods etc. are capital inputs into leisure or consumption activities. These are the true 'consumer durables'. A useful conceptual and practical way of distinguishing between these two types of household capital is to ask whether it is possible to distinguish between the production and consumption of a household activity. We can distinguish between the cooking of food and its consumption (and hence could sell the product on the market), but not between the production and consumption of television watching or backyard tennis playing (which cannot be marketed). The former is an economic activity, while the latter are leisure activities. This definition has been employed consistently throughout the book. Needless to say, as with the measurement of capital employed in the market sector, there are difficulties in determining whether certain durables are predominantly used in economic or leisure activities.

Owing to the lack of adequate data prior to 1901, only indirect methods can be employed to estimate household equipment in the nineteenth century. The estimates have been extended back to 1861 by applying the average ratio between capital expenditures on equipment and buildings (0.414) for 1901 and 1905, to the residential investment series, so that equipment in year $t$ is equal to 41.4 per cent of the average of residential investment for the three years $t$, $t-1$, and $t-2$.

A statistical comparison is made in Table 7.6 between capital formation in the household and market (both private and public) sectors, and for the Total Economy. To do this, residential investment has been transferred from the market sector (as estimated by N.G. Butlin before 1940 and the ABS thereafter) to its rightful place in the household sector. The relative size of these various components has also been provided in Table 7.7.

## Capital stock

### Household sector

Household capital stock for the period 1861 to 1990 has been estimated using the real investment series (1966/67 prices) for equipment and buildings (Table 9.5), together with estimates of base-year (1861) capital stock in both categories (Table 9.7), and the assumption that capital consumption occurs at a rate of 8 per cent per annum for equipment and 1.5 per cent per annum for housing. These assumptions are based on evidence presented in Butlin, *Australian domestic product*; M. Butlin, *Preliminary database*; Haig, *Capital stock*; and Snooks, 'Capital stock'.

The value of housing capital stock (in 1966/67 prices) for 1861 was estimated in the following way. Imputed housing rents taken from Butlin, *Australian domestic product* (ch. 15) for 1861 ($15.8 million) were capitalized using the bond rate of 4.0 per cent for the year (Pope, 'Private finance'), giving a stock estimate of $98.8 million in 1861 prices, or $893.3 million in 1966/67 prices. An examination of New South Wales government reports on housing for the early twentieth century suggested that one-quarter of this figure should be subtracted from the combined buildings/land total for land, leaving a housing stock figure in 1966/67 prices of $670 million. The stock of housing equipment in 1861 was taken to be one-third of capitalized rentals—as suggested by a comparison of flows of equipment and buildings over the period 1861 to 1990— which in 1966/67 prices amounted to $123.6 million. These base-year stock estimates should not be taken too seriously other than as a starting point for estimates of capital stock that are used to indicate, not levels of capital, but rather changes in this variable over time. It is expected that any error in the 1861 level will be overwhelmed by the cumulative addition of net real investment figures over the following 130 years. The stock estimates are given in Table 9.7.

### Market sector

A similar method was employed to estimate the plant and equipment capital stock for the market (both private and public) economy. This market capital stock series has been used in the analysis presented in Chapter 5. The plant and equipment investment series in nominal prices was constructed from the following sources:

- 1861 to 1900: N.G. Butlin, *Australian domestic product*, Part III
- 1901 to 1972: M. Butlin, *Preliminary database*
- 1973 to 1990: ABS, *Australian national accounts*

The nominal investment series was converted to 1966/67 prices using the private and public 'non-dwelling' price indices in Table 7.11. These price indices were also constructed from data in the above sources.

The base-year plant and equipment stock figure for 1861 was obtained by extrapolating M. Butlin's 1901 stock estimate backwards using N. G. Butlin's real investment series, and converting to 1966/67 prices. For estimates of capital consumption, a depreciation rate of 8 per cent per annum was used. The resulting estimates, obtained by cumulating the real investment series on the 1861 stock estimate (in 1966/67 prices), and retiring the growing stock figure at the rate of 8 per cent per annum, are presented in Table 9.10.

# Residential land

It is not possible to measure the quantity or value of residential land directly, even in more recent decades. While Scott, *The value of land*, is a valuable source, it cannot be employed for this purpose. Nevertheless a good index of changes in the quantity of residential land is provided by the number of households between 1788 and 1990 presented in Table 8.2. The assumption underlying the use of this index is that there is no significant change in the size of residential blocks. As is well known, the size of blocks in residential development since the 1950s declined due, in part, to the rising real costs of urbanization as Australian cities grew rapidly in this period, and in part to the changing nature of the relationship between the household and market sectors. Possibly partly offsetting this trend has been the move since the early 1970s of young middle-class families onto larger holdings in the rural fringes of our cities. Despite these qualifications, household numbers can be regarded as a reasonable proxy for the change in the quantity of residential land.

In any case the estimated quantity of residential land has been employed in this study only to check the preferred estimate based upon household rental data. As will be discussed in greater detail in the next section, our attempt to measure the contribution of residential land to household income is based on actual and imputed rents of all private dwellings in Australia. Residential rents take into account not only the nature of the residence, but also the quantity, quality, and location of the land, together with other aspects of the rental market.

# Household income

An attempt has been made in this study to measure household income on a factor-of-production basis. This can be done by measuring the opportunity cost of all factors of production employed in the household sector including labour, buildings, land, and equipment. While Chapter 8 outlines my estimate of the value of household labour services, the value of productive services provided by household buildings, land, and equipment needs to be discussed here in greater detail.

## Residential buildings and land

Clearly residential buildings and land are an important, indeed essential, input in the household economy. They are equivalent to the factory and office in the market sector. It is possible to measure the value of their productive services by measuring the opportunity cost of funds tied up in these assets. Conceptually there are two ways in which their opportunity cost can be captured: by measuring the actual and imputed rents paid on all dwellings, as a product of the household stock and market rentals in each year; and by estimating the opportunity cost of the capital tied up in residential land and buildings, as a product of the capital stock and the rate of interest on low-risk securities, such as government bonds. With perfect information we would expect both estimates to be approximately the same. (A comparison has been made in Figure 9.1.) As the information on rents is more reliable than data on residential capital stock (mainly owing to problems with the land variable) the former has been used in this study. The results, in current prices, are given in Table 9.8.

## Rents

It is fortunate that a continuous series of actual and imputed rents on residential buildings and land already exists for the entire period 1810 to the present. The value of house rents from 1810 to 1939 can be found in Noel Butlin's work, and official estimates are available since 1940.[3] Both sources use estimates of various types of housing stock and market rentals to construct gross rents from which are subtracted 'operating expenses'—such as municipal rates, maintenance, insurance, and commissions—in order to arrive at estimates of gross operating surpluses on dwellings. The official estimates from 1962/63 onwards provide information on imputed rents for corporate and government bodies as well as individuals. Using this information, adjustments were made to official data between 1939/40 and 1961/62. The results are presented in Table 9.8.

## The return on capital

In order to check the trend in the house rents series, I have employed the alternative method of estimating capital stock and valuing it by the government bond rate. While the techniques employed are approximate, the results are interesting. To construct a housing stock series we need to estimate a depreciated stock value in 1861 and to build this up by accumulating the available series of residential investment.[4] The 1861 base figure was calculated by capitalizing the value of house rents in that year by the bond rate, and this base was built up annually by adding in residential investment expenditures in current prices. The product is a capital stock series in *historical prices* which, owing to the effect of inflation, reflects the declining amenity of the ageing stock of housing. No attempt has been made to retire housing owing to the long life span of this asset and to its growing insignificance in the inflationary world of the post–Second World War period, when we know that some earlier stock was demolished. It is important to realize that we are not attempting to estimate the changing quantity of the housing stock for the purposes of calculating productivity change,[5] but rather the changing market value of that stock which, at any point of time, is composed of a bewildering variety of vintages. A housing stock valued at historical cost is an approx-imation of what we are looking for. The government bond rate was employed to calculate the opportunity cost of using capital in the household.[6]

Calculating the role of residential land is made difficult by the absence, as already noted, of sufficient direct data on quantities. The best that can be done is to inflate the return to capital in housing by an appropriate proportion. An examination of land and house values in housing department reports for New South Wales, Victoria, and South Australia during the early twentieth century suggests a mark-up of one-third applied to the value of housing stock.

A comparison between residential rents and this indirect estimate of the income accruing to land and buildings is made in Figure 9.1. Given the very different methods employed, it is interesting to see how close the two alternative series are. The main difference between them appears in the second half of the nineteenth century. What we know of these years—a period in which population increased at 3.4 per cent per annum—suggests that the preferred real rent series (land and buildings 1) is the appropriate series.

**Figure 9.1 Comparison of two estimates of household income accruing to residential land and buildings, 1861–1990**

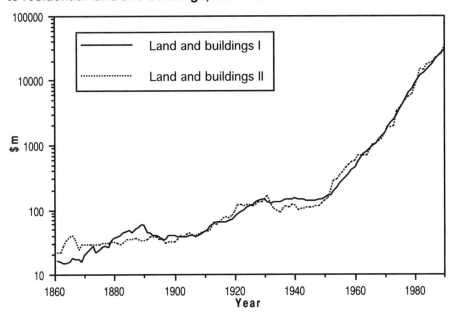

Notes:   Land and buildings I is from Table 9.8; Land and buildings II, which has not been employed in the estimates in this book, was constructed as an alternative series using capital stock estimates and an appropriate interest rate.

Source:   See text and Table 9.8.

## *Household equipment*

The opportunity cost of capital tied up in household equipment can be calculated in a similar way to the alternative method discussed above for household buildings. A base-year stock figure for 1861 was calculated by capitalizing the estimated amount required to lease the existing stock of housing equipment on the assumption that it was one-quarter of the total sum of house rents in 1861 (derived from the ratios between expenditures on buildings and equipment for the twenty years after 1900 when detailed data became available). The series of investment in household equipment from 1861 to 1985 was then used to construct a series of equipment stock at *historical cost*. Once again no attempt was made to retire this capital for the reasons discussed above, together with the fact that old household equipment is generally recycled through second-hand markets. To estimate the imputed return to this capital stock series, the government bond rate series discussed earlier was employed. Some confidence in this method is derived from the similar results for alternative approaches to land and buildings presented in Figure 9.1.

Estimates of household income from all sources are presented in Table 9.8.

# Gross Community Income and Capital Formation

It is now possible to compile a table presenting gross income generated by the Total Economy of Australia from 1788 to 1990. Gross Community Income is the aggregation of gross income from both the household and market sectors. But in order to present a consistent set of social accounts for the Total Economy it is necessary to transfer elements of the family economy from the official national accounts to the household sector. By subtracting house rents on owner-occupied dwellings from GDP we arrive at an acceptable measure of market activity. It will be recalled that house rents have already been included in our estimate of household income. This study presents the first attempt to measure the economic activity of the Total Economy—a measure I have called Gross Community Income—for the period 1788 to 1990. In a similar way, Gross Community Capital Formation for 1861 to 1990 can be estimated by combining my estimates of household investment (Table 9.2) with the Butlin/ABS estimates of Gross Domestic Capital Formation *minus* residential investment. The new set of total social accounts, for both income and investment, in current prices, is presented in Tables 7.1 and 7.6.

# Prices of output and investment

When dealing with time in economics it is essential to allow for changes in prices. This means constructing price indexes and deflating current price data in order to obtain constant price series. It must be emphasized that this can only ever be an approximate procedure but, equally, it must be done if we wish to say anything at all about changes in the quantities of inputs and outcomes in the process of economic change. The problems associated with the use of price indexes and deflation techniques are well known—the representativeness of the available prices, the use of shadow prices for goods not marketed, index number problems, fixed weights, quality changes, etc.— and they should be taken into account when the constant price series is examined. This is not to say that the procedure is invalid, just that it should be employed with sensitivity and imagination. No statistical series—or indeed any other piece of evidence whether quantitative or literary—should be subjected to more analytical pressure than it can bear. None have in this study.

## Output prices

There are two alternative deflation methods. The first is to employ the implicit GDP deflator to convert household, market, and total income to constant (1966/67) prices. This deflator was based on Butlin, 'Contours' for the period 1800 to 1860; Butlin, *Australian domestic product* for 1861 to 1900; M. Butlin, *Preliminary database* for 1901 to 1949; and ABS, *Australian national accounts* for 1950 to 1990. Second, household income can be deflated by the final consumption deflator (obtained from same sources) and market income by the implicit GDP deflator. While both methods have been employed, the latter is preferred as household income is largely spent on final consumption goods. The price indexes are presented in Table 7.10.

## Capital expenditure prices

Four different price indexes were used to deflate the current price series of household buildings, household equipment, private plant and equipment, and public plant and equipment. These indexes are presented in Table 7.11.

The price index for household buildings, or dwellings, has been obtained from Butlin, *Australian domestic product* for the period 1861 to 1990; M. Butlin, *Preliminary database* for 1901 to 1949; and ABS, *Australian national accounts* for 1950 to 1990. As the price series on which this index is based is detailed, and the methods employed in its reconstruction are sound, the reliability of the resulting index is high. The price index for household equipment is less specific, and the underlying data, at least for the nineteenth century, is less satisfactory. This does not apply to the period 1950 to 1990 for which we have an official price index (ABS, *Consumer price index*) for 'household equipment and operation'. Before 1950 I have relied on various consumer price indexes. These have been obtained from M. Butlin for the period 1901 to 1949 (implicit private consumption deflator), and N.G. Butlin for 1861 to 1900. While the twentieth century indexes are basically weighted averages for all capital cities, that for the nineteenth century is based on Sydney alone, owing to the absence of adequate data for other colonial capital cities. Owing to the importance of Sydney in the 'national' economy during the second half of the nineteenth century, this should not impose significant distortions.

The private plant and equipment series has been deflated using the implicit price deflator for private non-dwelling fixed capital expenditure. This has been calculated from the abovementioned sources. In a similar way the public plant and equipment series has been deflated using the implicit deflator for public non-dwelling fixed capital expenditure by employing the same sources. In the process, a few errors in these sources were discovered and corrected.

## Capital intensity and productivity

Finally, the above estimates have been employed to construct indexes for the ratio between capital stock and labour, and of labour productivity in the household and market sectors. These indexes are employed in the analysis in Part One, and are presented here for the first time in Tables 9.9 and 9.11 for the household sector, and in Tables 9.10 and 9.11 for the market sector. Relative factor prices, which influence these indexes, can be found, for both the household and market sectors, in Table 9.12.

**Table 9.2   Household capital formation, Australia, 1861–1990**

| Year ending 31st Dec. | Values in current prices ($m) | | | Shares (%) | | |
|---|---|---|---|---|---|---|
| | Equipment | Buildings | Total | Equipment | Buildings | Total |
| **1861** | 1.81 | 4.36 | 6.17 | 29.3 | 70.7 | 100 |
| **1862** | 1.80 | 4.31 | 6.11 | 29.5 | 70.5 | 100 |
| **1863** | 1.88 | 4.96 | 6.84 | 27.5 | 72.5 | 100 |
| **1864** | 2.17 | 6.48 | 8.65 | 25.1 | 74.9 | 100 |
| **1865** | 2.42 | 6.06 | 8.48 | 28.5 | 71.5 | 100 |
| **1866** | 2.42 | 5.00 | 7.42 | 32.6 | 67.4 | 100 |
| **1867** | 2.35 | 5.99 | 8.34 | 28.2 | 71.8 | 100 |
| **1868** | 2.22 | 5.11 | 7.33 | 30.3 | 69.7 | 100 |
| **1869** | 2.41 | 6.34 | 8.75 | 27.5 | 72.5 | 100 |
| **1870** | 2.42 | 6.05 | 8.47 | 28.6 | 71.4 | 100 |
| **1871** | 2.42 | 5.15 | 7.57 | 32.0 | 68.0 | 100 |
| **1872** | 2.62 | 7.75 | 10.37 | 25.3 | 74.7 | 100 |
| **1873** | 2.87 | 7.91 | 10.78 | 26.6 | 73.4 | 100 |
| **1874** | 3.23 | 7.73 | 10.96 | 29.5 | 70.5 | 100 |
| **1875** | 3.28 | 8.14 | 11.42 | 28.7 | 71.3 | 100 |
| **1876** | 3.75 | 11.30 | 15.05 | 24.9 | 75.1 | 100 |
| **1877** | 3.83 | 8.30 | 12.13 | 31.6 | 68.4 | 100 |
| **1878** | 3.77 | 7.75 | 11.52 | 32.7 | 67.3 | 100 |
| **1879** | 3.40 | 8.56 | 11.96 | 28.4 | 71.6 | 100 |
| **1880** | 2.92 | 7.86 | 10.78 | 27.1 | 72.9 | 100 |
| **1881** | 4.01 | 12.62 | 16.63 | 24.1 | 75.9 | 100 |
| **1882** | 4.64 | 13.11 | 17.75 | 26.1 | 73.9 | 100 |
| **1883** | 6.39 | 20.58 | 26.97 | 23.7 | 76.3 | 100 |
| **1884** | 7.35 | 19.60 | 26.95 | 27.3 | 72.7 | 100 |
| **1885** | 7.91 | 17.15 | 25.06 | 31.6 | 68.4 | 100 |
| **1886** | 7.13 | 14.91 | 22.04 | 32.4 | 67.6 | 100 |
| **1887** | 7.13 | 19.63 | 26.76 | 26.6 | 73.4 | 100 |
| **1888** | 7.73 | 21.49 | 29.22 | 26.5 | 73.5 | 100 |
| **1889** | 7.56 | 13.69 | 21.25 | 35.6 | 64.4 | 100 |
| **1890** | 7.13 | 16.51 | 23.64 | 30.2 | 69.8 | 100 |
| **1891** | 5.87 | 12.31 | 18.18 | 32.3 | 67.7 | 100 |
| **1892** | 5.32 | 9.74 | 15.06 | 35.3 | 64.7 | 100 |
| **1893** | 4.00 | 6.90 | 10.90 | 36.7 | 63.3 | 100 |
| **1894** | 3.45 | 8.33 | 11.78 | 29.3 | 70.7 | 100 |
| **1895** | 3.04 | 6.79 | 9.83 | 30.9 | 69.1 | 100 |
| **1896** | 3.07 | 7.15 | 10.22 | 30.0 | 70.0 | 100 |
| **1897** | 2.41 | 3.50 | 5.91 | 40.8 | 59.2 | 100 |
| **1898** | 2.59 | 8.13 | 10.72 | 24.2 | 75.8 | 100 |
| **1899** | 2.17 | 4.09 | 6.26 | 34.7 | 65.3 | 100 |
| **1900** | 2.20 | 3.73 | 5.93 | 37.1 | 62.9 | 100 |
| 30th June | | | | | | |
| **1901** | 5.25 | 9.08 | 14.33 | 36.6 | 63.4 | 100 |
| **1902** | 5.11 | 17.84 | 22.95 | 22.3 | 77.7 | 100 |
| **1903** | 5.15 | 12.76 | 17.91 | 28.8 | 71.2 | 100 |

**Table 9.2**  continued

| Year ending 30th June | Values in current prices ($m) | | | Shares (%) | | |
|---|---|---|---|---|---|---|
| | Equipment | Buildings | Total | Equipment | Buildings | Total |
| 1904 | 5.07 | 10.96 | 16.03 | 31.6 | 68.4 | 100 |
| 1905 | 5.19 | 11.56 | 16.75 | 31.0 | 69.0 | 100 |
| 1906 | 5.37 | 13.98 | 19.35 | 27.8 | 72.2 | 100 |
| 1907 | 5.89 | 16.22 | 22.11 | 26.6 | 73.4 | 100 |
| 1908 | 6.20 | 15.90 | 22.10 | 28.1 | 71.9 | 100 |
| 1909 | 6.13 | 14.14 | 20.27 | 30.2 | 69.8 | 100 |
| 1910 | 6.65 | 15.64 | 22.29 | 29.8 | 70.2 | 100 |
| 1911 | 7.24 | 19.22 | 26.46 | 27.4 | 72.6 | 100 |
| 1912 | 8.27 | 24.44 | 32.71 | 25.3 | 74.7 | 100 |
| 1913 | 8.20 | 32.84 | 41.04 | 20.0 | 80.0 | 100 |
| 1914 | 8.30 | 36.17 | 44.47 | 18.7 | 81.3 | 100 |
| 1915 | 8.20 | 31.53 | 39.73 | 20.6 | 79.4 | 100 |
| 1916 | 8.79 | 24.23 | 33.02 | 26.6 | 73.4 | 100 |
| 1917 | 8.71 | 20.04 | 28.75 | 30.3 | 69.7 | 100 |
| 1918 | 8.58 | 19.31 | 27.89 | 30.8 | 69.2 | 100 |
| 1919 | 10.65 | 26.40 | 37.05 | 28.7 | 71.3 | 100 |
| 1920 | 10.64 | 49.58 | 60.22 | 17.7 | 82.3 | 100 |
| 1921 | 13.89 | 58.11 | 72.00 | 19.3 | 80.7 | 100 |
| 1922 | 11.16 | 52.36 | 63.52 | 17.6 | 82.4 | 100 |
| 1923 | 12.04 | 68.66 | 80.70 | 14.9 | 85.1 | 100 |
| 1924 | 13.59 | 76.78 | 90.37 | 15.0 | 85.0 | 100 |
| 1925 | 13.31 | 74.39 | 87.70 | 15.2 | 84.8 | 100 |
| 1926 | 13.80 | 73.82 | 87.62 | 15.7 | 84.3 | 100 |
| 1927 | 16.58 | 82.56 | 99.14 | 16.7 | 83.3 | 100 |
| 1928 | 14.55 | 84.95 | 99.50 | 14.6 | 85.4 | 100 |
| 1929 | 14.88 | 74.88 | 89.76 | 16.6 | 83.4 | 100 |
| 1930 | 12.85 | 53.04 | 65.89 | 19.5 | 80.5 | 100 |
| 1931 | 8.98 | 25.61 | 34.59 | 26.0 | 74.0 | 100 |
| 1932 | 6.81 | 15.91 | 22.72 | 30.0 | 70.0 | 100 |
| 1933 | 8.44 | 22.62 | 31.06 | 27.2 | 72.8 | 100 |
| 1934 | 9.68 | 31.40 | 41.08 | 23.6 | 76.4 | 100 |
| 1935 | 11.34 | 37.62 | 48.96 | 23.2 | 76.8 | 100 |
| 1936 | 14.96 | 48.14 | 63.10 | 23.7 | 76.3 | 100 |
| 1937 | 15.01 | 55.37 | 70.38 | 21.3 | 78.7 | 100 |
| 1938 | 18.70 | 64.48 | 83.18 | 22.5 | 77.5 | 100 |
| 1939 | 20.94 | 65.55 | 86.49 | 24.2 | 75.8 | 100 |
| 1940 | 22.09 | 59.44 | 81.53 | 27.1 | 72.9 | 100 |
| 1941 | 19.90 | 55.42 | 75.32 | 26.4 | 73.6 | 100 |
| 1942 | 17.90 | 35.14 | 53.04 | 33.7 | 66.3 | 100 |
| 1943 | 14.64 | 15.34 | 29.98 | 48.8 | 51.2 | 100 |
| 1944 | 16.33 | 11.40 | 27.73 | 58.9 | 41.1 | 100 |
| 1945 | 17.93 | 19.02 | 36.95 | 48.5 | 51.5 | 100 |
| 1946 | 22.28 | 47.34 | 69.62 | 32.0 | 68.0 | 100 |
| 1947 | 39.18 | 97.66 | 136.84 | 28.6 | 71.4 | 100 |

**Table 9.2**  continued

| Year ending 30th June | Values in current prices ($m) | | | Shares (%) | | |
|---|---|---|---|---|---|---|
| | Equipment | Buildings | Total | Equipment | Buildings | Total |
| 1948 | 72.16 | 131.02 | 203.18 | 35.5 | 64.5 | 100 |
| 1949 | 88.45 | 201.12 | 289.57 | 30.5 | 69.5 | 100 |
| 1950 | 135.40 | 268.60 | 404.00 | 33.5 | 66.5 | 100 |
| 1951 | 156.45 | 376.40 | 532.85 | 29.4 | 70.6 | 100 |
| 1952 | 207.16 | 474.80 | 681.96 | 30.4 | 69.6 | 100 |
| 1953 | 144.53 | 472.20 | 616.73 | 23.4 | 76.6 | 100 |
| 1954 | 206.82 | 509.20 | 716.02 | 28.9 | 71.1 | 100 |
| 1955 | 226.57 | 544.80 | 771.37 | 29.4 | 70.6 | 100 |
| 1956 | 228.77 | 559.80 | 788.57 | 29.0 | 71.0 | 100 |
| 1957 | 210.91 | 544.20 | 755.11 | 27.9 | 72.1 | 100 |
| 1958 | 191.93 | 605.60 | 797.53 | 24.1 | 75.9 | 100 |
| 1959 | 247.41 | 666.80 | 914.21 | 27.1 | 72.9 | 100 |
| 1960 | 276.62 | 748.40 | 1025.02 | 27.0 | 73.0 | 100 |
| 1961 | 325.89 | 815.60 | 1141.49 | 28.5 | 71.5 | 100 |
| 1962 | 328.18 | 761.00 | 1089.18 | 30.1 | 69.9 | 100 |
| 1963 | 339.59 | 835.00 | 1174.59 | 28.9 | 71.1 | 100 |
| 1964 | 376.01 | 954.00 | 1330.01 | 28.3 | 71.7 | 100 |
| 1965 | 393.46 | 1109.00 | 1502.46 | 26.2 | 73.8 | 100 |
| 1966 | 394.19 | 1157.00 | 1551.19 | 25.4 | 74.6 | 100 |
| 1967 | 434.44 | 1244.00 | 1678.44 | 25.9 | 74.1 | 100 |
| 1968 | 455.19 | 1392.00 | 1847.19 | 24.6 | 75.4 | 100 |
| 1969 | 520.81 | 1573.00 | 2093.81 | 24.9 | 75.1 | 100 |
| 1970 | 566.52 | 1809.00 | 2375.52 | 23.8 | 76.2 | 100 |
| 1971 | 589.05 | 1915.00 | 2504.05 | 23.5 | 76.5 | 100 |
| 1972 | 635.87 | 2195.00 | 2830.87 | 22.5 | 77.5 | 100 |
| 1973 | 704.21 | 2588.00 | 3292.21 | 21.4 | 78.6 | 100 |
| 1974 | 919.59 | 3140.00 | 4059.59 | 22.7 | 77.3 | 100 |
| 1975 | 1092.27 | 3312.00 | 4404.27 | 24.8 | 75.2 | 100 |
| 1976 | 1271.99 | 4513.00 | 5784.99 | 22.0 | 78.0 | 100 |
| 1977 | 1454.66 | 5587.00 | 7041.66 | 20.7 | 79.3 | 100 |
| 1978 | 1446.65 | 5516.00 | 6962.65 | 20.8 | 79.2 | 100 |
| 1979 | 1590.00 | 5769.00 | 7359.00 | 21.6 | 78.4 | 100 |
| 1980 | 1744.78 | 6753.00 | 8497.78 | 20.5 | 79.5 | 100 |
| 1981 | 1875.78 | 8518.00 | 10393.78 | 18.0 | 82.0 | 100 |
| 1982 | 2264.91 | 9396.00 | 11660.91 | 19.4 | 80.6 | 100 |
| 1983 | 2374.43 | 8245.00 | 10619.43 | 22.4 | 77.6 | 100 |
| 1984 | 2634.66 | 9473.00 | 12107.66 | 21.8 | 78.2 | 100 |
| 1985 | 2943.12 | 11326.00 | 14269.12 | 20.6 | 79.4 | 100 |
| 1986 | 3433.30 | 12319.00 | 15752.30 | 21.8 | 78.2 | 100 |
| 1987 | 3891.83 | 11859.00 | 15750.83 | 24.7 | 75.3 | 100 |
| 1988 | 4046.10 | 13421.00 | 17467.10 | 23.2 | 76.8 | 100 |
| 1989 | 4049.86 | 18520.00 | 22569.86 | 17.9 | 82.1 | 100 |
| 1990 | 4393.93 | 20018.00 | 24411.93 | 18.0 | 82.0 | 100 |

**Table 9.3   Household equipment, Australia, 1901–1985 ($'000)**

| Year ending 30th June | Food preparation | Cooking | Food storage and cooling | House cleaning | Clothes washing | Water heating | Clothes making | Space heating and cooling | Gardening and house maintenance | Total household equipment |
|---|---|---|---|---|---|---|---|---|---|---|
| 1901 | 1664 | 532 | 153 | 924 | 882 | 264 | 47 | 123 | 659 | 5248 |
| 1902 | 1627 | 532 | 143 | 893 | 852 | 255 | 47 | 121 | 638 | 5107 |
| 1903 | 1590 | 530 | 164 | 918 | 867 | 263 | 48 | 120 | 654 | 5153 |
| 1904 | 1562 | 527 | 200 | 865 | 815 | 248 | 45 | 118 | 695 | 5074 |
| 1905 | 1628 | 503 | 172 | 872 | 822 | 249 | 45 | 116 | 777 | 5186 |
| 1906 | 1784 | 486 | 186 | 873 | 822 | 250 | 49 | 118 | 802 | 5369 |
| 1907 | 2008 | 497 | 221 | 924 | 886 | 264 | 65 | 122 | 906 | 5894 |
| 1908 | 2061 | 511 | 288 | 950 | 922 | 272 | 83 | 127 | 988 | 6201 |
| 1909 | 2018 | 552 | 276 | 968 | 933 | 277 | 84 | 132 | 889 | 6129 |
| 1910 | 2363 | 615 | 238 | 1007 | 984 | 288 | 101 | 140 | 918 | 6652 |
| 1911 | 2294 | 735 | 244 | 1115 | 1098 | 319 | 125 | 152 | 1159 | 7240 |
| 1912 | 2838 | 724 | 325 | 1215 | 1204 | 347 | 165 | 167 | 1283 | 8269 |
| 1913 | 2886 | 606 | 293 | 1219 | 1216 | 349 | 163 | 177 | 1289 | 8198 |
| 1914 | 2911 | 528 | 305 | 1287 | 1277 | 368 | 139 | 183 | 1303 | 8300 |
| 1915 | 2770 | 484 | 265 | 1365 | 1306 | 391 | 170 | 181 | 1272 | 8203 |
| 1916 | 2998 | 554 | 243 | 1492 | 1408 | 427 | 99 | 202 | 1365 | 8789 |
| 1917 | 2912 | 563 | 173 | 1510 | 1406 | 431 | 108 | 212 | 1394 | 8708 |
| 1918 | 2683 | 586 | 210 | 1561 | 1450 | 447 | 88 | 225 | 1330 | 8578 |
| 1919 | 3680 | 790 | 245 | 1712 | 1584 | 490 | 156 | 247 | 1746 | 10649 |
| 1920 | 3059 | 997 | 408 | 1770 | 1636 | 540 | 122 | 287 | 1818 | 10637 |
| 1921 | 4800 | 1486 | 323 | 1871 | 1761 | 605 | 433 | 373 | 2238 | 13888 |
| 1922 | 3606 | 1178 | 334 | 1705 | 1582 | 583 | 226 | 283 | 1667 | 11164 |
| 1923 | 3075 | 1420 | 510 | 1972 | 1704 | 687 | 427 | 349 | 1891 | 12037 |
| 1924 | 3448 | 1777 | 536 | 2086 | 1927 | 739 | 416 | 469 | 2191 | 13589 |
| 1925 | 3532 | 1863 | 516 | 2073 | 1935 | 766 | 361 | 517 | 1751 | 13314 |
| 1926 | 3426 | 2198 | 569 | 2101 | 1886 | 832 | 410 | 593 | 1788 | 13804 |
| 1927 | 3640 | 2445 | 620 | 3202 | 2100 | 870 | 634 | 696 | 2374 | 16581 |
| 1928 | 3233 | 2445 | 649 | 2669 | 1929 | 861 | 391 | 669 | 1706 | 14550 |
| 1929 | 3751 | 2479 | 530 | 2469 | 1725 | 868 | 424 | 673 | 1959 | 14877 |

**Table 9.3** continued

| Year ending 30th June | Food preparation | Cooking | Food storage and cooling | House cleaning | Clothes washing | Water heating | Clothes making | Space heating and cooling | Gardening and house maintenance | Total household equipment |
|---|---|---|---|---|---|---|---|---|---|---|
| **1930** | 3399 | 2328 | 411 | 2222 | 1003 | 565 | 395 | 707 | 1818 | 12849 |
| **1931** | 2299 | 1285 | 725 | 1616 | 489 | 446 | 205 | 348 | 1565 | 8976 |
| **1932** | 1742 | 1031 | 180 | 1370 | 378 | 437 | 103 | 243 | 1322 | 6805 |
| **1933** | 2221 | 1202 | 601 | 1543 | 392 | 476 | 114 | 350 | 1539 | 8439 |
| **1934** | 2194 | 1362 | 1156 | 1638 | 422 | 500 | 282 | 473 | 1649 | 9675 |
| **1935** | 2608 | 1746 | 1171 | 1880 | 485 | 552 | 251 | 733 | 1917 | 11343 |
| **1936** | 3023 | 2389 | 1790 | 2392 | 862 | 948 | 454 | 983 | 2120 | 14961 |
| **1937** | 3146 | 2235 | 1509 | 2283 | 947 | 1012 | 488 | 1242 | 2147 | 15008 |
| **1938** | 3009 | 3293 | 3212 | 2661 | 1081 | 1099 | 524 | 1481 | 2339 | 18699 |
| **1939** | 3200 | 3498 | 4550 | 2734 | 1149 | 1113 | 562 | 1981 | 2157 | 20944 |
| **1940** | 3517 | 3965 | 5052 | 2971 | 1027 | 739 | 769 | 1933 | 2113 | 22085 |
| **1941** | 3221 | 3986 | 4952 | 1960 | 582 | 778 | 606 | 1739 | 2074 | 19898 |
| **1942** | 3477 | 3239 | 3513 | 1983 | 604 | 822 | 513 | 1650 | 2094 | 17896 |
| **1943** | 3227 | 3275 | 711 | 1702 | 444 | 869 | 339 | 1238 | 2837 | 14643 |
| **1944** | 5266 | 2411 | 1520 | 1595 | 413 | 837 | 168 | 1968 | 2148 | 16326 |
| **1945** | 4064 | 2845 | 3460 | 1786 | 464 | 951 | 189 | 1863 | 2306 | 17926 |
| **1946** | 4119 | 3426 | 6348 | 2140 | 522 | 1157 | 364 | 1971 | 2237 | 22284 |
| **1947** | 7289 | 5177 | 11147 | 4095 | 1644 | 2011 | 900 | 3703 | 3217 | 39183 |
| **1948** | 11337 | 10543 | 20564 | 7551 | 4806 | 5385 | 1660 | 3560 | 6757 | 72162 |
| **1949** | 11789 | 15180 | 30024 | 6540 | 6260 | 5509 | 2069 | 4547 | 6532 | 88449 |
| **1950** | 14297 | 12099 | 67725 | 10111 | 9769 | 5523 | 2901 | 4812 | 8159 | 135397 |
| **1951** | 18030 | 19756 | 53332 | 11657 | 20367 | 9930 | 4933 | 8180 | 10261 | 156447 |
| **1952** | 22578 | 31620 | 62948 | 17128 | 30602 | 12614 | 5433 | 12791 | 11447 | 207161 |
| **1953** | 19365 | 14319 | 56854 | 10214 | 14966 | 9775 | 4796 | 7161 | 7079 | 144529 |
| **1954** | 22961 | 21394 | 87709 | 12890 | 23960 | 11591 | 6181 | 9207 | 10922 | 206815 |
| **1955** | 21442 | 27375 | 86723 | 15056 | 24940 | 12610 | 10693 | 11542 | 16190 | 226572 |
| **1956** | 28578 | 19997 | 77275 | 13587 | 24560 | 13937 | 10091 | 17474 | 23266 | 228766 |
| **1957** | 22495 | 28072 | 61779 | 15052 | 19155 | 14407 | 7460 | 14712 | 27778 | 210911 |
| **1958** | 27843 | 30969 | 34089 | 15110 | 21483 | 15611 | 8013 | 14305 | 24505 | 191927 |

**Table 9.3**  continued

| Year ending 30th June | Food preparation | Cooking | Food storage and cooling | House cleaning | Clothes washing | Water heating | Clothes making | Space heating and cooling | Gardening and house maintenance | Total household equipment |
|---|---|---|---|---|---|---|---|---|---|---|
| 1959 | 31104 | 33223 | 67453 | 15041 | 22346 | 17027 | 7579 | 18318 | 35315 | 247407 |
| 1960 | 33745 | 38364 | 73836 | 19701 | 24383 | 18606 | 6104 | 19320 | 42557 | 276617 |
| 1961 | 41810 | 35924 | 70851 | 18313 | 57751 | 19048 | 5981 | 47690 | 28524 | 325891 |
| 1962 | 39741 | 38281 | 66745 | 16424 | 66710 | 17807 | 8649 | 43843 | 29982 | 328182 |
| 1963 | 46559 | 41593 | 65464 | 17731 | 66370 | 19077 | 7084 | 41343 | 34364 | 339586 |
| 1964 | 52438 | 47412 | 72282 | 19020 | 76396 | 21691 | 5057 | 48624 | 33093 | 376012 |
| 1965 | 63819 | 49628 | 78452 | 21863 | 78767 | 23395 | 8742 | 36563 | 32227 | 393456 |
| 1966 | 62122 | 48106 | 75953 | 23008 | 72885 | 27815 | 10901 | 42491 | 30911 | 394192 |
| 1967 | 67553 | 51828 | 88500 | 23483 | 72748 | 30403 | 15193 | 50004 | 34726 | 434438 |
| 1968 | 67455 | 50574 | 96872 | 23112 | 75246 | 31650 | 17811 | 59672 | 32796 | 455189 |
| 1969 | 68997 | 54387 | 106525 | 24272 | 91422 | 34363 | 24440 | 81203 | 35198 | 520806 |
| 1970 | 80735 | 64702 | 113002 | 27996 | 102890 | 37652 | 23273 | 72597 | 43674 | 566521 |
| 1971 | 74087 | 64685 | 120312 | 33190 | 108402 | 42646 | 20866 | 77853 | 47013 | 589054 |
| 1972 | 83575 | 66355 | 132622 | 33656 | 109545 | 49374 | 24795 | 87834 | 48116 | 635871 |
| 1973 | 92966 | 73724 | 145441 | 38880 | 129468 | 50851 | 28418 | 86104 | 58359 | 704211 |
| 1974 | 111429 | 87251 | 204382 | 53130 | 156272 | 56618 | 37387 | 141513 | 71602 | 919585 |
| 1975 | 134896 | 104299 | 245741 | 61698 | 173935 | 60057 | 42244 | 184105 | 85299 | 1092274 |
| 1976 | 196436 | 134457 | 256964 | 82031 | 208285 | 79879 | 52501 | 163009 | 98426 | 1271987 |
| 1977 | 239849 | 161474 | 269354 | 106491 | 227036 | 99440 | 62262 | 185637 | 103116 | 1454659 |
| 1978 | 224908 | 191562 | 245472 | 93889 | 216704 | 103467 | 53625 | 218498 | 98530 | 1446655 |
| 1979 | 231536 | 197492 | 245776 | 92293 | 287625 | 109448 | 50604 | 251685 | 123533 | 1589994 |
| 1980 | 220309 | 208979 | 294558 | 125333 | 289988 | 139449 | 43521 | 290080 | 132562 | 1744780 |
| 1981 | 257355 | 237654 | 249090 | 102713 | 341542 | 169462 | 47814 | 327345 | 142804 | 1875779 |
| 1982 | 301538 | 283171 | 393852 | 129503 | 373951 | 184308 | 58121 | 383493 | 156960 | 2264905 |
| 1983 | 287293 | 369215 | 325537 | 128869 | 431280 | 202583 | 66541 | 417845 | 145266 | 2374429 |
| 1984 | 313069 | 456280 | 349148 | 144312 | 474414 | 210799 | 86879 | 425761 | 173994 | 2634656 |
| 1985 | 360918 | 515478 | 373705 | 156758 | 526025 | 229251 | 106428 | 481751 | 192804 | 2943117 |

**Table 9.4 Shares of household equipment, Australia, 1901–1985 (per cent)**

| Year ending 30th June | Food preparation | Cooking | Food storage and cooling | House cleaning | Clothes washing | Water heating | Clothes making | Space heating and cooling | Gardening and house maintenance | Total household equipment |
|---|---|---|---|---|---|---|---|---|---|---|
| 1901 | 31.7 | 10.1 | 2.9 | 17.6 | 16.8 | 5.0 | 0.9 | 2.3 | 12.6 | 100.0 |
| 1902 | 31.9 | 10.4 | 2.8 | 17.5 | 16.7 | 5.0 | 0.9 | 2.4 | 12.5 | 100.0 |
| 1903 | 30.9 | 10.3 | 3.2 | 17.8 | 16.8 | 5.1 | 0.9 | 2.3 | 12.7 | 100.0 |
| 1904 | 30.8 | 10.4 | 3.9 | 17.1 | 16.1 | 4.9 | 0.9 | 2.3 | 13.7 | 100.0 |
| 1905 | 31.4 | 9.7 | 3.3 | 16.8 | 15.9 | 4.8 | 0.9 | 2.2 | 15.0 | 100.0 |
| 1906 | 33.2 | 9.0 | 3.5 | 16.3 | 15.3 | 4.7 | 0.9 | 2.2 | 14.9 | 100.0 |
| 1907 | 34.1 | 8.4 | 3.8 | 15.7 | 15.0 | 4.5 | 1.1 | 2.1 | 15.4 | 100.0 |
| 1908 | 33.2 | 8.2 | 4.6 | 15.3 | 14.9 | 4.4 | 1.3 | 2.0 | 15.9 | 100.0 |
| 1909 | 32.9 | 9.0 | 4.5 | 15.8 | 15.2 | 4.5 | 1.4 | 2.2 | 14.5 | 100.0 |
| 1910 | 35.5 | 9.2 | 3.6 | 15.1 | 14.8 | 4.3 | 1.5 | 2.1 | 13.8 | 100.0 |
| 1911 | 31.7 | 10.1 | 3.4 | 15.4 | 15.2 | 4.4 | 1.7 | 2.1 | 16.0 | 100.0 |
| 1912 | 34.3 | 8.8 | 3.9 | 14.7 | 14.6 | 4.2 | 2.0 | 2.0 | 15.5 | 100.0 |
| 1913 | 35.2 | 7.4 | 3.6 | 14.9 | 14.8 | 4.3 | 2.0 | 2.2 | 15.7 | 100.0 |
| 1914 | 35.1 | 6.4 | 3.7 | 15.5 | 15.4 | 4.4 | 1.7 | 2.2 | 15.7 | 100.0 |
| 1915 | 33.8 | 5.9 | 3.2 | 16.6 | 15.9 | 4.8 | 2.1 | 2.2 | 15.5 | 100.0 |
| 1916 | 34.1 | 6.3 | 2.8 | 17.0 | 16.0 | 4.9 | 1.1 | 2.3 | 15.5 | 100.0 |
| 1917 | 33.4 | 6.5 | 2.0 | 17.3 | 16.1 | 5.0 | 1.2 | 2.4 | 16.0 | 100.0 |
| 1918 | 31.3 | 6.8 | 2.4 | 18.2 | 16.9 | 5.2 | 1.0 | 2.6 | 15.5 | 100.0 |
| 1919 | 34.6 | 7.4 | 2.3 | 16.1 | 14.9 | 4.6 | 1.5 | 2.3 | 16.4 | 100.0 |
| 1920 | 28.8 | 9.4 | 3.8 | 16.6 | 15.4 | 5.1 | 1.1 | 2.7 | 17.1 | 100.0 |
| 1921 | 34.6 | 10.7 | 2.3 | 13.5 | 12.7 | 4.4 | 3.1 | 2.7 | 16.1 | 100.0 |
| 1922 | 32.3 | 10.6 | 3.0 | 15.3 | 14.2 | 5.2 | 2.0 | 2.5 | 14.9 | 100.0 |
| 1923 | 25.5 | 11.8 | 4.2 | 16.4 | 14.2 | 5.7 | 3.6 | 2.9 | 15.7 | 100.0 |
| 1924 | 25.4 | 13.1 | 3.9 | 15.4 | 14.2 | 5.4 | 3.1 | 3.4 | 16.1 | 100.0 |
| 1925 | 26.5 | 14.0 | 3.9 | 15.6 | 14.5 | 5.8 | 2.7 | 3.9 | 13.2 | 100.0 |
| 1926 | 24.8 | 15.9 | 4.1 | 15.2 | 13.7 | 6.0 | 3.0 | 4.3 | 13.0 | 100.0 |
| 1927 | 22.0 | 14.7 | 3.7 | 19.3 | 12.7 | 5.2 | 3.8 | 4.2 | 14.3 | 100.0 |
| 1928 | 22.2 | 16.8 | 4.5 | 18.3 | 13.3 | 5.9 | 2.7 | 4.6 | 11.7 | 100.0 |
| 1929 | 25.2 | 16.7 | 3.6 | 16.6 | 11.6 | 5.8 | 2.8 | 4.5 | 13.2 | 100.0 |

**Table 9.4** continued

| Year ending 30th June | Food preparation | Cooking | Food storage and cooling | House cleaning | Clothes washing | Water heating | Clothes making | Space heating and cooling | Gardening and house maintenance | Total household equipment |
|---|---|---|---|---|---|---|---|---|---|---|
| 1930 | 26.5 | 18.1 | 3.2 | 17.3 | 7.8 | 4.4 | 3.1 | 5.5 | 14.1 | 100.0 |
| 1931 | 25.6 | 14.3 | 8.1 | 18.0 | 5.4 | 5.0 | 2.3 | 3.9 | 17.4 | 100.0 |
| 1932 | 25.6 | 15.2 | 2.6 | 20.1 | 5.6 | 6.4 | 1.5 | 3.6 | 19.4 | 100.0 |
| 1933 | 26.3 | 14.2 | 7.1 | 18.3 | 4.6 | 5.6 | 1.4 | 4.1 | 18.2 | 100.0 |
| 1934 | 22.7 | 14.1 | 11.9 | 16.9 | 4.4 | 5.2 | 2.9 | 4.9 | 17.0 | 100.0 |
| 1935 | 23.0 | 15.4 | 10.3 | 16.6 | 4.3 | 4.9 | 2.2 | 6.5 | 16.9 | 100.0 |
| 1936 | 20.2 | 16.0 | 12.0 | 16.0 | 5.8 | 6.3 | 3.0 | 6.6 | 14.2 | 100.0 |
| 1937 | 21.0 | 14.9 | 10.1 | 15.2 | 6.3 | 6.7 | 3.3 | 8.3 | 14.3 | 100.0 |
| 1938 | 16.1 | 17.6 | 17.2 | 14.2 | 5.8 | 5.9 | 2.8 | 7.9 | 12.5 | 100.0 |
| 1939 | 15.3 | 16.7 | 21.7 | 13.1 | 5.5 | 5.3 | 2.7 | 9.5 | 10.3 | 100.0 |
| 1940 | 15.9 | 18.0 | 22.9 | 13.5 | 4.6 | 3.3 | 3.5 | 8.8 | 9.6 | 100.0 |
| 1941 | 16.2 | 20.0 | 24.9 | 9.9 | 2.9 | 3.9 | 3.0 | 8.7 | 10.4 | 100.0 |
| 1942 | 19.4 | 18.1 | 19.6 | 11.1 | 3.4 | 4.6 | 2.9 | 9.2 | 11.7 | 100.0 |
| 1943 | 22.0 | 22.4 | 4.9 | 11.6 | 3.0 | 5.9 | 2.3 | 8.5 | 19.4 | 100.0 |
| 1944 | 32.3 | 14.8 | 9.3 | 9.8 | 2.5 | 5.1 | 1.0 | 12.1 | 13.2 | 100.0 |
| 1945 | 22.7 | 15.9 | 19.3 | 10.0 | 2.6 | 5.3 | 1.1 | 10.4 | 12.9 | 100.0 |
| 1946 | 18.5 | 15.4 | 28.5 | 9.6 | 2.3 | 5.2 | 1.6 | 8.8 | 10.0 | 100.0 |
| 1947 | 18.6 | 13.2 | 28.4 | 10.5 | 4.2 | 5.1 | 2.3 | 9.5 | 8.2 | 100.0 |
| 1948 | 15.7 | 14.6 | 28.5 | 10.5 | 6.7 | 7.5 | 2.3 | 4.9 | 9.4 | 100.0 |
| 1949 | 13.3 | 17.2 | 33.9 | 7.4 | 7.1 | 6.2 | 2.3 | 5.1 | 7.4 | 100.0 |
| 1950 | 10.6 | 8.9 | 50.0 | 7.5 | 7.2 | 4.1 | 2.1 | 3.6 | 6.0 | 100.0 |
| 1951 | 11.5 | 12.6 | 34.1 | 7.5 | 13.0 | 6.3 | 3.2 | 5.2 | 6.6 | 100.0 |
| 1952 | 10.9 | 15.3 | 30.4 | 8.3 | 14.8 | 6.1 | 2.6 | 6.2 | 5.5 | 100.0 |
| 1953 | 13.4 | 9.9 | 39.3 | 7.1 | 10.4 | 6.8 | 3.3 | 5.0 | 4.9 | 100.0 |
| 1954 | 11.1 | 10.3 | 42.4 | 6.2 | 11.6 | 6.8 | 3.0 | 4.5 | 5.3 | 100.0 |
| 1955 | 9.5 | 12.1 | 38.3 | 6.6 | 11.0 | 5.6 | 4.7 | 5.1 | 7.1 | 100.0 |
| 1956 | 12.5 | 8.7 | 33.8 | 5.9 | 10.7 | 6.1 | 4.4 | 7.6 | 10.2 | 100.0 |
| 1957 | 10.7 | 13.3 | 29.3 | 7.1 | 9.1 | 6.8 | 3.5 | 7.0 | 13.2 | 100.0 |
| 1958 | 14.5 | 16.1 | 17.8 | 7.9 | 11.2 | 8.1 | 4.2 | 7.5 | 12.8 | 100.0 |

**Table 9.4**   continued

| Year ending 30th June | Food preparation | Cooking | Food storage and cooling | House cleaning | Clothes washing | Water heating | Clothes making | Space heating and cooling | Gardening and house maintenance | Total household equipment |
|---|---|---|---|---|---|---|---|---|---|---|
| 1959 | 12.6 | 13.4 | 27.3 | 6.1 | 9.0 | 6.9 | 3.1 | 7.4 | 14.3 | 100.0 |
| 1960 | 12.2 | 13.9 | 26.7 | 7.1 | 8.8 | 6.7 | 2.2 | 7.0 | 15.4 | 100.0 |
| 1961 | 12.8 | 11.0 | 21.7 | 5.6 | 17.7 | 5.8 | 1.8 | 14.6 | 8.8 | 100.0 |
| 1962 | 12.1 | 11.7 | 20.3 | 5.0 | 20.3 | 5.4 | 2.6 | 13.4 | 9.1 | 100.0 |
| 1963 | 13.7 | 12.2 | 19.3 | 5.2 | 19.5 | 5.6 | 2.1 | 12.2 | 10.1 | 100.0 |
| 1964 | 13.9 | 12.6 | 19.2 | 5.1 | 20.3 | 5.8 | 1.3 | 12.9 | 8.8 | 100.0 |
| 1965 | 16.2 | 12.6 | 19.9 | 5.6 | 20.0 | 5.9 | 2.2 | 9.3 | 8.2 | 100.0 |
| 1966 | 15.8 | 12.2 | 19.3 | 5.8 | 18.5 | 7.1 | 2.8 | 10.8 | 7.8 | 100.0 |
| 1967 | 15.5 | 11.9 | 20.4 | 5.4 | 16.7 | 7.0 | 3.5 | 11.5 | 8.0 | 100.0 |
| 1968 | 14.8 | 11.1 | 21.3 | 5.1 | 16.5 | 7.0 | 3.9 | 13.1 | 7.2 | 100.0 |
| 1969 | 13.2 | 10.4 | 20.5 | 4.7 | 17.6 | 6.6 | 4.7 | 15.6 | 6.8 | 100.0 |
| 1970 | 14.3 | 11.4 | 19.9 | 4.9 | 18.2 | 6.6 | 4.1 | 12.8 | 7.7 | 100.0 |
| 1971 | 12.6 | 11.0 | 20.4 | 5.6 | 18.4 | 7.2 | 3.5 | 13.2 | 8.0 | 100.0 |
| 1972 | 13.1 | 10.4 | 20.9 | 5.3 | 17.2 | 7.8 | 3.9 | 13.8 | 7.6 | 100.0 |
| 1973 | 13.2 | 10.5 | 20.7 | 5.5 | 18.4 | 7.2 | 4.0 | 12.2 | 8.3 | 100.0 |
| 1974 | 12.1 | 9.5 | 22.2 | 5.8 | 17.0 | 6.2 | 4.1 | 15.4 | 7.8 | 100.0 |
| 1975 | 12.4 | 9.5 | 22.5 | 5.6 | 15.9 | 5.5 | 3.9 | 16.9 | 7.8 | 100.0 |
| 1976 | 15.4 | 10.6 | 20.2 | 6.4 | 16.4 | 6.3 | 4.1 | 12.8 | 7.7 | 100.0 |
| 1977 | 16.5 | 11.1 | 18.5 | 7.3 | 15.6 | 6.8 | 4.3 | 12.8 | 7.1 | 100.0 |
| 1978 | 15.5 | 13.2 | 17.0 | 6.5 | 15.0 | 7.2 | 3.7 | 15.1 | 6.8 | 100.0 |
| 1979 | 14.6 | 12.4 | 15.5 | 5.8 | 18.1 | 6.9 | 3.2 | 15.8 | 7.8 | 100.0 |
| 1980 | 12.6 | 12.0 | 16.9 | 7.2 | 16.6 | 8.0 | 2.5 | 16.6 | 7.6 | 100.0 |
| 1981 | 13.7 | 12.7 | 13.3 | 5.5 | 18.2 | 9.0 | 2.5 | 17.5 | 7.6 | 100.0 |
| 1982 | 13.3 | 12.5 | 17.4 | 5.7 | 16.5 | 8.1 | 2.6 | 16.9 | 6.9 | 100.0 |
| 1983 | 12.1 | 15.5 | 13.7 | 5.4 | 18.2 | 8.5 | 2.8 | 17.6 | 6.1 | 100.0 |
| 1984 | 11.9 | 17.3 | 13.3 | 5.5 | 18.0 | 8.0 | 3.3 | 16.2 | 6.6 | 100.0 |
| 1985 | 12.3 | 17.5 | 12.7 | 5.3 | 17.9 | 7.8 | 3.6 | 16.4 | 6.6 | 100.0 |

**Table 9.5   Real household capital formation (1966/67 prices), Australia, 1861–1990 ($m)**

| Year ending 31st Dec. | Equipment | Buildings | Total | Year ending 31st Dec. | Equipment | Buildings | Total |
|---|---|---|---|---|---|---|---|
| 1861 | 6.8 | 39.4 | 46.2 | 1894 | 21.8 | 116.8 | 138.6 |
| 1862 | 7.4 | 41.2 | 48.6 | 1895 | 19.5 | 92.9 | 112.4 |
| 1863 | 7.5 | 49.2 | 56.7 | 1896 | 19.4 | 97.7 | 117.1 |
| 1864 | 9.3 | 70.6 | 79.9 | 1897 | 15.4 | 48.5 | 63.9 |
| 1865 | 10.0 | 62.6 | 72.6 | 1898 | 16.7 | 98.2 | 114.9 |
| 1866 | 10.8 | 50.6 | 61.4 | 1899 | 12.8 | 46.3 | 59.1 |
| 1867 | 12.6 | 62.9 | 75.5 | 1900 | 13.7 | 40.9 | 54.6 |
| 1868 | 11.0 | 54.7 | 65.7 | 30th June | | | |
| 1869 | 13.9 | 72.4 | 86.3 | 1901 | 28.1 | 89.0 | 117.1 |
| 1870 | 13.4 | 58.7 | 72.1 | 1902 | 28.7 | 176.6 | 205.3 |
| 1871 | 13.7 | 54.0 | 67.7 | 1903 | 28.8 | 131.5 | 160.3 |
| 1872 | 16.2 | 75.5 | 91.7 | 1904 | 31.1 | 115.4 | 146.5 |
| 1873 | 16.1 | 66.0 | 82.1 | 1905 | 32.0 | 127.0 | 159.0 |
| 1874 | 16.7 | 70.7 | 87.4 | 1906 | 31.8 | 142.7 | 174.5 |
| 1875 | 16.4 | 84.4 | 100.8 | 1907 | 36.6 | 167.2 | 203.8 |
| 1876 | 19.5 | 111.4 | 130.9 | 1908 | 34.6 | 151.4 | 186.0 |
| 1877 | 19.1 | 87.6 | 106.7 | 1909 | 32.6 | 138.6 | 171.2 |
| 1878 | 19.7 | 80.3 | 100.0 | 1910 | 34.1 | 149.0 | 183.1 |
| 1879 | 19.9 | 87.8 | 107.7 | 1911 | 36.6 | 171.6 | 208.2 |
| 1880 | 17.2 | 80.6 | 97.8 | 1912 | 38.1 | 195.5 | 233.6 |
| 1881 | 23.5 | 121.8 | 145.3 | 1913 | 38.7 | 245.1 | 283.8 |
| 1882 | 22.2 | 131.5 | 153.7 | 1914 | 35.3 | 267.9 | 303.2 |
| 1883 | 31.2 | 206.0 | 237.2 | 1915 | 30.4 | 230.1 | 260.5 |
| 1884 | 37.8 | 202.9 | 240.7 | 1916 | 29.1 | 168.3 | 197.4 |
| 1885 | 39.6 | 165.5 | 205.1 | 1917 | 24.3 | 133.6 | 157.9 |
| 1886 | 34.1 | 151.8 | 185.9 | 1918 | 22.9 | 117.7 | 140.6 |
| 1887 | 36.8 | 202.0 | 238.8 | 1919 | 27.9 | 151.7 | 179.6 |
| 1888 | 40.0 | 219.7 | 259.7 | 1920 | 27.3 | 235.0 | 262.3 |
| 1889 | 39.6 | 132.1 | 171.7 | 1921 | 35.6 | 266.6 | 302.2 |
| 1890 | 37.4 | 158.9 | 196.3 | 1922 | 31.2 | 240.2 | 271.4 |
| 1891 | 31.4 | 120.1 | 151.5 | 1923 | 32.4 | 310.7 | 343.1 |
| 1892 | 28.8 | 118.3 | 147.1 | 1924 | 38.9 | 347.4 | 386.3 |
| 1893 | 22.2 | 92.0 | 114.2 | 1925 | 38.7 | 327.7 | 366.4 |

**Table 9.5** continued

| Year ending 30th June | Equipment | Buildings | Total | Year ending 30th June | Equipment | Buildings | Total |
|---|---|---|---|---|---|---|---|
| 1926 | 37.9 | 328.1 | 366.0 | 1959 | 262.1 | 783.5 | 1045.6 |
| 1927 | 45.8 | 363.7 | 409.5 | 1960 | 290.0 | 865.2 | 1155.2 |
| 1928 | 40.4 | 375.9 | 416.3 | 1961 | 337.4 | 912.3 | 1249.7 |
| 1929 | 40.4 | 329.9 | 370.3 | 1962 | 335.2 | 851.2 | 1186.4 |
| 1930 | 37.7 | 234.7 | 272.4 | 1963 | 347.6 | 934.0 | 1281.6 |
| 1931 | 27.9 | 118.0 | 145.9 | 1964 | 390.1 | 1043.8 | 1433.9 |
| 1932 | 22.9 | 77.6 | 100.5 | 1965 | 404.8 | 1177.3 | 1582.1 |
| 1933 | 28.7 | 109.3 | 138.0 | 1966 | 398.6 | 1191.6 | 1590.2 |
| 1934 | 33.5 | 153.9 | 187.4 | 1967 | 434.4 | 1244.0 | 1678.4 |
| 1935 | 35.7 | 184.4 | 220.1 | 1968 | 446.7 | 1352.8 | 1799.5 |
| 1936 | 47.0 | 233.7 | 280.7 | 1969 | 500.8 | 1486.8 | 1987.6 |
| 1937 | 46.3 | 255.2 | 301.5 | 1970 | 538.0 | 1650.5 | 2188.5 |
| 1938 | 54.8 | 290.5 | 345.3 | 1971 | 540.4 | 1666.7 | 2207.1 |
| 1939 | 55.1 | 285.0 | 340.1 | 1972 | 554.9 | 1775.9 | 2330.8 |
| 1940 | 54.5 | 242.6 | 297.1 | 1973 | 593.3 | 1901.5 | 2494.8 |
| 1941 | 47.0 | 198.6 | 245.6 | 1974 | 709.6 | 1898.4 | 2608.0 |
| 1942 | 40.7 | 121.2 | 161.9 | 1975 | 710.2 | 1640.4 | 2350.6 |
| 1943 | 30.8 | 45.1 | 75.9 | 1976 | 713.4 | 1911.5 | 2624.9 |
| 1944 | 34.3 | 32.1 | 66.4 | 1977 | 741.0 | 2120.3 | 2861.3 |
| 1945 | 38.6 | 53.3 | 91.9 | 1978 | 680.5 | 1967.9 | 2648.4 |
| 1946 | 45.1 | 128.6 | 173.7 | 1979 | 703.9 | 1993.4 | 2697.3 |
| 1947 | 79.0 | 266.1 | 345.1 | 1980 | 714.5 | 2181.2 | 2895.7 |
| 1948 | 136.9 | 349.4 | 486.3 | 1981 | 691.4 | 2457.6 | 3149.0 |
| 1949 | 157.1 | 469.9 | 627.0 | 1982 | 754.7 | 2421.6 | 3176.3 |
| 1950 | 219.1 | 564.3 | 783.4 | 1983 | 706.9 | 1929.1 | 2636.0 |
| 1951 | 230.8 | 641.2 | 872.0 | 1984 | 732.5 | 2114.0 | 2846.5 |
| 1952 | 256.7 | 737.3 | 994.0 | 1985 | 781.1 | 2355.7 | 3136.8 |
| 1953 | 166.3 | 646.0 | 812.3 | 1986 | 842.5 | 2352.8 | 3195.3 |
| 1954 | 234.2 | 691.8 | 926.0 | 1987 | 890.0 | 2126.4 | 3016.4 |
| 1955 | 257.2 | 703.9 | 961.1 | 1988 | 865.1 | 2265.9 | 3131.0 |
| 1956 | 259.1 | 681.0 | 940.1 | 1989 | 819.3 | 2691.9 | 3511.2 |
| 1957 | 229.3 | 650.2 | 879.5 | 1990 | 842.7 | 2620.5 | 3463.2 |
| 1958 | 205.5 | 711.6 | 917.1 | | | | |

**Table 9.6    Real value of equipment per household (1966/67 prices), Australia, 1861–1990 ($)**

| Year ending 31st Dec. | Equipment per household | Year ending 30th June | Equipment per household | Year ending 30th June | Equipment per household |
|---|---|---|---|---|---|
| 1861 | 27.8 | 1904 | 41.8 | 1948 | 71.3 |
| 1862 | 29.6 | 1905 | 42.3 | 1949 | 79.6 |
| 1863 | 29.1 | 1906 | 41.2 | 1950 | 107.9 |
| 1864 | 34.6 | 1907 | 46.1 | 1951 | 109.8 |
| 1865 | 35.6 | 1908 | 41.9 | 1952 | 117.6 |
| 1866 | 37.2 | 1909 | 38.2 | 1953 | 73.4 |
| 1867 | 42.3 | 1910 | 39.1 | 1954 | 99.9 |
| 1868 | 35.7 | 1911 | 40.9 | 1955 | 106.9 |
| 1869 | 44.0 | 1912 | 41.3 | 1956 | 105.0 |
| 1870 | 41.4 | 1913 | 40.6 | 1957 | 91.0 |
| 1871 | 41.3 | 1914 | 35.9 | 1958 | 79.8 |
| 1872 | 48.2 | 1915 | 30.2 | 1959 | 99.3 |
| 1873 | 46.9 | 1916 | 28.5 | 1960 | 107.0 |
| 1874 | 47.6 | 1917 | 23.6 | 1961 | 121.3 |
| 1875 | 46.0 | 1918 | 21.9 | 1962 | 117.8 |
| 1876 | 53.6 | 1919 | 26.2 | 1963 | 119.4 |
| 1877 | 51.0 | 1920 | 25.1 | 1964 | 130.7 |
| 1878 | 51.6 | 1921 | 32.2 | 1965 | 131.9 |
| 1879 | 50.9 | 1922 | 27.4 | 1966 | 126.5 |
| 1880 | 43.0 | 1923 | 27.4 | 1967 | 134.0 |
| 1881 | 57.4 | 1924 | 31.7 | 1968 | 133.8 |
| 1882 | 51.8 | 1925 | 30.4 | 1969 | 145.5 |
| 1883 | 70.4 | 1926 | 28.7 | 1970 | 151.2 |
| 1884 | 81.5 | 1927 | 33.4 | 1971 | 147.2 |
| 1885 | 82.1 | 1928 | 28.6 | 1972 | 147.5 |
| 1886 | 68.3 | 1929 | 27.9 | 1973 | 153.7 |
| 1887 | 71.4 | 1930 | 25.7 | 1974 | 179.3 |
| 1888 | 74.9 | 1931 | 18.9 | 1975 | 175.3 |
| 1889 | 71.8 | 1932 | 15.4 | 1976 | 172.3 |
| 1890 | 65.4 | 1933 | 19.0 | 1977 | 174.1 |
| 1891 | 53.2 | 1934 | 21.7 | 1978 | 156.0 |
| 1892 | 47.2 | 1935 | 22.7 | 1979 | 158.0 |
| 1893 | 35.8 | 1936 | 29.3 | 1980 | 156.7 |
| 1894 | 34.3 | 1937 | 28.3 | 1981 | 148.1 |
| 1895 | 30.1 | 1938 | 32.8 | 1982 | 158.0 |
| 1896 | 29.2 | 1939 | 32.3 | 1983 | 145.2 |
| 1897 | 22.9 | 1940 | 31.4 | 1984 | 147.5 |
| 1898 | 24.5 | 1941 | 26.6 | 1985 | 153.8 |
| 1899 | 18.6 | 1942 | 22.8 | 1986 | 162.4 |
| 1900 | 19.5 | 1943 | 17.2 | 1987 | 168.5 |
| 30th June | | 1944 | 19.1 | 1988 | 161.0 |
| 1901 | 39.4 | 1945 | 21.4 | 1989 | 149.2 |
| 1902 | 40.0 | 1946 | 24.6 | 1990 | 150.0 |
| 1903 | 39.5 | 1947 | 42.2 | | |

**Table 9.7    Real stock of buildings and household equipment (1966/67 prices), Australia, 1861–1990 ($m)**

| Year ending 31st Dec. | Equipment investment | Stock of equipment | Equipment depreciation | Buildings investment | Stock of buildings | Building depreciation |
|---|---|---|---|---|---|---|
| **1861** | 6.8 | 123.6 | | 39.4 | 670.0 | |
| **1862** | 7.4 | 121.1 | 9.9 | 41.2 | 701.2 | 10.1 |
| **1863** | 7.5 | 118.9 | 9.7 | 49.2 | 739.8 | 10.5 |
| **1864** | 9.3 | 118.7 | 9.5 | 70.6 | 799.3 | 11.1 |
| **1865** | 10.0 | 119.2 | 9.5 | 62.6 | 849.9 | 12.0 |
| **1866** | 10.8 | 120.5 | 9.5 | 50.6 | 887.8 | 12.7 |
| **1867** | 12.6 | 123.4 | 9.6 | 62.9 | 937.4 | 13.3 |
| **1868** | 11.0 | 124.6 | 9.9 | 54.7 | 978.0 | 14.1 |
| **1869** | 13.9 | 128.5 | 10.0 | 72.4 | 1035.7 | 14.7 |
| **1870** | 13.4 | 131.6 | 10.3 | 58.7 | 1078.9 | 15.5 |
| **1871** | 13.7 | 134.8 | 10.5 | 54.0 | 1116.7 | 16.2 |
| **1872** | 16.2 | 140.2 | 10.8 | 75.5 | 1175.5 | 16.8 |
| **1873** | 16.1 | 145.1 | 11.2 | 66.0 | 1223.8 | 17.6 |
| **1874** | 16.7 | 150.2 | 11.6 | 70.7 | 1276.2 | 18.4 |
| **1875** | 16.4 | 154.6 | 12.0 | 84.4 | 1341.4 | 19.1 |
| **1876** | 19.5 | 161.7 | 12.4 | 111.4 | 1432.7 | 20.1 |
| **1877** | 19.1 | 167.9 | 12.9 | 87.6 | 1498.8 | 21.5 |
| **1878** | 19.7 | 174.1 | 13.4 | 80.3 | 1556.6 | 22.5 |
| **1879** | 19.9 | 180.1 | 13.9 | 87.8 | 1621.1 | 23.3 |
| **1880** | 17.2 | 182.9 | 14.4 | 80.6 | 1677.4 | 24.3 |
| **1881** | 23.5 | 191.8 | 14.6 | 121.8 | 1774.0 | 25.2 |
| **1882** | 22.2 | 198.6 | 15.3 | 131.5 | 1878.9 | 26.6 |
| **1883** | 31.2 | 213.9 | 15.9 | 206.0 | 2056.7 | 28.2 |
| **1884** | 37.8 | 234.6 | 17.1 | 202.9 | 2228.8 | 30.9 |
| **1885** | 39.6 | 255.4 | 18.8 | 165.5 | 2360.8 | 33.4 |
| **1886** | 34.1 | 269.1 | 20.4 | 151.8 | 2477.2 | 35.4 |
| **1887** | 36.8 | 284.4 | 21.5 | 202.0 | 2642.1 | 37.2 |
| **1888** | 40.0 | 301.6 | 22.8 | 219.7 | 2822.1 | 39.6 |
| **1889** | 39.6 | 317.1 | 24.1 | 132.1 | 2911.9 | 42.3 |
| **1890** | 37.4 | 329.1 | 25.4 | 158.9 | 3027.1 | 43.7 |
| **1891** | 31.4 | 334.2 | 26.3 | 120.1 | 3101.8 | 45.4 |
| **1892** | 28.8 | 336.3 | 26.7 | 118.3 | 3173.6 | 46.5 |
| **1893** | 22.2 | 331.6 | 26.9 | 92.0 | 3218.0 | 47.6 |
| **1894** | 21.8 | 326.8 | 26.5 | 116.8 | 3286.5 | 48.3 |
| **1895** | 19.5 | 320.2 | 26.1 | 92.9 | 3330.1 | 49.3 |
| **1896** | 19.4 | 314.0 | 25.6 | 97.7 | 3377.9 | 50.0 |
| **1897** | 15.4 | 304.3 | 25.1 | 48.5 | 3375.7 | 50.7 |
| **1898** | 16.7 | 296.6 | 24.3 | 98.2 | 3423.3 | 50.6 |
| **1899** | 12.8 | 285.7 | 23.7 | 46.3 | 3418.2 | 51.3 |
| **1900** | 13.7 | 276.5 | 22.9 | 40.9 | 3407.8 | 51.3 |
| 30th June | | | | | | |
| **1901** | 28.1 | 282.5 | 22.1 | 89.0 | 3445.7 | 51.1 |
| **1902** | 28.7 | 288.6 | 22.6 | 176.6 | 3570.6 | 51.7 |

**Table 9.7** continued

| Year ending 30th June | Equipment investment | Stock of equipment | Equipment depreciation | Buildings investment | Stock of buildings | Building depreciation |
|---|---|---|---|---|---|---|
| **1903** | 28.8 | 294.3 | 23.1 | 131.5 | 3648.6 | 53.6 |
| **1904** | 31.1 | 301.9 | 23.5 | 115.4 | 3709.3 | 54.7 |
| **1905** | 32.0 | 309.7 | 24.2 | 127.0 | 3780.6 | 55.6 |
| **1906** | 31.8 | 316.7 | 24.8 | 142.7 | 3866.6 | 56.7 |
| **1907** | 36.6 | 328.0 | 25.3 | 167.2 | 3975.8 | 58.0 |
| **1908** | 34.6 | 336.4 | 26.2 | 151.4 | 4067.6 | 59.6 |
| **1909** | 32.6 | 342.1 | 26.9 | 138.6 | 4145.2 | 61.0 |
| **1910** | 34.1 | 348.8 | 27.4 | 149.0 | 4232.0 | 62.2 |
| **1911** | 36.6 | 357.5 | 27.9 | 171.6 | 4340.1 | 63.5 |
| **1912** | 38.1 | 367.0 | 28.6 | 195.5 | 4470.5 | 65.1 |
| **1913** | 38.7 | 376.3 | 29.4 | 245.1 | 4648.5 | 67.1 |
| **1914** | 35.3 | 381.5 | 30.1 | 267.9 | 4846.7 | 69.7 |
| **1915** | 30.4 | 381.4 | 30.5 | 230.1 | 5004.1 | 72.7 |
| **1916** | 29.1 | 380.0 | 30.5 | 168.3 | 5097.4 | 75.1 |
| **1917** | 24.3 | 373.9 | 30.4 | 133.6 | 5154.5 | 76.5 |
| **1918** | 22.9 | 366.9 | 29.9 | 117.7 | 5194.9 | 77.3 |
| **1919** | 27.9 | 365.4 | 29.4 | 151.7 | 5268.7 | 77.9 |
| **1920** | 27.3 | 363.5 | 29.2 | 235.0 | 5424.6 | 79.0 |
| **1921** | 35.6 | 370.0 | 29.1 | 266.6 | 5609.9 | 81.4 |
| **1922** | 31.2 | 371.6 | 29.6 | 240.2 | 5765.9 | 84.1 |
| **1923** | 32.4 | 374.3 | 29.7 | 310.7 | 5990.1 | 86.5 |
| **1924** | 38.9 | 383.2 | 29.9 | 347.4 | 6247.7 | 89.9 |
| **1925** | 38.7 | 391.3 | 30.7 | 327.7 | 6481.6 | 93.7 |
| **1926** | 37.9 | 397.9 | 31.3 | 328.1 | 6712.5 | 97.2 |
| **1927** | 45.8 | 411.9 | 31.8 | 363.7 | 6975.5 | 100.7 |
| **1928** | 40.4 | 419.3 | 32.9 | 375.9 | 7246.8 | 104.6 |
| **1929** | 40.4 | 426.2 | 33.5 | 329.9 | 7468.0 | 108.7 |
| **1930** | 37.7 | 429.8 | 34.1 | 234.7 | 7590.7 | 112.0 |
| **1931** | 27.9 | 423.3 | 34.4 | 118.0 | 7594.8 | 113.9 |
| **1932** | 22.9 | 412.3 | 33.9 | 77.6 | 7558.5 | 113.9 |
| **1933** | 28.7 | 408.0 | 33.0 | 109.3 | 7554.4 | 113.4 |
| **1934** | 33.5 | 408.9 | 32.6 | 153.9 | 7595.0 | 113.3 |
| **1935** | 35.7 | 411.9 | 32.7 | 184.4 | 7665.5 | 113.9 |
| **1936** | 47.0 | 425.9 | 33.0 | 233.7 | 7784.2 | 115.0 |
| **1937** | 46.3 | 438.2 | 34.1 | 255.2 | 7922.6 | 116.8 |
| **1938** | 54.8 | 457.9 | 35.1 | 290.5 | 8094.3 | 118.8 |
| **1939** | 55.1 | 476.4 | 36.6 | 285.0 | 8257.9 | 121.4 |
| **1940** | 54.5 | 492.8 | 38.1 | 242.6 | 8376.6 | 123.9 |
| **1941** | 47.0 | 500.3 | 39.4 | 198.6 | 8449.6 | 125.6 |
| **1942** | 40.7 | 501.0 | 40.0 | 121.2 | 8444.0 | 126.7 |
| **1943** | 30.8 | 491.7 | 40.1 | 45.1 | 8362.5 | 126.7 |
| **1944** | 34.3 | 486.7 | 39.3 | 32.1 | 8269.1 | 125.4 |
| **1945** | 38.6 | 486.4 | 38.9 | 53.3 | 8198.4 | 124.0 |
| **1946** | 45.1 | 492.5 | 38.9 | 128.6 | 8204.0 | 123.0 |

**Table 9.7**   continued

| Year ending 30th June | Equipment investment | Stock of equipment | Equipment depreciation | Buildings investment | Stock of buildings | Building depreciation |
|---|---|---|---|---|---|---|
| **1947** | 79.0 | 532.1 | 39.4 | 266.1 | 8347.0 | 123.1 |
| **1948** | 136.9 | 626.5 | 42.6 | 349.4 | 8571.2 | 125.2 |
| **1949** | 157.1 | 733.5 | 50.1 | 469.9 | 8912.6 | 128.6 |
| **1950** | 219.1 | 893.9 | 58.7 | 564.3 | 9343.2 | 133.7 |
| **1951** | 230.8 | 1053.2 | 71.5 | 641.2 | 9844.2 | 140.1 |
| **1952** | 256.7 | 1225.6 | 84.3 | 737.3 | 10433.9 | 147.7 |
| **1953** | 166.3 | 1293.9 | 98.0 | 646.0 | 10923.4 | 156.5 |
| **1954** | 234.2 | 1424.6 | 103.5 | 691.8 | 11451.3 | 163.9 |
| **1955** | 257.2 | 1567.8 | 114.0 | 703.9 | 11983.4 | 171.8 |
| **1956** | 259.1 | 1701.5 | 125.4 | 681.0 | 12484.7 | 179.8 |
| **1957** | 229.3 | 1794.7 | 136.1 | 650.2 | 12947.6 | 187.3 |
| **1958** | 205.5 | 1856.6 | 143.6 | 711.6 | 13465.0 | 194.2 |
| **1959** | 262.1 | 1970.2 | 148.5 | 783.5 | 14046.5 | 202.0 |
| **1960** | 290.0 | 2102.5 | 157.6 | 865.2 | 14701.0 | 210.7 |
| **1961** | 337.4 | 2271.7 | 168.2 | 912.3 | 15392.8 | 220.5 |
| **1962** | 335.2 | 2425.2 | 181.7 | 851.2 | 16013.1 | 230.9 |
| **1963** | 347.6 | 2578.8 | 194.0 | 934.0 | 16706.9 | 240.2 |
| **1964** | 390.1 | 2762.6 | 206.3 | 1043.8 | 17500.1 | 250.6 |
| **1965** | 404.8 | 2946.4 | 221.0 | 1177.3 | 18414.9 | 262.5 |
| **1966** | 398.6 | 3109.3 | 235.7 | 1191.6 | 19330.3 | 276.2 |
| **1967** | 434.4 | 3294.9 | 248.7 | 1244.0 | 20284.3 | 290.0 |
| **1968** | 446.7 | 3478.0 | 263.6 | 1352.8 | 21332.9 | 304.3 |
| **1969** | 500.8 | 3700.6 | 278.2 | 1486.8 | 22499.7 | 320.0 |
| **1970** | 538.0 | 3942.5 | 296.0 | 1650.5 | 23812.7 | 337.5 |
| **1971** | 540.4 | 4167.5 | 315.4 | 1666.7 | 25122.2 | 357.2 |
| **1972** | 554.9 | 4389.0 | 333.4 | 1775.9 | 26521.3 | 376.8 |
| **1973** | 593.3 | 4631.2 | 351.1 | 1901.5 | 28025.0 | 397.8 |
| **1974** | 709.6 | 4970.3 | 370.5 | 1898.4 | 29503.0 | 420.4 |
| **1975** | 710.2 | 5282.9 | 397.6 | 1640.4 | 30700.8 | 442.5 |
| **1976** | 713.4 | 5573.7 | 422.6 | 1911.5 | 32151.8 | 460.5 |
| **1977** | 741.0 | 5868.8 | 445.9 | 2120.3 | 33789.8 | 482.3 |
| **1978** | 680.5 | 6079.8 | 469.5 | 1967.9 | 35250.9 | 506.8 |
| **1979** | 703.9 | 6297.3 | 486.4 | 1993.4 | 36715.5 | 528.8 |
| **1980** | 714.5 | 6508.0 | 503.8 | 2181.2 | 38346.0 | 550.7 |
| **1981** | 691.4 | 6678.8 | 520.6 | 2457.6 | 40228.4 | 575.2 |
| **1982** | 754.7 | 6899.2 | 534.3 | 2421.6 | 42046.6 | 603.4 |
| **1983** | 706.9 | 7054.1 | 551.9 | 1929.1 | 43345.0 | 630.7 |
| **1984** | 732.5 | 7222.3 | 564.3 | 2114.0 | 44808.8 | 650.2 |
| **1985** | 781.1 | 7425.6 | 577.8 | 2355.7 | 46492.4 | 672.1 |
| **1986** | 842.5 | 7674.1 | 594.0 | 2352.8 | 48147.8 | 697.4 |
| **1987** | 890.0 | 7950.1 | 613.9 | 2126.4 | 49552.0 | 722.2 |
| **1988** | 865.1 | 8179.2 | 636.0 | 2265.9 | 51074.6 | 743.3 |
| **1989** | 819.3 | 8344.2 | 654.3 | 2691.9 | 53000.4 | 766.1 |
| **1990** | 842.7 | 8519.4 | 667.5 | 2620.5 | 54825.9 | 795.0 |

**Table 9.8   Household income by factor (current prices), Australia, 1788–1990 ($m)**

| Year ending 31st Dec. | Labour | Land, buildings and equipment | Total | Year ending 31st Dec. | Labour | Land, buildings and equipment | Total |
|---|---|---|---|---|---|---|---|
| 1788 | 0.01 | 0.00 | 0.01 | 1822 | 0.55 | 0.29 | 0.84 |
| 1789 | 0.01 | 0.00 | 0.01 | 1823 | 0.60 | 0.31 | 0.91 |
| 1790 | 0.03 | 0.00 | 0.03 | 1824 | 0.71 | 0.34 | 1.05 |
| 1791 | 0.04 | 0.00 | 0.04 | 1825 | 0.77 | 0.36 | 1.13 |
| 1792 | 0.05 | 0.00 | 0.05 | 1826 | 0.79 | 0.39 | 1.18 |
| 1793 | 0.06 | 0.00 | 0.06 | 1827 | 0.84 | 0.41 | 1.25 |
| 1794 | 0.06 | 0.01 | 0.07 | 1828 | 0.87 | 0.42 | 1.29 |
| 1795 | 0.06 | 0.01 | 0.07 | 1829 | 0.93 | 0.49 | 1.42 |
| 1796 | 0.06 | 0.01 | 0.07 | 1830 | 1.06 | 0.56 | 1.62 |
| 1797 | 0.06 | 0.01 | 0.07 | 1831 | 1.16 | 0.62 | 1.78 |
| 1798 | 0.07 | 0.01 | 0.08 | 1832 | 1.29 | 0.72 | 2.01 |
| 1799 | 0.07 | 0.01 | 0.08 | 1833 | 1.52 | 0.78 | 2.30 |
| 1800 | 0.07 | 0.01 | 0.08 | 1834 | 1.72 | 0.91 | 2.63 |
| 1801 | 0.09 | 0.01 | 0.10 | 1835 | 1.94 | 1.12 | 3.06 |
| 1802 | 0.10 | 0.01 | 0.11 | 1836 | 2.11 | 1.35 | 3.46 |
| 1803 | 0.10 | 0.01 | 0.11 | 1837 | 2.32 | 1.88 | 4.20 |
| 1804 | 0.12 | 0.01 | 0.13 | 1838 | 2.69 | 2.19 | 4.88 |
| 1805 | 0.12 | 0.01 | 0.13 | 1839 | 3.24 | 2.64 | 5.88 |
| 1806 | 0.12 | 0.02 | 0.14 | 1840 | 3.90 | 3.01 | 6.91 |
| 1807 | 0.13 | 0.02 | 0.15 | 1841 | 3.94 | 2.85 | 6.79 |
| 1808 | 0.15 | 0.03 | 0.18 | 1842 | 3.82 | 2.80 | 6.62 |
| 1809 | 0.18 | 0.04 | 0.22 | 1843 | 3.48 | 2.95 | 6.43 |
| 1810 | 0.18 | 0.05 | 0.23 | 1844 | 3.53 | 3.29 | 6.82 |
| 1811 | 0.18 | 0.06 | 0.24 | 1845 | 4.48 | 3.79 | 8.27 |
| 1812 | 0.19 | 0.08 | 0.27 | 1846 | 5.34 | 3.99 | 9.33 |
| 1813 | 0.21 | 0.09 | 0.30 | 1847 | 6.32 | 4.18 | 10.50 |
| 1814 | 0.21 | 0.11 | 0.32 | 1848 | 6.58 | 4.53 | 11.11 |
| 1815 | 0.22 | 0.13 | 0.35 | 1849 | 6.29 | 4.72 | 11.01 |
| 1816 | 0.26 | 0.15 | 0.41 | 1850 | 7.39 | 5.18 | 12.57 |
| 1817 | 0.31 | 0.18 | 0.49 | 1851 | 9.23 | 5.25 | 14.48 |
| 1818 | 0.39 | 0.19 | 0.58 | 1852 | 12.83 | 7.46 | 20.29 |
| 1819 | 0.46 | 0.21 | 0.67 | 1853 | 18.94 | 15.54 | 34.48 |
| 1820 | 0.49 | 0.24 | 0.73 | 1854 | 34.72 | 24.07 | 58.79 |
| 1821 | 0.52 | 0.26 | 0.78 | 1855 | 32.38 | 17.51 | 49.89 |

**Table 9.8** continued

| Year ending 31st Dec. | Labour | Land and buildings | Equipment | Total |
|---|---|---|---|---|
| 1856 | 32.54 | | 13.98 | 46.52 |
| 1857 | 36.43 | | 13.53 | 49.96 |
| 1858 | 40.32 | | 16.34 | 56.66 |
| 1859 | 38.28 | | 17.06 | 55.34 |
| 1860 | 42.73 | | 18.08 | 60.81 |
| 1861 | 44.92 | 15.80 | 4.00 | 64.72 |
| 1862 | 49.39 | 15.20 | 4.00 | 68.59 |
| 1863 | 50.00 | 14.80 | 5.10 | 69.90 |
| 1864 | 52.75 | 14.80 | 6.30 | 73.85 |
| 1865 | 45.86 | 15.60 | 7.20 | 68.66 |
| 1866 | 53.28 | 18.00 | 7.70 | 78.98 |
| 1867 | 55.16 | 17.00 | 6.70 | 78.86 |
| 1868 | 63.16 | 16.80 | 4.60 | 84.56 |
| 1869 | 62.36 | 15.60 | 5.50 | 83.46 |
| 1870 | 63.74 | 19.60 | 5.80 | 89.14 |
| 1871 | 60.90 | 21.40 | 5.80 | 88.10 |
| 1872 | 66.82 | 24.80 | 5.80 | 97.42 |
| 1873 | 70.60 | 26.80 | 5.90 | 103.30 |
| 1874 | 74.06 | 21.60 | 5.90 | 101.56 |
| 1875 | 82.01 | 23.40 | 5.90 | 111.31 |
| 1876 | 89.57 | 26.20 | 6.30 | 122.07 |
| 1877 | 94.36 | 27.20 | 6.30 | 127.86 |
| 1878 | 96.94 | 25.60 | 6.30 | 128.84 |
| 1879 | 97.36 | 32.60 | 6.70 | 136.66 |
| 1880 | 94.03 | 35.60 | 6.80 | 136.43 |
| 1881 | 100.66 | 37.80 | 6.40 | 144.86 |
| 1882 | 107.62 | 40.00 | 6.10 | 153.72 |
| 1883 | 110.82 | 42.80 | 6.60 | 160.22 |
| 1884 | 113.63 | 46.20 | 7.40 | 167.23 |
| 1885 | 116.22 | 48.60 | 7.60 | 172.42 |
| 1886 | 124.59 | 44.60 | 7.90 | 177.09 |
| 1887 | 132.93 | 50.20 | 8.20 | 191.33 |
| 1888 | 123.06 | 53.00 | 7.80 | 183.86 |
| 1889 | 128.69 | 56.80 | 7.50 | 192.99 |

| Year ending 31st Dec. | Labour | Land and buildings | Equipment | Total |
|---|---|---|---|---|
| 1890 | 141.96 | 59.20 | 7.70 | 208.86 |
| 1891 | 144.52 | 43.80 | 8.20 | 196.52 |
| 1892 | 121.61 | 44.00 | 9.20 | 174.81 |
| 1893 | 118.75 | 39.40 | 9.30 | 167.45 |
| 1894 | 121.94 | 39.60 | 9.10 | 170.64 |
| 1895 | 134.08 | 37.40 | 8.50 | 179.98 |
| 1896 | 130.03 | 35.00 | 8.60 | 173.63 |
| 1897 | 129.86 | 34.40 | 7.40 | 171.66 |
| 1898 | 127.71 | 39.60 | 7.70 | 175.01 |
| 1899 | 129.52 | 39.80 | 7.60 | 176.92 |
| 1900 | 127.13 | 40.20 | 7.90 | 175.23 |
| *30th June* | | | | |
| 1901 | 144.97 | 38.40 | 8.60 | 191.97 |
| 1902 | 146.05 | 37.20 | 10.10 | 193.35 |
| 1903 | 142.54 | 37.40 | 9.40 | 189.34 |
| 1904 | 126.43 | 38.00 | 10.40 | 174.83 |
| 1905 | 157.79 | 38.80 | 11.10 | 207.69 |
| 1906 | 164.98 | 39.00 | 9.80 | 213.78 |
| 1907 | 176.54 | 38.20 | 9.80 | 224.54 |
| 1908 | 183.89 | 40.20 | 10.60 | 234.69 |
| 1909 | 197.70 | 42.40 | 11.00 | 251.10 |
| 1910 | 214.17 | 45.40 | 11.80 | 271.37 |
| 1911 | 237.57 | 49.00 | 11.50 | 298.07 |
| 1912 | 260.04 | 54.00 | 12.40 | 326.44 |
| 1913 | 279.51 | 59.60 | 16.10 | 355.21 |
| 1914 | 290.32 | 64.20 | 14.50 | 369.02 |
| 1915 | 299.22 | 64.40 | 15.60 | 379.22 |
| 1916 | 320.65 | 63.20 | 18.10 | 401.95 |
| 1917 | 345.82 | 64.40 | 19.50 | 429.72 |
| 1918 | 366.16 | 66.60 | 18.50 | 451.26 |
| 1919 | 431.58 | 71.20 | 20.40 | 523.18 |
| 1920 | 529.58 | 78.20 | 23.20 | 630.98 |
| 1921 | 550.75 | 85.20 | 29.60 | 665.55 |
| 1922 | 586.00 | 91.80 | 28.50 | 706.30 |

**Table 9.8** continued

| Year ending 30th June | Labour | Land and buildings | Equipment | Total | Year ending 30th June | Labour | Land and buildings | Equipment | Total |
|---|---|---|---|---|---|---|---|---|---|
| 1923 | 624.33 | 99.00 | 27.20 | 750.53 | 1957 | 4745 | 313 | 127 | 5185 |
| 1924 | 646.80 | 107.40 | 26.80 | 781.00 | 1958 | 4922 | 352 | 134 | 5408 |
| 1925 | 681.77 | 113.40 | 27.40 | 822.57 | 1959 | 5372 | 401 | 146 | 5919 |
| 1926 | 720.84 | 120.60 | 24.60 | 866.04 | 1960 | 5699 | 455 | 155 | 6309 |
| 1927 | 757.96 | 128.60 | 26.20 | 912.76 | 1961 | 6040 | 537 | 189 | 6766 |
| 1928 | 787.47 | 133.60 | 27.40 | 948.47 | 1962 | 6145 | 611 | 189 | 6945 |
| 1929 | 806.60 | 140.00 | 27.30 | 973.90 | 1963 | 6360 | 701 | 199 | 7260 |
| 1930 | 799.24 | 139.60 | 29.70 | 968.54 | 1964 | 6860 | 779 | 197 | 7836 |
| 1931 | 709.07 | 129.00 | 35.30 | 873.37 | 1965 | 7219 | 857 | 237 | 8313 |
| 1932 | 664.06 | 123.00 | 25.70 | 812.76 | 1966 | 7782 | 936 | 277 | 8995 |
| 1933 | 660.49 | 127.00 | 21.80 | 809.29 | 1967 | 8515 | 1059 | 291 | 9865 |
| 1934 | 686.12 | 130.80 | 20.40 | 837.32 | 1968 | 9457 | 1191 | 319 | 10967 |
| 1935 | 707.31 | 132.20 | 19.10 | 858.61 | 1969 | 10507 | 1340 | 333 | 12180 |
| 1936 | 739.13 | 135.80 | 22.20 | 897.13 | 1970 | 11478 | 1544 | 414 | 13436 |
| 1937 | 804.34 | 140.60 | 24.40 | 969.34 | 1971 | 13944 | 1823 | 509 | 16276 |
| 1938 | 848.86 | 142.40 | 23.10 | 1014.36 | 1972 | 15640 | 2108 | 489 | 18237 |
| 1939 | 886.10 | 144.00 | 25.30 | 1055.40 | 1973 | 19612 | 2429 | 492 | 22533 |
| 1940 | 926 | 148 | 25 | 1099 | 1974 | 28143 | 2844 | 813 | 31800 |
| 1941 | 1006 | 146 | 21 | 1173 | 1975 | 33943 | 3483 | 907 | 38333 |
| 1942 | 1122 | 146 | 23 | 1291 | 1976 | 39834 | 4318 | 1061 | 45213 |
| 1943 | 1188 | 142 | 23 | 1353 | 1977 | 45158 | 5264 | 1233 | 51655 |
| 1944 | 1239 | 138 | 24 | 1401 | 1978 | 49226 | 6352 | 1280 | 56858 |
| 1945 | 1263 | 136 | 25 | 1424 | 1979 | 51735 | 7509 | 1442 | 60686 |
| 1946 | 1384 | 133 | 25 | 1542 | 1980 | 59740 | 8677 | 1868 | 70285 |
| 1947 | 1496 | 133 | 26 | 1655 | 1981 | 69290 | 10014 | 2288 | 81592 |
| 1948 | 1766 | 140 | 28 | 1934 | 1982 | 78382 | 11600 | 3178 | 93160 |
| 1949 | 1962 | 146 | 31 | 2139 | 1983 | 83242 | 13150 | 3143 | 99535 |
| 1950 | 2548 | 150 | 35 | 2733 | 1984 | 88286 | 14609 | 3630 | 106525 |
| 1951 | 3181 | 161 | 40 | 3382 | 1985 | 95470 | 16016 | 3920 | 115406 |
| 1952 | 3711 | 161 | 55 | 3927 | 1986 | 101651 | 18145 | 4099 | 123895 |
| 1953 | 3901 | 186 | 74 | 4161 | 1987 | 104846 | 20593 | 4793 | 130232 |
| 1954 | 4020 | 218 | 81 | 4319 | 1988 | 119050 | 23440 | 4857 | 147347 |
| 1955 | 4286 | 256 | 93 | 4635 | 1989 | 128111 | 26645 | 5369 | 160125 |
| 1956 | 4591 | 282 | 104 | 4977 | 1990 | 139558 | 29649 | 6436 | 175643 |

**Table 9.9 Household capital/labour ratios, Australia, 1861–1990 ($/worker)**

| Year ending 31st Dec. | Equipment | Buildings | Total | Year ending 31st Dec. | Equipment | Buildings | Total |
|---|---|---|---|---|---|---|---|
| 1861 | 379.0 | 2054.6 | 2433.6 | 1894 | 305.2 | 3067.8 | 3373.0 |
| 1862 | 356.8 | 2065.7 | 2422.5 | 1895 | 292.1 | 3037.3 | 3329.4 |
| 1863 | 332.9 | 2071.1 | 2404.0 | 1896 | 279.8 | 3009.2 | 3289.0 |
| 1864 | 312.1 | 2101.8 | 2413.9 | 1897 | 266.7 | 2957.7 | 3224.4 |
| 1865 | 296.3 | 2112.6 | 2408.9 | 1898 | 255.8 | 2951.8 | 3207.6 |
| 1866 | 285.9 | 2106.3 | 2392.2 | 1899 | 242.7 | 2903.2 | 3145.9 |
| 1867 | 283.7 | 2153.5 | 2437.2 | 1900 | 229.9 | 2832.5 | 3062.4 |
| 1868 | 274.8 | 2156.6 | 2431.3 | 30th June | | | |
| 1869 | 274.2 | 2210.2 | 2484.4 | 1901 | 231.2 | 2818.6 | 3049.7 |
| 1870 | 271.8 | 2228.2 | 2500.0 | 1902 | 234.1 | 2895.6 | 3129.8 |
| 1871 | 269.6 | 2233.4 | 2503.0 | 1903 | 234.5 | 2906.7 | 3141.3 |
| 1872 | 273.0 | 2288.6 | 2561.5 | 1904 | 235.6 | 2894.4 | 3130.0 |
| 1873 | 273.7 | 2308.6 | 2582.3 | 1905 | 237.4 | 2897.9 | 3135.3 |
| 1874 | 274.4 | 2331.6 | 2606.1 | 1906 | 237.8 | 2903.5 | 3141.3 |
| 1875 | 274.9 | 2385.1 | 2660.0 | 1907 | 239.1 | 2898.0 | 3137.1 |
| 1876 | 278.3 | 2465.9 | 2744.2 | 1908 | 236.1 | 2854.7 | 3090.7 |
| 1877 | 275.7 | 2461.5 | 2737.2 | 1909 | 232.3 | 2814.5 | 3046.8 |
| 1878 | 276.5 | 2470.8 | 2747.3 | 1910 | 231.6 | 2809.9 | 3041.5 |
| 1879 | 275.8 | 2480.6 | 2756.4 | 1911 | 231.2 | 2806.4 | 3037.6 |
| 1880 | 270.5 | 2479.5 | 2750.0 | 1912 | 229.3 | 2792.8 | 3022.1 |
| 1881 | 273.0 | 2523.8 | 2796.8 | 1913 | 226.9 | 2803.3 | 3030.3 |
| 1882 | 271.3 | 2565.8 | 2837.1 | 1914 | 222.9 | 2832.3 | 3055.3 |
| 1883 | 282.1 | 2710.8 | 2992.9 | 1915 | 217.3 | 2851.3 | 3068.7 |
| 1884 | 297.2 | 2822.2 | 3119.4 | 1916 | 212.6 | 2851.8 | 3064.4 |
| 1885 | 312.3 | 2885.7 | 3198.0 | 1917 | 206.2 | 2842.6 | 3048.8 |
| 1886 | 318.7 | 2933.0 | 3251.7 | 1918 | 198.7 | 2813.9 | 3012.7 |
| 1887 | 326.8 | 3035.0 | 3361.9 | 1919 | 194.2 | 2799.5 | 2993.6 |
| 1888 | 335.5 | 3137.8 | 3473.2 | 1920 | 188.4 | 2810.8 | 2999.2 |
| 1889 | 342.2 | 3141.2 | 3483.4 | 1921 | 187.7 | 2846.3 | 3034.0 |
| 1890 | 343.8 | 3161.5 | 3505.3 | 1922 | 184.2 | 2858.5 | 3042.7 |
| 1891 | 338.6 | 3141.4 | 3479.9 | 1923 | 179.5 | 2873.2 | 3052.8 |
| 1892 | 329.1 | 3104.4 | 3433.4 | 1924 | 177.9 | 2899.8 | 3077.7 |
| 1893 | 317.7 | 3082.1 | 3399.8 | 1925 | 176.0 | 2914.9 | 3090.9 |

**Table 9.9**  continued

| Year ending 30th June | Equipment | Buildings | Total | Year ending 30th June | Equipment | Buildings | Total |
|---|---|---|---|---|---|---|---|
| 1926 | 173.2 | 2921.4 | 3094.6 | 1959 | 500.2 | 3566.2 | 4066.4 |
| 1927 | 173.6 | 2940.1 | 3113.8 | 1960 | 522.1 | 3650.2 | 4172.3 |
| 1928 | 172.3 | 2978.5 | 3150.9 | 1961 | 551.3 | 3735.4 | 4286.7 |
| 1929 | 171.7 | 3009.3 | 3181.1 | 1962 | 579.9 | 3828.5 | 4408.3 |
| 1930 | 171.6 | 3031.2 | 3202.8 | 1963 | 609.2 | 3946.8 | 4556.0 |
| 1931 | 169.3 | 3037.1 | 3206.3 | 1964 | 642.1 | 4067.2 | 4709.3 |
| 1932 | 164.4 | 3014.5 | 3178.9 | 1965 | 668.6 | 4178.3 | 4846.9 |
| 1933 | 160.8 | 2977.2 | 3138.0 | 1966 | 691.1 | 4296.3 | 4987.4 |
| 1934 | 158.4 | 2941.6 | 3100.0 | 1967 | 707.0 | 4352.3 | 5059.3 |
| 1935 | 156.8 | 2917.1 | 3073.8 | 1968 | 721.7 | 4426.3 | 5148.0 |
| 1936 | 159.5 | 2914.2 | 3073.7 | 1969 | 743.2 | 4518.3 | 5261.5 |
| 1937 | 161.2 | 2914.5 | 3075.7 | 1970 | 760.9 | 4595.4 | 5356.3 |
| 1938 | 165.2 | 2919.6 | 3084.8 | 1971 | 776.5 | 4680.7 | 5457.1 |
| 1939 | 168.7 | 2924.3 | 3093.0 | 1972 | 805.8 | 4869.1 | 5674.9 |
| 1940 | 171.9 | 2922.6 | 3094.6 | 1973 | 829.8 | 5021.0 | 5850.8 |
| 1941 | 172.1 | 2905.3 | 3077.4 | 1974 | 867.7 | 5150.2 | 6017.8 |
| 1942 | 170.6 | 2875.4 | 3046.0 | 1975 | 894.1 | 5196.0 | 6090.2 |
| 1943 | 166.6 | 2832.8 | 2999.4 | 1976 | 925.6 | 5339.1 | 6264.7 |
| 1944 | 164.4 | 2791.9 | 2956.2 | 1977 | 951.4 | 5477.3 | 6428.7 |
| 1945 | 164.1 | 2764.5 | 2928.6 | 1978 | 970.5 | 5627.1 | 6597.6 |
| 1946 | 165.5 | 2756.4 | 2921.9 | 1979 | 994.1 | 5795.6 | 6789.6 |
| 1947 | 176.4 | 2765.4 | 2941.8 | 1980 | 1000.7 | 5896.4 | 6897.1 |
| 1948 | 204.2 | 2793.0 | 2997.1 | 1981 | 1008.9 | 6077.0 | 7085.9 |
| 1949 | 233.7 | 2839.4 | 3073.1 | 1982 | 1029.1 | 6271.4 | 7300.4 |
| 1950 | 278.3 | 2908.5 | 3186.8 | 1983 | 1041.4 | 6398.5 | 7439.9 |
| 1951 | 318.6 | 2977.3 | 3295.8 | 1984 | 1050.3 | 6515.9 | 7566.2 |
| 1952 | 359.7 | 3062.1 | 3421.8 | 1985 | 1064.7 | 6665.8 | 7730.4 |
| 1953 | 370.9 | 3131.4 | 3502.4 | 1986 | 1075.8 | 6749.3 | 7825.1 |
| 1954 | 397.4 | 3194.0 | 3591.4 | 1987 | 1078.2 | 6719.8 | 7798.0 |
| 1955 | 427.8 | 3269.5 | 3697.3 | 1988 | 1084.3 | 6770.7 | 7855.0 |
| 1956 | 454.6 | 3335.6 | 3790.2 | 1989 | 1076.6 | 6838.5 | 7915.1 |
| 1957 | 472.2 | 3406.5 | 3878.7 | 1990 | 1067.5 | 6869.5 | 7937.0 |
| 1958 | 480.2 | 3482.3 | 3962.4 | | | | |

**Table 9.10   Market capital/labour ratios, Australia, 1861–1990**

| Year ending 31st Dec. | Market capital stock (plant and equipment) ($m) | Total workforce ('000) | Capital/labour ratio | Year ending 31st Dec. | Market capital stock (plant and equipment) ($m) | Total workforce ('000) | Capital/labour ratio |
|---|---|---|---|---|---|---|---|
| 1861 | 315 | 485 | 649.48 | 1894 | 1289 | 954 | 1351.15 |
| 1862 | 312 | 518 | 602.32 | 1895 | 1247 | 1052 | 1185.36 |
| 1863 | 318 | 523 | 608.03 | 1896 | 1246 | 1258 | 990.46 |
| 1864 | 317 | 547 | 579.52 | 1897 | 1220 | 1308 | 932.72 |
| 1865 | 317 | 574 | 552.26 | 1898 | 1228 | 1273 | 964.65 |
| 1866 | 318 | 578 | 550.17 | 1899 | 1244 | 1356 | 917.40 |
| 1867 | 322 | 554 | 581.23 | 1900 | 1244 | 1441 | 863.29 |
| 1868 | 334 | 539 | 619.67 | 30th June | | | |
| 1869 | 341 | 554 | 615.52 | 1901 | 1275 | 1426 | 894.11 |
| 1870 | 341 | 600 | 568.33 | 1902 | 1360 | 1458 | 932.78 |
| 1871 | 344 | 597 | 576.21 | 1903 | 1409 | 1445 | 975.09 |
| 1872 | 351 | 688 | 510.17 | 1904 | 1399 | 1499 | 933.29 |
| 1873 | 361 | 710 | 508.45 | 1905 | 1394 | 1492 | 934.32 |
| 1874 | 378 | 727 | 519.94 | 1906 | 1408 | 1523 | 924.49 |
| 1875 | 413 | 717 | 576.01 | 1907 | 1440 | 1588 | 906.80 |
| 1876 | 442 | 717 | 616.46 | 1908 | 1452 | 1641 | 884.83 |
| 1877 | 505 | 716 | 705.31 | 1909 | 1468 | 1690 | 868.64 |
| 1878 | 559 | 755 | 740.40 | 1910 | 1491 | 1763 | 845.72 |
| 1879 | 600 | 767 | 782.27 | 1911 | 1576 | 1782 | 884.40 |
| 1880 | 649 | 762 | 851.71 | 1912 | 1639 | 1898 | 863.54 |
| 1881 | 717 | 813 | 881.92 | 1913 | 1679 | 1937 | 866.80 |
| 1882 | 767 | 891 | 860.83 | 1914 | 1723 | 2017 | 854.24 |
| 1883 | 814 | 932 | 873.39 | 1915 | 1723 | 1956 | 880.88 |
| 1884 | 871 | 831 | 1048.13 | 1916 | 1698 | 1929 | 880.25 |
| 1885 | 929 | 949 | 978.93 | 1917 | 1684 | 1896 | 888.19 |
| 1886 | 1024 | 997 | 1027.08 | 1918 | 1651 | 1893 | 872.16 |
| 1887 | 1103 | 998 | 1105.21 | 1919 | 1673 | 1924 | 869.54 |
| 1888 | 1184 | 1059 | 1118.04 | 1920 | 1751 | 1999 | 875.94 |
| 1889 | 1268 | 1131 | 1121.13 | 1921 | 1873 | 2037 | 919.49 |
| 1890 | 1300 | 1176 | 1105.44 | 1922 | 1950 | 2104 | 926.81 |
| 1891 | 1369 | 1160 | 1180.17 | 1923 | 2025 | 2187 | 925.93 |
| 1892 | 1353 | 1059 | 1277.62 | 1924 | 2121 | 2230 | 951.12 |
| 1893 | 1316 | 956 | 1376.57 | 1925 | 2203 | 2302 | 956.99 |

**Table 9.10**  continued

| Year ending 30th June | Market capital stock (plant and equipment) ($m) | Total workforce ('000) | Capital/labour ratio | Year ending 30th June | Market capital stock (plant and equipment) ($m) | Total workforce ('000) | Capital/labour ratio |
|---|---|---|---|---|---|---|---|
| 1926 | 2274 | 2338 | 972.63 | 1959 | 10863 | 3978 | 2730.77 |
| 1927 | 2341 | 2402 | 974.60 | 1960 | 11639 | 4095 | 2842.25 |
| 1928 | 2390 | 2398 | 996.66 | 1961 | 12426 | 4288 | 2897.85 |
| 1929 | 2440 | 2389 | 1021.35 | 1962 | 13184 | 4335 | 3041.29 |
| 1930 | 2470 | 2300 | 1073.91 | 1963 | 14060 | 4396 | 3198.36 |
| 1931 | 2441 | 2131 | 1145.47 | 1964 | 15068 | 4496 | 3351.42 |
| 1932 | 2358 | 2086 | 1130.39 | 1965 | 16360 | 4683 | 3493.49 |
| 1933 | 2292 | 2208 | 1038.04 | 1966 | 17692 | 4903 | 3608.40 |
| 1934 | 2249 | 2313 | 972.33 | 1967 | 18997 | 5020 | 3784.26 |
| 1935 | 2270 | 2417 | 939.18 | 1968 | 20301 | 5137 | 3951.92 |
| 1936 | 2292 | 2504 | 915.34 | 1969 | 21653 | 5262 | 4114.98 |
| 1937 | 2318 | 2565 | 903.70 | 1970 | 22993 | 5474 | 4200.40 |
| 1938 | 2418 | 2655 | 910.73 | 1971 | 24363 | 5608 | 4344.33 |
| 1939 | 2655 | 2682 | 989.93 | 1972 | 25689 | 5754 | 4464.55 |
| 1940 | 2821 | 2677 | 1053.79 | 1973 | 26836 | 5889 | 4556.97 |
| 1941 | 2906 | 2662 | 1091.66 | 1974 | 28033 | 5996 | 4675.28 |
| 1942 | 2933 | 2628 | 1116.06 | 1975 | 29086 | 6120 | 4752.61 |
| 1943 | 2906 | 2572 | 1129.86 | 1976 | 30092 | 6191 | 4860.60 |
| 1944 | 2915 | 2600 | 1121.15 | 1977 | 30952 | 6355 | 4870.50 |
| 1945 | 2961 | 2637 | 1122.87 | 1978 | 31885 | 6404 | 4978.92 |
| 1946 | 3222 | 2775 | 1161.08 | 1979 | 33197 | 6456 | 5142.04 |
| 1947 | 3603 | 3034 | 1187.54 | 1980 | 34332 | 6676 | 5142.60 |
| 1948 | 3991 | 3167 | 1260.18 | 1981 | 35946 | 6774 | 5306.47 |
| 1949 | 4477 | 3282 | 1364.11 | 1982 | 37983 | 6841 | 5552.26 |
| 1950 | 5095 | 3439 | 1481.54 | 1983 | 39396 | 6928 | 5686.49 |
| 1951 | 5834 | 3551 | 1642.92 | 1984 | 40865 | 7070 | 5780.06 |
| 1952 | 6501 | 3626 | 1792.88 | 1985 | 42652 | 7248 | 5884.66 |
| 1953 | 6992 | 3617 | 1933.09 | 1986 | 44536 | 7516 | 5925.49 |
| 1954 | 7616 | 3659 | 2081.44 | 1987 | 46367 | 7694 | 6026.38 |
| 1955 | 8298 | 3737 | 2220.50 | 1988 | 48163 | 7892 | 6102.76 |
| 1956 | 8976 | 3835 | 2340.55 | 1989 | 50693 | 8197 | 6184.34 |
| 1957 | 9603 | 3886 | 2471.18 | 1990 | 53124 | 8413 | 6314.51 |
| 1958 | 10233 | 3952 | 2589.32 | | | | |

**Table 9.11   Household and market labour productivity, Australia, 1861–1990** ($/worker)

| Year ending 31st Dec. | Household | Market | Year ending 30th June | Household | Market | Year ending 30th June | Household | Market |
|---|---|---|---|---|---|---|---|---|
| 1861 | 1144 | 1347 | 1904 | 1100 | 2184 | 1948 | 1612 | 3057 |
| 1862 | 1158 | 1251 | 1905 | 1274 | 2195 | 1949 | 1585 | 3082 |
| 1863 | 1176 | 1280 | 1906 | 1244 | 2240 | 1950 | 1814 | 3192 |
| 1864 | 1257 | 1364 | 1907 | 1289 | 2479 | 1951 | 1737 | 3283 |
| 1865 | 1094 | 1288 | 1908 | 1202 | 2247 | 1952 | 1877 | 3335 |
| 1866 | 1175 | 1348 | 1909 | 1209 | 2172 | 1953 | 1699 | 3311 |
| 1867 | 1259 | 1588 | 1910 | 1243 | 2274 | 1954 | 1669 | 3471 |
| 1868 | 1279 | 1732 | 1911 | 1320 | 2355 | 1955 | 1742 | 3591 |
| 1869 | 1236 | 1718 | 1912 | 1283 | 2123 | 1956 | 1775 | 3672 |
| 1870 | 1280 | 1667 | 1913 | 1356 | 2266 | 1957 | 1705 | 3690 |
| 1871 | 1230 | 1583 | 1914 | 1275 | 2228 | 1958 | 1746 | 3699 |
| 1872 | 1228 | 1528 | 1915 | 1162 | 1870 | 1959 | 1875 | 3940 |
| 1873 | 1200 | 1652 | 1916 | 1165 | 2055 | 1960 | 1869 | 4036 |
| 1874 | 1169 | 1713 | 1917 | 1128 | 2225 | 1961 | 1902 | 3964 |
| 1875 | 1277 | 1926 | 1918 | 1101 | 2182 | 1962 | 1900 | 3952 |
| 1876 | 1363 | 1894 | 1919 | 1188 | 2189 | 1963 | 1942 | 4157 |
| 1877 | 1386 | 1971 | 1920 | 1206 | 1986 | 1964 | 1988 | 4352 |
| 1878 | 1411 | 2073 | 1921 | 1284 | 2398 | 1965 | 2007 | 4480 |
| 1879 | 1440 | 2021 | 1922 | 1406 | 2340 | 1966 | 2065 | 4360 |
| 1880 | 1403 | 2117 | 1923 | 1364 | 2253 | 1967 | 2117 | 4539 |
| 1881 | 1446 | 2131 | 1924 | 1373 | 2285 | 1968 | 2214 | 4602 |
| 1882 | 1405 | 1925 | 1925 | 1360 | 2445 | 1969 | 2303 | 4900 |
| 1883 | 1368 | 1999 | 1926 | 1396 | 2281 | 1970 | 2336 | 4983 |
| 1884 | 1411 | 2227 | 1927 | 1425 | 2144 | 1971 | 2611 | 5111 |
| 1885 | 1418 | 2113 | 1928 | 1422 | 2226 | 1972 | 2713 | 5236 |
| 1886 | 1429 | 2023 | 1929 | 1427 | 2206 | 1973 | 2990 | 5328 |
| 1887 | 1545 | 2297 | 1930 | 1559 | 2281 | 1974 | 3575 | 5450 |
| 1888 | 1424 | 2194 | 1931 | 1552 | 2229 | 1975 | 3536 | 5449 |
| 1889 | 1404 | 2195 | 1932 | 1558 | 2266 | 1976 | 3552 | 5508 |
| 1890 | 1456 | 2006 | 1933 | 1556 | 2269 | 1977 | 3567 | 5498 |
| 1891 | 1388 | 2175 | 1934 | 1530 | 2258 | 1978 | 3588 | 5463 |
| 1892 | 1274 | 2094 | 1935 | 1492 | 2216 | 1979 | 3510 | 5729 |
| 1893 | 1250 | 2174 | 1936 | 1466 | 2249 | 1980 | 3569 | 5652 |
| 1894 | 1317 | 2228 | 1937 | 1473 | 2313 | 1981 | 3689 | 5751 |
| 1895 | 1402 | 1979 | 1938 | 1487 | 2385 | 1982 | 3775 | 5819 |
| 1896 | 1280 | 1872 | 1939 | 1489 | 2283 | 1983 | 3613 | 5625 |
| 1897 | 1203 | 1666 | 1940 | 1480 | 2684 | 1984 | 3560 | 5851 |
| 1898 | 1194 | 1968 | 1941 | 1545 | 2869 | 1985 | 3601 | 6006 |
| 1899 | 1175 | 1864 | 1942 | 1659 | 3392 | 1986 | 3539 | 6017 |
| 1900 | 1137 | 2102 | 1943 | 1643 | 3831 | 1987 | 3515 | 6030 |
| 30th June | | | 1944 | 1648 | 3754 | 1988 | 3431 | 6150 |
| 1901 | 1180 | 1799 | 1945 | 1611 | 3470 | 1989 | 3313 | 6146 |
| 1902 | 1224 | 1936 | 1946 | 1613 | 3172 | 1990 | 3347 | 6191 |
| 1903 | 1142 | 1857 | 1947 | 1558 | 2856 | | | |

**Table 9.12   Relative factor prices (equipment to labour) in the household and the market, Australia, 1861-1990** (1966/67 = 1.0)

| Year ending 31st Dec. | Household | Market | Year ending 30th June | Household | Market | Year ending 30th June | Household | Market |
|---|---|---|---|---|---|---|---|---|
| 1861 | 4.5 | 1.6 | 1904 | 2.8 | 1.2 | 1948 | 1.7 | 1.0 |
| 1862 | 4.0 | 1.5 | 1905 | 2.8 | 1.2 | 1949 | 1.7 | 1.0 |
| 1863 | 4.5 | 1.7 | 1906 | 2.9 | 1.2 | 1950 | 1.4 | 0.9 |
| 1864 | 4.4 | 1.7 | 1907 | 2.6 | 1.2 | 1951 | 1.3 | 0.9 |
| 1865 | 4.3 | 1.8 | 1908 | 2.9 | 1.2 | 1952 | 1.4 | 1.0 |
| 1866 | 4.1 | 1.5 | 1909 | 2.9 | 1.2 | 1953 | 1.4 | 1.1 |
| 1867 | 3.3 | 1.4 | 1910 | 2.8 | 1.2 | 1954 | 1.5 | 1.1 |
| 1868 | 3.6 | 1.6 | 1911 | 2.6 | 1.1 | 1955 | 1.4 | 1.1 |
| 1869 | 3.2 | 1.4 | 1912 | 2.7 | 1.2 | 1956 | 1.3 | 1.1 |
| 1870 | 3.3 | 1.5 | 1913 | 2.5 | 1.2 | 1957 | 1.4 | 1.2 |
| 1871 | 3.4 | 1.4 | 1914 | 2.8 | 1.2 | 1958 | 1.3 | 1.2 |
| 1872 | 2.8 | 1.8 | 1915 | 3.2 | 1.3 | 1959 | 1.3 | 1.1 |
| 1873 | 2.9 | 1.7 | 1916 | 3.5 | 1.5 | 1960 | 1.2 | 1.1 |
| 1874 | 3.1 | 1.8 | 1917 | 3.8 | 1.6 | 1961 | 1.2 | 1.1 |
| 1875 | 3.1 | 1.7 | 1918 | 3.8 | 1.7 | 1962 | 1.2 | 1.1 |
| 1876 | 2.9 | 1.6 | 1919 | 3.4 | 1.3 | 1963 | 1.2 | 1.1 |
| 1877 | 2.9 | 1.4 | 1920 | 2.9 | 1.3 | 1964 | 1.1 | 1.0 |
| 1878 | 2.9 | 1.4 | 1921 | 2.8 | 1.2 | 1965 | 1.1 | 1.0 |
| 1879 | 2.6 | 1.4 | 1922 | 2.4 | 1.3 | 1966 | 1.0 | 1.0 |
| 1880 | 2.7 | 1.4 | 1923 | 2.5 | 1.2 | 1967 | 1.0 | 1.0 |
| 1881 | 2.7 | 1.4 | 1924 | 2.3 | 1.2 | 1968 | 1.0 | 0.9 |
| 1882 | 3.2 | 1.2 | 1925 | 2.2 | 1.2 | 1969 | 0.9 | 0.9 |
| 1883 | 3.2 | 1.3 | 1926 | 2.3 | 1.2 | 1970 | 0.9 | 0.9 |
| 1884 | 3.0 | 1.2 | 1927 | 2.2 | 1.2 | 1971 | 0.8 | 0.8 |
| 1885 | 3.0 | 1.2 | 1928 | 2.2 | 1.2 | 1972 | 0.7 | 0.8 |
| 1886 | 3.3 | 1.2 | 1929 | 2.2 | 1.2 | 1973 | 0.6 | 0.8 |
| 1887 | 2.9 | 1.1 | 1930 | 2.1 | 1.1 | 1974 | 0.5 | 0.6 |
| 1888 | 3.0 | 1.1 | 1931 | 2.2 | 1.3 | 1975 | 0.5 | 0.7 |
| 1889 | 3.0 | 1.2 | 1932 | 2.2 | 1.3 | 1976 | 0.5 | 0.7 |
| 1890 | 3.0 | 1.2 | 1933 | 2.2 | 1.3 | 1977 | 0.5 | 0.7 |
| 1891 | 2.9 | 1.2 | 1934 | 2.1 | 1.3 | 1978 | 0.5 | 0.7 |
| 1892 | 2.9 | 1.1 | 1935 | 2.3 | 1.3 | 1979 | 0.5 | 0.8 |
| 1893 | 3.0 | 1.1 | 1936 | 2.2 | 1.2 | 1980 | 0.5 | 0.8 |
| 1894 | 2.6 | 1.0 | 1937 | 2.1 | 1.2 | 1981 | 0.4 | 0.7 |
| 1895 | 2.7 | 1.0 | 1938 | 2.2 | 1.2 | 1982 | 0.4 | 0.7 |
| 1896 | 2.7 | 1.0 | 1939 | 2.4 | 1.0 | 1983 | 0.5 | 0.7 |
| 1897 | 2.7 | 1.0 | 1940 | 2.4 | 1.0 | 1984 | 0.5 | 0.7 |
| 1898 | 2.6 | 1.1 | 1941 | 2.4 | 1.0 | 1985 | 0.5 | 0.7 |
| 1899 | 2.9 | 1.2 | 1942 | 2.2 | 1.1 | 1986 | 0.5 | 0.8 |
| 1900 | 2.8 | 1.4 | 1943 | 2.3 | 1.1 | 1987 | 0.5 | 0.8 |
| 30th June | | | 1944 | 2.2 | 1.1 | 1988 | 0.5 | 0.8 |
| 1901 | 3.1 | 1.3 | 1945 | 2.1 | 1.1 | 1989 | 0.5 | 0.8 |
| 1902 | 3.0 | 1.2 | 1946 | 2.0 | 1.0 | 1990 | 0.5 | 0.8 |
| 1903 | 3.0 | 1.2 | 1947 | 1.9 | 1.0 | | | |

# 10

---

# *Retrospective*

*T*his study is a first step in the attempt to analyse the dynamic processes which transform the Total Economy in the longrun. As shown, this process involves an interactive relationship between the household and market sectors. Inevitably there will be differences of opinion about the methods and interpretations in the book, but hopefully this will stimulate others to refine the general picture of the Total Economy presented here, and to apply it to other countries. If so, this should significantly change our view of the longrun dynamics of human society.

## Timescapes

The objective of the book has been twofold: to construct a new set of historical social accounts covering the Total Economy for the period of European–Asian settlement in Australia; and to use these building blocks to create a new picture of the longrun process of household–market dynamics: a picture of the family within the Total Economy. The first of these objectives has led to the household, market, and total sector timescapes which have been presented throughout the book. The second objective has resulted in a sequence of existential models of reality that have been exposed using these timescapes.

Timescapes are the building blocks of existential models. Herein lies the importance of timescapes and, hence, of quantitative economic history. Without timescapes there would be no existential models; no way of showing what logical models cannot show—the longrun process by which real-world economies are transformed. This book has attempted to provide a new set of timescapes for the household and total economies over the period 1788 to 1990. They build upon, and extend, the longrun estimates of the market economy that have been undertaken variously by Charles Feinstein in the UK, Simon Kuznets in the USA, Timothy Coghlan and Noel Butlin in Australia, and by others throughout the world.[1] It is argued that these wider social accounts provide a significantly different perspective of the economy. The hope is that this different perspective will be applied to other countries.

# Existential models

Timescapes are the means to higher ends. They enable the construction of existential models—models of existence—which are contrasted here with logical models. A major claim in this study is that it is possible to develop complex and relevant models of human society through the observation of reality. If so, a partial realization of the historicist dream may be possible. But we must avoid the temptation that ultimately defeated the historicists of the late nineteenth century—the attempt to compete with economists at what they do best, namely the construction (and econometric testing) of simple static models. Instead we should focus on what deductive economics cannot do—the reconstruction of existential models of the longrun dynamic process of human society. This is a role that quantitative economic history can and should play.

A beginning has been made here, by showing how the Total Economy operates over the longrun through an interaction between the household and market sectors. As we have seen, the driving force in this process is dynamic economic man, and the headquarters of dynamic economic man is the household. The transformation of human society can, it is suggested, take two forms: environmental dynamic change (EDC), and technological dynamic change (TDC). Of these, EDC is the traditional process by which human society, down through the ages, has increased and spread throughout the world. It is a process of economic expansion, or household multiplication, that occurs by bringing previously unused natural resources into the process of production. TDC, on the other hand, involves a transformation of the technological base of the economy, thereby producing economic growth as well as economic expansion. In contrast to EDC, it depends on a more intensive use of natural resources. More specifically, economic change is the result of an interaction between the household and market economies—or at a more disaggregated level, between the household, private, and public sectors—which is orchestrated by the household as the ultimate centre of all economic activity.

While I have no intention of further summarizing work in this book, it may be helpful to compare the interpretation reached here with other studies of longrun economic change.

## International studies

This is, as far as I am aware, the first study of longrun dynamic processes in the Total Economy for any country. The attempt has been to analyse quantitatively—using a set of total social accounts—the longrun process of interaction between the household, private, and public sectors, and to construct an empirically-based longrun existential model that integrates the household and market sectors into an analysis of economic growth and economic expansion as component parts of a wider dynamic process. Other scholars have focused on the growth of the market economy, generally within a comparative-static growth-accounting framework, rather than on the Total Economy, in a dynamic framework. Because there were no other models to follow in this matter, it has been necessary to develop a number of new definitions and concepts to explain the dynamics of human society. These concepts should be useful in explaining the emergence of other societies over very long periods of time.

## Australian studies

In the main, the empirically-based interpretations of Australian economic development can be regarded as part of the Coghlan tradition, with variations of emphasis that reflect changing fashions in economic thought. These include the interpretations of T.A. Coghlan (1918), E.O.G. Shann (1930), N.G. Butlin (1964), and W.A. Sinclair (1976).[2] Basically the Coghlan tradition has strong links with the approach to growth taken by the classical economists and by Schumpeter. This approach focuses on outcomes generated by the application of increasing quantities of capital and labour to the supply of natural resources. If investment occurs too rapidly, or if it is misdirected, then the development process will break down and lead to depression. Only once depression has forged equilibrium can economic growth be resumed. Scholars following Coghlan have developed variations on this central theme: Shann provided a neoclassical focus on the efficiency of markets; Butlin saw the growth process through a Schumpeterian–Harrodian lens; and Sinclair has adopted a classical–neoclassical synthesis.

The tradition began with Coghlan. In *Labour and industry*, Coghlan, when discussing the process of development—or 'progress'—in the Australian colonies during the 1880s that led to downturn after 1889 and financial crisis in 1893, wrote:

> During the earlier years capital was brought to the colonies in readily absorbable amounts, and this may be said to have continued until about 1885, with excellent results for the whole community. After 1885, in certain years and by certain colonies there was amazing recklessness both on the part of the governments and of the financial institutions . . . Australia could have absorbed freely and advantageously all the money that it received, if there had been time given for its assimilation, but to bring in seventy-three millions of money to a community numbering between two and three millions, as was done in the five years 1881–85, and 100 millions during 1886–90 was to provoke extravagance and invite wastefulness . . . [with the result that] there was more or less wild speculation, an arrest of industry and the withdrawal of large bodies of men from productive pursuits, followed later by a derangement of the labour market, with strikes, lock-outs, and industrial unrest.

Victoria, he claimed, was most at fault—as indeed it is one hundred years later—while 'New South Wales with its large area, more extensive natural resources, and inferior development, was better able to absorb capital'.[3] Coghlan used (implicitly) the national accounting framework that he had pioneered in the 1880s to examine this relationship between population, capital, and natural resources. He was concerned with the process of 'progress' in Australia.[4]

Shann (1930) took up the Coghlan theme of the application of capital and labour to the natural resources of the Australian continent, but he viewed this process through a neoclassical lens. He thought that the optimal rate of progress could be achieved, and economic crisis avoided, if factor and commodity markets were allowed to operate freely. Only if a nation's institutional structure allowed the entrepreneur full scope, to pursue his own 'self-interest and hope', and thereby introduce new ideas into the production process, could uninterrupted growth become a reality. Government involvement would merely lead to a misallocation of resources, an increase in production costs, and a breakdown of the development process. This, Shann reminded his readers, had occurred in the 1890s and would occur again in the 1930s.[5] Subsequent events proved him correct.

Butlin (1964) drew together the main strands of the Australian tradition initiated by Coghlan and Shann. He took up where Coghlan left off, by linking the official Australian estimates of GDP and GDCF, that resumed in the 1940s, with his own estimates for earlier years. Butlin employed this national accounting framework to examine the outcome of private and public investment in rural and urban areas in the second half of the nineteenth century. His theme is that Australian economic development in the second half of the nineteenth century was determined largely by Australian rather than British decisionmakers in the light of Australian conditions (part of the Coghlan–Shann tradition), and that the deep depression of the 1890s was the logical outcome of this development process. The long boom from 1860 to 1890, which is a process involving both private and public entrepreneurs, sows the seeds of its own destruction as, progressively, local investment criteria deteriorates, speculation emerges, and the old leading sectors starve new sectors of funds. Clearly Butlin was influenced by his early interest in Schumpeter, but much of this story is contained within Coghlan.[6] Butlin's contribution was to tell that story in a more precise, a more explicitly economic, and a more modern way. There are differences between them but the similarities suggest that *Investment in Australian economic development* is the type of book Coghlan would have written in the early 1960s.

Interest in Sinclair's *Economic development* (1976) arises from his concern with the *process* of economic change, his attempt in an early chapter to model it explicitly (the models of all former scholars remain implicit in their work), and the parallels with the classical growth model it contains. Sinclair sees the development of Australia from the 1820s to the 1920s as a response to a 'fundamental disequilibrium' in the distribution of international factors of production when, in 1813, the Blue Mountains were crossed and the vast 'unused' land resources of Australia were discovered. In a situation where the demand for export staples exceeded their supply, the 'full' utilization of this land was determined on the supply side by restrictions in the supply of capital and effective transport. By the 1920s 'a previously unused natural resource had been adapted to yield what appeared to be the full range of products of which it was capable, involving as intensive a use of land as was permitted by the technical and institution conditions of the day'.[7] After the 1920s development was increasingly determined by a protected manufacturing sector.

What my model has in common with the entire Coghlan tradition is a shared interest in the central role played by natural resources—particularly in the company of capital, population, and real wages—in the process of Australian economic development. A major difference, however, is the role given to technological change. While it is a central part of my model, it does not play a major role in the Coghlan tradition. As Sinclair has constructed an explicit model of Australian economic development, and as he is concerned with a longer period of time (1788 to the early 1970s) than the others, I will briefly contrast my approach with his. But most of the following comments apply equally to the tradition as a whole.

First, my concern is not just with the market sector, but with the Total Economy. This implies a very different model of economic development, involving a household/expansion–market/growth distinction. In turn this depends on an analysis of extensive and intensive resource use. Second, Sinclair has employed a comparative static model, which is based on classical and neoclassical theory with its old vision of static, or analytical, economic man. In contrast, I have developed a dynamic model, which is based on the economic timescapes presented in this book, and on a new vision of dynamic, or historical, economic man. This is largely a distinction between the use of logical models and existential models in history. Third, technological change is a central part of my explanation of economic development. While Sinclair considers technological change, it is relegated to the background, as it is by all other contributors to the Coghlan tradition. This is a curious characteristic of this school's interpretation, and is probably explained by the mutual perception that the massive application of outside factors of production overwhelms the effects of innovation. Fourth, I am not persuaded by Sinclair's argument about the operation of a 'fundamental disequilibrium' for the hundred years after the 1820s. There were a number of transitional stages in the dynamic process of change (that those accustomed to seeing the world through static models might regard as equilibria) determined by the state of technology during this century. A crucial one, for example, occurred around 1860—that remarkable kink in the upward path of household multiplication (or economic expansion)—and was a watershed between extensive and intensive processes of development. Finally, it is unnecessarily restrictive to argue that natural resources prior to 1788 were 'unused'. Resources were fully used given the prevailing state of technology in Australia before 1788. After

1788, given the technology of the Industrial Revolution, resources were underutilized and, as a result, a phase of rapid European economic expansion (or household multiplication) was initiated. Only once these resources were again fully utilized, which was achieved by the early 1860s, did further economic change depend on a change in the economy's technological base rather than the absorption of underutilized natural resources. This is not merely an 'academic' point. Rather it is central to my longer-term model of economic development over the past 60,000 years.

The dynamic model of the Total Economy presented in this book has been useful in composing a new portrait of the Australian economy. And this portrait could help to avoid unsoundly based policy measures that merely frustrate the dynamics of the Total Economy. I embrace the idea of Adam Smith that we need to understand the fundamental economic process in human society in order to remove impediments to its effective operation. It is hoped that this analysis might also assist in providing a new direction for future studies of the economies of other countries. Much work remains to be done, however, before we will have a clear picture of the longrun dynamics of the global Total Economy.

# Glossary of new terms
# and concepts

Owing to some novel aspects of this study a number of new terms and concepts had to be developed and employed in the text. A few familiar concepts have also been redefined to make them more appropriate to the wider analysis adopted here. To assist the reader, these terms and concepts have been brought together and are briefly defined in this Glossary. When a new term or concept is first mentioned in the text it has been printed in bold type. Italics in the Glossary has been used to indicate that additional concepts are also defined here.

**Analytical economic man.** See *static economic man.*

**Cooperative behaviour** is the term substituted in this study for Becker's misnamed concept, 'altruism'. It occurs when individuals attempt to maximize their separate utility functions by maximizing a joint objective function. This is not altruistic behaviour in the normal sense of the word, and should not be contrasted with the, equally misnamed, 'selfish' action of individuals in the market. Individual and cooperative actions are just different means applied in different circumstances by decisionmakers to achieve the same end—the maximization of individual utility. The market and household sectors are characterized by both strategies. Also see *dynamic economic man.*

**Dynamic economic man.** If economics is to improve its understanding of the dynamics of human society it needs not only to adopt a *longrun analytical* focus, but also to develop a more realistic discussion of human motivation to complement its present preoccupation with shortrun hypothetical behavioural outcomes. The working assumption in this study is that the major driving force in human society throughout time is economic man— but an economic man of real historical substance. A major focus here is the search for dynamic (or historical) economic man as the substance and not the shadow of dynamic change in human society. A model of dynamic economic man, who occupies *both* the household and market sectors (contrast *static economic man* in Becker's *Treatise*) and who presides over longrun change, is developed in Chapter 3.

**Economic activity** is work done either to earn income or to produce substitutes for income. It involves, therefore, the production of goods and services that are either marketed or could be marketed. These goods and services are produced in both the market and household sectors. A distinction must be made between family time employed on work, both paid and unpaid, and leisure—see *household economy*. Also see *Total Economy*.

**Economic distance** is a measure of the strength of the relationship between an economically rational individual and any other individual or group with whom he/she interacts. Economic distance, which varies inversely with the importance of any other individual or group to the central individual in maximizing his/her utility, is always positive. Also see *dynamic economic man*.

**Economic expansion** refers to economic change that is not encompassed by the concept of *economic growth*. It has been defined in this study as an increase in the number of households without any increase in real household income. This can occur, either by bringing unutilized natural resources into the system of production, or by a more *intensive* use of existing resources through technological change (broadly envisioned), or by both. The household is the source of economic expansion. In short, economic expansion is household multiplication. Also see *technological dynamic change (TDC)*, and *environmental dynamic change (EDC)*.

**Economic feminization** is the degree to which female workers participate in a firm, industry, sector, or economy; and it is measured as a ratio between female market workers and either the total market workforce, or the male market workforce. Also see *market/household workers*.

**Economic growth** is defined as a change in GDP or GCI *per household* rather than the more conventional measure of GDP per capita. Also see *technological dynamic change*, *environmental dynamic change*, and *economic expansion*.

**Economic man.** See *static economic man*, and *dynamic economic man*.

**Economic resilience** is the command that nations have over material goods and services, and it is measured conventionally by GDP per capita or, better, by GCI per household. It is a measure of a society's ability to compete and to survive, and should be contrasted with the concept of *quality of life*, which has little to do with survival in the longrun. Economic resilience is the power of nations over longrun survival.

**Economic timescapes** are those portraits of economic reality provided by visual presentations of longrun time-series data concerning key macroeconomic variables. They show us the nature of real-world relationships; and seeing is the beginning of understanding. For example, they provide a glimpse of the dynamic processes operating in society. They are the building blocks of *existential models*.

**Environmental dynamic change (EDC)** is economic change achieved via an increase in household numbers by the exploitation of unutilized natural resources with a given state of technology. This is *economic expansion* without *economic growth*, which dominated human experience in pre-market societies. It is contrasted with *technological dynamic change (TDC)*.

**Existential models** are empirical models of reality, and are contrasted with *logical models* that are merely constructs of the mind. An existential model has many of the characteristics of a scaled-down representation of physical reality, and can be constructed from an examination of quantitative *economic timescapes*. The reason for constructing an existential model is to portray reality through the correspondences between the characteristics or structure of the model and those of the real world both past and present. It shows visually what reality is like. It is argued in Chapter 1 that seeing is the beginning of understanding.

**Great waves of economic change.** This term describes the very longrun fluctuations in real GDP per capita of about 300 years in duration (detected for England over the last millennium in Snooks, *Economics without time*). In these great waves—contrary to the conventional wisdom—real GDP per capita is positively correlated with population as well as real GDP and prices. Also see *technological paradigm*.

**Gross Community Capital Formation (or GCCF)** is a measure of annual investment in plant, machinery, equipment, and buildings in both the household and market sectors. It is an extension of the concept of GDCF to the *Total Economy*.

**Gross Community Income (or GCI)** is a measure of the total economic activity that takes place in both the *household* and *market sectors* on an annual basis. It is an extension of the concept of GDP to the *Total Economy*.

**Household economy** involves the production of economic goods and services that could be marketed, but are not. These goods and services include the preparation of meals and the associated clearing away and dishwashing, laundry, house cleaning, child-care and informal education, the production of clothing and furnishings, garden care, house repairs, and other activities such as shopping, record keeping, and payment of household accounts. A clear distinction must be made between activities that are economic—the production of goods and services that could be marketed—and non-economic—the production of 'commodities' for which it is not possible to separate the acts of production and consumption (such as TV watching). These economic goods and services are produced using unpaid household labour together with household buildings, equipment, and land. The household economy plays a unique role in the *Total Economy* because at the beginning of civilization it gave rise to the *market economy*, and it still is the strategic centre of the *Total Economy* and of society as a whole. It is the source of *economic expansion* in society. Also see *market economy*.

**Logical models** are constructs of the mind that are intended to synthetically establish the probable relationship between key variables abstracted from reality. They are constructed not from data corresponding to real-world features, but from abstract mathematical symbols that are brought together deductively into a logical system. Logical models correspond to reality only in the minds of those who create them and who continue to have faith in them even when they are shown empirically to have little explanatory power and to be a poor basis for policy advice. Their importance lies not in what they tell us about, but what to look for in reality, as well as being tools for reconstructing *existential models* that show us what reality is like.

**Longrun analysis** involves an approach to the study of economics that focuses on the process of change over significant periods of time. The benefits of this approach include the identification of some of the larger issues that emerge from dynamic change in society, and an understanding of the dynamic process itself. In this study, 'longrun' is a single word for an important concept in economic history; a single word to raise the editorial hackles.

**Market economy** had its early origins in the *household economy*, but has long since gained an independence and momentum of its own. Unlike the household, it is able to achieve economies of scale and to apply a large-scale technology to the production process. Accordingly, it is the source of *economic growth* in society. As is well known it consists of the private and public sectors. Also see *technological dynamic change* and *household economy*.

**Market/household dynamics** involves an ebb and flow of resources between the household and market sector of a longrun structural, and a shortrun cyclical, kind. The prime mover in this interaction is the changing technological base of the market sector, but it is also influenced by the internal dynamics of the household sector. A major aspect of this interaction is the shift of female household workers to and from the market economy. The impact of this shift on the *Total Economy* will depend on the nature of three effects: the labour-shift effect, which changes the size of the market sector; the factor-substitution effect, by which households attempt to maintain family income at former levels; and the wealth effect, which increases the stock of housing and household equipment. The outcome depends on the prevailing economic circumstances.

**Market/household workers** are those females who work either part-time or full-time in the market place, yet are still primarily responsible for work in the home. This group has risen from negligible levels in the 1950s to include about 40 per cent of all *primary household workers* in the last decade of the twentieth century.

**New economic revolution.** The modern period has experienced two 'revolutions'—the Industrial Revolution during the late eighteenth and early nineteenth centuries, and the new economic revolution during the mid twentieth century. The revolutionary characteristic of the first of these was not in terms of rates of growth (as has often been claimed) but rather in structural terms—of the overthrow of the medieval nexus between population and natural resources based on a technologically-induced structural change from agriculture to manufacturing; the massive redistribution of income from an aristocratic elite to the middle and, later, working classes; and the great change in the gender division of labour on a market–household basis leading to a decline in female market participation. The main characteristics of the new economic revolution were also structural, and involved a major, technologically-induced, shift from manufacturing to service activities, together with a great change in the gender structure of labour demand that caused a rapid increase in the market participation rates of females—particularly 'married' females—after a century of relative stasis.

**Primary household workers** are those workers (largely female) who are responsible for unpaid economic activities in the home. They include both full-time household workers and, increasingly, females who also work in the market sector on a part-time or full-time basis (called here *market/household workers*). The composition of this category of labour in the *Total Economy* has changed so radically since the 1950s that it should be regarded as part of a wider economic and social revolution in society—the *new economic revolution*. Also see *secondary household workers*.

**Productivity gap** is the difference in average labour productivity levels between the household and market sectors. Productivity levels are higher in the market sector because of an ability to transcend the size limitations (of about five persons over the millennium prior to the First World War) of individual households, owing to the application of more effective systems of supervision. As productive units (firms) in the market sector are able to exploit economies of scale and to apply large-scale technology to the production of economic goods and services, they can achieve higher levels of labour productivity.

**Quality of life** is a concept that, in this study, is contrasted with the ability of nations to handle the conditions of life—the *economic resilience* of society. While real GDP (or GCI) per capita (household) may not be a particularly appropriate measure of the quality of life, it is a good reflection of the material power of society. It is unlikely that we will ever be able to quantify happiness—which is a subjective rather than an objective state—only the material inputs into the quality of life. Further, a preoccupation of society with the quality of life—of 'happiness'—*may* even undermine its economic resilience—its ability to survive in the longrun. The ultimate objective of a society that is successful in the longrun is survival rather than quality of life. This does not deny, however, that quality of life is an important objective, just that it is not *the* most important objective of society.

**Secondary household workers** are those workers (largely male) who work full-time in the market and part-time in the household economy. They tend to specialize in household activities related to the market human capital they have acquired, such as landscaping, gardening, the building and maintenance of structures, mechanical repairs, and record keeping and financial matters. Also see *primary household workers*.

**Static economic man** is a convenient assumption made in economic theory. Static economic man is not a dynamic force in society, but rather an abstract collection of preferences and rational choices about consumption and production. In divorcing these behavioural outcomes from more fundamental motivational impulses, economic theorists have created an analytical version of economic man that has little real-world substance. In the process they have lost sight of the wellspring of economic change. It is argued in this study that the discipline of economics needs to rediscover an economic man of real substance, and that this can only be achieved through *longrun analysis*. Also see *dynamic economic man*.

**Technological dynamic change (TDC).** In (modern) societies where all natural resources are 'fully' utilized with the existing state of technology (in its broadest sense), *economic growth* (an increase in GCI per household), and *economic expansion* (an increase in the number of households) can be regarded as component parts of a wider dynamic process of economic change that I have called technological dynamic change. The balance between growth and expansion will depend on the nature of the aggregate production function in a particular society at a particular time, which in turn will be influenced by the internal dynamics (family fertility and consumption) of the household. TDC, which only became possible with the emergence of market economies, has been experienced from time to time in human society over the last 6,000 years, whereas *environmental dynamic change (EDC)* is as old as the human race itself. Also see *EDC, economic expansion,* and *economic growth*.

**Technological paradigm.** This describes the technological foundation for a single *great wave of economic change* of up to 300 years in duration. It consists of an interacting set of innovations in production, transport, communications, and economic organization at various levels, that liberate human society from the constraining effect of natural resources. While this liberation may last for up to twelve generations, it will always come to an end. Once a technological paradigm has been exhausted, further population increase will bring the very-long upswing to an end as the pressure on natural resources will reduce GDP per capita. A new equilibrium between population and resources will be achieved. For human society to break free from this equilibrium, a new technological paradigm must emerge based on a radically different set of techniques. Although this has occurred in the past, there is no guarantee it will occur in the future.

**Total Economy** is the sum of all *economic activity* taking place within society. There are three main sectors—the household, private, and public sectors— that interact to generate the *Total Economy*. As the *Total Economy* is a single economy and not a dual economy, no one sector can be meaningfully examined without taking interactions with the other sectors into account. In the case of Australia over the last two centuries, these three sectors have been of approximately equal quantitative importance. Economic activity in the Total Economy is measured by *Gross Community Income (GCI)* and *Gross Community Capital Formation (GCCF)*. Also see *household economy* and *market economy*.

# *Notes*

## 1 *Economic portraits or reality exposed*

1 This is absolute in the longrun economic sense, and relative in the theoretical and applied sense. The bibliography contains the exceptions—including Becker, Mincer, and their followers—in the latter case.

2 Even Butlin's final work, which I have read in manuscript form, is cast entirely in market terms. While Butlin's scope has increased in his final work—reaching out to Australia's European origins—its objective and structure are very similar to what they were in the early 1960s. He maintains his Schumpeterian vision of booms leading to busts (in this instance the 1820–40 boom with the 1840s bust), and he uses the familiar output/input scenario.

3 This is not to deny the important recent work of some applied economists such as Eisner, Kendrick, Murphy, and others to estimate contemporary non-market economic activity. Their work will be discussed in Chapter 7.

4 It may be helpful to quote briefly from the Introduction in *Economics without time* (pp. 1–3):

### *Ideas and reality*

Casual observation suggests that, throughout the social sciences, abstract ideas are either more 'respectable', 'successful', or 'popular' than empirical accounts of reality. Why should this be so? The answer throws modest light upon the problems facing the use of the social sciences to understand reality and it may prevent society from taking the least optimal development path. The primary objective of the social sciences is to understand man in society, in the past, present, and future. Its conduct is based upon the premise that there is an objective reality that can be explored albeit approximately; understood however imperfectly; and modified with difficulty. The major problem we face is that the social activities of mankind are extremely complex, interactive, and overwhelmingly difficult to understand through observation alone. In order to make the intellectual task easier to handle within the social sciences, the main activities of man in society—economic, social, and political—have been isolated and subjected to separate study; simple models of the various aspects of human society have been developed; and techniques for handling empirical evidence have been standardised. These abstract models serve a number of functions: to sidestep the complexity of social reality by developing persuasive 'stories' about cause and effect; to explore social reality so as to create order out of apparent chaos; and, in conjunction with historical analysis, to formulate 'social' policy. Theory, then, constitutes the necessary (but not sufficient) tools to assist in the understanding, and modification, of the present social reality.

The history of the social sciences has involved an intense struggle between those who think that theory should be developed inductively from observations of the past and present using historical and statistical techniques, and those who believe that it should be developed deductively with the aid of mathematics. In this struggle, the inductionists had the upper hand until the mid to late nineteenth century, but thereafter the deductionists, through their impressive development of abstract ideas—particularly in the discipline of economics—began to surge ahead with, in Miltonian language, 'blind zeal' until they ultimately eclipsed the inductionists. The success of the deductionists was so overwhelming that the social sciences have become distinctly unbalanced in their approach to reality. Indeed, there are even times when deductive theory is mistaken for—certainly preferred to—reality. In other words, in some circles, theory in the social sciences has come to be regarded as a better guide to reality than direct empirical studies of man in society. Policy in the social sciences, for example, is normally derived directly from simple theoretical models with little empirical analysis and no historical insight. Apart from being a precarious procedure, it is highly irresponsible, as human welfare is at stake. Social scientists, however, are not alone in this; ecologists, who are determined to remodel human society even more dramatically (despite their lack of expertise in the social sciences), also base their policies on unverified deductive models.

But what is it that accounts for the dominance of ideas, many of them unsubstantiated, in the social sciences? My general argument, which has been applied in more detail to the economics discipline . . . begins with the fact that the social sciences attract scholars of two extreme types: those who prefer to explore worlds of their own making—the 'gameplayer' in theoretical disciplines or the 'mythmaker' in history; and those who prefer to explore the real world—the 'realist'. Naturally there are rare individuals who can work brilliantly at both ends of the spectrum, such as W.S. Jevons the English neoclassical economist, and there are a few more who feel happy in the role of competent all-rounder; but the great majority tend to specialise at either end of the spectrum. Needless to say, a sound social science requires the application of both approaches: theory is required to make sure that the right questions are being asked, and to isolate potentially relevant relationships; while empirical/historical work is essential to test the relevance of theory and to suggest modifications to it, to suggest general causal relationships, and to provide a sound basis for policy advice. But even more importantly, the role of history is to raise and analyse the big issues that lie beyond the scope of economics—issues concerning the forces that determine the very longrun processes of economic change that are sweeping human society out of the past and into the future. Economists merely focus upon the ripples that briefly flit across the surface of these great waves (of 300 years or more in duration) of economic change. But the tools of economists are essential to historians who are attempting to analyse these forces. The exclusion of either approach, therefore, will lead to the impoverishment of the social sciences. Hence the fact that the triumph of deductive theory has marginalised empirical/historical work in the social sciences is cause for considerable concern. This concern, as it relates to the discipline of economics, is a central message of *Economics without time*.

5 The word 'existential' is used in its more traditional sense of pertaining to 'existence' or reality (as opposed to 'appearance') and should not be associated with the more recent school of philosophy initiated by Søren Kierkegaard and popularized by Jean-Paul Sartre.

6 Wittgenstein, *Tractatus*, p. 15.

7 See for example the 'historical chapters' in Alfred Marshall's *Principles*. These chapters were moved from the beginning of the first edition to appendixes in later

additions owing to the attack on Marshall by Cunningham in 'The perversion of economic history'.

8 Becker, *Treatise*, p. 76 (my emphasis). References to this work are to the enlarged edition of 1991.

9 Becker, *Treatise*, p. 54.

10 An interesting illustration of Becker's appeal to evidence is a footnote reference (p. 77) to the film *Kramer vs Kramer*, in which the actor Dustin Hoffman loses his job when he takes over responsibility for his child following the desertion of his wife! This suggests that, for Becker, 'evidence' is only required to 'illustrate' a theoretical point. For the purposes of illustration—rather than demonstration—fiction is just as useful as fact.

11 Becker, *Treatise*, p. 3.

12 For example, his discussion of 'effort' leads him to see a future in which 'A person's sex would . . . no longer be a valid predictor of earnings and household activities' (Becker, *Treatise*, p. 79). The content of the prediction is not being questioned, just the way in which it was achieved.

13 An interesting attempt has recently been made—Winston, *Timing of economic activities* (written before Becker, *Treatise*, but after Becker, 'Allocation of time')—to locate the usual static production theory for both the firm and household, where everything is determined instantaneously, in a 'time-specific' framework. Winston is concerned with 'processes' and 'flows'. In two chapters on the household, he describes a 'time-specific household model that sees work and consumption activities as processes in time' (p. 157): a model 'to analyse the process of household choice in time that must underly those atemporal models' (p. 158) of Becker, 'Allocation of time'; Lancaster, 'Technology of consumption'; and Linder, *Leisure class*. Clearly this is a step in the right direction, but Winston is still a captive of *analytical* time. He does not consider the medium of *real* time, which can show the dynamic process of economic activity. Hence his model is still a *deductive* model, rather than an *existential* model as developed in this study. And even this extension of analytical time focuses solely on 'stylized' *shortrun* rhythms of the day, the week, and the year. *Longrun* historical rhythms are ignored. It is with longrun historical rhythms that this study is concerned.

14 Mincer, 'Married women'.

15 For a review of this literature see Killingsworth and Heckman, 'Female labour supply'.

16 Gregory, McMahon, and Whittingham, 'Women'.

17 Gregory, McMahon, and Whittingham, 'Women', p. S308.

18 Sontag, *On photography*, pp. 23 and 111.

19 Cunningham, 'The perversion of economic history'.

## 2 The Total Economy

1 King, *Observations*, p. 31.

2 In British mines prior to the Industrial Revolution, males did the heaviest, most dangerous, and most skilled work at the coal face, while their female relatives worked as 'drawers'. As Angela John in *Sweat of their brow* says: 'In the eighteenth century the employment of women was still part of a family concern, male members utilising the help of their female relatives wherever possible . . . Their main task was to work as drawers. This involved pulling sledges or tubs along the pit floor

or on planks from the coal face to the bottom of the shaft' (p. 20). Training in more skilled work was denied women because of the shorter time they were engaged in pit work (and hence the reduced return on investment in these skills) and the physical demands made by the extremely arduous work at the coal face. Work on the surface, however, which was relatively unskilled and less physically demanding, meant that women could, and did, compete effectively with men. See John, *Sweat of their brow*, chs 3 and 4. And in the agricultural sector the men undertook more enervating tasks like scything, while the women did the raking and stacking of the harvested crop. See Snell, *Labouring poor*. More generally, see Pinchbeck, *Women workers*.

3 Richards, 'Women in the British economy'.

4 A major effect of massive post-war reconstruction was to increase female participation rates in West Germany, France, and Japan to between 45 and 60 per cent in the early 1950s, at a time when other Western countries experienced participation rates between only 25 and 40 per cent. But during the second half of the 1950s these rates began to fall, and by the late 1960s they reached a low point at about 40 per cent—a level comparable to that achieved in non-devastated Western countries. From the late 1960s they increased in line with participation rates elsewhere, until by the early 1990s they were in the vicinity of 50–60 per cent.

5 Apart from the modern pioneering theoretical work of Mincer (1962) and Becker (1965, 1981)—which has its roots in earlier neoclassical work by Jevons (1882, 1894)—and the contemporary national accounting work of Eisner ('Extended accounts' and *Total incomes system*) and others, little formal attention has been given to the operation of the Total Economy by leading economists, and virtually no attention at all by analytical economic historians. Neither have general historians and feminists attempted to place the household in a wider social accounting context and certainly not over the longrun. This is not to say, however, that in terms of their own objectives these works are other than highly valuable and interesting.

6 A halfway house—a diagrammatic model of the feudal economy of Anglo-Norman England—is presented in Snooks, *Economics without time*, ch. 5 (p. 203). This is where a large dependent subsistence economy (60 per cent of GDP) is appended to the demesne market economy.

7 This diagram also illustrates the three ways in which GDP and GCI are measured. The household, private, and public boxes represent the production of the goods and services; the arrows indicating returns to factors of production from the market sector to the household represent the income approach; and the arrows indicating cash payments represent the expenditure approach.

8 For a discussion of timeless 'growth' models, see Snooks, *Economics without time*, ch. 3.

9 The attempt to retouch this picture, by McLean and Pincus, 'Living standards', and Haig, 'International comparisons', is unconvincing for reasons discussed throughout the text. In particular, it is pertinent that my estimate of gross household income, which is based on census rather than production data, describes a profile similar to Butlin's estimates of GDP for the period 1861 to 1939.

10 McLean and Pincus, 'Living standards'; and Haig, 'International comparisons'.

11 Snooks, 'Development in adversity'; McLean and Pincus, 'Living standards'.

12 The sequence of shedding and acquiring market labour in Australia during the Great Depression is discussed in Snooks, 'Unemployment relief', particularly pp. 328–34. I used the expression 'robbing Peter to pay Paul' to encapsulate this process; see Snooks, 'Robbing Peter to pay Paul'.

13 See Australian Bureau of Statistics (ABS) unemployment statement for April 1992. The difference between the Great Depression and the recessions of the early 1980s and early 1990s—apart from gender—is that the shift between full-time and part-time market employment in the 1930s was government inspired, whereas in the last decade it has been driven by the private sector.

14 I have employed the gender wage ratio as an explanatory variable in three econometric models in this book—see Tables 2.3, 3.1, and 4.1. In two of these models I attempt to explain processes or interactive relationships. Table 2.3 is concerned with the interaction between the household and market sectors, and Table 4.1 is concerned with the participation rates of married females. In the third I analyse an absolute outcome—the average size of Australian households. While the level of the female/male wage ratio is appropriate when explaining absolute outcomes, changes in the level of this ratio are appropriate when explaining interactive relationships.

15 The diagnostic tests (using Microfit) for the household/market interaction model, for 1946 to 1990, are as follows:

| Test statistics | LM version | F version |
|---|---|---|
| A: Serial correlation | CHI-SQ $(1) = 2.4701[0.116]$ | $F(1, 38) = 2.2602[0.141]$ |
| B: Functional form | CHI-SQ $(1) = 0.21209[0.645]$ | $F(1, 38) = 0.18406[0.670]$ |
| C: Normality | CHI-SQ $(2) = 3.6137[0.164]$ | Not applicable |
| D: Heteroskedasticity | CHI-SQ $(1) = 1.4824[0.223]$ | $F(1, 42) = 1.4643[0.233]$ |

A: Lagrange multiplier test of residual serial correlation.
B: Ramsey's RESET test using the square of the fitted values.
C: Based on a test of skewness and kurtosis of residuals.
D: Based on the regression of squared residuals on squared fitted values.

These results suggest that in the above model there is no significant autocorrelation, that the functional form is appropriate, that the errors are normally distributed, and that the disturbances are homoskedastic (i.e. have uniform variances).

16 See Snooks, *Economics without time*.

17 This issue is taken up by Snooks in 'A new portrait of economic development'.

18 Jackson, *Nineteenth century*, p. 93.

19 Butlin, *Investment*, ch. 4.

20 See Snooks, *Depression and recovery*, chs 3 and 8; and Sinclair, 'Capital formation'.

## 3 The household economy

1 While I have used the terms 'family economy' and 'household economy' interchangeably, it must be stressed that the data in this study are constructed on a household rather than a family basis. Where two or more unrelated families live in the same household, this is not a strictly accurate equation. But, on

the whole, it will not introduce any significant distortion owing to the fact that Australian families have been largely successful in their persistent desire to live in their own homes.

2  The household economy did attract some attention from earlier economists, such as Jevons, Thorold Rogers, Sidgwick, and even Marshall, in the late nineteenth century (see note 2 for Chapter 4), and Reid (*Household production*) in the 1930s.

3  For surveys of recent work on the household, see Gronau, 'Home production'; and Eisner, 'Extended accounts'.

4  Becker, *Treatise*, p. 303.

5  The idea of altruism motivating economic agents is not new. Becker's contribution in *Treatise* has been to draw a sharp distinction between 'selfishness' in the market and 'altruism' as the motivating force in the home. For earlier discussions of altruism, see Boulding, *Love and fear* (1973); Phelps, *Altruism* (1975); Becker, 'Altruism' (1976); and Collard, *Altruism* (1978).

6  Becker, *Treatise*, p. 278.

7  Becker, *Treatise*, p. 279.

8  Becker, *Treatise*, p. 299.

9  Different aspects of longrun analysis, together with its importance in economics, are discussed in Snooks, *Economics without time*, and Snooks, *Historical analysis in economics*.

10  Snooks, *Economics without time*, ch. 6.

11  For European landings, see McIntyre, *Secret discovery of Australia*; Sigmond and Zuiderbaan, *Dutch discoveries*; Collingridge, *Discovery of Australia*; Keniha, *Journal of Abel Jansz Tasman*; Beaglehole, *Journals of Captain James Cook*; and Dunmore, *French explorers*. And for Southeast Asian contacts, see Lloyd-Warner, 'Malay influence'; Macknight, 'Macassans and Aborigines'; and Macknight, *Voyage to Marege'*.

12  For a discussion of Aboriginal economy, see Butlin, *Our original aggression*; Butlin, *Economics and the Dreamtime*; Butlin, *Forming an economy*; and Dingle, *Aboriginal economy*.

13  See Butlin, *Forming an economy*. It is not clear from his discussion that this estimate takes into account the consumption in England of services from durables. For a discussion of the importance of this aspect of consumption, see Snooks, *Economics without time*, ch. 7, and Table 7.6.

14  There is abundant evidence that Aboriginal society had responded creatively to changes in their environment over long periods of time. See Butlin, *Dreamtime*, and Dingle, *Aboriginal economy*.

15  The generally accepted date of 60,000 years has recently been challenged by Monash University's Department of Geography and Environmental Science. After examining charcoal and pollen samples in a drill core covering the last 1.5 million years taken from the edge of the continental shelf 80 km east of Cairns, they claim that human settlement of Australia began at least 140,000 years ago. This has yet to be confirmed by other scientists. See 'Education Review', *Weekend Australian*, 20–21 June 1992.

16  See Finley, *Ancient economy*, and Phillips, *Medieval expansion*.

17  There is also a biological parallel that has exacerbated the costs of the clash

between cultures: isolation weakens the body's defences against the introduction of outside diseases.

18 As with other species that live by hunting, conflict tends to be ritualistic because even relatively minor wounds can lead to the death through infection of a few key providers which in turn could endanger the entire kinship group.

19 See Snooks, *Economics without time*, ch. 6.

20 There are competing theories to the one developed in this chapter about the motivation of individuals within firms. First, there is the so-called 'cooperative games theory' pioneered in 1944 by von Neumann and Morgenstern, *Theory of games* and later developed by Shubik, *Game theory*. Second, there are those who argue for the importance of 'fair play', 'benevolence', or 'moral economic behaviour' in economic activity, such as: Collard, *Altruism and economy*; Collard, 'Love is not enough'; Phelps, *Altruism*; Sugden, 'Philanthropy'; Sen, 'Rational fools'; Sen, *Ethics*; and Sen, 'Beneconfusion'. Third, there are a range of non-economic, or political and psychological theories of cooperative behaviour that need not concern us here. Yet even the most sympathetic economist, who wishes to take a broader approach to economic man, is 'unsure whether the practical wisdom of this thoughtful economic man fits happily into the orthodox model of rational choice . . . or whether a radical upheaval in economic analysis is needed to accommodate him' (Meeks, *Thoughtful economic man*, p. 1).

Such a radical upheaval in economics may well be overdue but, in my opinion, not for this reason. No doubt some individuals are motivated by all the forces nominated in the above publications, but small groups of individuals cannot drive economic systems. The dynamics of human society derive energy from the 'typical' person, not the 'deviant' person; and my reading of the historical evidence suggests that the typical person is rational economic man. But, there is a need, as I have suggested in the text, to develop a model of dynamic economic man if we are to explain longrun economic change.

21 See Butlin, 'Contours', p. 107.

22 See Durnin and Passmore, *Energy, work, and leisure*, p. 52; and ch. 4. Also in his 'enlarged edition' (1991) Becker draws attention to this point.

23 Forster, *Industrial development in Australia*, pp. 103–15.

24 See Becker, *Treatise*; Laslett, *Household*.

25 For example, the use of fencing rather than shepherds in the pastoral industry from the 1860s, and the conversion of pastoral land to wheat land with the use of various types of machinery and superphosphates from the turn of the century. See Butlin, *Investment*, ch. 2, and Dunsdorfs, *Wheatgrowing*, ch. 5.

26 Coghlan, *Wealth and progress*, and ABS, *Manufacturing industry*.

27 See Becker, *Treatise*, ch. 2, and particularly pp. 52–3. While he is correct about the capital intensity of some firms, this is not as true today as it once was. It has already been noted that Becker tends to ignore the role of physical capital in the household.

28 King, *Observations*, p. 31.

29 See Moore, 'Anglo-Norman family', p. 193.

30 See Postan, *Medieval economy*, p. 32, and Dyer, *Standards of living*, p. 134.

31 Laslett, *Household*, p. 76.

32 See Alford, *Production or reproduction?*
33 Laslett, 'Introduction'.
34 The lags are not arbitrary, but were determined using a lag-deletion test.
35 The diagnostic tests for the corrected regression results (using Microfit) for 1946 to 1990 are as follows:

| Test statistics | LM version | F version |
|---|---|---|
| A: Serial correlation | CHI-SQ (1) = 0.011620[0.914] | $F(1, 37) =$ 0.010002[0.921] |
| B: Functional form | CHI-SQ (1) = 5.4222[0.020] | $F(1, 37) = 5.3389[0.027]$ |
| C: Normality | CHI-SQ (2) = 0.26834[0.874] | Not applicable |
| D: Heteroskedasticity | CHI-SQ (1) = 2.0291[0.154] | $F(1, 41) = 2.0305[0.162]$ |

A: Lagrange multiplier test of residual serial correlation.
B: Ramsey's RESET test using the square of the fitted values.
C: Based on a test of skewness and kurtosis of residuals.
D: Based on the regression of squared residuals on squared fitted values.

36 See, for example, Becker, *Treatise*, chs 4–6.
37 Sinclair, 'Economic growth and well-being'.
38 Lancaster and Gordon, 'Health and medicine', p. 315.

## 4 Household workers

1 There is a large and rapidly growing literature in this field. For recent surveys see Ferber, *Women and work*; Bridenthal *et al.*, *Becoming visible*; and Borchardt, *Australians*.
2 See in particular: Jevons, *The state*; Thorold Rogers, *The economic interpretation*; Sidgwick, *Political economy*; Marshall, *Principles*. This particular interest of late nineteenth century economists was brought to my attention by Chris Nyland.
3 Becker, *Treatise*, p. 39.
4 Becker, *Treatise*, p. 64.
5 Becker, *Treatise*, p. 56.
6 Becker, *Treatise*, p. 57.
7 Becker, *Treatise*, p. 63.
8 While human capital theory has provided major insights regarding economic decision-making, it should not be regarded as a panacea. It has its limitations and should not be employed beyond them. This first became clear to me in the mid 1970s from a study of the earnings of visual artists; see Snooks, 'Determinants of earnings inequality amongst Australian artists'. In the process of preparing this paper for an economics journal, it was necessary to argue that artists were a special case. To the theorist, all failures of theory *must* be special cases.
9 Becker, *Treatise*, p. 40.
10 Becker, *Treatise*, p. 69.
11 Chris Nyland brought this literature to my notice.
12 See Durnin and Passmore, *Energy, work and leisure*, ch. 4.
13 Gregory, McMahon and Whittingham, 'Women'.

14 There is an extensive literature: Lewis, *Victorian and Edwardian England*; Kent, 'Sex, power and politics'; Pankhurst, *The suffragette*; and Ostrogorski, *Rights of women*—are but a few.

15 For economic analysis, it matters not that female market workers are married or single, but whether they are also primary household workers.

16 For a discussion of the participation of married women in the US market sector, see Goldin, *Gender gap*, ch. 5. The more gradual increase in the USA reflected the earlier structural and technological change in that economy.

17 In the real world, in contrast to the world of theory, it is impossible to distinguish between technological change and the substitution of factors of production—between a shift in the production function, and a movement along the function—because both involve a change in the production process, and both are reflected in a change in relative factor prices and a change in the capital/labour ratio. Accordingly, the market K/L ratio can be employed as an index of the complex change in the technological foundations (interpreted in its broadest sense) of the market economy over time. It is instructive to remember that this index is an aggregation of many types of physical and human capital that are growing and decaying at various rates in the economy. This, however, is the nature of macroeconomic history.

18 The diagnostic tests (using Microfit) for 1946 to 1990 are as follows:

| Test statistics | LM version | F version |
|---|---|---|
| A: Serial correlation | CHI-SQ (1) = 0.0038920[0.950] | F(1, 36) = 0.0032588[0.955] |
| B: Functional form | CHI-SQ (1) = 0.20362[0.652] | F(1, 36) = 0.17128[0.681] |
| C: Normality | CHI-SQ (2) = 2.0885[0.352] | Not applicable |
| D: Heteroskedasticity | CHI-SQ (1) = 1.3452[0.246] | F(1, 41) = 1.3240[0.257] |

A: Lagrange multiplier test of residual serial correlation.
B: Ramsey's RESET test using the square of the fitted values.
C: Based on a test of skewness and kurtosis of residuals.
D: Based on the regression of squared residuals on squared fitted values.

Tests were also undertaken for possible stability problems in the model. Basically we wish to know whether the parameter estimates are valid throughout the period of analysis. The two tests employed were CUSUM and the square of CUSUM. The test is to ensure that the recursive residuals do not exceed upper and lower confidence bounds over time. If the residuals remain within these confidence bounds for the period under examination—if there is no structural break—then the system is stable, and the coefficients are valid for the entire period. Each explanatory variable was examined separately and in each case there were structural changes around the 1890s and the Second World War (and for ΔFMW, around 1973). In the periods defined by these structural breaks, the recursive residuals were highly stable and, hence, the coefficients for these periods were valid throughout. It is interesting to note that this structural change was evident from the economic timescapes presented in Chapter 2, and the periodization used in this study was determined before the econometric tests were undertaken. This appears to confirm the argument in Chapter 1, that the standardized rules and conventions of econometrics are a generally accepted method of testing the objectivity of our seeing in the process of induction. But seeing should come before testing.

19 Two lags of the dependent variable fully describe the lagged process. Further lags were not significant and did not survive a lag-detection test.

20 Gregory, McMahon and Whittingham, 'Women', p. 308.

21 Mincer, 'Married women'.

22 For a comprehensive review of the female labour supply literature, see Killingsworth and Heckman, 'Female labour supply', particularly pp. 185–197. Also see Smith and Ward, *Women's wages*.

23 Goldin, *Gender gap*, ch. 5.

24 Goldin, *Gender gap*, chs 6 and 7.

25 Long, 'Comment', p. 105 (my emphasis). There has been some recent work on 'dynamic'—or life cycle—labour supply models. In these models, while wage rates are endogenously determined, they depend on the accumulation of human capital. They are, in other words, supply-side models, which ignore the real dynamics of the market economy—i.e. demand-side forces. Also, according to a recent survey, they are still in their 'infancy'. See Killingsworth and Heckman, 'Female labour supply', pp. 144–78.

26 No attempt has been made in this study to estimate the value of human capital, owing to the absence of suitable data prior to the Second World War. While the data on formal education, particularly during the nineteenth century, is poor, it is totally absent for on-the-job training during all but the last few decades. Also, the suggestion that the production and rearing of children is an act of investment in human capital is open to serious objections. As there is no economic return to individuals who spend their time and income in this way, procreation/child-rearing should be regarded as consumption rather than investment. In any case, it is not possible to value the time devoted to rearing children prior to the time-budget surveys of the 1970s and 1980s. Hence, in this chapter I have used—as Matthews, Feinstein and Odling-Smee, *British economic growth*, have done—proxies for the main forms of investment in human capital. It seems, therefore, more sensible to continue to think of an increase in population as just that—an increase in people rather than as an increase in productive capital. Certainly the variable is easier to measure in these terms.

27 Sinclair, 'Economic growth and well-being'.

28 The 1950s and 1960s have been regarded as 'normal' by those who lived through these years, and who could not remember the Great Depression. But the period should be regarded as historically atypical, owing to the important role played by exogenous forces in the preceding generation. A period of comparable growth and prosperity in the UK occurred in the first half of the sixteenth century also under the influence of exogenous forces in the preceding 150 years. The next occurrence could be centuries into the future. See ch. 6 above; Snooks, *Economics without time*, ch. 7; and Snooks, 'Great waves'.

29 All education data are from Grundy and Yuan, 'Education and science', and population data in the censuses. This ratio is inflated by the fact that after 1950 a growing proportion of students were older than 14 years.

30 Calculated from ABS, *Year book Australia*.

31 Higher education data are from DEET, *Selected higher education statistics 1990*, and population data from ABS, *Estimated resident population.*

32 Sinclair, 'Economic growth and well-being'. He argues persuasively, however, that investment in deep sewerage was not undertaken until it was considered at least as economic as the existing pan system.

33 See Snooks, 'Innovation', pp. 20–2.

34 Lancaster and Gordon, 'Health and medicine', p. 314.

35 For a discussion of the spread of baby-care centres in the rural districts of New South Wales—and of the role of private organizations—see Country Women's Association, *The golden years: the story of fifty years of the Country Women's Association of New South Wales, 1922–1972.*

36 Very casual empiricism over four Australian generations by those of us in our mid forties, suggests a significant increase in heights between those born in the 1880s or 1890s and their grandchildren born in the 1940s, and again between the latter and those born in the 1970s. It is not clear, however, that the generation born in the 1910s and 1920s was any taller than its parents. However, detailed data on this issue are required.

37 Lancaster and Gordon, 'Health and medicine', pp. 317–25.


## 5 *The market and the household*

1 This is the reversal of the creation story of Adam and Eve.

2 A very different interpretation about the role of 'cultural' influences is contained in Goldin, *Gender gap*. She claims that job, and hence wage, discrimination was 'reinforced by a long history of occupational segregation and by a society that had formed a consensus around the virtue of sex segregation and the appropriateness of differentiating on the basis of sex. They were also enabled by the absence of an opposing ideology that would eventually lead women as individuals to become discontent with their treatment as a group' (p. 118). Goldin's main evidence on this issue is of a literary rather than a quantitative kind, and it includes policy statements by governments (ch. 7), businessmen (ch. 6), and unions (p. 104). It is essential, however, to test the realworld impact of policy statements of this type, because the desire to discriminate is not the same as the act of discrimination, and policy statements may merely reflect underlying economic conditions rather than irrational discrimination. The residual method for estimating gender wage differentials (which Goldin calls, rather suggestively, 'wage discrimination') is not conclusive, as the residual may merely be the result of inadequately measured and omitted explanatory variables.

3 In a very interesting study of women in the British coalmining industry, entitled *By the sweat of their brow*, Angela John demonstrates quite clearly that, although women played a vital part in the family economy of mining communities in the eighteenth century by undertaking physically demanding work in the mines, this work was not *as* physically demanding as that done by their menfolk. She shows that they assisted their husbands, fathers, and brothers by carrying out the less skilled and less physically demanding jobs such as 'drawing' and sometimes 'hauling'. This is not to say that the work done by females in the family was not physically demanding, just that it was not *as* physically

demanding in an absolute sense (although it was in a relative sense) as work at the coal face. Family members, both male and female, undertook work according to their comparative advantage, in order to maximize family utility. The point is that females could not, and did not, compete with males in the most physically demanding work, but they could and did, compete with males in less physically demanding surface, or 'pit-brow', work involving sorting, washing, and preparing coal for the market (John, *Sweat of their brow*, chs 3 and 4).

The coalmining industry also illustrates the interactive nature of human and physical capital. Work at the coalface, which was more highly skilled than other work in the mine, was undertaken only by men. Human capital theory would explain this in terms of the longer working life of males owing to the child-bearing role of women. But this is only part of the answer. As coalface work was both more skilled and very demanding physically, a high degree of physical strength was required before mining skills could be acquired. Clearly, both physical strength and manual skills were, and are, required in acquiring certain forms of human capital.

4 Goldin, *Gender gap* (pp. 63, 103–4) also recognizes that physical strength has played a role in manufacturing (but not, she claims, in the service sector) in the past, and she takes it into account when considering the question of 'wage discrimination'. But she views it not as a skill requiring investment of time and income and receiving an anticipated rate of return, but merely as a matter of 'brute' strength (p. 103) or 'brawn' (p. 109) that one either does or does not possess. Goldin concludes that, while significant, strength is not as important in determining gender wage differences as is discrimination in the form of occupational barriers. Goldin also recognizes that, during the course of the twentieth century, capital has been substituted for human strength (p. 63), but does not quantitatively test the impact of this on the changing gender demand for labour.

5 Primitive machinery in the Industrial Revolution was often dangerous and difficult to handle. It also increased the speed and duration of both industrial and agricultural work, which in turn increased the demand for strength and stamina. Machines, unlike horses and oxen, did not need to rest, and would continue well into the night. See Hobsbawm and Rudé, *Captain Swing*; Mantoux, *Industrial Revolution*, ch. 3; and Deane, *Industrial Revolution*, chs 3, 6, 7.

6 Crafts, *Industrial Revolution*, ch. 4; Matthews, Feinstein and Odling-Smee, *British economic growth*, p. 378.

7 Davis *et al.*, *American economic growth*, p. 287.

8 Byrne, *The health and safety of women in industry*, p. 19.

9 This important evidence, which has been neglected in the discussion of the gender division of labour, was brought to my attention by Chris Nyland.

10 Monod and Zerbib, 'Sex-related differences', pp. 125 and 127.

11 Strandberg, 'Falling and overexertion accidents', p. 131.

12 David, 'Lumbar injuries at work', p. 15.

13 Hull, 'Cervical, dorsal and lumbar spine syndromes', pp. 1–102.

14 Snook, 'Psychophysical acceptability', p. 332.

15 Anderson, 'Permissible loads', p. 324.

16 Checkland, *Industrial society in England*, pp. 246–51; and John, *Sweat of their brow*, ch. 1.

17 Byrne, *Women in industry*, pp. 4, 9, 19. This was a report prepared by the Women's Bureau in the US Department of Labor.

18 Snook, 'Psychophysical acceptability', p. 334.

19 Rutenfranz, 'Energy expenditure', p. 117.

20 Viscusi, *Employment hazards*, p. 234.

21 See Van Cott *et al.*, *Human engineering*, p. 549; Bishop *et al.*, 'Sex difference', pp. 675–87. This issue is discussed more fully in an unpublished research paper (1988) by Snooks and Nyland, 'The physical demands of the labour process'.

22 McLean and Pincus, 'Living standards'. They employ a consumer price index rather than an implicit GDP deflator. The main problem with this procedure is that it ignores the differential price change in the important non-consumption sector.

23 By Shann in *The boom of 1890 and now*, and in the polemical final section of Shann, *An economic history of Australia*.

24 Many of those who retained their jobs experienced an increase in real income as prices fell faster than money wages and other sources of income.

25 The capital stock variable employed here is for plant and machinery (and does not include buildings) because it is plant and machinery (and not buildings) that are substituted for labour. The capital price series used is also that for plant and machinery.

26 See Salter, *Productivity*, chs 2, 3, 5, but particularly pp. 29–45.

27 A logarithmic function for the period 1861 to 1990 generated the following results:
$$LKLR = 7.587 - 2.810 \, LRFP, \text{ with } \bar{R}^2 = 0.756.$$
$$(209.6) \quad (-19.998)$$
The $t$ statistics are in parenthesis and $L$ indicates logs.

28 Snooks, 'Growth and productivity'.

29 Snooks, 'Innovation and the growth of the firm'; and Snooks, 'Hume enterprises in Australia'.

30 Snooks, 'Growth and productivity'.

31 Goldin, *Gender gap*, pp. 106–7, and Gershuny and Miles, *Service economy*, pp. 15–17 and 52–7.

32 Interesting work has been done on the recent emergence of part-time work on a large scale (part-time work has always been with us) in Britain by Beechey and Perkins, *Hours*. They also associate it with the emergence of a 'new' technology.

33 ABS, *Labour statistics*.

34 The employment data have been taken from the various population censuses, which record all persons employed during the week of the census according to 'main' occupation and industry.

35 Goldin, *Gender gap*, pp. 106–7.

36 In Australia, females replaced (among others) male bank tellers because of the substitution of a new electronic technology for labour skills, not, as some have argued, because the Second World War demonstrated to clients that 'women could be trustworthy tellers' (Goldin, *Gender gap*, p. 117).

37 Considerable adjustment of the official data is required in order to obtain

consistent series of male and female employment in manufacturing. This has been done in Snooks, 'Manufacturing', pp. 286–301, where there is also a discussion of problems and solutions, pp. 458–60. These data are examined here in detail for the first time. The manufacturing census includes all employees and working proprietors recorded as being on the pay-roll at the end of the period in question (either the financial year or each month).

38 These factory census percentages differ slightly from those based on the population census and quoted above, owing to different definition of 'manufacturing'.

39 See Butlin, Barnard, and Pincus, *Government*, pp. 146–7.

40 See Sheridan, *Mindful militants*; Forster, *Industrial development*; S.J. Butlin, *War economy 1939–1942*.

41 See ABS, *Labour statistics, Australia, 1989*, p. 4.

## 6  *A new portrait of the Australian economy*

1 It is indeed unfortunate that Noel Butlin did not write the promised analytical account of the economic growth of the Australian market sector. In the preface to *Investment in Australian economic development, 1861–1900* (C.U.P. 1964), Butlin wrote: 'This book is intended to be primarily an institutional and historical account of Australian investment and economic development. I hope to follow it with a third essay, a strictly analytical study of growth', p. xiv. This third essay (the first was *Australian Domestic Product*) did not appear. In contrast I have attempted to provide a statistical and analytical account, but on this occasion for the Total Economy rather than the market economy.

2 See Snooks, *Economics without time*, ch. 7.

3 For a discussion of growth theory in this context, see Snooks, *Economics without time*, ch. 3.

4 See Snooks, *Economics without time*, ch. 7; and Snooks, 'Great waves of economic change'.

5 The interpretation of Australian economic development in this chapter is based on the author's estimates of GCI. As discussed in Chapter 7, these estimates employ the opportunity-cost principle of valuation, which is most meaningful when there is little involuntary unemployment of productive resources. As explained in Chapter 7, market rates during depressions overvalue (in the sense that they are higher than the clearing rate) economic activity in both the market and the household sectors, thereby leaving sector relativities substantially unaffected. This is not a problem in longrun analysis if economic performance is measured between successive peak years, as has been done throughout Chapters 1 to 6. When focusing on the interdepression years between the 1890s and 1930s, however, it should be remembered that true performance is *even worse* than recorded performance.

6 The process of migration is discussed in Butlin, 'Palaeoeconomic history'.

7 For a reconstruction of Aboriginal population 1788 to 1850, see Butlin, *Original aggression*.

8 In Snooks, *Economics without time*, ch. 7, I show that relatively rapid average growth rates had been achieved in England at certain times during the 700 years prior to 1788.

9 By 1860 the Aboriginal population had been reduced by disease, economic competition, and violence to between 300,000 and 400,000.

10 See Sinclair, *Economic development*, for discussion of manufacturing demand.

11 Sinclair, *Economic development*, ch. 1.

12 Schedvin, *Great depression*; Snooks, *Depression and recovery*; and Snooks, 'Development in adversity'.

13 For a discussion of public and relief works in the interwar period, see Snooks, 'Government unemployment relief'; and Snooks, *Depression and recovery*, ch. 7.

14 See Forster, *Industrial development*.

15 See Forster, *Industrial development*, ch. 5.

16 See Snooks, *Depression and recovery*, chs 3 and 7; and Sinclair, *Economic development*.

17 See Sinclair, 'Capital formation'; Sinclair, *Economic development*, ch. 6; and Snooks, 'Manufacturing'.

18 This is a rough estimate obtained by the aggregation of annual numbers of net male (15–65 years) immigration from 1947 to 1989/90 (inclusive).

19 Segmented labour market 'theory' should be seen as a conspiracy-based alternative view of the world to mainstream economics. It is based on a different view of human motivation to that underlying mainstream economics—that social groups (not just individuals) are prepared to systematically implement their prejudices even when it significantly affects their material gains. There is, however, no evidence for this in open, market-oriented economies. For a survey of this literature, see Cain, 'Segmented labor market theories', and Taubman and Wachter, 'Segmented labour markets'.

20 Some aspects are briefly discussed by Whitwell, *Making the market*.

21 The only official Australian household surveys are those very limited surveys of 1911 (222 responses) and 1913 (392 responses) and those since 1984. See Knibbs, *Cost of living*; and ABS, *Household expenditure survey*.

## 7  A new approach to historical social accounting

1 For a survey see Eisner, ' Extended accounts' and Eisner, *Total incomes system*. The growing interest of official statisticians from around the world in measuring non-market economic activity is reflected in the increasing number of exploratory papers given at the 1992, 22nd General Conference of the International Association for Research in Income and Wealth (IARIW), Flims, Switzerland.

2 Clark, 'Coghlan, Timothy (1855–1926)', pp. 469–70.

3 See Butlin, 'An early estimate of Australian national income'. Studenski's *Income of nations* overlooks W.C. Wentworth, whose approach was similar to that of G. Tucker, but who predates the American by twenty-four years.

4 See Mulhall, *Dictionary of statistics*; and Butlin, *Australian domestic product*, pp. 36–7.

5 Coghlan, *Wealth and progress*.

6 Victoria, *Census* (Melbourne, 1891).

7 See successive volumes of Coghlan, *Wealth and progress*.

8 For a full discussion of Coghlan's methods, see Arndt, 'A pioneer of national income estimates', pp. 616–25, who had access to Coghlan's working sheets. Studenski, *Income of nations* relies heavily on information from Arndt on Coghlan.

9 See these authors in Bibliography.

10 Just before this text went to press, Stan Engerman brought to my attention an article by Nancy Folbre, 'The unproductive housewife', which mentions an earlier (1985) article by Desley Deacon, 'Political arithmetic', on the distinction between breadwinners and dependents in the Australian census. Both authors insist that neoclassical economists and economic statisticians at the turn of the century regarded housework as 'unproductive'. This is not true of most orthodox economists of that time, and certainly not of Coghlan. Unpaid housework was ignored because it could not be analysed by an approach to economic activity based on market models. It was ignored, not because of chauvinism, but because it was too difficult to handle. Only since the 1960s has economic theory developed sufficiently to make possible an analysis of non-market work. It was, therefore, a pragmatic, not an ideological response. They also appear unaware of the important point that Coghlan's 1890 classification of population was driven by his pioneering work on national accounts. Also see Katrina Alford, 'Women's employment' on Coghlan.

11 Coghlan, *Census of 1891: Statistician's Report*, p. 270.

12 Coghlan, *Census of 1891*, p. 272 (my emphasis).

13 Coghlan, *Census of 1891*, p. 273 (my emphasis).

14 The earlier focus on money incomes in the work of Petty, Davenant, and King was not for economic theoretic reasons as it was for Coghlan, but for the very practical reason of assessing the taxable capacity of the nation. However, by the end of the nineteenth century economists and statisticians elsewhere were, like Coghlan, beginning to draw a distinction between economic activities based on remuneration.

15 Coghlan, *Census of 1891*, p. 279.

16 Coghlan, *Census of 1891*, pp. 276–9.

17 For the timeless approach see Eisner, 'Extended accounts'; and Eisner, *Total incomes system*. My book is the first longrun approach.

18 Even at the 1992 IARIW Conference, European bureaucrats had got no further than cautiously suggesting that the value of household income be included in 'satellite' accounts. The prospect of forging a new measure of total economic activity still appears too daunting.

19 For early discussion and estimates of the contribution of household services see Mitchell *et al.*, *Income* (1921) [US]; Lindahl *et al.*, *National income* (1937) [Sweden]; Kuznets, *National income* (1937) [US]; and Clark, 'House-work' (1958) [UK]. Also see Studenski, *Income of nations*, p. 177.

20 See Gronau, 'Home production'; Kendrick, 'Expanding imputed values'; Hawrylyshyn, 'Household services'; Murphy, 'Household work'; Eisner, 'Extended accounts'; and Eisner, *Total incomes system*. For applied work on recent decades in Australia, see Ironmonger, *Household work*.

21 See Becker, 'Allocation of time'; Becker, *Treatise*; and ABS, *Time use*.

22 Hawrylyshyn, 'Household services', pp. 108–9; ABS, *Measuring unpaid household work*, p. 17.

23 Nordhaus and Tobin, 'Is growth obsolete?'.

24 Studenski, *Income of nations*, p. 177.

25 Weinrobe, 'Household production'.

26 See Hawrylyshyn, 'Household services', p. 102; Kendrick, 'Expanding imputed values', p. 350; Murphy, 'Household work', p. 30.

27 Murphy, 'Household work', p. 30.

28 An alternative but equally experimental indirect method has been suggested by Gronau, 'Home production', based on the estimation of a marginal productivity function using imputed wage rates and 'a vector of variables affecting the value of marginal productivity at home' (including the education and experience of wives and details of their children). Little, to my knowledge, has come of this.

29 Mitchell, *Income*; Lindahl *et al.*, *National Income*; Kuznets, *National Income*; and Clark, *National income*.

30 For a survey of these studies see Hawrylyshyn, 'Household services'; and Murphy, 'Household work'.

31 See Hawrylyshyn, 'Household services', p.26; and Kendrick, 'Expanding imputed values', p. 352.

32 Ferber and Birnbaum, 'Housework', after employing a number of conceptual and empirical tests, claim that this procedure is superior to the other two. Also Mitchell, *Income*, Kuznets *National income*, Lindahl *et al.*, *National income*, and Kendrick, 'Expanding imputed values', have used this method.

33 In the case of household repairs, for example, should we use the wage rates of a master craftsman or his apprentice? Further, it has been suggested by Gronau, 'Home production', p. 414, that no type of market price valuation is appropriate in those cases where the household does not consume market services, precisely for the reason that they have rejected these prices as a measure of its productivity. But what proportion of households would this involve? A very small proportion.

34 See Nordhaus and Tobin, 'Is growth obsolete?'; Weinrobe, 'Household production'; and Murphy, 'Household Work'.

35 Becker, *Treatise*, pp. 20–33.

36 Becker, *Treatise*, p. 23.

37 McCloskey, *Applied theory*, pp. 536–7.

38 McCloskey, *Applied theory*, p. 537.

39 See Snooks, 'Regional estimates'; Snooks, *Depression and recovery*; Snooks, 'Arithmetic'; and Snooks 'Capital stock'.

40 See Butlin, *Australian domestic product*; Snooks, 'Regional estimates'; and Sinclair, 'Gross domestic product'.

41 See Kuznets, *National income*; Feinstein, *National income*; and Feinstein, 'National statistics'.


*8 Households and household workers*

1 See Thompson, 'Australian manufacturing'.

2 Becker, *Treatise*, pp. 23–5.

3 Butlin, *Australian domestic product*, chs 16 and 17; and Butlin and Sinclair, 'Australian GDP'.

4 Butlin, *Australian domestic product*, pp. 251–64, and 302–7.

5 See Krupinski, 'Quality of life'; and ABS, *Time use*.

6 It has been suggested to me that there are also market occupations that involve 'on-the-job leisure', such as academic work and publishing. Even if true, these occupations are atypical and are usually characterized by relatively low salaries

(in relation to the human capital required to do them) and working weeks up to double the community standard.

7 This suggestion was made by one of the publisher's readers.
8 See Krupinski, 'Quality of life', ABS, *Time use*.
9 Bittman, *Juggling time*.
10 For confirmation see Bittman, *Juggling time*, p. 7.
11 Alford, *Production or reproduction?*, p. 208.
12 See Snooks, 'Household services'.
13 Murphy, 'Household work'.

## 9 Capital, land, and income in the Total Economy

1 See Butlin, *Australian domestic product*, chs 16 and 17; and ABS, *Australian national accounts*.
2 Butlin, *Australian domestic product*; and Haig, *Capital stock*.
3 See Butlin, 'Australian national accounts', pp. 130 and 133; and ABS, *Australian national accounts*.
4 Butlin, 'Australian national accounts', p. 139; and Norton and Kennedy, *Australian economic statistics*, pp. 38 and 133.
5 For a discussion of methods employed in calculating capital stock for the estimation of productivity change, see Snooks, 'Growth and productivity change', and Snooks, 'Capital stock'.
6 Pope, 'Private finance', p. 240; and Foster and Stewart, *Australian economic statistics*, p. 146.

## 10 Retrospective

1 See Studenski, *Income of nations*, for a survey of the important work on national accounting for the market sector over the last 300 years, and see Snooks, *Economics without time*, ch. 5, for an evaluation of Domesday Book as the first set of national accounts in Europe, 600 years before Gregory King.
2 See Coghlan, *Labour and industry*; Shann, *Australia*; Butlin, *Investment*; and Sinclair, *Economic development*.
3 Coghlan, *Labour and industry*, p. 1417.
4 For a more detailed discussion of Coghlan's work, see Snooks, *Economics without time*, pp. 143–50.
5 For a more complete discussion of Shann's work, see Snooks, *Economics without time*, pp. 150–4; Snooks, 'Bond or free?'; and Snooks, 'Interpretations'.
6 For a discussion of the influences on Butlin's work see Snooks, 'Interpretations' and Snooks, 'In my beginning'.
7 Sinclair, *Economic development*, pp. 4–5.

# Bibliography

Alford, K., *Production or reproduction? An economic history of women in Australia, 1788-1850* (Melbourne: Oxford University Press, 1984).

Alford, K., 'Colonial women's employment as seen by nineteenth-century statisticians and twentieth-century economic historians', *Labour History*, 51 (November 1986), pp. 1-10.

Anderson, G.B.J., 'Permissible loads: biomechanical considerations', *Ergonomics*, vol. 28, no. 1 (1985), pp. 323-26.

Anderson, M., *Approaches to the history of the Western family, 1500-1914* (London: Macmillan, 1980).

Arndt, H.W., 'A pioneer of national income estimates', *Economic Journal*, 59 (December 1949), pp. 616-25.

Ashenfelter, O. and Layard, R. (eds), *Handbook of labour economics* (Amsterdam: North-Holland, 1986).

Australia, *Census* (Canberra: CBCS/ABS, 1911, 1921, 1933, 1947, 1954, 1961, 1966, 1971, 1976, 1981, 1986).

Australia, Australian Bureau of Statistics, *Australian national accounts: national income and expenditure* (cat. no. 5234.0; Canberra: ABS, various issues).

Australia, Australian Bureau of Statistics, *Award rates of pay indexes, Australia* (cat. no. 6312.0; Canberra: ABS, various issues).

Australia, Australian Bureau of Statistics, *Consumer price index* (cat. no. 6401.0; Canberra: ABS, various issues).

Australia, Australian Bureau of Statistics, *Household expenditure survey, Australia: detailed expenditure items* (cat. no. 6535.0; Canberra: ABS, 1984 and 1988/89).

Australia, Australian Bureau of Statistics, *Imports cleared for home consumption, Australia* (cat. nos 5412.0 and 5413.0; Canberra: ABS, various issues).

Australia, Australian Bureau of Statistics, *Labour statistics, Australia, 1989* (cat. no. 6101.0; Canberra: ABS, 1989).

Australia, Australian Bureau of Statistics, *Manufacturing commodities: principal articles produced, Australia* (cat. no. 8303.0; Canberra: ABS, various issues).

Australia, Australian Bureau of Statistics, *Manufacturing industry: details of operations, Australia* (cat. no. 8203.0; Canberra: ABS, various issues).

Australia, Australian Bureau of Statistics, *Measuring unpaid household work: issues and experimental estimates* (cat. no. 5236.0; Canberra: ABS, 1990).

Australia, Australian Bureau of Statistics, *Quarterly estimates of national income and expenditure, Australia* (cat. no. 5206.0; Canberra: ABS, various issues).

Australia, Australian Bureau of Statistics, *Schools, Australia* (cat. no. 4202.0; Canberra: ABS, various issues).

Australia, Australian Bureau of Statistics, *Time use pilot survey, Sydney , May–June 1987* (cat. no. 4111.1; Sydney: ABS, 1987).

Australia, Australian Bureau of Statistics, *Year book Australia* (cat. no. 1301.0; Canberra: ABS, various issues).

Australia, Commonwealth Bureau of Census and Statistics, *Building and construction: bulletin* (ref. no. 3.1; Canberra: CBCS, various issues).

Australia, Commonwealth Bureau of Census and Statistics, *Labour report* (Canberra: CBCS, various issues).

Australia, Commonwealth Bureau of Census and Statistics, *Monthly bulletin of overseas trade statistics* (ref. no. 8.9; Canberra: CBCS, various issues).

Australia, Commonwealth Bureau of Census and Statistics, *Production: bulletin* (Canberra: CBCS, various issues).

Australia, Commonwealth Bureau of Census and Statistics, *Secondary industries: bulletin* (Canberra: CBCS, various issues).

Australia, Department of Employment, Education and Training, *Apprenticeship statistics* (Canberra: AGPS, various years).

Australia, Department of Employment, Education and Training, *Selected higher education statistics* (Canberra: AGPS, various years).

Australia, Department of the Prime Minister and Cabinet, Office of the Status of Women, *Selected findings from 'Juggling time: how Australian families use time'* (Canberra: Office of the Status of Women, Department of the Prime Minister and Cabinet, 1991).

Australia, Parliament, *Report of the Commissioner of Taxation* (Parliamentary Papers; Canberra: Government Printer, various years).

Australia, TAFE National Centre for Research and Development & Department of Employment, Education and Training, *Selected TAFE statistics* (Canberra: AGPS, various years).

Beaglehole, J.C. (ed.), *The journals of Captain James Cook on his voyages of discovery*, 4 vols (Cambridge: Cambridge University Press, for the Hakluyt Society, 1955–74).

Becker, G.S., 'A theory of the allocation of time', *Economic Journal*, 75 (1965), pp. 493–517.

Becker, G.S., 'Altruism, egoism, and genetic fitness: economics and sociology', *Journal of Economic Literature*, 14 (1976), pp. 817–26.

Becker, G.S., *A treatise on the family* (Cambridge, Mass.: Harvard University Press, 1981; enlarged edition 1991).

Beechey, V. and Perkins, T., *A matter of hours: women, part-time work and the labour market* (Oxford: Polity Press/Blackwell, 1987).

Benham, F.C., *The prosperity of Australia: an economic analysis* (London: P.S. King and Son Ltd, 1928).

Bishop, P. *et al.*, 'Sex difference in muscular strength in equally-trained men and women', *Ergonomics*, vol. 30, no. 4 (1987), pp. 675–87.

Bittman, M., *Juggling time: how Australian women use time* (Canberra: Office of the Status of Women, Department of the Prime Minister and Cabinet, 1991).

Blau, F.D., 'Gender', in J. Eatwell, M. Milgate and P. Newman (eds), *The new Palgrave: a dictionary of economics* (London: Macmillan, 1987), vol. 2, pp. 492–8.

Boehm, E.A., *Twentieth century economic development in Australia* (2nd edn, Melbourne: Longman Cheshire, 1979; first published 1971).

Borchardt, D.H. (ed.), *Australians: a guide to sources* (Broadway, NSW: Fairfax, Syme & Weldon, 1987).

Bose, C.E. *et al.*, 'Household technology and the social construction of housework', *Technology and Culture*, 25 (1984), pp. 53–82.

Boulding, K.E., *The economy of love and fear* (Belmont, Calif.: Wadsworth, 1973).

Bridenthal, R., Koonz, C. and Stuard, S (eds), *Becoming visible: women in European history* (2nd edn; Boston: Houghton Mifflin, 1987).

Brownlee, W.E., 'Household values, women's work, and economic growth, 1800–1930', *Journal of Economic History*, 39 (1979), pp. 199–209.

Butlin, M.W., 'A preliminary annual database 1900/01 to 1973/74', *Research Discussion Paper* 7701 (Reserve Bank of Australia, May 1977).

Butlin, N.G., *Australian domestic product, investment and foreign borrowing: 1861–1938/39* (Cambridge: Cambridge University Press, 1962).

Butlin, N.G., *Investment in Australian economic development, 1861–1900* (Cambridge: Cambridge University Press, 1964).

Butlin, N.G., *Our original aggression: Aboriginal populations of southeastern Australia, 1788–1850* (Sydney: George Allen & Unwin, 1983).

Butlin, N.G., 'Contours of the Australian economy 1788–1860', *Australian Economic History Review*, vol. 26, no. 2 (September 1986), pp. 96–125.

Butlin, N.G., 'Australian national accounts', in W. Vamplew (ed.), *Australians: historical statistics* (Broadway, NSW: Fairfax, Syme and Weldon, 1987), pp. 126–44.

Butlin, N.G., 'The palaeoeconomic history of Aboriginal migration', *Australian Economic History Review*, vol. 29, no. 2 (September 1989), pp. 3–57.

Butlin, N.G., 'Australian public sector wages, 1786 to 1850', *Source Papers in Economic History*, no. 21, ANU, (December 1992).

Butlin, N.G., *Economics and the dreamtime* (Cambridge University Press, forthcoming).

Butlin, N.G., *Forming an economy* (Cambridge University Press, forthcoming).

Butlin, N.G., Barnard, A. and Pincus, J.J., *Government and capitalism: public and private choice in twentieth century Australia* (Sydney: George Allen & Unwin, 1982).

Butlin, N.G. and Dowie, J.A., 'Estimates of Australian workforce and employment 1861–1961', *Australian Economic History Review*, vol. 9, no. 2 (September 1969), pp. 38–55.

Butlin, N.G. and Sinclair, W.A., 'Australian gross domestic product 1788–1860: estimates, sources and methods', *Australian Economic History Review*, vol. 26, no. 2 (September 1986), pp. 126–47.

Butlin, S.J., 'An early estimate of Australian national income', *Economic Record*, vol. 14, no. 27 (December 1938), pp. 266–8.

Butlin, S.J., *War economy, 1939–1942* (Canberra: Australian War Memorial, 1955).

Byrne, H.A., *The health and safety of women in industry* (Washington: Women's Bureau, US Department of Labor, 1935).

Cain, G.G., 'The challenge of segmented labour market theories to orthodox theory: a survey', *Journal of Economic Literature*, vol. 14, no. 4 (December 1976), pp. 1215–57.

Caldwell, J.C., 'Population', in W. Vamplew (ed.), *Australians: historical statistics* (Broadway, NSW: Fairfax, Syme & Weldon, 1987), pp. 23–41.

Carter, M., 'Issues in the hidden economy: a survey', *Economic Record*, vol. 60, no. 170 (September 1984), pp. 209–21.

Carter, M. and Maddock, R., 'Leisure and Australian wellbeing, 1911-1981', *Australian Economic History Review*, vol. 27, no. 1 (March 1987), pp. 30-43.

Checkland, S.G., *The rise of industrial society in England, 1815-1885* (London: Longmans, 1964).

Clark, C.G., *National income and outlay* (London: Macmillan, 1937).

Clark, C.G., 'The economics of house-work', *Bulletin of the Oxford University Institute of Statistics*, vol. 20, no. 1 (May 1958), pp. 205-11.

Clark, C.G., *The national income, 1924-1931* (London: F. Cass & Co., 1965; first published London: Macmillan, 1932).

Clark, C.G., 'Coghlan, Timothy (1855-1926)', in J. Eatwell, M. Milgate and P. Newman (eds), *The new Palgrave: a dictionary of economics* (London: Macmillan, 1987), vol. 1, pp. 469-70.

Clark, C.G. and Crawford, J.G., *The national income of Australia* (Sydney: Angus & Robertson, 1938).

Coghlan, T.A., *The wealth and progress of New South Wales* (Sydney: Government Printer, 1887-1902).

Coghlan, T.A., *General report on the eleventh census of New South Wales [Census of 1891: Statistician's report]* (Sydney: Government Printer, 1894).

Coghlan, T.A., *Labour and industry in Australia*, vol. 1 (London: Oxford University Press, 1918).

Collard, D.A., *Altruism and economy* (Oxford: Martin Robertson, 1978).

Collard, D.A., 'Love is not enough', in J.G.T. Meeks (ed.), *Thoughtful economic man: essays on rationality, moral rules and benevolence* (Cambridge: Cambridge University Press, 1991), pp. 17-28.

Collingridge, G., *The discovery of Australia: a critical, documentary and historic investigation concerning the priority of discovery in Australasia by Europeans before the arrival of Lieut. James Cook, in the 'Endeavour', in the year 1770* (Gladesville, NSW: Golden Press, 1983).

Country Women's Association, N.S.W., *The golden years: the story of fifty years of the Country Women's Association of New South Wales 1922-1972.* (n.p.: Country Women's Association, N.S.W., n.d.).

Crafts, N.F.R., *British economic growth during the Industrial Revolution* (Oxford: Clarendon Press ; New York : Oxford University Press, 1985).

Cunningham, W., 'The perversion of economic history', *Economic Journal*, 2 (1892), pp. 491-506.

David, G.C., 'U.K. National statistics on handling accidents and lumbar injuries at work', *Ergonomics*, vol. 28, no. 1 (1985), pp. 9-16.

Davis, L.E. *et al.*, *American economic growth: an economist's history of the United States* (New York: Harper & Row, 1972).

Deacon, D., 'Political arithmetic: the nineteenth-century Australian census and the construction of the dependent woman', *Signs*, 11 (1985), pp. 27-47.

Deane, P., *The first industrial revolution* (2nd edn; Cambridge: Cambridge University Press, 1979; first published 1965).

Dingle, A.E., *Aboriginal economy* (Melbourne: McPhee Gribble/Penguin Books, 1988).

Dunlop, Y., Healy, T., and McMahon, P., 'Australian models of labour force participation: a critical review', in Andre J. Kaspura (ed.), *Labour force participation in Australia: the proceedings of a conference* (Canberra: Australian Government Publishing Service, 1984), pp. 17-38.

Dunmore, J., *French explorers in the Pacific*, 2 vols (Oxford: Clarendon Press, 1965, 1969).

Dunsdorfs, E., *The Australian wheat-growing industry, 1788–1948* (Melbourne: Melbourne University Press, 1956).

Durnin, J.V.G.A. and Passmore, R., *Energy, work and leisure* (London: Heinemann Educational Books Ltd., 1967).

Dyer, C., *Standards of living in the later Middle Ages* (Cambridge: Cambridge University Press, 1990).

Eisner, R., 'Extended accounts for national income and product', *Journal of Economic Literature*, 26 (December, 1988), pp. 1611–84.

Eisner, R., *The total incomes system of accounts* (Chicago: University of Chicago Press, 1989).

Feinstein, C.H., *National income, expenditure and output of the United Kingdom, 1855–1965* (Cambridge: Cambridge University Press, 1972).

Feinstein, C.H., 'National statistics, 1760–1920', in C.H. Feinstein and S. Pollard, (eds), *Studies in capital formation in the United Kingdom, 1750–1920* (Oxford: Clarendon Press, 1988), pp. 257–401.

Ferber, M., *Women and work, paid and unpaid: a selected, annotated bibliography* (New York: Garland, 1987).

Ferber, M.A. and Birnbaum, B.G., 'Housework: priceless or valueless', *Review of Income and Wealth*, ser. 26 (1980), pp. 387–400.

Finley, M.I., *The ancient economy* (2nd edn; Berkeley: University of California Press, 1985; first published 1973).

Flandrin, J.L., *Families in former times: kinship, household and sexuality* (Cambridge: Cambridge University Press, 1979).

Folbre, N., 'The unproductive housewife: her evolution in nineteenth-century economic thought', *Signs*, 16 (1991), pp. 463–84.

Forster, C., *Industrial development in Australia, 1920–30* (Canberra: Australian National University Press, 1964).

Foster, R.A. and Stewart, S.E., *Australian economic statistics, 1949–50 to 1989–90* (Occasional Paper No. 8; [Sydney]: Reserve Bank of Australia, 1991).

Gandevia, B., *Tears often shed: child health and welfare in Australia from 1788* (Sydney: Pergamon, 1978).

Gershuny, J.I., *Social innovation and the division of labour* (Oxford: Oxford University Press, 1983).

Gershuny, J.I. and Miles, I.D., *The new service economy* (New York: Praeger, 1983).

Goldin, C., *Understanding the gender gap: an economic history of American women* (New York: Oxford University Press, 1990).

Gregory, R.G., McMahon, P., and Whittingham, B., 'Women in the Australian labor force: trends, causes, and consequences', *Journal of Labor Economics*, vol. 3, no. 1, (supplements, 1985), pp. S293–S309.

Gronau, R., 'Home production: a forgotten industry', *Review of Economics and Statistics*, 62 (1980), pp. 408–16.

Gronau, R., 'Home production: a survey', in O. Ashenfelter and R. Layard (eds), *Handbook of labour economics* (Amsterdam: North-Holland, 1986), pp. 273–304.

Grundy, D. and Yuan, F.F.F., 'Education and science', in W. Vamplew (ed.), *Australians: historical statistics* (Broadway, NSW: Fairfax, Syme & Weldon, 1987), pp. 328–46.

Haig, B.D., *Capital stock in Australian manufacturing* (Canberra: Department of Economics, RSSS, Australian National University, 1980).

Haig, B.D., 'International comparisons of Australian GDP in the 19th century', *Review of Income and Wealth*, 35 (1989), pp. 151–62.

Hawrylyshyn, O., 'The value of household services: a survey of empirical estimates', *Review of Income and Wealth*, 22 (1976), pp. 101–31.

Hobsbawm, E.J. and Rudé, G., *Captain Swing* (London: Lawrence and Wishart, 1969).

Hull, L., 'Cervical, dorsal and lumbar spine syndromes', *Acta Orthopaedica Scandinavica*, suppl. 17 (1954), pp. 1–102.

Humphries, J., 'Women and work', in J. Eatwell, M. Milgate and P. Newman (eds), *The new Palgrave: a dictionary of economics* (London: Macmillan, 1987), vol. 4, pp. 925–8.

Ironmonger, D.S. (ed.), *Households work: productive activities, women and income in the household economy* (Sydney: Allen & Unwin, 1989).

Jackson, R.V., *Australian economic development in the nineteenth century* (Canberra: Australian National University Press, 1977).

Jackson, R.V. (ed.), *Cambridge economic history of Australia* (Cambridge University Press, forthcoming 1994).

Jevons, W.S., *The state in relation to labour* (London: Macmillan, 1882).

Jevons, W.S., *Money and the mechanism of exchange* (New York: D. Appleton & Co., 1894).

John, A.V., *By the sweat of their brow: women workers at Victorian coal mines* (London: Croom Helm, 1980).

Juster, F.T., *Household capital formation and financing, 1897–1962* (New York: National Bureau of Economic Research, distributed by Columbia University Press, 1966).

Juster, F.T. and Stafford, F.P., 'The allocation of time: empirical findings, behavioural models, and problems of measurement', *Journal of Economic Literature*, 29 (1991), pp. 471–522.

Keating, M., 'Australian work force and employment, 1910–11 to 1960–61', *Australian Economic History Review*, vol. 7, no. 2 (September 1967), pp. 150–71.

Kendrick, J.W., 'Expanding imputed values in the national income and product accounts', *Review of Income and Wealth*, 25 (1979), pp. 349–64.

Kendrick, J.W., assisted by Carol S. Carson, *Economic accounts and their uses* (New York: McGraw-Hill, [1972]).

Keniha, G.H. (ed.), *The journal of Abel Jansz Tasman 1642, with documents relating to his exploration of Australia in 1644* (Adelaide: Australian Heritage Press, 1964).

Kent, S.K., *Sex, power and politics: the women's suffrage campaign in Britain, 1860–1914* (PhD thesis, Brandeis University, 1984).

Keynes, J.M., *The general theory of employment, interest, and money* (London: Macmillan, 1936).

Killingsworth, M.R. and Heckman, J.J., 'Female labour supply: a survey', in O. Ashenfelter and R. Layard (eds), *Handbook of labour economics* (Amsterdam: North-Holland, 1986), pp. 103–204.

King, Gregory, *Natural and political observations and conclusions upon the state and condition of England*, in G.E. Barnett (ed.), *Two tracts by Gregory King* (Baltimore: The Johns Hopkins Press, 1936).

Knibbs, G.H., *Inquiry into the cost of living in Australia, 1910–11* (Melbourne: Commonwealth Bureau of Census and Statistics, 1911).

Krupinski, J., 'Quality of life', in J. Krupinski and A. Mackenzie (eds), *The health and social survey of the north-west region of Melbourne* (Melbourne: Institute of Mental Health Research and Post-graduate Training, Mental Health Division, Health Commission of Victoria, 1979), pp. 61–76.

Kuznets, S., *National income and capital formation, 1919–1935* (New York: National Bureau of Economic Research, 1937).

Kuznets, S., *Commodity flow and capital formation* (New York: National Bureau of Economic Research, 1938).

Kuznets, S., assisted by L. Epstein and E. Jenks, *National income and its composition, 1919–1938* (New York: National Bureau of Economic Research, 1941).

Lancaster, H. and Gordon, D., 'Health and medicine', in W. Vamplew (ed.), *Australians: historical statistics* (Broadway, NSW: Fairfax, Syme & Weldon, 1987), pp. 314–27.

Lancaster, K., 'Change and innovation in the technology of consumption', *American Economic Review*, 56 (1966), pp. 14–42.

Laslett, P. (ed.), *Household and family in past time* (Cambridge: Cambridge University Press, 1972).

Laslett, P., 'Introduction: the history of the family', in P. Laslett (ed.), *Household and family in past time* (Cambridge: Cambridge University Press, 1972), pp. 1–89.

Lewis, J., *Women and social action in Victorian and Edwardian England* (Aldershot: Edward Elgar, 1991).

Lindahl, E.R., 'National income, the concept and methods of estimation', in E.R. Lindahl, E. Dahlgren and K. Kock (eds), *National income of Sweden, 1861–1930* (London: King & Son; Stockholm: Nortedt & Soner, 1937), pp. 1–25.

Lindahl, E.R., Dahlgren, E. and Kock, K. (eds), *National income of Sweden, 1861–1930* (London: King & Son; Stockholm: Nortedt & Soner, 1937).

Linder, S.B., *The harried leisure class* (New York: Columbia University Press, 1970).

Linge, G.J.R., *Industrial awakening: a geography of Australian manufacturing, 1788–1890* (Canberra: Australian National University Press, 1979).

Lloyd-Warner, W., 'Malay influence on the Aboriginal cultures of north-eastern Arnhem Land', *Oceania*, 2 (1932), pp. 476–95.

Long, C.D., 'Labor force participation of married women: comment', in H.G. Lewis (ed.), *Aspects of labour economics* (Princeton: Princeton University Press for the National Bureau of Economic Research, 1962), pp. 98–105.

McCloskey, D.N., *The applied theory of price* (New York: Macmillan, 1982).

McIntyre, K.G., *The secret discovery of Australia: Portuguese ventures 200 years before Captain Cook* (Adelaide: Souvenir Press, 1977).

Macknight, C.C., 'Macassans and Aborigines', *Oceania*, vol. 42, no. 4 (June 1972), pp. 283–321.

Macknight, C.C., *The voyage to Marege': Macassan trepangers in northern Australia* (Melbourne: Melbourne University Press, 1976).

McLean, I.W. and Pincus, J.J., 'Did Australian living standards stagnate between 1890 and 1940?', *Journal of Economic History*, 43 (1983), pp. 193–202.

Mantoux, P., *The Industrial Revolution in the eighteenth century: an outline of the beginnings of the modern factory system in England* (trans. Marjorie Vernon; London: Jonathan Cape, 1928).

Marshall, Alfred, *Principles of economics* (London: Macmillan, 1890).

Matthews, R.C.O., Feinstein, C.H. and Odling-Smee, J.C., *British economic growth, 1856–1973* (Oxford: Clarendon Press, 1982).

Meeks, J.G.T. (ed.), *Thoughtful economic man: essays on rationality, moral rules and benevolence* (Cambridge: Cambridge University Press, 1991).

Mincer, J., 'Labour force participation of married women', in H.G. Lewis (ed.), *Aspects of labour economics* (Princeton: Princeton University Press for the National Bureau of Economic Research, 1962), pp. 63–97.

Mitchell, W.C. *et. al.*, *Income in the United States: its amount and distribution, 1909–1919*, 2 vols (New York: Harcourt, Brace and Co., 1921).

Monod, H. and Zerbib, T., 'Sex-related differences in the manual carriage of loads', *Ergonomics*, vol. 28, no. 1 (1985), pp. 125–9.

Moore, J.S., 'The Anglo-Norman family: size and structure', in M. Chibnall (ed.), *Anglo-Norman Studies XIV: the Battle conference of 1991* (Woodbridge, Suffolk: Boydell Press, 1992), pp. 152–96.

Mulhall, M.G., *The dictionary of statistics* (London: George Routledge & Sons, 1884).

Murphy, M., 'Comparative estimates of the value of household work in the United States for 1976', *Review of Income and Wealth*, vol. 28, no. 1 (March 1982), pp. 29–43.

New South Wales, *Census* (Sydney: Government Printer, 1828, 1833, 1836, 1841, 1846, 1851, 1856, 1861, 1871, 1881, 1891, 1901).

New South Wales, Department of Housing, *Report* (Sydney: Department of Housing, various years).

New South Wales, *Musters*, various years.

New South Wales, *Statistical registers* (Sydney: Government Printer, various years).

Nordhaus, W. and Tobin, J., 'Is growth obsolete?', in National Bureau of Economic Research, *Economic research: retrospect and prospect—fiftieth annual colloquium V: Economic growth* (New York: National Bureau of Economic Research, 1972), pp. 1–80.

Norton, W.E. and Kennedy, P.J., *Australian economic statistics 1949–50 to 1984–85: I, Tables* (Occasional Paper No. 8A; [Sydney]: Reserve Bank of Australia, 1985).

Norton, W.E. and Kennedy, P.J., *Australian economic statistics 1949–50 to 1984–85: II, Graphs* (Occasional Paper No. 8B; [Sydney]: Reserve Bank of Australia, 1985).

Organisation for Economic Co-operation and Development, *Labour force statistics* (Paris: OECD, various years).

Ostrogorski, M., *The rights of women: a comparative study in history and legislation* (London: S.Sonnenschein, 1893).

Pahl, R.E., *Divisions of labour* (Oxford: Basil Blackwell, 1984).

Palgrave, R.H.I. (ed.), *Dictionary of political economy*, 3 vols (London: Macmillan, 1894, 1896, and 1899).

Pankhurst, E.S., *The suffragette: the history of the Women's Militant Suffrage Movement, 1865–1910* ([NewYork]: Source Book Press, [1970]; first published 1911).

Phelps, E.S. (ed), *Altruism, morality, and economic theory* (New York: Sage, 1975).

Phillips, J.R.S., *The medieval expansion of Europe* (Oxford/New York: Oxford University Press, 1988).

Pinchbeck, I., *Women workers and the Industrial Revolution, 1750–1850* (London: Routledge, 1930).

Pollak, R.A. and Wachter, M.L., 'The relevance of the household production function and its implications for the allocation of time', *Journal of Political Economy*, 38 (1975), pp. 255–77.

Pope, D., 'Private finance', in W. Vamplew (ed.), *Australians: historical statistics* (Broadway, NSW: Fairfax, Syme and Weldon, 1987), pp. 238–53.

Postan, M.M., *The medieval economy and society: an economic history of Britain in the Middle Ages* (Harmondsworth: Penguin, 1972).

Queensland, *Census* (Brisbane: Government Printer, 1861, 1864, 1868, 1871, 1876, 1881, 1886, 1891, 1901).

Queensland, *Statistical registers* (Brisbane: Government Printer, various years).

Reid, M.G., *Economics of household production* (New York: J. Wiley & Sons, 1934).

Reiger, K.M., *The disenchantment of the home: modernizing the Australian family, 1880–1940* (Melbourne: Oxford University Press, 1985).

Richards, E.S., 'Women in the British economy since about 1700: an interpretation', *History*, vol. 59, no. 197 (October 1974), pp. 337–57.

Roberts, M., 'Sickles and scythes: women's work and men's work at harvest time', *History Workshop*, 7 (Spring 1979), pp. 3–28.

Robinson, J.P., *How Americans use time: a social-psychological analysis of everyday behavior* (New York: Praeger, 1977).

Rogers, J. E. Thorold, *The economic interpretation of history* (London: Unwin, 1888).

Rutenfranz, J., 'Energy expenditure constrained by sex and age', *Ergonomics*, vol. 28, no. 1 (1985), pp.115–18.

Sahlins, M., *Stone age economics* (Chicago: Aldine-Atherton, 1972).

Salter, W.E.G., *Productivity and technical change* (Cambridge: Cambridge University Press, 1960).

Schedvin, C.V., *Australia and the great depression: a study of economic development and policy in the 1920s and 1930s* (Sydney: Sydney University Press, 1970).

Scott, R.H., *The value of land in Australia* (Canberra: Centre for Research on Federal Financial Relations, Australian National University, 1986).

Sen, AK., 'Rational fools: a critique of the behavioural foundations of economic theory', *Philosophy and Public Affairs*, 6 (1977), pp. 317–44.

Sen, A.K., *On ethics and economics* (Oxford: Blackwell, 1987).

Sen, A.K., 'Beneconfusion', in J.G.T. Meeks (ed.), *Thoughtful economic man: essays on rationality, moral rules and benevolence* (Cambridge: Cambridge University Press, 1991), pp. 12–16.

Shann, E., *The boom of 1890 and now: a call to Australia to put her house in order lest drought and falling prices for wool and wheat overtake us* (Sydney: Cornstalk, 1927).

Shann, E., *An economic history of Australia* (Cambridge: Cambridge University Press, 1948).

Sheridan, T., *Mindful militants: the Amalgamated Engineering Union in Australia, 1920–1972* (Cambridge: Cambridge University Press, 1975).

Shubik, M., *Game theory in the social sciences: concepts and solutions* (Cambridge, Mass.: MIT Press, 1982).

Sidgwick, H., *The principles of political economy* (London: Macmillan, 1883).

Sigmond, J.P. and Zuiderbaan, L.H., *Dutch discoveries of Australia: shipwrecks, treasures and early voyages off the west coast* (Adelaide: Rigby, 1979).

Sinclair, W.A., 'Capital formation', in C. Forster (ed.), *Australian economic development in the twentieth century* (London: George Allen & Unwin, 1970), pp. 11–65.

Sinclair, W.A., 'Economic growth and well-being: Melbourne 1870–1914', *Economic Record*, vol. 51, no. 134 (June 1975), pp. 153–73.

Sinclair, W.A., *The process of economic development in Australia* (Melbourne: Cheshire, 1976).

Sinclair, W.A., 'Women at work in Melbourne and Adelaide since 1871', *Economic Record*, vol. 57, no. 159 (December 1981), pp. 344–53.

Sinclair, W.A., 'Gross domestic product', in W. Vamplew, E. Richards, D. Jaensch and J. Hancock (eds), *South Australian historical statistics*, Historical Statistics Monograph No. 3, University of New South Wales, 1984.

Smith, J.P. and Ward, M.P., *Women's wages and work in the twentieth century* (Santa Monica, Calif.: Rand Corporation, 1984).

Snell, K.D.M., 'Agricultural seasonal unemployment, the standard of living, and women's work in the South and East, 1690-1860', *Economic History Review*, 34 (1981), pp. 407-37.

Snell, K.D.M., *Annals of the labouring poor: social change and agrarian England, 1660-1900* (Cambridge: Cambridge University Press, 1985).

Snook, S.H., 'The design of manual handling tasks', *Ergonomics*, vol. 21, no. 12 (1978), pp. 963-85.

Snook, S.H., 'Psychophysical acceptability as a constraint in manual working capacity', *Ergonomics*, vol. 28, no. 1 (1985), pp. 331-5.

Snooks, G.D., 'Household services and national income in Australia, 1891-1981: some preliminary results', in A. Barnard (ed.), *First Spring Workshop in Australian Economic History 1983* (Department of Economic History, RSSS, Australian National University, September 1983), pp. 1-28.

Snooks, G.D., Towards a new approach to the Australian economy: household and market investment, 1900-1985 (Economic History Joint Seminar, Australian National University, 11 November 1988).

Snooks, G.D., 'Estimating Australian household labour services, 1881-1986', *Working Papers in Economic History*, no. 130 (RSSS, Australian National University, December, 1989).

Snooks, G.D., The dynamic relationship between the household and market sectors in longrun economic development: the Australian case, 1788-1990 (ESRC Quantitative Economic History Conference, St Anthony's College, Oxford, 18-19 September 1992).

Snooks, G.D., 'A new portrait of economic development', in R.V. Jackson (ed.), *The Cambridge economic history of Australia*, vol. 2 (Cambridge/Sydney: Cambridge University Press, forthcoming 1994).

Snooks, G.D., 'Regional estimates of gross domestic product and capital formation: Western Australia, 1923/24-1938/39', *Economic Record*, vol. 48, no. 124 (December 1972), pp. 536-53.

Snooks, G.D., 'The arithmetic of regional growth: Western Australia, 1912/13 to 1957/58', *Australian Economic History Review*, vol. 19, no. 1 (March 1979), pp. 63-74.

Snooks, G.D., *Depression and recovery in Western Australia, 1928/29-1938/39: a study in cyclical and structural change* (Perth: University of Western Australia Press, 1974).

Snooks, G.D., 'Development in adversity, 1913 to 1946', in C.T. Stannage (ed.), *A new history of Western Australia* (Perth: University of Western Australia Press, 1981), pp. 237-65 and 713-16.

Snooks, G.D., 'Robbing Peter to pay Paul: Australian unemployment relief in the thirties', *Working Papers in Economic History*, no. 41 (RSSS, Australian National University, August 1985).

Snooks, G.D., 'Government unemployment relief in the 1930s: aid or hindrance to recovery?', in R.G. Gregory and N.G. Butlin (eds), *Recovery from the depression:*

*Australia and the world economy in the 1930s* (Cambridge/Melbourne: Cambridge University Press, 1988), pp. 311–34.

Snooks, G.D., Hume Enterprises in Australia 1910–1940 (PhD. thesis, Australian National University, 1971).

Snooks, G.D., 'Innovation and the growth of the firm: Hume Enterprises, 1910–40', *Australian Economic History Review*, vol. 13, no. 1 (March 1973), pp. 16–40.

Snooks, G.D., 'Growth and productivity change in the Australian mechanical engineering industry, 1910–1940', *Australian Economic History Review*, vol. 24, no. 1 (March 1984), pp. 53–70.

Snooks, G.D., 'Capital stock in the Australian mechanical engineering industry, 1908/09–1938/39, *Australian Historical Statistics*, 7 (1983), pp. 3–37.

Snooks, G.D., 'Manufacturing, 1860–1982', in W. Vamplew (ed.), *Australians: historical statistics* (Broadway, NSW: Fairfax, Syme and Weldon, 1987), pp. 286–301 and 458–460.

Snooks, G.D., 'Determinants of earnings inequality amongst Australian artists', *Australian Economic Papers*, vol. 22, no. 41 (December 1983), pp. 322–32.

Snooks, G.D., 'Orthodox and radical interpretations of the development of Australian capitalism', *Labour History*, 28 (May 1975), pp. 1–11.

Snooks, G.D., ' "In my beginning is my end": the life and work of Noel George Butlin, 1921–1991', *Australian Economic History Review*, vol. 31, no. 2 (September 1991), pp. 3–27.

Snooks, G.D., 'Bond or free? The life, work, and times of Edward Shann, 1884–1935', in A. Siddique (ed.), *The Shann Memorial Lectures and the Australian economy* (Singapore: Academic Press International, 1993).

Snooks, G.D., *Economics without time: a science blind to the forces of historical change* (London: Macmillan, 1993).

Snooks, G.D. (ed.), *Historical analysis in economics* (London: Routledge, 1993).

Snooks, G.D., 'Great waves of economic change: an historical perspective for the Industrial Revolution', in G.D. Snooks (ed.), *Was the Industrial Revolution necessary?* (London: Routledge, 1994).

Snooks, G.D. and Nyland, C., The physical demands of the labour process (Flinders University research paper, 1988).

Sontag, S., *On photography* (Harmondsworth: Penguin Books, 1979).

South Australia, *Census* (Adelaide: Government Printer, 1844, 1846, 1851, 1855, 1861, 1866, 1871, 1876, 1881, 1891, 1901).

South Australia, *Statistical registers* (Adelaide: Government Printer, various years).

South Australia, Department of Housing, *Report* (Adelaide: Department of Housing, various years).

Strandberg, L., 'The effect of conditions underfoot on falling and overexertion accidents', *Ergonomics*, vol. 28, no. 1 (1985), pp. 131–47.

Studenski, Paul, *The income of nations: theory, measurement, and analysis, past and present: a study in applied economics and statistics* (New York: New York University Press, 1958).

Sugden, R., 'On the economics of philanthropy', *Economic Journal*, 92 (1982), pp. 341–50.

Sutcliffe, J.T., *The national dividend* (Melbourne: Melbourne University Press, 1926).

Tasmania, *Census* (Hobart: Government Printer, 1842, 1848, 1851, 1857, 1861, 1870, 1881, 1891, 1901).

Tasmania, *Statistical registers* (Hobart: Government Printer, various years).

Taubman, P. and Wachter, M.L., 'Segmented labour markets', in O. Ashenfelter and R. Layard (eds), *Handbook of labour economics* (Amsterdam: Elsevier Science Publishers, 1986), pp. 1183–1217.

Thompson, A., 'The enigma of Australian manufacturing, 1851–1901', *Australian Economic Papers*, vol. 9, no. 14 (June 1970), pp. 76–92.

Tilly, L.A. and Scott, J.W., *Women, work and family* (New York: Holt, Rinehard & Winston, 1978).

United Nations, *Demographic Yearbook* (New York: UN, various years).

Van Cott, H.P. and Kinkade, R.G., *Human engineering guide to equipment design* (Washington: Department of Defence, US Government Printing Office, 1972).

Victoria, *Census* (Melbourne: Government Printer, 1854, 1857, 1861, 1871, 1881, 1891, 1901).

Victoria, *Statistical registers* (Melbourne: Government Printer, various years).

Victoria, Department of Housing, *Report* (Melbourne: Department of Housing, various years).

Viscusi, W.K., *Employment hazards: an investigation of market performance* (Cambridge, Mass.: Harvard University Press, 1979).

Von Neumann, J. and Morgenstern, O., *The theory of games and economic behavior* (Princeton: Princeton University Press, 1944).

Weinrobe, M., 'Household production and national production: an improvement in the record', *Review of Income and Wealth*, 20 (1974), pp. 89–102.

Wentworth, W.C., *A statistical, historical and political description of the colony of New South Wales and its dependent settlements in Van Diemen's Land* (London: G. & W.B. Whittaker, 1819).

Western Australia, *Census* (Perth: Government printer, 1848, 1854, 1859, 1861, 1870, 1881, 1891, 1901).

Western Australia, *Statistical registers* (Perth: Government Printer, various years).

Whitwell, G, *Making the market: the rise of consumer society* (Fitzroy, Vic.: McPhee Gribble, 1989).

Willis, R.J., 'What have we learned from the economics of the family?' *American Economic Review*, 77 (1987), pp. 68–81.

Wilson, R., Public and private investment in Australia (ANZAAS paper, 1939).

Winston, G.C., *The timing of economic activities: firms, households, and markets in time-specific analysis* (Cambridge [Cambridgeshire]/New York: Cambridge University Press, 1982).

Wittgenstein, L., *Tractatus logico-philosophicus* (London: Routledge & Kegan Paul, 1961; first German edn 1921; first English edn 1922).

# Index